COLLECTED ESSAYS IN LAW



# The Jurisprudence of Law's Form and Substance

*Robert S. Summers is William G. McRoberts Research Professor of Law, Cornell Law School, and Arthur L. Goodhart Visiting Professor of Legal Sciences, Cambridge University, 1991–92. B.S. 1955 University of Oregon; L.L.B. 1959, Harvard Law School, Doctor of Laws, Honoris Causa, University of Helsinki, 1990; Doctor of Laws, Honoris Causa, University of Göttingen.*

**The Collected Essays in Law Series**
*General Editor: Tom D. Campbell*

Law's Premises, Law's Promise:
Jurisprudence after Wittgenstein

*Thomas Morawetz*

ISBN: 0 7546 2013 1

Constitutional Interpretation

*Frederick Schauer*

ISBN: 0 7546 2039 5

Regulation, Crime, and Freedom

*John Braithwaite*

ISBN: 0 7546 2005 0

Legal Rules and Legal Reasoning

*Larry Alexander*

ISBN: 0 7546 2004 2

Robert S. Summers

# The Jurisprudence of Law's Form and Substance

Routledge
Taylor & Francis Group
LONDON AND NEW YORK

First published 2000 by Dartmouth Publishing Company and Ashgate Publishing

Reissued 2018 by Routledge
2 Park Square, Milton Park, Abingdon, Oxon OX14 4RN
711 Third Avenue, New York, NY 10017, USA

*Routledge is an imprint of the Taylor & Francis Group, an informa business*



A Library of Congress record exists under LC control number: 99039720

ISBN 13: 978-1-138-70032-1 (hbk)
ISBN 13: 978-1-138-70031-4 (pbk)
ISBN 13: 978-1-315-20479-6 (ebk)

# Contents

# Series Editor's Preface

Collected Essays in Law makes available some of the most important work of scholars who have made a major contribution to the study of law. Each volume brings together a selection of writings by a leading authority on a particular subject. The series gives authors an opportunity to present and comment on what they regard as their most important work in a specific area. Within their chosen subject area, the collections aim to give a comprehensive coverage of the authors' research. Care is taken to include essays and articles which are less readily accessible and to give the reader a picture of the development of the authors' work and an indication of research in progress.

The initial volumes in the series include collections by Professors Frederick Schauer (Harvard), *Constitutional Interpretation*, John Braithwaite (ANU), *Regulation, Crime and Freedom*, Tom Morawetz, *Law's Premises, Law's Promise*, Robert Summers (Cornell), *Law's Form and Substance*, and Larry Alexander (San Diego), *Legal Rules and Legal Reasoning*. These collections set a high standard for future volumes in the series and I am most grateful to all of these distinguished authors for being in at the start of what it is hoped will become a rich and varied repository of the achievements of contemporary legal scholarship

# Preface

In the introductory essay I explain the content of this collection of essays in jurisprudence and legal theory. I also explain how a number of them came to be written. Here I wish to record my gratitude and indebtedness to several categories of persons and to several individuals.

Over many years, I have benefited enormously from the aid of numerous research assistants, all students at the Cornell Law School. I have also been privileged to be served by several extraordinary administrative assistants and secretaries. One of the foremost of these is Mrs. Pam Finnigan, who has enabled me to achieve many things, and has, in particular helped in all ways to put this collection together. Various deans and colleagues at the Cornell Law School have also been generous with support and advice. Prof. Dr. Okko Behrends of the University of Göttingen has also been most generous with his thoughts, especially in regard to Chapter Two. My thanks to all is heartfelt, and my gratitude permanent.

I wish, in closing, to thank Mr. John Irwin, of this publishing house, for his encouragement. I first came to know him through Professor D. Neil MacCormick who arranged with Mr. Irwin to have the two books of The Bielefelder Kreis on statutory interpretation and precedent published by this house. When John Irwin and I, rather later, took a long walk together in Oxford's Port Meadow, I promised him I would put this collection of essays together. I thank him for his interest and his patience.

I have dedicated this book to my mother, Estella Robertson Summers, of Scottish descent, and living alone on the family farm in Halfway, Oregon, where she continues, at the age of 88, to chop her own wood.

ROBERT S. SUMMERS

*Oxford,*
*Spring 1999*

For my Mother:

ESTELLA ROBERTSON SUMMERS

Born March 11, 1911
Near Halfway, Oregon,
USA

# Introduction

The five extended essays collected here were written over a period of thirty two years (1965–1997). Though in that period I devoted over half of my research and writing to matters of positive law – primarily American contract and commercial law, all of the present essays, save the last on good faith, fall entirely within jurisprudence and legal theory. As I will later explain, the essay on good faith itself owes its inspiration to the writings of an Oxford philosopher, J. L. Austin.

All of the essays treat basic issues of wide-ranging significance and all but the first appear, quite to my surprise, to have been influential in their own way. From having taught all of the essays as parts of classes and seminars, I can testify that each is readily accessible to the serious student. With the exception of one essay, what is collected here still represents my central views on the key issues addressed. This is not to say I believe these essays are perfect. They are not. It is rather that I still stand by all of their central themes.

The exception is the essay in Chapter Two entitled 'How Law is Formal and Why It Matters'. This essay is the most recent of the lot and represents the general state of my thought as of 1996 on the most complex subject with which I have ever grappled. The essay is in the nature of a general report on issues I had theretofore been thinking about continuously since the early nineteen eighties when Professor Patrick Atiyah and I began our work, *Form and Substance in Anglo-American Law* (OUP 1987, 1991). My further, more theoretical, work on form, will eventually appear as a book tentatively entitled 'The Place of Form in the Fundamentals of Law'. While I still adhere to most of the main outlines of the essay that appears here as Chapter Two my views continue to evolve in ways that, to me, at least, are not minor. By the time I wrote this essay, I had come to believe that the formal character of law is by far the most important of several neglected branches of jurisprudence and legal theory. Not even Kelsen and Hart plumbed the depths of this rich subject so revelatory of the fundamentals of law. I am sure I shall not be able to do so with any finality. Yet I believe the essay here is significantly redirective, provides some conceptual foundations, and points to ways in which we should give due credit to law's forms, formal dimensions, and formal features.

The essays may be grouped in three categories: methodological questions, issues of the form and process of law, and issues concerned with the character of law's substance or content. The essay in Chapter One entitled 'The New Analytical Jurists' treats basic methodological issues in jurisprudence and legal theory. The essays in Chapters Two and Three are on the formal character of law. Chapter Two is on what legal form is and how it matters, and is followed by the essay in Chapter Three in which I concentrate more specifically on process values, and thus treat procedural form in the law. This essay also differentiates between the instrumentalist and constitutive functions of legal process, and demonstrates that some process values, such as adjudicative fairness, are constituted by the process itself and so are realized in the very course of the workings of such a process rather than in their outcomes. What I failed to see at the time of writing the essay is that major credit must be given to appropriate form here. The procedural form of an institution is not merely means but also ends or values insofar as it is constitutive of procedural fairness. Such form defines, structures, and expresses fairness. Here, form is both means and ends. This is a generalizeable point about form of major import, itself never better captured than in a stanza written by the nineteenth century German socialist thinker, Ferdinard Lasalle:

> Show us not the aim without the way.
> For ends and means on earth are so entangled
> That changing one, you change the other too;
> Each different path brings other ends in view.

The final two essays treat fundamental topics pertaining to the substance or content of the law. Chapter Four presents a general account of the distinction between formal, i.e., authoritative reasons for decisions and actions of citizens and officials on the one hand, and on the other, substantive reasons for such decisions and actions, i.e., moral, equitable, economic, institutional, and other social considerations. The chapter focuses on substantive reasons and provides an extended analysis of their scope, limits, and justificatory force. The chapter also demonstrates how such reasons necessarily figure in the workings of a legal order. Among other things, it is simply fallacious to hold that formal legal reasons for decision and action are the only type of reason of major significance for law. Substantive reasons must figure, too, in all sorts of ways, and not merely in filling gaps in the law.

The essay on good faith in Chapter Five addresses a major substantive doctrine of private law, one that is part of the content of all major

Western legal systems. I wrote this essay while sitting at what had been the desk of the Oxford philosopher, J.L. Austin, during the academic year 1964–65.[1] The proximity was inspiring in a very specific way. Austin had written important work on a significant category of words and phrases which he called 'excluders'. Instead of having a positive meaning of their own, such words and phrases are characteristically used on a specific occasion to rule out one of a heterogeneous array of 'opposite' possibilities in the circumstances. Austin argued that the word 'real', for example, was an excluder. Thus, when we say 'that is a real duck', we do not positively affirm any given attribute, but instead rule out, say, that it is a decoy duck, or a dummy duck, or the like. On reflection, I came to see that the common law courts of the U.S.A. (and of other countries, too) actually use the wide-ranging expression 'good faith' in numerous legal doctrines much less to affirm any positive meaning than to rule out a heterogeneous variety of forms of bad faith. Accordingly, I wrote the essay that appears as Chapter Five here and it, along with an early essay by Professor Alan Farnsworth of Columbia, had the effect of redirecting much American doctrinal study of the substance of this subject, and led to the discovery that American common law actually recognized a vast body of good faith case law. The essay that appears here as Chapter Five also influenced the conceptualization of good faith in the new Restatement of Contracts, 2d.

This naturally leads to matters of method in general, and I will now offer some remarks on the subject of the first essay included here, the one entitled 'The New Analytical Jurists'. The title derives from a category widely in use earlier in this century when legal theorists regularly wrote of 'analytical' jurisprudence, 'natural law' jurisprudence, 'sociological' jurisprudence, and 'historical' jurisprudence. Since this terminology is now not so widely used, I offer some elaboration. Among the principal legal theorists classed as 'analytical' were the nineteenth century English jurist, John Austin, and the late H.L.A. Hart. There were also thinkers classified as 'analytical' jurists in the United States, as well, including Oliver Wendell Holmes, Jr., John Chipman Gray, and the philosopher Morris Cohen. These 'analytical' jurists were diverse, yet they shared an interest in the form and structure of law, in fundamental legal ideas such as duty and sanction, and in basic legal concepts generally. Misconceptions about analytical jurisprudence still abound, and all would do well to read Hart's writings on the nature of that type of theoretical interest.[2]

The first essay here, on the new analytical jurists, was also written mainly during the year 1964–65 when I studied for a year at the University of Oxford under Professor H.L.A. Hart. The new analytical jurists included Hart, and many studying under or with him, such as A.M. Honoré, Geoffrey Marshall, Neil MacCormick, Joseph Raz, and the Americans, Kent Greenawalt, and Ronald Dworkin. These theorists were new not only in the sense that they were relatively new to the jurisprudential scene. They were also new in the sense that they were applying techniques of philosophical method characteristic of what came to be known as 'Oxford analytical philosophy', a movement that was influenced also by developments in Cambridge, especially the work of Russell, Moore, and Wittgenstein. Just what were these techniques? Chapter One systematically addresses that question, as do the two lengthy introductions I wrote to two collections of specimens of such work that were published as books in 1968 and 1971, and which the reader may also wish to consult. Chapter Five on good faith is also a specimen insofar as it conceptualizes good faith as an excluder. Moreover, all of the other chapters in this book reflect at least the indirect influence of the techniques which I discuss in Chapter One.

It is well known that Hart himself was also a 'legal positivist'. It does not, however, follow that a so-called 'new analytical jurist' must also be a positivist, though some theorists inhabit both of these categories. Hart once defined legal positivism as 'the doctrine ... that no reference need be made to morality or natural justice in either the definition of 'law properly so called' or a determination of whether or not a given rule is a 'valid' rule of law'.[3] It should be evident that a theorist can 'do' analytical jurisprudence without espousing the foregoing positivist doctrines, and many have, including, in addition to myself, Ronald Dworkin, John Finnis, Charles Fried, and Philip Soper.

For the assistance of those who wish to pursue my further writings on each of the topics treated in the several chapters here, I have included an Appendix with relevant references.

## Endnotes

1 Professor H.L.A. Hart had arranged my rental of a flat owned by the widow of J.L. Austin.

2 See, e.g., H.L.A. Hart, Analytical Jurisprudence in Mid-Twentieth Century: A Reply to Professor Bodenheimer, 105 *U. of Pa. Law Review* **953** (1957).

3 Paul Edwards, ed., *The Encyclopedia of Philosophy* Vol. 1 p. 110 (1967).

# [1]
# The *New* Analytical Jurists

## I

### Introduction

IT seems appropriate to introduce an article of this nature by describing what it is to be a jurist.[1] A jurist is not a lawyer, although he may be and often is. A jurist is not a teacher of substantive law, although he may be, and usually is. Instead of drafting contracts or trying cases, instead of researching and teaching the elements of a crime or the theory of consideration, the jurist studies jurisprudence. Jurisprudence is concerned with the nature of law, its functions, the means by which it performs these functions, the limits of law, the relation of law to justice and morality, the modes by which law changes and develops, and more.[2]

Jurisprudence, like many other branches of philosophy, has its schools of thought, among which are the "historical," the "sociological," the "evaluative," and the "analytical."[3] This scheme of classification is, in important ways, an unhappy one,[4] but it has served to differentiate those jurists who are primarily

---

Robert S. Summers is Associate Professor of Law, University of Oregon School of Law. The author wishes to record his gratitude to the Social Science Research Council for a research fellowship in legal philosophy that enabled him to spend the academic year 1964-1965 at Oxford University. He is also grateful to the University of Oregon Office of Scientific and Scholarly Research for research support.

1. There is no up-to-date law review article on what a jurist is. But a chap named Anon. has recently written a brilliant piece on how to become a jurist in which, among other things, the learned author says:

> Perhaps the best tip that can be given is to cultivate a general air of vagueness and other worldliness. . . .
>
> A large part of [any article written by a would-be jurist] . . . should be taken up by quotations, preferably in foreign tongues, from the least comprehensible legal philosophies . . . . and remember that it is the footnotes that count.

Anon., How To Become a Jurist, 7 J. of Soc'y of Public Teachers of Law 129, 130, 133 (1963).

2. See 13 Encyclopedia Britannica 149 (1965) (entry by "L.L.F." (Lon L. Fuller)).

3. See Urmson, A Concise Encyclopedia of Western Philosophy and Philosophers 199-200 (1960) (entry by H. L. A. Hart). For detailed treatment of these schools of thought see Pound, Jurisprudence (1959) (5 vols.).

4. Unhappy because (1) all jurisprudential work must be in some sense "analytical" to be of any value at all, (2) few, if any, jurists are exclusively interested in one type of inquiry, (3) any "schools" scheme invites lumping quite different thinkers into the same category, and (4) such a scheme invites some thinkers to "take sides." On the last point see the thoughtful article by Ryle, Taking Sides in Philosophy, 12 Philosophy 317 (1937).

interested in approaching the problems of jurisprudence historically, those primarily interested in approaching them sociologically, those concerned with the evaluative or normative side of these problems, and those whose interest in such problems is "analytical."

Each of the foregoing general types of jurisprudential inquiry has its own distinctive history and its own hall of fame. Thus, Anglo-American[5] *analytical* jurisprudence may be said to have started with Hobbes[6] and to have achieved its zenith in the nineteenth century in the works of the British jurist, John Austin,[7] and his successors in the English-speaking world. But it is not the object of this article to trace the history of analytical jurisprudence. Rather, this article is addressed to two seemingly simple questions: What are the new analytical jurists doing? How does this differ from what their predecessors did?

Contrary to what is very widely assumed, even by interested legal scholars,[8] it is now both possible and important to distinguish between, on the one hand, the work of "old" analytical jurists—John Austin and his successors,[9] including Gray,[10] Hohfeld,[11] and Kocourek[12] in the United States—and, on the other hand, the published efforts of a group of Anglo-American analyti-

5. The work of contemporary continental analytical jurists such as Hans Kelsen, Alf Ross, and Norberto Bobbio is beyond the scope of this article.

6. See Hobbes, A Dialogue Between a Philosopher and a Student of the Common Laws of England (circa 1670); Hobbes, Leviathan (1651).

7. See Austin, The Province of Jurisprudence Determined (Library of Ideas ed. 1954). Austin was born in 1790 and died in 1859.

8. Only two scholars have been discovered who even recognize that there might be some significant difference between the old and the new in analytical jurisprudence. See Friedmann, Legal Theory 223-27 (4th ed. 1960); Bodenheimer, Analytical Positivism, Legal Realism, and the Future of Legal Method, 44 Va. L. Rev. 365 (1958).

9. See Sheldon Amos (1835-1886), The Science of Law (9th ed. 1909); Amos, Systematic View of the Science of Jurisprudence (1872); E. C. Clark (1835-1917), Practical Jurisprudence: A Comment on Austin (1883); William Hearn (1826-1888), The Theory of Legal Duties and Rights (1883); Sir Thomas Holland (1835-1926), Elements of Jurisprudence (13th ed. 1924); Sir William Markby (1829-1914), Elements of Law Considered With Reference to Principles of General Jurisprudence (4th ed. 1889); Sir John Salmond (1862-1924), Jurisprudence: The Theory of the Law (3d ed. 1910). An important predecessor of Austin, Jeremy Bentham (1748-1832), is not, for the purposes of this article, considered one of the old analytical jurists. Here, as in most other respects, Bentham was far ahead of his time. His best work on analytical jurisprudence consists of the following: The Comment on the Commentaries (Everett ed. 1928); A Fragment on Government (Montague ed. 1891); An Introduction to the Principles of Morals and Legislation (Hafner Library ed. 1948); The Limits of Jurisprudence Defined (Everett ed. 1945).

10. See Gray, The Nature and Sources of Law (2d ed. 1921).

11. See Hohfeld, Fundamental Legal Conceptions (1923).

12. See Kocourek, An Introduction to the Science of Law (1930); Kocourek, Jural Relations (1927).

cal jurists that has emerged since World War II. This latter group includes H. L. A. Hart,[13] Glanville L. Williams,[14] and Graham B. J. Hughes,[15] all Britons, and Ronald M. Dworkin,[16] Charles Fried,[17] Herbert Morris,[18] and Richard A. Wasserstrom[19] of the United States.[20] Inasmuch as the work of these new jurists is in the analytical vein, it plainly has more in common with the efforts of earlier analysts than with that of adherents of other modern "schools." Yet this fact should not be allowed to obscure the very great differences between the old and the new. The new is broader in scope, more sophisticated in methodology, less doctrinaire and positivistic, and more likely to be of practical utility.

13. Hart's most important writings include: Hart & Honoré, Causation in the Law (1959); The Concept of Law (1961); Bentham: Lecture on a Master Mind, 48 Proceedings of the British Academy 297 (1962); Definition and Theory in Jurisprudence, 70 L.Q. Rev. 37 (1954); Positivism and the Separation of Law and Morals, 71 Harv. L. Rev. 593 (1958); Prolegomenon to the Principles of Punishment, 60 Proceedings of the Aristotelian Soc'y 1 (1960); Book Review, 78 Harv. L. Rev. 1281 (1965). On his work generally see Pannam, Professor Hart and Analytical Jurisprudence, 16 J. Legal Ed. 379 (1964); Summers, Professor H. L. A. Hart's Concept of Law, 1963 Duke L.J. 629.

14. See the following works by Williams: Salmond on Jurisprudence (11th ed. 1957); Carelessness, Indifference and Recklessness: Two Replies, 25 Modern L. Rev. 49, 55 (1962); The Concept of Legal Liberty, 56 Colum. L. Rev. 1129 (1956); International Law and the Controversy Concerning the Word "Law," 22 Brit. Yb. Int'l L. 146 (1945); Language and the Law (pts. 1-5), 61 L.Q. Rev. 71, 179, 293, 384 (1945), 62 L.Q. Rev. 387 (1946).

15. See the following works by Hughes: The Concept of Crime: An American View (pts. 1, 2), 1959 Crim. L. Rev. 239, 331; Criminal Omissions, 67 Yale L.J. 590 (1958); The Existence of a Legal System, 35 N.Y.U.L. Rev. 1001 (1960); Jurisprudence, 1965 Ann. Survey Am. L. 639 (1966); Jurisprudence, 1964 Ann. Survey Am. L. 685 (1965); Professor Hart's Concept of Law, 25 Modern L. Rev. 319 (1962); Book Review, 9 Natural L.F. 164 (1964); Book Review, 17 Stan. L. Rev. 547 (1965); Book Review, 16 Stan. L. Rev. 470 (1964).

16. See the following works by Dworkin: Does Law Have a Function? A Comment on the Two-Level Theory of Decision, 74 Yale L.J. 640 (1965); Judicial Discretion, 60 J. Philosophy 624 (1963); Lord Devlin and the Enforcement of Morals, 75 Yale L.J. 986 (1966); Philosophy, Morality and Law—Observations Prompted by Professor Fuller's Novel Claim, 113 U. Pa. L. Rev. 668 (1965).

17. See the following works by Fried: Justice and Liberty, 6 Nomos (Justice) 126 (1963); Moral Causation, 77 Harv. L. Rev. 1258 (1964); Natural Law and the Concept of Justice, 74 Ethics 237 (1964); Two Concepts of Interests: Some Reflections on the Supreme Court's Balancing Test, 76 Harv. L. Rev. 755 (1963).

18. See the following works by Morris: Freedom and Responsibility: Readings in Philosophy and Law (Morris ed. 1961); Imperatives and Orders, 26 Theoria 183 (1966); Punishment for Thoughts, 49 Monist 342 (1965); Verbal Disputes and the Legal Philosophy of John Austin, 7 U.C.L.A.L. Rev. 27 (1960).

19. See the following works by Wasserstrom: The Judicial Decision: Toward a Theory of Legal Justification (1961); The Obligation To Obey the Law, 10 U.C.L.A.L. Rev. 780 (1963); Rights, Human Rights, and Racial Discrimination, 61 J. Philosophy 628 (1964); Strict Liability in the Criminal Law, 12 Stan. L. Rev. 731 (1960).

20. Of course, there are other new analysts of importance.

Before discussing each of these differences in turn, several caveats must be entered to forestall misunderstanding. First, it is not claimed that what is new in the recent analytical jurisprudence is new to the philosophical world generally. Many of the new analytical jurists have drawn on techniques, distinctions, and ideas already familiar in philosophy, particularly twentieth century analytic philosophy.[21] Most of what is new in their work is characterized as such only because of its novelty within the tradition of analytical jurisprudence as a branch of scholarship. Second, while the "new analysts" are grouped together for the purposes of this article, it must not be assumed that they agree on specific solutions to any of the problems they have been seeking to resolve. There is not yet any evidence of such agreement. Hence they do not, doctrinally, form a "school." They form a school only in the limited sense that a major part of the work of each is analytical in nature. This leads naturally to a third caveat. From the fact that these thinkers are concerned with analytical studies, it should not be concluded that they have no interest in sociological or evaluative inquiries. There is no evidence that any of them is exclusively occupied with analysis. Finally, it is not suggested that the new analytical jurists have a monopoly. They plainly do not. A significant number of professional philosophers interested in law are now pursuing what they call "legal philosophy."[22] Moreover, in spite of the rampages of behavioralism

21. The writings of the new jurists include many references to works of contemporary analytic philosophers. Figures who have profoundly influenced twentieth century analytic philosophy include Bertrand Russell (1872- ), G. E. Moore (1873-1959), Ludwig Wittgenstein (1889-1951), J. L. Austin (1911-1960), and Gilbert Ryle (1900- ). Russell, Moore, and Wittgenstein taught at Cambridge; Austin and Ryle taught at Oxford. It was not until the 1930's that the Cam began to flow into the Isis and the center of analytic philosophy moved from Cambridge to Oxford.

For introductory treatments of aspects of twentieth century analytic philosophy see Quinton, Contemporary British Philosophy, in A Critical History of Western Philosophy 530 (O'Conner ed. 1964); Urmson, Philosophical Analysis: Its Development Between the Two World Wars (1956); Warnock, English Philosophy Since 1900 (1958); The Age of Analysis: Twentieth Century Philosophers (White ed. 1955); British Analytical Philosophy (Williams & Montefiore eds. 1966).

22. A partial list follows:

(1) H. Bedau: The Death Penalty in America (Bedau ed. 1964); Justice and Classical Utilitarianism, 6 Nomos (Justice) 284 (1963); Law, Legal Systems, and Types of Legal Rules, Memorias del XIII Congreso Internacional de Filosofia, 7 Communicaciones Libres 17 (1964); On Civil Disobedience, 58 J. Philosophy 653 (1961).

(2) L. Boonin: Concerning the Authoritative Status of Legal Rules, 74 Ethics 219 (1964); Concerning the Defeasibility of Legal Rules, 26 Philosophy & Phenomenological Research 371 (1966); The Logic of Legal Decisions, 75 Ethics 179 (1965); The Meaning and Existence of Rules, 76 Ethics 212 (1966); The

within the discipline of political science, there are still some political "theorists."[23] While these thinkers are not, for the purposes of this article, called analytical jurists, there are no substantial differences between what they do and the work of the new jurists, all of whom are or have been members of law faculties.

## II

## SCOPE OF THE NEW ANALYTICAL JURISPRUDENCE

The new jurists are performing a wider variety of analytical activities than did most of their predecessors. These activities can be divided into four main types (a good philosophical number): (1) analysis of the existing conceptual framework of and about law; (2) construction of new conceptual frameworks with accompanying terminologies; (3) rational justification of insti-

Theoretical and Practical Approaches to Legal Reasoning, 49 Archiv für Rechts und Sozialphilosophie 433 (1963).

(3) M. Cohen: Law, Morality and Purpose, 10 Vill. L. Rev. 640 (1965).

(4) J. Feinberg: Action and Responsibility, in Philosophy in America 134 (Black ed. 1965); Justice and Personal Deserts, 6 Nomos (Justice) 69 (1963); Problematic Responsibility in Law and Morals, 71 Philosophical Rev. 340 (1962).

(5) M. Golding: Causation in the Law, 59 J. Philosophy 85 (1961); Kelsen and the Concept of "Legal System," 47 Archiv für Rechts und Sozialphilosophie 355 (1961); Principled Decision-Making and the Supreme Court, 63 Colum. L. Rev. 35 (1963); Principled Judicial Decision-Making, 73 Ethics 247 (1963).

(6) J. Rawls: Legal Obligation and the Duty of Fair Play, in Law and Philosophy 3 (Hook ed. 1964); Constitutional Liberty and the Concept of Justice, 6 Nomos (Justice) 98 (1963); Justice as Fairness, 67 Philosophical Rev. 164 (1958); Two Concepts of Rules, 64 Philosophical Rev. 3 (1955).

(7) M. Singer: Hart's Concept of Law, 60 J. Philosophy 197 (1963); Negative and Positive Duties, 15 Philosophy Q. 97 (1965).

The following remarks of one of the new analytical jurists are pertinent:

> Nowadays in philosophy departments in British and American universities, graduate students are busily writing dissertations on legal concepts or concepts having a close connection with law. The philosophy journals contain a growing sprinkling of articles on themes having relevance to the law. This development is very welcome. Jurisprudence, at least in its Anglo-American version, has suffered for too long through having little or no contact with professional philosophy. Competent legal scholars who venture into the field of legal theory often make blunders that a disciplined training in philosophy would have led them to avoid. But, correspondingly, philosophers may make very naive or misconceived appraisals of problems in legal theory simply through knowing too little law. They need to work together if only to correct each other's mistakes and there are now plenty of encouraging signs that, if not actually collaborating, lawyers and philosophers are at least paying attention to what the other has to say.

Hughes, Jurisprudence, 1964 Ann. Survey Am. L. 685, 687-88 (1965).

23. A representative cross section of their writings can be found in the annual publication of the recently formed American Society of Political and Legal Philosophy. This publication is called Nomos, and, to date, annual volumes have appeared devoted to the following topics: Authority, Community, Responsibility, Liberty, The Public Interest, Justice, Revolution, and Rational Decision.

tutions and practices, existing and proposed; and (4) "purposive implication"—tracing out what the acceptance of social purposes "implies" in terms of social arrangements and social ordering. All analytical jurists have been interested in the first of the foregoing activities—conceptual analysis. In fact, conceptual analysis has been a main, if not the primary, interest of analytical jurists, old and new. But, compared to most of the older analysts, the new are analyzing a wider range of concepts and performing a wider variety of analytical activities. These represent significant differences of scope.

### A. *Analysis of the Conceptual* Status Quo

At least to philosophers, conceptual analysis is important because clarity and insight are important.[24] Concepts, and their interrelations, often turn out to be far more complex than is supposed. Through analysis, it is often possible to achieve better understanding. But this is not all that analysis accomplishes. As the philosopher J. L. Austin was fond of observing, a sharpened awareness of the uses of words can sharpen our awareness of phenomena.[25] This is not, by any means, a new idea. Plato, in the *Cratylus*, had Socrates ask of Cratylus: "What is the force of names, and what is the use of them?" To this, Cratylus replied: "The use of names, Socrates, as I should imagine, is to inform: the simple truth is, that he who knows names knows also the things which are expressed by them."[26]

What is conceptual analysis? Whether we speak of "con-

24. What is insight? There is, of course, no Platonic "form" of insight, and what is insight for one person may be old hat to another. An insight may be presented in such forms as (1) a sharpened awareness, (2) an exposed presupposition, (3) a novel line of argument, (4) a new distinction, (5) a relationship or a similarity or a contrast not previously seen, (6) a new technique or method, (7) an unseen implication, (8) an exemplification of something more general.

25. See J. L. Austin, A Plea for Excuses, 57 Proceedings of the Aristotelian Soc'y 1, 8 (1956).

26. 1 Dialogues of Plato 224 (Jowett transl. Random House 1937). H. L. A. Hart has made this point similarly:

> The question "Is analytical jurisprudence concerned with words or with things?" incorporates a most misleading dichotomy. Perhaps its misleading character comes out in the following analogy. Suppose a man to be occupied in focusing through a telescope on a battleship lying in the harbor some distance away. A friend comes up to him and says, "Are you concerned with the image in your glass or with the ship?" Plainly (if well advised) the other would answer "Both. I am endeavoring to align the image in the glass with the battleship in order to see it better." It seems to me that similarly in pursuing analytical inquiries we seek to sharpen our awareness of what we talk about when we use our language. There is no clarification of concepts which can fail to increase our understanding of the world to which we apply them.

Hart, Analytical Jurisprudence in Mid-Twentieth Century: A Reply to Professor Bodenheimer, 105 U. Pa. L. Rev. 953, 967 (1957).

ceptual analysis" or of "analyzing the *uses* of words," it all comes to much the same. The phrase "linguistic analysis," though often used, is less appropriate. It implies that language itself is the relevant subject matter, and this is not so. The relevant subject matter consists of concepts or ideas currently used by either laymen or professionals in dealing with law. Language, of course, is necessary, but only as the means by which, and the medium in which, concepts or ideas are dealt with.[27] It is possible to hint meaningfully at the range and variety of relevant concepts or ideas for conceptual analysis. Consider the following inexhaustive list:

(1) Concepts used in formulating theories of law, *e.g.*, sources of law, adjudication, minimum efficacy, sanctions.

(2) Concepts used in characterizing theories of law, *e.g.*, imperative, positivist.

(3) Concepts that are more or less creatures of law, *e.g.*, ownership, corporation.

(4) Concepts widely used in formulations of substantive laws, *e.g.*, intention, causation, possession.

(5) Concepts used to demarcate basic legal relations, *e.g.*, right-duty, power-liability.

(6) Concepts central to the administration of law, *e.g.*, interpretation, *ratio decidendi*, discretion, stare decisis, justification.

(7) Concepts used in classifying laws, *e.g.*, criminal, civil, substantive, procedural, public, private.

(8) Concepts used in criticism of law and its administration, *e.g.*, justice, freedom, equality, morality, natural law, "the rule of law."

So much for subject matter. What activities are involved in the "analysis" of this subject matter? Like most cover words, "analysis" suggests more unity than exists. For analysis is not a single activity, but rather a family of related activities. It includes breaking down concepts, differentiating related concepts, correlating and/or unifying related concepts, classifying them in some way, and charting their implications—their "logical bearings."[28] Perhaps "analysis" is not an ideal word,[29] but in the

27. This is not to say that idioms of language may not be useful as "pointers" to important distinctions or ideas. See Warnock, English Philosophy Since 1900, at 149-52 (1958).

28. In the course of these activities, various methodological techniques, distinctions, or ideas may come into play. For discussion of some of these as they figure in Hart's work see Summers, Professor H. L. A. Hart's Concept of Law, 1963 Duke L.J. 629, 661.

29. For those familiar with jurisprudence, it should be plain that "analysis," as used here, does not mean the formulation of logically equivalent definitions à

interest of brevity some cover word is essential, and "analysis" seems better than any other.

We should take an example—"justice"[30]—and, without attempting detailed elaboration, illustrate the general nature of conceptual analysis. After assembling representative examples of uses of "just" and "justice," an analytical jurist might try to establish that there is only one basic concept embedded in this usage, *e.g.*, the concept of just desert. Thus, he might try to show that a principle embodying this concept—each man shall have his due—in fact accounts for, or "ties together," the diverse uses we make of the terms "just" and "justice." Then, too, he might decide that no single principle ties them together, and that usage reflects not one unitary concept of justice but several distinct, though cognate, concepts. Thus, the principle that each man shall have his due may account for some uses, the principle that like cases are to be treated alike may account for others, and the principle that humans are to be treated humanely may account for still others. If this should be so, our jurist would want to stress that, since each of these principles embodies a different concept, there are distinct, though cognate, concepts of justice. Having identified and differentiated these, our jurist might then consider precisely how they are related—how they are cognate. He might go on to compare and contrast justice with allied concepts of evaluation such as utility. Though much more is involved, enough has been said to illustrate the technique of conceptual analysis. What will be the end result? Presumably a better understanding of some important domain within our conceptual scheme.

Because of vague similarities, conceptual analysis is not uncommonly confused with legal interpretation.[31] But when the jurist engages in conceptual analysis he is simply not doing the kind of work that the lawyer does when he interprets a statute or some other authoritative text. Although there are many differences, three will suffice for illustration. First, the sources of their problems are very different. The lawyer's interpretational problem arises because, for example, there is inconsistent usage of the same word in the text, syntactical ambiguity, or evidence of a difference between what the authority intended and the usual

la Russell and Moore. (The uninitiated would not know of and therefore not worry about this possible meaning anyway.)

30. Actually, analysts have done a great deal of work on this topic. See, e.g., 6 Nomos (Justice) (1963).

31. See, e.g., Bodenheimer, Modern Analytical Jurisprudence and the Limits of Its Usefulness, 104 U. Pa. L. Rev. 1080, 1085 (1956); Dunlop, Developments in English Jurisprudence 1953-1963, 3 Alberta L. Rev. 63, 72 (1963); Jones, A View From the Bridge, Law & Society, Summer 1965, pp. 39, 40.

meanings of the words used. The conceptual analyst's problem does not arise in this manner. Instead, it may arise because he is genuinely puzzled or confused about what is involved in the general content of some concept or about how it contrasts with and relates to other concepts. Alternatively, his problem may arise not because he is antecedently puzzled or in a fog, but rather because he simply wants to articulate a clear analysis of something he has set out to investigate.[32] Second, the lawyer can almost always frame his issue in terms of a choice between two alternative interpretations each of which he readily grasps and fully understands. This cannot be true of the jurist whose problem arises because of antecedent confusion or puzzlement. Moreover, the jurist's analysis—his "solution," if it can be called that —can hardly be described in terms of a choice between alternatives. The complexity of the activities involved in analysis defies such simplicity of description. Third, the lawyer will use techniques in his "analysis" that are hardly appropriate for the analytical jurist. Thus, interpreting a statute, the lawyer can be expected to invoke canons of statutory construction, canons obviously foreign to conceptual analysis. Also, the lawyer might involve himself in the old methodological dispute between purposive and literal interpretation.[33] But the jurist, qua analyst, could not even be a party to this dispute if he is analyzing the conceptual *status quo*, or, indeed, even if he is recommending the adoption of a better conceptual framework for representing reality.[34] In both cases, he is plainly not trying to determine what a specific person on a particular occasion meant by a specific use of a term. Furthermore, the lawyer, in interpreting a statute, may quite rightly marshal and rely on relevant arguments of public

32. See Warnock, English Philosophy Since 1900, at 147-57 (1958).

33. See generally Heydon's Case, 3 Coke 7a, 76 Eng. Rep. 637 (Ex. 1584). Every article on jurisprudence must include a citation to at least one case, for, as Holmes is supposed to have said, "Philosophising about the law does not amount to much until one has soaked in the details," quoted in J. Stone, Legal System and Lawyers' Reasonings 287 (1964).

34. Professor Lon L. Fuller appears to think the contrary. Thus, he has recently said that Professor Hart, in giving an account of judicial interpretation, is really "proposing" literal as opposed to purposive interpretation. See Fuller, Positivism and Fidelity to Law—A Reply to Professor Hart, 71 Harv. L. Rev. 630, 661-69 (1958). Professor Hart, however, is not, in the relevant passages, proposing a theory of judicial interpretation at all. Rather, he is indicating his preference for one conceptual schema over another for the purpose of representing the nature of the process of judicial interpretation, and this he is doing in the context of conveying what he thinks is of value in the work of legal realists. Of course, he might be wrong in his preference, but this would be to adopt a framework that misrepresents reality, and not to adopt an indefensible theory of judicial interpretation. See Hart, Positivism and the Separation of Law and Morals, 71 Harv. L. Rev. 593, 606-08 (1958).

policy. But it would be inappropriate, indeed, for a jurist to try to establish a *conceptual* connection between, say, the concept of law and the concept of general rules, by invoking considerations of "public policy." Similarly, it would be queer, indeed, for him to differentiate the concepts of purposive and reckless behavior "as a matter of public policy." It is proper that within *the substantive law's* own conceptual scheme, connections and distinctions be influenced by specific policies and purposes of duly constituted authorities. But it does not follow, in fact it is surely false, that all connections and distinctions within any conceptual scheme are exclusively creatures of specific human policies or purposes of the moment.[35] Whether or not there is a conceptual connection between the concept of law and the concept of general rules, and whether or not the general concepts of purposive or reckless behavior can be differentiated, are *not*, as such, questions arising within the conceptional scheme of the substantive law. Moreover, while over the long run such connections and distinctions are influenced by general human purposes, they have a reality of their own[36] which is not governed by short-run, transitory, practical policies or purposes of the moment. Of course, whether or not these connections and distinctions are to be recognized and embodied in the substantive law, and thus made subject to such policies and purposes, is an entirely different question, and itself one of policy.

With respect to conceptual analysis, how do the old analysts differ from the new? The new are methodologically more sophisticated, a point that will be developed later in this article.[37] Of equal, if not greater, importance is the fact that the new analysts are engaged in analyzing a wider range of concepts than their predecessors. John Austin very broadly defined the range of concepts jurists might investigate.[38] But most of his successors

35. From the tenor of Professor Fuller's article, it appears he believes that the very existence of any distinction between law "as it is" and law "as it ought to be" must ultimately turn somehow on the relevance of some specific and practical purpose. He suggests that the only "real" reason Professor Hart might have for insisting on this distinction is not conceptual in nature. Rather, it is a more specific and practical reason, namely, that Professor Hart believes strongly in "fidelity to law." Fuller, Positivism and Fidelity to Law—A Reply to Professor Hart, 71 Harv. L. Rev. 630 (1958).

36. For a useful general discussion of the "theory of distinctions" in which the interplay between purposes and less transient factors is perceptively analyzed see Crawshay-Williams, Methods and Criteria of Reasoning 103-27 (1957).

37. See pp. 877-87 infra.

38. He said their study encompassed "principles, notions, and distinctions" that are "necessary" to law, and others not necessary but which, because of their "utility," "extend through all communities." Austin, The Province of Jurisprudence Determined 367-69 (Library of Ideas ed. 1954).

actually worked within far narrower bounds. This is especially true of analytical jurists in the United States, who by the mid-1930's had become almost exclusively preoccupied with analyzing concepts of "jural relations" such as "right," "duty," "power," and "liability."[39] In 1937, the then leading American analytical jurist, Albert Kocourek, proclaimed that "the jural relation is the central theme of analytic jurisprudence."[40] And so it was. This myopic narrowness contrasts strikingly with the wide-ranging interests of the new jurists. Already they have published studies of such varied subjects as justice,[41] discretion,[42] strict liability,[43] imperatives,[44] responsibility,[45] causation,[46] and the nature of law itself.[47]

### *B. Construction of a Conceptual Framework or Schema*

If the analytical jurist is to provide the illumination and insight of which he is capable, he must commonly go beyond the conceptual *status quo*. He must go beyond analyzing concepts within our conceptual scheme as it is, and devise improved ways of more adequately representing reality.[48] The necessity for

39. See Hohfeld, Fundamental Legal Conceptions (1923); Kocourek, Jural Relations (1927); Cook, Hohfeld's Contributions to the Science of Law, 28 Yale L.J. 721 (1919); Cook, The Utility of Jurisprudence in the Solution of Legal Problems, 5 Lectures on Legal Topics 337 (1928); Corbin, Jural Relations and Their Classification, 30 Yale L.J. 226 (1921); Corbin, Legal Analysis and Terminology, 29 Yale L.J. 163 (1919); Corbin, Rights and Duties, 33 Yale L.J. 501 (1924); Corbin, What Is a Legal Relation?, 5 Ill. L.Q. 50 (1922); Goble, Affirmative and Negative Legal Relations, 4 Ill. L.Q. 94 (1922); Goble, Negative Legal Relations Re-examined, 5 Ill. L.Q. 36 (1922); Goble, A Redefinition of Basic Legal Terms, 35 Colum. L. Rev. 535 (1935); Goble, The Sanction of a Duty, 37 Yale L.J. 426 (1928); Goble, Terms for Restating the Law, 10 A.B.A.J. 58 (1924); Radin, A Restatement of Hohfeld, 51 Harv. L. Rev. 1141 (1938); Terry, The Arrangement of the Law (pts. 1, 2), 17 Colum. L. Rev. 291, 365 (1917); Terry, Duties, Rights and Wrongs, 10 A.B.A.J. 123 (1924).

For explicit statements of the scope of analytical jurisprudence as Hohfeld and Kocourek saw it see their remarks as quoted in Hall, Readings in Jurisprudence 336-39 (1938).

One brilliant American analytical jurist who was not preoccupied with the topic of jural relations during this period was John Dickinson. See, in particular, the following articles: The Law Behind Law (pts. 1, 2), 29 Colum. L. Rev. 113, 285 (1929); Legal Rules—Their Application and Elaboration, 79 U. Pa. L. Rev. 1052 (1931).

40. Kocourek, The Century of Analytic Jurisprudence Since John Austin, in 2 Law, A Century of Progress: 1835-1935, at 195, 216 (1937).

41. Fried, Justice and Liberty, 6 Nomos (Justice) 126 (1963).

42. Dworkin, Judicial Discretion, 60 J. Philosophy 624 (1963).

43. Wasserstrom, Strict Liability in the Criminal Law, 12 Stan. L. Rev. 731 (1960).

44. Morris, Imperatives and Orders, 26 Theoria 183 (1960).

45. Hughes, Book Review, 16 Stan. L. Rev. 470 (1964).

46. Hart & Honoré, Causation in the Law (1959).

47. Hart, The Concept of Law (1961).

48. On the general nature of this task see Hall, Conceptual Reform—One

such creative and constructive effort stems from two sources. First, our existing conceptual framework does not always have things right initially. Second, things change, and our concepts sometimes lag behind, thus becoming outmoded. Just as the nineteenth century concept of travel is outmoded today, so too is its concept of law.

Not all concepts, not all ideas, are about things. But some are, and we sometimes have the wrong *idea* of a thing. Thus, some do not have the right idea of what it is to have an obligation, or what it is to exercise discretion, or what constitutes punishment, or what morality involves. Instead, they have *mis*conceptions. Usually, misconceptions such as these can be cleared up by someone who has "got things right." But it is conceivable that no one has yet got some things right. Some things none of us yet understands. Our puzzlement exists not because we do not have enough facts about these things; rather, it is that our existing conceptual framework is inadequate—it does not take satisfactory account of what we are puzzled about. A different schema or framework is needed. While providing this involves going beyond the conceptual *status quo*, it does not necessarily involve introducing wholly new concepts or devising new terminologies in which to express these concepts. Frequently, it will involve combining old ideas or old and new ideas. Sometimes a new word or phrase will be invented, or an old word or phrase will be put to a new use.

In the following illustrative passages, Herbert Morris, one of the new analytical jurists, is striving to formulate an improved picture (conceptual schema) of the nature of what Dean Pound called "mechanical jurisprudence."

> First, why does Dean Pound say that "there was *usually* no logical compulsion" [in cases decided by judges]? What types of cases does he have in mind in which there is in fact the logical compulsion to "take the starting point"? Must we not keep steadily before us a fundamental distinction between reasoning logically and regarding oneself as bound by one's duty as a judge? It is not logic that "binds" a judge to apply rules or to decide cases. It is his obligation as a judge to do so. He might fail in his duties as a judge without reasoning illogically. Next, Dean Pound holds that once we "take the starting point" we are logically compelled to reach a result. But it is not clear what is involved for Dean Pound in a judge's "taking a starting point" or in this "logically compelling a result."
>
> Suppose a judge believes that a rule is clearly applicable to the facts of the case before him. Logic does not compel him to apply that rule. If he does not decide one way or the other he is an

Task of Philosophy, 61 Proceedings of the Aristotelian Soc'y 169 (1961); Nowell-Smith, Philosophical Theories, 48 Proceedings of the Aristotelian Soc'y 165 (1948).

irresponsible judge, not illogical in his reasoning. If he should overrule a line of decisions, he is not illogical, though he may be, of course, unreasonable. It is not logic, but *stare decisis* that directs him and in such cases he may be disregarding that principle but not necessarily reasoning invalidly. The judge may agree with counsel that the rule is, for example, that two witnesses are required to the signing of the will; he may agree that there was only one witness to the signing of the will in the case before him, and he still need not be "logically compelled" to reach any result. It is always open to him to take any feature of the situation and treat it as a relevant difference. He may select any difference as relevant without being logically inconsistent. There is a difference between logical inconsistency, involving the holding of two contradictory views, and making unreasonable or absurd distinctions. This is why the expression "carrying concepts to their logical extreme" makes little sense. As far as logic is concerned a judge can stop anywhere. But suppose that he does not overrule nor does he distinguish, what role is then played by logic in the result reached? Judges may, indeed, set their opinions out in a form such that, given the rule and given an additional premise, the conclusion follows logically. But is this what Dean Pound means by "the starting point logically compelling a result"? The impression his language gives is that once a judge has selected a rule, he is compelled by logic to reach a certain conclusion, and that is not so. Logic does not compel that a valid conclusion be drawn, for logic does not tell people to do anything. A person who agreed that "all men are mortal and that Socrates is a man" would not be compelled by logic to do anything further. He can stop talking and he would not be inconsistent. But if he draws the conclusion that Socrates is immortal, then we may say that he is inconsistent. Neither "starting points" nor "logic" compels any decisions.

It is, then, still not clear from Dean Pound's presentation precisely what role is played by logic in mechanical jurisprudence. But there are other difficulties. If we characterize mechanical jurisprudence as a judge's selecting a rule or conception and deriving implications from it without considering the effects of so doing, the following question may remain: First, must the judge in fact believe that logic requires him to choose a certain rule or conception and derive certain implications? Or is it sufficient that in his written opinion he gives the impression that logic is directing the result? To be sure that we have an instance of mechanical jurisprudence, must we first interview a judge or have independent knowledge of the thought processes which led him to his result? When we charge someone with mechanical jurisprudence are we objecting to the way he has written an opinion, setting forth his justification for a decision, or to the way we believe he has reached a particular result? Second, are judges who abide by *stare decisis*, and who apply rules without considering the social effects of so doing, guilty of mechanical jurisprudence? Third, suppose a judge concludes that justice in a particular case requires one kind of decision and the applicable rule another. Suppose, further, that he thinks it more important that a bad rule be applied and predictability furthered in the legal system than that a particular case be decided on the equities. If he writes his opinion solely in conceptual terms, is he guilty of mechanical jurisprudence? Fourth, suppose the judge believes the rule a desirable one but recognizes that in the case before him its application will not be in accord with the equities. Suppose he decides to apply the rule but does not mention in his opinion any considerations other than conceptual ones. Is this mechanical jurisprudence?

We have all had occasion to object to mechanical jurisprudence. We can pick out instances of it. What is rather more difficult to do is to pick out its essential characteristics so that we have a precise idea of what it is that we are objecting to.[49]

In the foregoing passages, the jurist tries to clarify something that is complex and only imperfectly understood. No readily available concept, no *use* of a familiar phrase or phrases seems to do the trick. Yet it is plain that there is an important phenomenon to be characterized. The only question is: How? In this example, the analyst has not, in the end, offered anything by way of a positive conceptualization of his own. Nor has he invented any words or recommended any new uses for old ones. Presumably, a positive account will eventually be presented. When it appears, it will, in one sense, be new. It will be an addition to, indeed a revision of, our existing conceptual scheme. The present scheme relies on "mechanical jurisprudence" and "logic" to represent the reality at hand, and in the foregoing passages we are shown that these are inadequate.

It is essential to stress that conceptual lag, as well as the failure to get things right in the beginning, gives rise to the necessity of constructing conceptual frameworks. To illustrate: One of the central problems of jurisprudence is the problem of explicating the nature of law itself. Law—the phenomenon of law—unlike elephants or triangles, is a mode of social organization and therefore is itself subject to some change, even fundamental change over long periods. Because of this, our understanding of law, our conceptions of it, may ultimately require revision.[50] Hence, in criticizing a theory such as John Austin's that law consists of sovereign commands, there are two possible dimensions of criticism. It is not merely that Austin might have gotten it wrong in the first place back in 1828. It is also possible that some features of his theory might need to be revised specifically to account for basic developments since that date.[51] For example, any account

49. Morris, Book Review, 13 Stan. L. Rev. 185, 203-04 (1960). (Reprinted with the permission of the Stanford Law Review.)

50. See generally Corbett, Innovation and Philosophy, 68 Mind 289 (1959). See also note 48 supra.

51. See generally Hexner, The Timeless Concept of Law, 52 J. Politics 48, 62-63 (1943).

of the nature of law in modern industrial societies must make a place for the pervasive impact of new administrative institutions with their varied structures and paraphernalia of orders, rulings, and regulations.

This, then, explains in a general way what is involved in constructing a conceptual framework, and explains what occasions this kind of creative analytical activity. With respect to this activity, how do the old and the new analysts compare? It cannot be said that old analysts did not engage in this activity. John Austin certainly did. His lectures are filled with formulations which he apparently thought more faithfully represented the nature of law than any framework theretofore devised.[52] But it can be said that, to date, conceptual revision, that is, the construction of new conceptual frameworks, appears to be a far more central interest of the new analysts as a whole than it was of their predecessors. Hart and all of the other principal analysts have been concerned with it, at one time or another.[53] Furthermore, since the nature of this kind of analytical work is much better understood today, it should be performed more perspicaciously.

### C. *Rational Justification*

Rational justification is a third main type of activity that is, in its own way, analytical. Consider the following illustrative questions: What, if any, is the rational justification—the "case" —for civil disobedience? What, if any, is the rational justification—the "case"—for punishment as such? What, if any, is the rational justification—the "case"—for stare decisis? Questions of this type call upon the jurist to "make out a general case"—to marshal and articulate general justifying arguments, rather than to analyze the conceptual *status quo* or construct new conceptual schemes with their accompanying terminologies. Rational justification differs in two ways from the familiar day-to-day practical justification employed by the man of action. First, the analytical jurist works on a general type of question, *e.g.*, what, if any, is the rational justification—the "case"—for civil disobedience? The man of action, however, addresses himself to a more immediate and specific form of this general question, *e.g.*, is it justified to

52. See Austin, The Province of Jurisprudence Determined (Library of Ideas ed. 1954).

53. See, e.g., Hart, The Concept of Law (1961); Wasserstrom, The Judicial Decision: Toward a Theory of Legal Justification (1961); Dworkin, Judicial Discretion, 60 J. Philosophy 624 (1963); Fried, Moral Causation, 77 Harv. L. Rev. 1258 (1964); Williams, Concept of Legal Liberty, 56 Colum. L. Rev. 1129 (1956); Hughes, Book Review, 16 Stan. L. Rev. 470 (1964); Morris, Book Review, 13 Stan. L. Rev. 185 (1960).

disobey the local ordinance against mixing races in public hotels? Second, the man of action, in the nature of things, takes a stand on the merits of his specific question, whereas the analytical jurist need not take a stand at all. His job is completed when he has formulated and marshalled the relevant arguments. While this task necessarily requires that he evaluate the *rational* plausibility of possible arguments, it does not *call* on him to take a stand on the ultimate question or to grind an axe of any kind. Rational justification is analytical at least in the positive respect that it involves differentiating, constructing, and marshalling rational arguments.

While rational justification does not appear to have engaged the old analytical jurists to any significant extent, it is a main interest of the new. Hart has written on the justification of punishment as a social practice,[54] Wasserstrom on the justification of judicial decisions,[55] and Dworkin on justified and unjustified uses of law to enforce morality.[56] This broadening of interests to include rational justification is a welcome development in an age incessantly plagued by forces fostering irrationalism.[57] It is simply not true that just anything can serve as a reason for anything else, nor is it true that all reasons are fungible, that one is always just as good as any other. Also, reasons count. They are seldom rationalizations.

### D. *Purposive Implication*

Though of less significance than the activities already discussed, "purposive implication"[58] is another kind of analytical endeavor that has interested some of the new jurists. There is little or no evidence, however, that it occupied any of their pred-

54. See Hart, Prolegomenon to the Principles of Punishment, 60 Proceedings of the Aristotelian Soc'y 1 (1960).

55. See Wasserstrom, The Judicial Decision: Toward a Theory of Legal Justification (1961).

56. Dworkin, Lord Devlin and the Enforcement of Morals, 75 Yale L.J. 986 (1966).

57. For the record, it is worth identifying some of these forces. First, the tag end, at least, of logical positivism remains. Some positivists thought rational justification was not even possible. Second, there is misplaced libertarianism: "A man is *free* to adopt any position." Third, there is misplaced egalitarianism: "One man's view is just as good as any other man's." Fourth, Freud gets into the act: "We don't know what our *real* reasons are, so they cannot be all that important." And, just to end this particular list, we have the alarming result-orientation of a few modern political scientists: "It's the result that counts, not the reasons; reasons have little to do with results anyway."

58. This phrase was very recently introduced into the literature by Professor Lon L. Fuller. See Fuller, The Morality of Law 184 (1964). While Professor Fuller's book and his other works are full of insights of interest to analytical jurists, he would probably not want to be considered one of them.

ecessors. Its general character can be briefly explained. Consider the following illustrative questions: Given a purpose to have an effective system of law, does it *follow* that, in general, there must be rules? Known rules? Rules that are prospectively applicable? Given man's purpose to survive, his nature, and the conditions under which he lives, does it *follow* that he must have rules proscribing theft and violence? Given a purpose to have a humane and liberal society, does it *follow* that the legal system in such a society must recognize some version of the doctrine of *mens rea*? Questions of this nature call for work different from rational justification. In addressing such questions, the jurist does not build up a general case for or against some general proposition, institution, practice, or idea; instead, he traces what the acceptance of social purposes, aims, or values *commits* us to in terms of social arrangements and social ordering.[59] This activity is "analytical" at least in the positive respect that it involves tracing implications of what may be called "social premises."[60]

Thus, in addition to conceptual analysis, some or all of the new jurists are interested in what we have called the construction of conceptual frameworks, rational justification, and purposive implication, each of which may be plausibly characterized as analytical in nature. In these latter three types of work, most earlier analytical jurists displayed little or no interest. In summary, it can be said that the concerns of the new analytical jurists are broader in at least two important respects—they are performing a wider variety of analytical activities and, in doing conceptual analysis, always a major concern of analytical jurists, they are focusing on a much wider range of problems.

## III

## Methodology of the New Analytical Jurists

With respect to methodology and approach, the new analytical jurists are more sophisticated than their predecessors. This is largely because the new analysts, as performers of what

59. Actually, the most outstanding contemporary example of this kind of work appears in Fuller, The Morality of Law 33-94 (1964). But see Hart, The Concept of Law 189-95 (1961), for an apt example from the work of an avowed analyst.

60. While this work is in one sense deductive, it differs from strictly formal deduction. It would be inappropriate to say that valid conclusions of purposive implication derive their validity—their "necessity"—from compliance with formal rules of logical inference. It is better to say, simply, that our shared purposes, our knowledge or assumptions concerning relevant facts, and our practical wisdom "demand" these conclusions. Cf. Hart, The Concept of Law 195 (1961), where the author discusses the concept of "natural" as opposed to "definitional" or "formal" necessity.

is essentially a philosophical enterprise, have been able to take advantage of important methodological advances in philosophy generally, advances which had either not yet occurred or were not so widely understood when the older analysts were at work.

It is not possible to present these advances in the form of positive "how to do it" formulas. There are no such formulas. Rather, the new-found methodological sophistication is best described in terms of a deeper insight into the basic nature of analytical work,[61] and a greater awareness of certain sources of error that have traditionally plagued analytical jurists. It is important to explain several of these sources of error in some detail. Examples will be given to show how these sources of error affected earlier analysts, but no attempt will be made to "prove" that the new jurists as a whole have escaped them. This would invite all the notorious difficulties of "proving a negative," and would require more space than is available. It is enough to say that the new analysts are cognizant of these sources of error,[62] and try to avoid them. So far they seem, on the whole, to have been rather successful. These things cannot be said of the early analytical jurists.

The sources of error to be explained are (1) the urge to convert conceptual questions into straightforward questions of fact, (2) the urge to "grind axes," (3) the influence of misleading models, (4) the reductionist impulse, (5) essentialism, and (6) misuse of definition *per genus et differentiam*. It is not claimed that no other influences are at work in the examples that will be used to illustrate the foregoing. Nor is it claimed that the errors involved are errors *because* of the influence of the sources of error identified. Whether an example illustrates an error obviously depends on the merits. For present purposes, however, it is not necessary to argue merits; error is therefore assumed in each example, and the focus is on its source.

### *A. The Urge To Convert Conceptual Questions Into Straightforward Questions of Fact*

There is a difference between conceptual questions and straightforward questions of empirical fact. It may be true that,

61. Some say this insight has itself come to philosophers generally only in this century. Thus, it has been remarked, "it is only quite recently that the subject-matter, or rather the tasks, of philosophy have come to be clearly distinguished from those of other disciplines." Warnock, English Philosophy Since 1900, at 172 (1958).

62. Their own publications include many references to the works of thinkers who clarified the nature of these sources of error. Several of these earlier thinkers are referred to in note 21 supra.

despite the long history of philosophy, this difference has never been satisfactorily drawn.[63] But it is clear that a difference exists. For example, we must first decide what constitutes intentional behavior, before setting out empirically to find particular instances of it. For reasons we shall not try to explore, early analytical jurists seem to have succumbed to the urge to convert conceptual questions into straightforward questions of empirical fact. To cite an important example, John Austin and some of his followers were led to say that having an obligation consists merely of being threatened by a sanction if one does not act or forbear as indicated.[64] This is a faulty analysis, for one may quite rightly say a person has an obligation even if there is no possibility that a sanction will be imposed for noncompliance. What very likely accounts for this analysis is the urge to translate the conceptual question, "What constitutes having an obligation?" into the straightforward empirical or sociological question, "What is likely to happen if citizens do not act or forbear as indicated?" Unlike the former question, this is plainly a *straightforward* empirical question calling for sociological research into human behavior other than verbal behavior. Once such research (or, more often, speculation) shows that, as a matter of cold, hard, empirical fact, sanctions normally follow noncompliance, then it is but a short step to the erroneous conclusion that "having an obligation" consists merely of being threatened by a sanction and that, therefore, it is not possible to have an obligation if no sanction for noncompliance is likely.

A recent example, and therefore one not involving an earlier analytical jurist, superbly illustrates the widespread tendency to convert conceptual questions into straightforward empirical ones. It arises in one of the celebrated exchanges between Professor Lon L. Fuller and Professor H. L. A. Hart, one of the leading modern analysts. Hart wrote:

> If social control . . . [through legal rules] is to function, the rules must satisfy certain conditions: they must be intelligible and within the capacity of most to obey, and in general they must not be retrospective, though exceptionally they may be. . . . Plainly these features of control by rule are closely related to the requirements

63. Professor Gilbert Ryle has recently said: "We, too, know in our bones how philosophical problems differ in kind from scientific problems; but our statements of the differences continue to be inadequate." Ryle, Dialectic in the Academy, in New Essays on Plato and Aristotle 39, 67 (Bambrough ed. 1965). To add one remark, it seems plain that both are empirical, though in different ways. Hence, the use of the word "straightforward" in this paper. But it is not suggested that the word solves any problems.

64. For a faithful statement and incisive criticism of this view see Hart, The Concept of Law 79-88 (1961).

of justice which lawyers term principles of legality. Indeed one critic of positivism has seen in these aspects of control by rules, something amounting to a necessary connexion between law and morality, and suggested that they may be called "the inner morality of law". Again, if this is what the necessary connexion of law and morality means, we may accept it. It is unfortunately compatible with very great iniquity.[65]

Interpreting this passage, Professor Fuller concludes that: "Certainly one could not wish for a more explicit denial of any possible interaction between the internal and external moralities of law than that contained in the last sentence."[66] This, however, is a false interpretation. Hart is not saying, as Fuller takes him to be saying, that law and morality do not, in fact, affect each other. He is only saying that they do not *necessarily* affect each other and that good law in the sense of intelligible, prospective law is *logically* "compatible with very great iniquity." Yet Fuller wants to convert Hart's proposition into a straightforward empirical proposition of fact.

### B. *The Urge To Grind an Axe*

Conceptual questions are also sometimes, consciously or unconsciously, converted into questions of value. Analytical jurists have, from time to time, smuggled their own value preferences into what they seem to want to present as conceptual analysis. While purporting to analyze concepts, they have really been evaluating and recommending. Examples of this abound; one of the most spectacular appears in the work of Thomas Hobbes, the earliest thinker of importance in the history of analytical jurisprudence. Hobbes published his *Leviathan* in 1651, a period of great civil strife and turmoil. In this book, Hobbes' value preference for order emerges with luminous clarity, yet he pretends to be analyzing the concept of law within the framework of his day.[67] Thus, Hobbes wrongly contended that it would be conceptually illegitimate to speak of limited sovereignty[68] or a right to revolt.[69] While we may sympathize with Hobbes' desire for order in a time of great civil disorder, his is not really an analysis; rather, it is an indirect way of endorsing values. There is nothing conceptually illegitimate in the notion that sovereign power may

65. Id. at 202.
66. Fuller, The Morality of Law 154 (1964).
67. He renders his pretense explicit. See Hobbes, Leviathan 172 (Oakeshott ed. 1960), where he says he is showing "what is law."
68. Id. at 130, 173.
69. Id. at 113-15.

be limited, or the notion that citizens living under law have a right to revolt. These notions do not have the same kind of sound that "round-square" has.

Of course, the urge to grind an axe is not necessarily inconsistent with sound conceptual analysis. Indeed, it may provide the motivation for careful and, on its merits, wholly defensible analysis. But it may also distort an analysis, particularly if the axe at hand is one the analyst holds dear.

### C. *The Influence of Misleading or Irrelevant Models*

Models play an important role in human thought. As ideal types, they provide something to anchor to and even to judge by. But not everything can be assimilated to a model. Moreover, not all relevant models are equally relevant. Finally, a model is nothing more than that. And it can blind us.

The influence of irrelevant or misleading models has been a fertile source of error in analytical and other kinds of jurisprudence. Thus, the model of scientific knowledge embodied in general laws has sometimes led jurists to seek more unity and universality than exists in the nature of the case. Austin, for example, was led to think that there *must* be certain principles of positive law common to all developed systems.[70] Mathematical models have played their part. Indeed, Kocourek lamented that jurisprudence had not sufficiently imitated mathematics and formal logic.[71] Because of this, he was sometimes led to insist on what *he* conceived to be "logic" at the expense of conceptual felicity. For example, he wrote as late as 1937 that the "proposition, 'that "sovereign power is incapable of legal limitation," ' while often denied, is an inescapable proposition of logical truth."[72] Similarly, Bentham thought that the activity of rational justification was essentially a process of calculation. We are to *add up* the pleasures and pains involved, *count* the number of persons affected, *multiply* this number by the relevant pleasures and pains, and act accordingly.[73] "The law giver . . . [and] the geometrician . . . are both solving problems by sober calculation," according to Bentham.[74] At the other extreme, some jurists have

70. See Austin, The Province of Jurisprudence Determined (Library of Ideas ed. 1954).

71. Kocourek, The Century of Analytic Jurisprudence Since John Austin, in 2 Law, A Century of Progress: 1835-1935, at 195, 210, 221 (1937).

72. Id. at 200.

73. Bentham, An Introduction to the Principles of Morals and Legislation 30-31 (Hafner Library ed. 1948).

74. 2 Bentham, Works 19 (Bowring ed. 1859).

been influenced by the so-called "Boo-Hurrah" model of "justification," according to which *rational* justification is simply not possible.[75]

Architectural models have played a part. Both Hobbes and Austin were inclined to apply a simple top and bottom framework to the analysis of law, with the sovereign on top "laying down" the law to the citizenry at the bottom.[76] This, combined with the influence of the "command" model drawn from the military,[77] probably kept Austin, at least, from seeing that "valid law" is a concept that can be most effectively analyzed in terms of the compliance of specific rules with generally accepted criteria for the identification of laws rather than in terms of whether the rules are commands of an uncommanded commander.

The influence of the criminal-law model has been pervasive. Among other things, it has led some thinkers to neglect the vital role in a legal system of rules that, unlike the rules of the criminal law, confer powers rather than impose duties.[78]

The foregoing are only some of the many models that have led analytical jurists astray. The new jurists are cognizant of this basic source of error, more so, it seems, than any of their predecessors, but this is not, of course, any *guarantee* that their work will always be free of it.

### *D. The Reductionist Impulse*

Reductionism is not all bad. For example, generalization or systematization may be in order, and for purposes such as these it may be necessary to throw *different* things into the *same* category—to "reduce" one thing to another thing.[79] But for other purposes, distinctions may be more important than similarities. Succumbing to the reductionist impulse, the analyst may obscure important differences, and even ignore some things altogether. Thus, reductionism can be a vice. As such, it plagued the efforts

75. The outstanding instance today is Hans Kelsen. See, e.g., Kelsen, General Theory of Law and State xvi (Wedberg transl. 1945), where it is said that the problem of justification is rooted "in the emotional, not in the rational." Kocourek also said that "in its pure form morals is an emotional reaction." Kocourek, An Introduction to the Science of Law 132 (1930).

76. Austin, The Province of Jurisprudence Determined 191-361 (Library of Ideas ed. 1954); Hobbes, Leviathan 188, 210 (Oakeshott ed. 1960).

77. Austin, The Province of Jurisprudence Determined 13-18 (Library of Ideas ed. 1954). Austin was in the army from the ages of sixteen to twenty-two.

78. For extended discussion of this see Hart, The Concept of Law 27-41 (1961).

79. For extended discussion of the nature of reductionism see Symposium—Reducibility, in Men and Machines, Aristotelian Society Supplementary Vol. XXVI, 87-138 (1952). See also Hart, Analytical Jurisprudence in Mid-Twentieth Century: A Reply to Professor Bodenheimer, 105 U. Pa. L. Rev. 953, 956 (1957).

of earlier analytical jurists such as Austin who sought, for example, to reduce all types of directives having authoritative force in a system of law to "commands."[80] This obscured the very great differences between such things as orders, rules, rulings, principles, and regulations. He sought to reduce the various factors that account for compliance with a system of law to "habits."[81] This obscured the differences between, and indeed ignored altogether, such differing factors as the desire for order, the inclination simply to do as others do, the wish to be respected, and so forth. Austin sought to reduce the diverse things citizens do with legal rules to that of "obeying" them,[82] whereas what is done with rules includes many other activities as well.

These examples suffice to show that the analytical jurist must be wary of the reductionist impulse. As Bishop Butler said, "Everything is what it is, and not another thing."[83]

### E. *Essentialism*

Plato thought most things have an "ideal form." In *The Republic* he even said there was an ideal form for beds.[84] For Plato, to analyze a concept was to search for an ideal form—an essence. He assumed that all of the diverse things to which any general term is applied must have some defining property or properties in common.[85] While it may be true that essences can be found for some concepts, it is doubtful that an essence can be found for all concepts. Yet there is evidence that some philosophers, legal and nonlegal, have assumed this.

Austin seems to have been a searcher for essences where none could be found.[86] Consider, for example, his analysis of the concept of law. In Austin's day, many diverse societies existed to which this word was applied. Austin undertook to determine properties these societies had in common by virtue of which they were said to have law.[87] He concluded that it was not possible to con-

80. Austin, The Province of Jurisprudence Determined 10-33 (Library of Ideas ed. 1954).

81. Id. at 191-361.

82. Ibid.

83. See Moore, Principia Ethica iii (1903).

84. Plato, The Republic bk. X, in 1 The Dialogues of Plato 852-53 (Jowett transl. Random House 1937).

85. See, e.g., Plato, Meno, in 1 The Dialogues of Plato 352-53 (Jowett transl. Random House 1937).

86. This similarity between what classical jurists sometimes did and what Austin sometimes did has been noticed by others. See 4 Mill, Dissertations and Discussions 223 (1868); Chloros, Some Aspects of the Social and Ethical Element in Analytical Jurisprudence, 67 Juridical Rev. 79 (1955); Morris, Verbal Disputes and the Legal Philosophy of John Austin, 7 U.C.L.A.L. Rev. 27, 36 (1960).

87. Austin, The Province of Jurisprudence Determined 367-68 (Library of Ideas ed. 1954).

ceive of a system of law without the following properties as "constituent parts": duty, right, liberty, injury, punishment, sovereignty, and independent political existence.[88] This was Austin's "essence" of law. He was apparently led to search for such an essence because he assumed that the propriety of using the same term for diverse phenomena must inevitably turn on the presence of some property or properties *common to all the things* to which the term is applied. But with many terms of interest to analytical jurists, a search for an essence is likely to prove fruitless. This is certainly true of "law" itself. Of course, the various societies to which the term "law" is applied cannot lack all or even very many of the properties normally present in legal systems and still be legal systems. Yet even at this date no one has established that there is some defining property or properties which all things properly called legal systems have in common and which must therefore be present for the term to be correctly applied. Austin seems to have stressed the property of "unlimited sovereignty" more than any other, but even this is not present in many legal systems.

The influential Ludwig Wittgenstein, in one of his attacks on essentialism,[89] offered "family resemblances" as an alternative type of unifying factor. While there are still other types,[90] Wittgenstein's has been more widely discussed in philosophical literature than any other and is therefore singled out for explanation. He should be allowed to speak for himself:

> Consider for example the proceedings that we call "games". I mean board-games, card-games, ball-games, Olympic games, and so on. What is common to them all?—Don't say: "There *must* be something common, or they would not be called 'games' "—but *look and see* whether there is anything common to all.—For if you look at them you will not see something that is common to *all*, but similarities, relationships, and a whole series of them at that. To repeat: don't think, but look!—Look for example at board-games, with their multifarious relationships. Now pass to card-games; here you find many correspondences with the first group, but many common features drop out, and others appear. When we pass next to ball-games, much that is common is retained, but much is lost. —Are they all "amusing"? Compare chess with noughts and crosses. Or is there always winning and losing, or competition between players? Think of patience. In ball games there is winning and losing; but when a child throws his ball at the wall and catches

88. Id. at 367.

89. On essentialism generally see Wittgenstein, The Blue and Brown Books 17-18 (1958). See also Pitcher, The Philosophy of Wittgenstein 215-27 (1964) (chapter entitled The Attack on Essentialism).

90. The best concise discussion of several others is in J. L. Austin, Philosophical Papers 37-43 (1961).

it again, this feature has disappeared. Look at the parts played by skill and luck; and at the difference between skill in chess and skill in tennis. Think now of games like ring-a-ring-a-roses; here is the element of amusement, but how many other characteristic features have disappeared! And we can go through the many, many other groups of games in the same way; can see how similarities crop up and disappear.

And the result of this examination is: we see a complicated network of similarities overlapping and criss-crossing: sometimes overall similarities, sometimes similarities of detail.

I can think of no better expression to characterize these similarities than "family resemblances"; for the various resemblances between members of a family: build, features, colour of eyes, gait, temperament, etc. etc. overlap and criss-cross in the same way.—And I shall say: "games" form a family.[91]

### *F. Misuse of Definition* Per Genus et Differentiam

There is evidence that Austin and some of his successors tried to use the technique of definition *per genus et differentiam* to explicate concepts of and about law.[92] The new jurists recognize, however, that this technique cannot be used illuminatingly on many such concepts, for it presupposes that the concepts to be analyzed are not sui generis, that they fall within familiar and well understood genuses, and that they can be meaningfully isolated as single words or expressions which can be relatively straightforwardly correlated with counterparts in the world of fact and then differentiated accordingly from other species of the same genus.[93] These conditions are met in the case of concepts such as "dog" or "chair." These are not sui generis; "animal" is the genus for one and "furniture" for the other and each genus is itself familiar and well understood. Moreover, the terms "dog" or "chair" can be taken in isolation from whole sentences in specific contexts and be more or less straightforwardly correlated with counterparts in the world of fact which can then be differentiated from other species of the same genus. But what of words such as "corporation," "ownership," "right," or "discretion"? The conditions for use of the technique of definition *per genus et differentiam* to explicate the uses of terms such as these are simply not present. Even if not sui generis, they cannot be assigned to a general and well understood genus. Moreover, it is not possible to take these words singly and correlate them straight-

91. Wittgenstein, Philosophical Investigations 31e-32e (1953).

92. See, e.g., Austin, The Province of Jurisprudence Determined (Library of Ideas ed. 1954). See also Holland, Elements of Jurisprudence passim (13th ed. 1924); Kocourek, An Introduction to the Science of Law 215-16 (1927).

93. Cf. Hart, Analytical Jurisprudence in Mid-Twentieth Century: A Reply to Professor Bodenheimer, 105 U. Pa. L. Rev. 953, 960-63 (1957).

forwardly with counterparts in the world of fact. To explicate the uses of such terms, the new analytical jurist can invoke other techniques, one of which we shall call "contextual explication."[94] Pursuant to this method, he assembles examples of the relevant uses of the term within whole sentences in specific contexts.[95] In this way, he reveals what these words do—the concepts they convey in the context of their use within specific sentences.

This process can be lucidly illustrated by reference to games. Consider, for example, the sentence: "The batter is out," and suppose that someone wonders what being "out" is. This cannot be explained by assigning "outness" to some familiar genus, correlating it straightforwardly with a counterpart in the world of fact, and then differentiating it accordingly from other species of the same genus. The analyst can, however, confront his questioner with examples of sentences in which the relevant expression is used and then identify the relevant conditions present in the context of these uses. Thus, to explicate "right," the analytical jurist would, among other things, put this term in the context of sentences such as "*A* has a right that *B* pay him $50." Once the characteristic uses of this expression are identified, he would then show how they presuppose such things as (1) the existence of a relationship between persons, (2) the existence of a system of law, (3) the existence of a rule of the system such that *B* must do something for *A*. It is an explication of this nature that many concepts demand, for they cannot be readily assigned to a familiar genus, and are, relatively speaking, far more "context dependent" —far more intricately bound up with the whole context of their use in sentences in specific instances—than are words such as "dog" or "chair."[96]

It is misleading to describe conceptual studies as definitional anyway. Consider, for example, the problem of constructing a theory of law. In some texts on jurisprudence, this problem is called "The Definition of Law."[97] Such talk of "defining" ought

94. Cf. Hart, Definition and Theory in Jurisprudence, 70 L.Q. Rev. 37 (1954).

95. Lawyers must be cautioned that this is quite different from *inferring from context* what some particular person most likely meant by the use of a term or expression on a particular occasion.

96. Bentham was aware of the limitations of "defining" *per genus et differentiam* and suggested an alternative procedure along the lines indicated in the text. Bentham, Fragment on Government 232-36 (Montague ed. 1891). Professor H. L. A. Hart engrafted onto this procedure a step that involves showing what is the logical "function" of the sentence in which the word appears, e.g., descriptive, ascriptive, conclusion-drawing, and so on. What this additional step adds is not clear. One thinker has recently argued against it. See Simpson, The Analysis of Legal Concepts, 80 L.Q. Rev. 535, 555-57 (1965).

97. See, e.g., G. Paton, Jurisprudence 62-93 (3d ed. 1964).

to be abandoned for the following reasons. First, for many persons, definitions are sought to clear up doubt about usage. But theories of law do not originate in doubts of this kind. Second, definition is, for many, something one finds in a dictionary. Yet legal theorists, even at Oxford, seldom rely on dictionaries. Third, a definition is typically something concise. But theories of law, though they can be summed up, are almost never concise. Fourth, to many, definition is a matter of drawing boundaries. Yet most theories of law are concerned not only with boundaries between, say, law and morals, but also with the internal complexities of legal systems. Finally, ordinary definitions may be criticized as accurate or inaccurate reports of usage, but theories of law are criticized primarily as adequate or inadequate for the purpose of representing the basic features of actual legal systems.

The conversion of conceptual questions into straightforward questions of empirical fact, the process that we have called "axe grinding," the use of irrelevant and misleading models, reductionism, essentialism, and misuse of definition *per genus et differentiam*, are, then, all basic errors or sources of error in analytical jurisprudence. The new jurists are cognizant of these, and of still others of perhaps equal significance.[98] Because of this, more can be expected of them than of their predecessors.

98. Other sources of error include:

(1) The assumption that all concepts have "positive" content only. Not all do. Some function as "excluders." See the important article by Hall, Excluders, 20 Analysis 1 (1959). For the argument that the concept "voluntary," in the criminal law, "serves to exclude a heterogeneous range of cases such as physical compulsion, coercion by threats, accidents, mistakes, etc., and not to designate a mental element or state . . ." see Hart, The Ascription of Responsibility and Rights, 49 Proceedings of the Aristotelian Soc'y 171, 180 (1949).

(2) The assumption that dichotomies are truly dichotomies. Often they are not. For general remarks on this source of error in philosophy and in jurisprudence see J. L. Austin, Philosophical Papers 138-41 (1961). For a recent attack on the "rule vs. discretion" dichotomy in jurisprudence see Dworkin, Judicial Discretion, 60 J. Philosophy 624 (1963).

(3) The assumption that the object of inquiry can, without distortion, be analyzed from only one point of view. For discussion of the inadequacies of the "legislative point of view" toward the nature of law see Summers, Professor Fuller on Morality and Law, 18 J. Legal Ed. 1, 19-21 (1956).

(4) The assumption that the object of study is static rather than dynamic in nature. Many objects of study are continually changing. For general discussion see Rescher, Revolt Against Process, 59 J. Philosophy 410 (1962). For an effort to show why the nature of law itself must be analyzed as in "a continuous process of *becoming*" see H. M. Hart, Holmes' Positivism—An Addendum, 64 Harv. L. Rev. 929, 930 (1951).

(5) The assumption that "if we can only discover the true meanings of each of a cluster of key terms . . . that we use in some particular field . . . then it must without question transpire that each will fit into place in some single, interlocking, consistent conceptual scheme." J. L. Austin, Philosophical Papers 151 n.1 (1961). This assumption is false. Among analytical jurists who have succumbed to it, Hohfeld is an outstanding example. Hohfeld assumed that the "true"

## IV

## Doctrinal Commitment and Positivistic Bias

The new analytical jurists are less doctrinaire and less positivistic than were Austin and his successors.

### A. *Less Doctrinaire*

The new jurists are not committed to any particular doctrines, that is, they are not committed, as a group, to any particular solutions to the problems they confront. Indeed, as we remarked earlier, there is very little evidence of agreement between any of them on any solutions.

This cannot be said of John Austin and many of his successors. Explaining the nature of law may be said to be the central problem of jurisprudence. For many of the early jurists, the "party line" became Austin's "imperative" theory of the nature of law.[99] Essentially, this theory is that law consists of sovereign commands of an uncommanded commander.[100] Analysts became so closely associated with the imperative theory that some observers identified the whole discipline of analytical jurisprudence with this crude and simple account of law. Thus, the phrases "analytical jurisprudence" and the "imperative theory" were sometimes used interchangeably.[101] This was and is a mistake. Analytical jurisprudence is a discipline, not a doctrine, let alone a doctrine about the nature of law, and its problems include many besides this one.

It goes without saying that none of the new jurists adopts Austin's theory of law. In fact, the only new jurist to publish a general and systematic account of the nature of law has extensively criticized and rejected Austin's analysis.[102]

analysis of "right" neatly yields four relations, each with its "correlative" and its "opposite." See Hohfeld, Fundamental Legal Conceptions (1923). For criticism see J. Stone, Legal System and Lawyers' Reasonings 156-61 (1964).

(6) The influence of doctrines current in philosophy generally. For a general discussion of this source of error in jurisprudence see Bobbio, Nature et Fonction de la Philosophie du Droit, 7 Archive de Philosophie du Droit 1, 4 (1937). For illustrations of specific ways such doctrines can lead to error in jurisprudence see Hart, Scandinavian Realism, 1959 Camb. L.J. 233.

99. See Amos, The Science of Law (9th ed. 1909); Amos, Systematic View of the Science of Jurisprudence (1872); Holland, Elements of Jurisprudence (13th ed. 1924); Markby, Elements of Law Considered With Reference to Principles of General Jurisprudence (4th ed. 1889). See generally Brown, The Austinian Theory of Law (1906).

100. See Austin, The Province of Jurisprudence Determined passim (Library of Ideas ed. 1954).

101. See, e.g., E. W. Patterson, Jurisprudence: Men and Ideas of the Law 14-15 (1953).

102. See Hart, The Concept of Law 1-120 (1961).

### *B. Less Positivistic*

What is "legal positivism"? Today, this phrase is used to describe so many different things that it surely deserves to be junked. Here are some of the differing views the phrase is used to refer to:[103] (1) that law as it is can be clearly differentiated from law as it ought to be,[104] (2) that only the concepts of existing positive law are fit for analytical study,[105] (3) that force or power is the essence of law,[106] (4) that law is a self-sufficient closed system which does not draw on other disciplines for any of its premises,[107] (5) that laws and legal decisions cannot, in any ultimate sense, be rationally defended,[108] (6) that a logically self-consistent Utopia exists to which positive law ought to be made to conform,[109] (7) that, in interpreting statutes, considerations of what the law ought to be have no place,[110] (8) that judicial decisions are logical deductions from preexisting premises,[111] (9) that certainty is the "chief end of law,"[112] and (10) that there is an absolute duty to obey evil laws.[113]

Most of the new jurists are very likely legal positivists in the first of the foregoing senses. That is, most of them would probably say that the law as it is can be clearly differentiated from the law as it ought to be.[114] In this, they are at one with their predecessors. But, thereafter, the new and the old part company. There is no evidence that the new are "legal positivists"

103. In surveying the relevant literature, wholly novel senses of "legal positivism" have been disregarded. One such example quite recently appeared. See Ehrenzweig, Psychoanalytical Jurisprudence: A Common Language for Babylon, 65 Colum. L. Rev. 1331, 1336-37, 1353 (1965). While the matter is not free of interpretational difficulties, what the author seems to be saying is that the two "philosophies," "positivism" and "natural law," are, analytically at least, *identical*. Similarly novel (and similarly questionable) is the author's suggestion that "positivism" does not have as strong an "emotional preference" for justice as does "natural law." Id. at 1342.

104. See generally Hart, Positivism and the Separation of Law and Morals, 71 Harv. L. Rev. 593 (1958).

105. See Kelsen, General Theory of Law and State xiii (Wedberg transl. 1961); Ehrenzweig, supra note 103, at 1355.

106. See Friedmann, Legal Theory 221 (4th ed. 1960).

107. See Bodenheimer, Analytical Positivism, Legal Realism, and the Future of Legal Method, 44 Va. L. Rev. 365 (1958).

108. See Hart, Positivism and the Separation of Law and Morals, 71 Harv. L. Rev. 593, 624 (1958). Cf. Ehrenzweig, supra note 103, at 1335, 1346.

109. See Kahn-Freund, Introduction to Renner, The Institutions of Private Law and Their Social Functions 8 (1949).

110. See Berman, The Nature and Functions of Law 23-25 (1958).

111. See Morison, Some Myth About Positivism, 68 Yale L.J. 212 (1958).

112. See Friedmann, Legal Theory 163 (4th ed. 1960).

113. See Shuman, Legal Positivism, Its Scope and Limitations 177-209 (1963).

114. The most comprehensive presentation of this view by one of them is in Hart, Positivism and the Separation of Law and Morals, 71 Harv. L. Rev. 593 (1958).

in any of the other foregoing senses of this expression. But were their predecessors? There is evidence that some of them were legal positivists in senses (1), (2), (3), and (5).[115] It is largely for this reason that it is possible to say that the new jurists are *less* "positivistic." But, in truth, very little evidence has been found that Austin or any of his successors were "legal positivists" in the other senses of this expression. It would not, however, be possible to *demonstrate* this without writing a series of articles comparable to Morison's *Some Myth About Positivism*,[116] in which the author shows that, contrary to conventional understanding,[117] Austin did not believe that judicial decisions were logical deductions from preexisting premises (sense (8) above).

The opportunity must not be missed to point to a further moral of this story. The phrases "analytical jurisprudence" and "legal positivism" are not uncommonly used interchangeably in contemporary legal literature.[118] From what has been said, it follows that this practice should be discontinued. Logically, a scholar can engage in analytical work without espousing any of the foregoing "positivist" doctrines. Moreover, many have.

## V

## Practical Utility of the New Analytical Jurisprudence

It is one of the important lessons of the history of inquiry in the physical sciences that many things turn out to have practical uses not foreseen at the investigatory stage. Moreover, things can have practical value in different ways. Thus, although an idea may not appear to have any immediate and specific practical use, it may influence a thinker's general outlook or approach and thus better equip him to do his work. Furthermore, what sometimes seems initially to be practical may turn out to be very impractical.

All this is widely understood. It would seem to follow that scholars, at least, would be wary of condemning systematic intellectual endeavors as of "no practical value." But the late Dean Roscoe Pound, the leading American jurisprudential scholar in

115. Thus, Austin for one certainly believed that law as it is could be differentiated from the law as it ought to be. Austin, The Province of Jurisprudence Determined 365-69 (Library of Ideas ed. 1954). It is not clear that he thought force or power to be the "essence" of law, but his predecessor, Hobbes, came near to saying this. See Hobbes, Leviathan (1651). Kocourek seemed to think that preferences for specific laws and legal decisions could not be rationally defended. See Kocourek, An Introduction to the Science of Law 132 (1930).

116. 68 Yale L.J. 212 (1958).

117. See, e.g., the widely read book J. Stone, The Province and Function of Law 55-73 (1946).

118. See, e.g., Hall, Studies in Jurisprudence and Criminal Theory 13 (1958).

this century, thought analytical jurists were wasting their time in "Cloudcuckootown" and said so.[119] In a recent book by one of Dean Pound's students and for which Dean Pound wrote an introduction, the author quotes some lines that express Dean Pound's own judgment of analytical jurisprudence better than anything he wrote himself. These lines open with a question put to an analytical jurist who is assumed to reside in a "heaven of juristic concepts":

> Permit me still another question: are the difficult judicial problems, which you have set out up there, practical, have they any importance in life?
>
> There you show once again that you have absolutely no understanding for our heaven. Practical? You mustn't even use that word here; if another than I had heard the word you would have been ejected at once. Importance of the problems for life? Is there any life here? Here pure science, pure legal logic rules supreme, and the condition of this supremacy . . . is precisely this, that all this has nothing in the least to do with life.[120]

Against a background of life-long attacks on earlier analytical jurisprudence by the leading sociological jurist of this century, it should not be surprising to find that there are those who are similarly skeptical of the ultimate practical significance of the work of the new analytical jurists.[121] At times, it seems almost as if the skeptic really wants to say that analytical work, by its very nature, cannot possibly have practical relevance. In this concluding section, an effort will be made, through several examples, to demonstrate that there is nothing inherent in analytical work as such that necessarily deprives it of all practical significance. Perhaps the skeptic should not be taken so seriously. Perhaps he does not himself intend to be. But he cannot have it both ways.

It is appropriate to begin with the effect that efforts to explicate the concept of law can have on practical affairs, because it is commonly assumed that work of this generality can have no practical significance whatever. Ronald M. Dworkin, one of the new jurists, has quite recently demonstrated the falsity of this

119. See Pound, The Progress of the Law: Analytical Jurisprudence, 1914-1927, 41 Harv. L. Rev. 174, 184 (1927).

120. The remarks are by Rudolph Von Ihering, as translated and quoted in Von Mehren, The Civil Law System 79 (1957). Incidentally, the identification of analytical jurisprudence with logic is and was a common thing. *One* of the problems with this is that "logic" is often used by such writers in a variety of senses. A spectacular example of this, a book in which the word is used in *many* different ways, is J. Stone, Legal System and Lawyers' Reasonings (1964). See Summers, Book Review, 53 Calif. L. Rev. 386, 393-95 (1965).

121. See, e.g., Fuller, The Morality of Law 131, 95-151 passim (1964); Jones, A View From the Bridge, Law & Society, Summer 1965, pp. 39, 40.

assumption in terms that can scarcely be improved. Hence we quote at length, for the point cannot be meaningfully made briefly:

> Suppose a court finds itself faced in a particular case with two inconsistent lines of authority, one favoring the plaintiff and one the defendant. After study and reflection the two lines appear almost equally persuasive and sound. The court, hard pressed to decide which to adopt, resolves its dilemma by awarding the plaintiff *half* of the damages to which he would have been entitled had his arguments prevailed.
>
> . . . .
>
> Consider now a different form of objection: the decision is wrong because it is a *compromise* rather than an *adjudication*. It is not a decision "of law," and hence it is an improper result for a *court of law*, constituted and seized of the matter as such, to reach. These are jurisprudential contentions; they involve claims about the nature of the law and its related words and concepts. Of course, they might be unsound jurisprudential contentions. But if we assume that the decision *can* be shown to be a compromise and therefore *not* a decision "of law," what sort of rebuttal can now be made?
>
> A defender of the decision now faces not simply a principle or a policy which he might reject, or against which he might produce countervailing principles or policies in the light of particular circumstances. He faces instead a set of rules defining a pertinent institution and thus structuring the background against which his argument is being made. So long as he perceives himself, and wishes others to take him, as participating in or criticizing the workings of *that* institution (as distinguished from some other which it might have been or might become), he cannot step outside those rules.
>
> Of course, he can propose and argue that the conceptual frame of the institution be broken and rearranged, so that bodies otherwise constituted like courts may compromise some arguments instead of adjudicating them. But he would labor under some distinct burdens in urging this. First, one feature of his position (indeed, one way of describing his position) is that the other participants will normally be excused by the logic of the context from acknowledging and responding to his argument—it will be, in this sense, *out of order*. Second, his argument must acknowledge and accommodate the fact that any recognizable conceptual change must entail vast, possibly incalculable ramifications. We cannot alter, for particular cases only, conceptual notions of what a court is and should do. Third, he is likely (depending on how closely his proposals touch the core of the concepts involved) to have a special sort of difficulty in finding principles or policies of wide appeal in the community which support his proposal. What principles, for example, would support the argument that tribunals of compulsory jurisdiction should be allowed to dictate compromises in ordinary law suits? The likely candidates (principles of political justice, or of good public order, for example) cannot easily be made to serve. For these principles each *include* or *reflect* our concept of law—we cannot use them without im-

porting the practice to be tested into the standards used to test it. So these principles, far from aiding the attack on the concept of law, must be indicted, at least in part, along with it. The more deeply the ground rule in point is set into the concept of law, the greater becomes the Archimedean predicament of being unable to find a point to stand and a fulcrum for a lever.

In these ways and to this extent standards entering into and forming the concept of law operate differently from, and independently of, the standards of fairness, policy, or strategy more often used in criticism of the legal process. Once they are perceived as in point, in the absence of pertinent and successful challenge of the sort imagined in the last paragraph, these conceptual standards function as reasons in their own right and not simply as signals that the particular decisions they indict are unfair or unwise. . . .

. . . .

A statute is passed in terms so ambiguous as to leave extensive doubt about its proper application. A court adopts and applies a novel rule of law flatly inconsistent with another rule recently promulgated, with no recognition of the contradiction. Price ceilings are established retroactively, making illegal sales which have already taken place. These are the shadow cases in which the institutional and conceptual commitments of the law's vocabulary are ranged against policies and purposes, noble or ignoble, best served by their breach. . . .

These shadow cases in part explain why the business of arguing about the concept of law and other central terms of the legal vocabulary thrives and turns up in outpockets all over the legal terrain, despite lawyers' supposed sophistication in avoiding "verbal" arguments. There are at stake, in each academic confrontation about the meaning of law, groups of choices and decisions whose number and even whose nature is largely unforeseeable, but which will swing one way or the other depending upon which priority, which emphasis, which modulation now predominates.[122]

A second and less subtle example illustrating how the work of the new jurists can have practical relevance involves what we have called rational justification. When, for example, the analytical jurist sorts out and constructs general arguments for or against civil disobedience,[123] he is formulating arguments that can also be particularized and brought to bear on the solution of the specific practical problems of civil disobedience. Thus, general considerations such as the possibility of harm to others

122. Dworkin, Philosophy, Morality, and Law—Observations Prompted by Professor Fuller's Novel Claim, 113 U. Pa. L. Rev. 668, 679-83 (1965). (Reprinted with the permission of the University of Pennsylvania Law Review.)

123. See Wasserstrom, The Obligation To Obey the Law, 10 U.C.L.A.L. Rev. 780 (1963). See also the perceptive Maccabaean Lecture on the topic of civil disobedience delivered on June 16, 1965, to the British Academy by the too little-known Scottish analytical jurist, A. H. Campbell. The Lecture will be published in the Academy Proceedings for 1965.

and the feasibility of rapidly reforming the law are relevant to the man of action who must, for instance, decide whether to disobey a law against abortions in a case in which a young girl has been raped, or whether to disobey a local ordinance prohibiting the mixing of races in restaurants.

A third example reveals the profound practical significance that careful conceptual differentiation and explication can have. One scholar of the criminal law has recently written of "the disorderly state of traditional criminal law with respect to the mental element in the definition of offenses, a highly complex cluster of problems, for which the tag of *mens rea* stands as a convenient but elliptical symbol."[124] Since the differentiation and explication of different possible states of mind that figure in human action interests them, some of the new analysts can be expected to help solve this tangle of problems.[125] This should not be surprising, for "voluntarily," "intentionally," "purposefully," "knowingly," and "recklessly," to name some of the relevant concepts, are all well within the family of general notions that make up the daily diet of conceptual analysts.[126] Once the relevant conceptual possibilities are carefully differentiated and explicated, the legislator can be expected to enact less confusing statutes and statutes more consistent with his objectives. The lawyer, with a relevant scheme of distinct logical possibilities firmly in mind, should be able to determine better what specific mental element is embodied in the statute at hand.

A final example that shows how the work of the new jurists can bear on practical affairs involves both conceptual differentiation and rational justification. The problem of justifying judicial decisions can be broken down into the problem of justifying decisions that extend doctrine, that create exceptions to doctrine, that abolish doctrine, and so on. Once the analytical jurist identifies and differentiates these types, he can identify and articulate

124. Packer, Mens Rea and the Supreme Court, 1962 Sup. Ct. Rev. 107, 108.

125. The lawyers responsible for the Model Penal Code have themselves recently made substantial progress. See Model Penal Code §§ 2.01-.02, § 2.02, comment 2 (Tent. Draft No. 4, 1955).

126. See generally the collection of materials edited by one of the new jurists: Freedom and Responsibility: Readings in Philosophy and Law (Morris ed. 1961). See also Hart, Acts of Will and Responsibility, in Jubilee Lectures of the Faculty of Law, University of Sheffield 113 (Marshall ed. 1960); Hart, Negligence, Mens Rea and Criminal Responsibility, in Oxford Essays in Jurisprudence 29 (Guest ed. 1961); Dubin, *Mens Rea* Reconsidered: A Plea for a Due Process Concept of Criminal Responsibility, 18 Stan. L. Rev. 322 (1966) (drawing in part on recent analytical jurisprudence); Morris, Punishment for Thoughts, 49 Monist 342 (1965); Samek, The Concepts of Act and Intention and Their Treatment in Jurisprudence, 41 Australasian J. Philosophy 198 (1963).

the kinds of considerations that ought to figure in each.[127] This, in turn, may help Judge and Co. write more relevant, more persuasive, and more articulate opinions. To illustrate: It should be of value to a judge seeking to justify the creation of an exception to have before him an account of the factors that can plausibly be said to figure in the best possible "case" that could be made out in favor of creating an exception to any doctrine. Among such factors would be the following: (1) that when the doctrine itself was being formulated, it was not foreseen that its terms could apply to the facts at hand, (2) that the exception would interfere little, if at all, with the policy or policies of the doctrine, (3) that an independently significant policy can be furthered by recognizing the exception, (4) that the facts of the exception can be ascertained judicially without making significantly more mistakes (as to the facts) than would be made if no exception were recognized,[128] (5) that the exception can be formulated in such terms that it will not be likely to "swallow" up the doctrine itself, (6) that the boundaries of the exception can be formulated in nonarbitrary terms, and (7) that exceptions have similarly been made elsewhere in the law without adverse consequences.

## VI

## Conclusion

The new analytical jurisprudence is an autonomous discipline with practical relevance and promise. In closing, two questions naturally present themselves: What explains the rise of the new analytical jurisprudence? What are its prospects for the future? The answer to each question must, of necessity, be speculative and incomplete.

Several factors probably explain the flourish of interest in analytical studies. To begin with, in 1945 the problems of analytical jurisprudence were far from solved. Austin and his followers had left much work to be done. Furthermore, professional philosophers had, by the end of the war, become enamored of analytical philosophy generally. It was only natural that this interest should eventually manifest itself in such special branches of the field as legal philosophy. There is a further factor of a more accidental

127. The author of the present article is at work on a book along these lines.

128. For perceptive clarification of this important factor see Wasserstrom, The Judicial Decision: Toward a Theory of Legal Justification 162-71 (1961); Ross, The Value of Blood Tests as Evidence in Paternity Cases, 71 Harv. L. Rev. 466, 482-84 (1958).

nature. In 1952, H. L. A. Hart, who is a lawyer and a philosopher, became Professor of Jurisprudence at the University of Oxford. A powerful and articulate analytical jurist, Hart gave special impetus to the resurgence of his discipline, not only in Britain but also in the United States where he lectured extensively in the 1950's and 1960's. Undoubtedly other factors help explain the rise of the new analytical jurisprudence, but the foregoing seem the most significant.

What of the future? Although the new jurists are making headway, their discipline is not likely to be established, at least in American law schools, for some time. This seems true for several reasons. First, the work of the new jurists is not yet generally being differentiated from the old analytical jurisprudence, and the old had less than a good press. Second, some law teachers believe they already perform the work of analytical jurists. Third, analytical jurisprudence, as a branch of philosophy, must make its way against the whole range of familiar charges against philosophical work as such, including the "Armchair Speculation" charge, the "Excessive Generality" charge, the "No Progress" charge, and the "Triviality" charge. In spite of all this, professional interest in the new analytical jurisprudence grows each year.

# [2]
# How Law is Formal and Why it Matters

## INTRODUCTION

So far as I have been able to determine, the literature of Western jurisprudence and legal philosophy lacks any comprehensive and systematic treatment of the formal character of law in developed societies.[1] Later in this Article, I will explain at length what I mean by "the formal character of law." For now, I will merely suggest what I mean. By "the formal character of law," I mean first, that rules and other legal precepts, basic functional elements of law such as legislatures and courts, and the legal system taken as a whole, are all formal in the sense that, in their very existence, they conform to accepted conceptions of their essential forms.[2] For example, for a precept to conform to the essential form of a rule, it must be at least minimally prescrip-

---

1 This is a further preliminary formulation of my general thesis that one of the fundamental characteristics of law is that it is formal. This and the prior formulations set forth themes that will be developed much more fully in a book I am writing. A reader who turns to the earlier versions will see that I have altered some of my earlier views considerably, and that my overall thesis is in the course of evolution. *See* Robert S. Summers, *The Formal Character of Law*, 51 CAMBRIDGE L.J. 242 (1992); Robert S. Summers, *Der formale Charakter des Rechts II*, 80 ARCHIV FÜR RECHTS UND SOZIALPHILOSOPHIE 66 (1994); Robert S. Summers, *The Formal Character of Law III*, 25 RECHTSTHEORIE 125 (1994); *see also* Robert S. Summers, *The Juristic Study of Law's Formal Character*, 8 RATIO JURIS 237 (1995); Robert S. Summers, *A Formal Theory of the Rule of Law*, 6 RATIO JURIS 127 (1993).

I am much indebted to several established scholars in the U.S.A., in Great Britain, in Germany and elsewhere for ideas, stimulation, and encouragement, including especially Professor Dr. Okko Behrends of the University of Göttingen and Professor D. Neil MacCormick of the University of Edinburgh. In my forthcoming book, I will record these substantial debts, and my gratitude, in full. For now, I wish to thank my secretary, Mrs. Pam Finnigan, and my most recent student assistants and graduate students: Marshal Grant, Cornell Law School Class of 1996; James Hannon, Cornell Law School Class of 1996; Eric Jacobs, Cornell Law School Class of 1997; Matthew Michaels, Cornell Law School Class of 1997; Donald Stepka, Cornell Law School Class of 1997; and Laura McClellan, Cornell Law School Class of 1998. In addition, Andrew Siff, Cornell Law School Class of 1997; Ted McCutcheon, Cornell Law School Class of 1998; and Mitchell Wong, Cornell Law School Class of 1998 have been especially helpful. I also wish to thank a graduate student who was at Cornell during 1996, Okko Hendrik Behrends, for discussion of themes in the Article. In addition, I wish to record my special indebtedness to the faculty of the University of Florida College of Law for their contributions to my thinking about the formal character of law. On November 19, 1992, April 12, 1995, and March 21, 1996, I conducted research seminars on various aspects of this subject with this faculty, and on March 22, 1996, I gave the Dunwody Distinguished Lecture in Law at the University of Florida on this subject.

2 Though I use the expression "essential form," I do not intend to take sides in the ancient nominalist-realist debate, nor do I mean to commit myself to any one model for the analysis of concepts.

tive, minimally general, definite, and complete. But beyond this most fundamental sense of "formal" in which legal phenomena at least minimally satisfy their defining essential forms as accepted in the society, these phenomena are formal in still other ways.

Prescriptiveness, and some degrees of generality, definiteness, and completeness are defining features of rules. Yet, in rules actually created, such features typically go beyond the essential definitional minimum. Such defining features and their extra-essential elaborations and variations are also formal in the further basic sense that they are structural. These features together structure the form and content of a rule. But some formal features of rules are not defining features. For example, the degree of simplicity (or complexity) of a rule is not a defining feature. Yet, it is a formal feature in the sense that it, too, is structural. Rules are also formal in their mode of encapsulation: some take common law form, some statutory form, some constitutional form, and so on. Thus, features of rules are formal in the foregoing three senses: "essentially," structurally, and encapsulatorily. Rules are formal in still further distinct senses that I will explain.

At the same time, all other phenomena of the law besides rules and other precepts are likewise formal in various senses apart from their conformity to accepted minimal essential forms. For example, basic functional elements of a legal system such as legislatures and courts are formal in the sense that they, too, have structural features. They are formal in the sense that they have procedural features. They are formal in the sense that their institutional features overall are relatively definitive. They are formal in the sense that they are, to an extent, fixed according to rules or other precepts, and so, are "preceptually" formal. Similar truths also apply, *mutatis mutandis*, to a legal system considered as a functioning whole. A legal system is formal in its structure, in its coherence, and in its methodical nature. In sum, the phenomena of law are formal, in various senses which are all well-established in the English language. Thus, as I will demonstrate, formality is a pervasive, varied, and complex general characteristic of law. Moreover, the formality of law in all its varieties poses countless choices of form in the construction and operation of any legal system, choices that implicate not merely problem-specific policies, but also fundamental political values, general legal values, equitable considerations, private preferences, and more.

Because form in the law is a means to such ends, it may or may not be appropriate to those ends. In a particular rule or in a basic functional element such as a court, a formal feature may be ill-designed and so, inappropriate. But it does not follow that "form," "formal," "formality," and "formalism" generally have pejorative meanings in the English language, or even in legal usage. They do not. Yet some inhabitants of the American legal academy tend not to differentiate between the formal and the formalistic. They also tend to collapse the formal into the formalistic, and frequently end up using "form," "formal," "formality," and "formalism" pejoratively.[3] I do not follow them here.

In relation to rules, specific phenomena of law such as legislatures and courts, and the system as a whole, I use form and its derivatives neither pejoratively nor honorifically, but neutrally. However, I do distinguish between form that is appropriate and form that is inappropriate, in light of the ends to be served and other factors. Plainly, within a particular system, a particular formal feature may at a given time be inappropriate. Thus, such a feature may be overformal, and so formalistic; or it may be underformal, and so substantivistic; or it may be malformed in some other way. What is, or is not, appropriate form is a complex question. But it is certainly true that "more formal" does not necessarily translate into "appropriately formal," and "less formal" does not necessarily translate into "inappropriately formal." I wish at the outset to make clear, too, that I do not embrace pre-realist formalism.[4]

This, however, is primarily a jurisprudential article, and I will not concern myself with issues of legal reform, i.e., with reforming the formalistic, or the substantivistic, or whatever, in any particular system. Nor will I be concerned with comparing two or more systems in overall degrees of formality.[5] Rather, my focus will be on formality as a general characteristic of law in Western systems of law, more particularly, in Anglo-American and Western European systems, for these are the systems with which I am most familiar. My main questions will be these: How is law formal? What are the main varieties of formality in law? Why is appropriate form in the law important? Of course, I do not hold that appropriate form in the law is all that is required for law to be good and effective. Substantive policy and other values must play major roles. So, too, must societal attitudes of agreement, acceptance, and acquiescence in the law's methodology and its operation. Also, a legal system requires trained personnel, material resources, knowledge, language, and more. Thus, there is obviously much more to an effective legal system than form. But form is indispensable, and it may even be said that it is appropriate form that binds all the requisite ingredients into operational law.

3 *See, e.g.*, Richard A. Posner, The Problems of Jurisprudence, *passim* (1990); Duncan Kennedy, *Legal Formality*, 2 J. Legal Stud. 351, *passim* (1975).

4 *See* Robert S. Summers, Instrumentalism and American Legal Theory 136-75 (1982) (explaining and criticizing pre-realist formalism at length).

5 For such an effort, see generally P.S. Atiyah & Robert S. Summers, Form and Substance in Anglo-American Law (1987) (comparing U.S. and U.K. legal systems).

To my knowledge, no Western legal theorist has ever given due credit to the formal character of law.[6] Even the European and British

6 The general thesis that one of law's fundamental characteristics is that it is formal in character, has not, so far as I am aware, been the subject of any extended systematic study in English, German, French, Italian or Spanish. My Scandinavian colleagues tell me the same is true of their literature. The formal character of law is not the thesis of ATIYAH & SUMMERS, *supra* note 5. Rather, in that book, Professor Atiyah and I identified a variety of types of formality in law and compared their differing manifestations in the English and American systems, and offered explanations for the differences. In that book, we also used a different typology of form from that which I use here. We did, however, treat tangentially much that is relevant to my present thesis, and I am, accordingly, indebted to that work and to Professor Atiyah as well. My own first published work on themes associated with law's formal nature is: Robert S. Summers, *Working Conceptions of "The Law,"* 1 L. & PHIL. 263 (1982).

In my thinking about the formal character of law, I have found the writings of the nineteenth-century German jurist, Rudolf von Jhering, to be the most useful. *See* 2 RUDOLF VON JHERING, GEIST DES RÖMISCHEN RECHTS (Darmstadt 1993) [hereinafter JHERING, GEIST]; RUDOLF VON JHERING, LAW AS A MEANS TO AN END (Isaac Husik trans., 1913) (1903) [hereinafter JHERING, LAW AS A MEANS]. I have also found certain works of Max Weber useful, especially in avoiding pitfalls. *See* MAX WEBER, CRITIQUE OF STAMMLER *passim* (Guy Oakes trans., 1977) (1907).

There are important jurisprudential works that address in a general way one or more facets of law's formal character without advancing a general thesis to that effect. *See, e.g.*, H.L.A. HART, THE CONCEPT OF LAW *passim* (2d ed. 1994); HANS KELSEN, GENERAL THEORY OF LAW AND STATE *passim* (Anders Wedberg trans., 1945) (1905); HANS KELSEN, INTRODUCTION TO THE PROBLEMS OF LEGAL THEORY *passim* (Bonnie Litschewski Paulson & Stanley L. Paulson trans., 1992) (1934); *see also* LON L. FULLER, THE MORALITY OF LAW *passim* (2d ed. 1969) (addressing one major facet of the formal character of law, namely, the principles of legality (often also called the rule of law)).

This is not to say there are no jurisprudential books with such words as "form" or "formal" in the title! There are. *See, e.g.*, THOMAS ERSKINE HOLLAND, ESSAYS UPON THE FORM OF THE LAW (1870); GIORGIO DEL VECCHIO, THE FORMAL BASES OF LAW (John Lisle trans., 1914). The first of these works is in the Benthamite spirit and advocates that law be expressed largely in statutory or code form. The second book, especially at pages 68-125, addresses what the author calls "the logical form of law" and a "formal analysis of the concept of law," but one does not find a systematic and extended development of the varieties of form in law and how they matter.

There are various jurisprudential works on "legal formalism," a phrase that, like the word "formal," is sometimes used pejoratively. *See supra* note 3. One theorist who does not use the word formal pejoratively is Professor Ernest Weinrib. *See, e.g.*, Ernest J. Weinrib, *Legal Formalism: On the Immanent Rationality of Law*, 97 YALE L.J. 949, 950-57 (1988) [hereinafter Weinrib, *Legal Formalism*]; Ernest J. Weinrib, *The Jurisprudence of Legal Formalism*, 16 HARV. J.L. & PUB. POL'Y 583, 583-89 (1993) [hereinafter Weinrib, *Jurisprudence*]. Professor Weinrib describes the "project of legal formalism" in these terms: "Formalism is a theory of legal justification. As a theory of *justification*, formalism considers law to be not merely a collection of posited norms or an exercise of official power, but a social arrangement responsive to moral argument." Weinrib, *Jurisprudence, supra*, at 583. My own work on the formal character of law, while not inconsistent with some aspects of the foregoing formulation, nevertheless differs in major ways. First, one of Professor Weinrib's primary aims is to refute a thesis of the Critical Legal Studies Movement (the inseparability of law and politics). *See* Weinrib, *Legal Formalism, supra*, at 950-52. My thesis is not so motivated. Second, Weinrib views form as including the full "ensemble of characteristics that constitute" law. *Id.* at 958. My thesis focuses on formality as one basic overall characteristic of law, and within that focus treats a number of varieties of formality in addition to what I call essential form. I focus on the conceptual and descriptive far more than he does. Third, Weinrib uses as fundamental units of analysis such notions as "juridical relationship," "immanent positivists, whose interests have been more formal than other theorists, have failed to address this subject systematically and in depth. I believe that one major explanation for the neglect of law's formal character in Western jurisprudence is that we have never enjoyed a satisfactory conceptual account of what it is in law that is truly formal.[7] With such an account, we would be in a better position to see form in the law for what it is, and to give it its due. To some, this explanation might seem quite implausible, for whatever the extent and importance of form in the law, this must be right in front of us for everyone to see. Yet, no less a figure in twentieth-century philosophy than Ludwig Wittgenstein stressed that:

> The aspects of things that are most important for us are hidden because of their simplicity and familiarity. (One is unable to notice something—because it is always before one's eyes.)[8]

rationality," "intelligibility," and "coherence." *See id. passim.* My own fundamental units of analysis are quite different. Fourth, Weinrib generally resists conceiving of law in instrumentalist terms. *See id.* at 966-72. While I criticize crude instrumentalism, I treat appropriate form as an indispensable means to policy and other values.

There is also a large body of books and legal periodical literature addressed partly to specific aspects of the role of form in law. Some of these books are highly illuminating. *See, e.g.*, FRANCIS A. ALLEN, THE HABITS OF LEGALITY: CRIMINAL JUSTICE AND THE RULE OF LAW 27-56 (1996); FULLER, *supra*, *passim*; FREDERICK SCHAUER, PLAYING BY THE RULES *passim* (1991). Professor Schauer's book may be the best book ever written on rules. While much of what I now say and will say in my book about rules is compatible with his work, there are major differences. For example, I emphasize more than he does the perspective of citizens and others on the front lines of human interaction who must apply rules in advance of and in the absence of particular disputes. I also give more of a place than he does to what I call general legal values (for him, "formal values") in response to charges of "rule-worship." *See* SCHAUER, *supra*, at 132-33, 135-66. Further, I attempt to provide a more systematic and comprehensive account of how rules are formal than he does. For example, I treat in detail the "internal" formal features of rules: generality, definiteness, completeness, simplicity (complexity), and more. One (but not the only) additional difference is that I treat empirical generalizations (e.g., "dogs annoy restaurant patrons") as merely one source of the substantive content for legal rules.

In addition to various articles by the law trained on form, formality, and formalism, which I have not sought to catalog here, there are articles by persons trained in economic analysis of relevance to the formal character of law. *See, e.g.*, Isaac Ehrlich & Richard A. Posner, *An Economic Analysis of Rulemaking*, 3 J. LEGAL STUD. 257 (1974); Werner Z. Hirsch, *Reducing Law's Uncertainty and Complexity*, 21 UCLA L. REV. 1233 (1974); Louis Kaplow, *Rules Versus Standards: An Economic Analysis*, 42 DUKE L.J. 557 (1992).

7 The subject is a conceptual minefield. *See, e.g.*, DEL VECCHIO, *supra* note 6, at 113 ("No word is understood in so many ways as the word form."); WEBER, *supra* note 6, at 79 ("As everyone knows, there is no expression more ambiguous than the word 'formal' and no dichotomy more ambiguous than the distinction between form and content.") Some published accounts of form in the law are also distortions. *See, e.g.*, Kennedy, *supra* note 3, at 355-60 (describing formality as mechanical adherence to rigid rules).

8 LUDWIG WITTGENSTEIN, PHILOSOPHICAL INVESTIGATIONS ¶ 129, at 50 (G.E.M. Anscombe trans., 1953).

Wittgenstein also entered a general plea for "insight into what lies in front of everyone's eyes."[9] In this Article, I seek to identify, to remind us of, to explicate, and to characterize the familiar so that we may recognize formality for what it is, understand it more fully, appreciate it better, and ultimately, give it its due. As Oliver Wendell Holmes, Jr. once emphasized, what we often need is not "investigation of the obscure," but rather "education in the obvious."[10]

Some, perhaps many, readers will find, in the end, what I characterize as formal in the law to be quite obviously formal. But even for these perceptive analysts, some of what I say may not be quite so obvious, at least *at the outset* (and the outset is what Wittgenstein and Holmes had in mind). In particular, the variety of senses of the word formal applicable to law may not be quite so obvious. Precisely how one or more of these senses applies to rules, institutions, and other legal phenomena may not be quite so obvious. Also, the overall cumulative effect of applying these senses of formal to the phenomena of law—the aggregate quantum of form in law—may not be quite so obvious. Further, the extent of credit that should be given to appropriate form in working the law's will may not be quite so obvious. In addition, the interplay between the formal and the non-formal may not be quite so obvious. And that form and substance do not exhaust the ingredients of law may not be quite so obvious.

The overall place of form in the law and the credit to be given it has not totally escaped all legal theorists. For me, the work of the great nineteenth-century German thinker, Rudolph von Jhering of the University of Göttingen, has been the most suggestive. He saw that form is grounded in the innermost essence of law ("im innersten Wesen des Rechts begründet"),[11] and he appeared to think that form can be found all over the law.[12] Although he did not develop these theses, he was right. Of course, if form is "grounded in the innermost essence of law" and if form is to be found all over the law, this will embarrass those legal theorists who are extreme substantivists. These theorists use the words "form" and "formal" pejoratively, and find little place for appropriate form in the law. But law's formal character ought not to trouble the moderate substantivist who insists merely on seeing that substance gets its due. Appropriate form and due substance can and should co-exist (though even these together are by no means enough for law to exist, let alone work its will).

9 LUDWIG WITTGENSTEIN, VERMISCHTE BERMERKUNGEN 121 (1977) (translation my own).

10 OLIVER WENDELL HOLMES, JR., COLLECTED LEGAL PAPERS 292 (1921).

11 JHERING, GEIST, *supra* note 6, at 479 (translation my own).

12 *See* JHERING, LAW AS A MEANS, *supra* note 6, at 230-325.

In this Article, I try to give due credit to form (1) by introducing, mainly from general English usage of the words "form" and "formal,"[13] a stock of concepts that may be used faithfully to represent or portray the major varieties of form in the phenomena of Western legal systems; (2) by introducing a uniform and felicitous nomenclature for designating and articulating these concepts of form; and (3) by demonstrating, albeit only suggestively, the jurisprudential and practical significance of the varieties of form in the law. In demonstrating the significance of form, I also emphasize that appropriate form must be distinguished from inappropriate form, that appropriate form should not, even in the course of its application, generally collapse into something else, such as "substance," or "policy," or "equity;" and that issues of appropriate form pose many significant choices in legal ordering, ones that implicate fundamental political values, basic policies, general legal values, equitable considerations, private preferences, and more. Thus, my general theory of form in the law may be said to be prescriptive and normative in its implications, as well as conceptual and descriptive. The theory provides concepts and terminology for the perspicuous representation of the varieties and complexities of form in positive law and other legal phenomena, and provides concepts and terminology for the jurisprudential characterization of law's basic nature as formal (a characterization that rests on more than merely an aggregation of the varieties of form in law). The theory also identifies the main types of choices of appropriate form, the types of considerations relevant thereto, and standards for the evaluation of form. Jurisprudentially, the theory exposes

13 Although I have consulted several dictionaries, including historical and etymological dictionaries, I rely mainly on the OXFORD ENGLISH DICTIONARY (2d ed. 1989) [hereinafter OED] and WEBSTER'S THIRD NEW INTERNATIONAL DICTIONARY (1993) [hereinafter WEBSTER'S]. Of course, the latter draws to some extent on the former. It is enough for my present purposes to consult only usages in the English language. These dictionaries represent the best of British and American lexicographic scholarship. Such dictionaries indicate how the linguistic community generally understands the use of words such as "form" and "formal." (Both dictionaries record non-pejorative uses of "form" and "formal" ahead of pejorative ones.) *See* 6 OED *supra*, at 78-83; WEBSTER'S, supra, at 892-93. One well-known defense of my extensive reliance here on general usage is as follows:

> [O]ur common stock of words embodies all the distinctions men have found worth drawing, and the connexions they have found worth marking, in the lifetimes of many generations: these surely are likely to be more numerous, more sound, since they have stood up to the long test of the survival of the fittest, and more subtle, at least in all ordinary and reasonably practical matters, than any you and I are likely to think up in our arm-chairs of an afternoon—the most favored alternative method.
>
> . . . When we examine what we should say when, what words we should use in what situations, we are looking again not *merely* at words (or 'meanings' whatever they may be) but also at the realities we use the words to talk about: we are using a sharpened awareness of words to sharpen our perception of, though not as the final arbiter of, the phenomena.

JOHN L. AUSTIN, PHILOSOPHICAL PAPERS 130 (J.O. Urmson & G.J. Warnock eds., 1961).

the intimate relations between form and values in a system of law, and gives due credit to form in the law, overall. My effort here, however, is only a preliminary one. A book will follow in which I develop my theory more fully. In that work, I will also expound the view that appropriate form is hardly enough, for a functioning system of law is necessarily a fusion of many varieties of form with policy and other value content, with trained personnel, with material resources, and with much else.

## I
## How Law is Formal

I use the word "law" to include rules and other precepts, and also legal devices such as particular rulings and orders. I also use "law" to encompass all the basic functional elements in a legal system that together provide for the creation and implementation of law. These basic functional elements include elections, legislatures, courts, administrative agencies, the institutions of private law, and state sanctioning processes. Such elements also include criteria of validity; bodies of state-made law; privately made creations such as contracts, wills, and property arrangements; interpretive methodologies; a precedent system; and recognized entities such as the state, corporations, business and other associations, ordinary legal persons, and a legal profession. Further, I use "law" to refer to the legal system as a whole, which includes its basic functional elements; its general operational techniques which systematically order, integrate, and coordinate these basic functional elements; its system-wide principles of legality securing the rule of law; its systematic ranking of sources of valid law, whereby constitutional law is prioritized over all other law, statute law over merely judge made law, and so on. As I will explain, the varieties of form, the choices involved, and the values at stake vary somewhat depending on whether the object of study consists of rules or the like, of basic functional elements such as a legislature or a court, or of the system taken as a whole.

### A. The Formal Character of Rules

Rules are of special importance. Rules are the primary means we use to prescribe the internal organizational features and subject matter of basic functional elements for creating and implementing law. As I have said, these basic elements include electoral processes, legislatures, courts, and interpretive methodologies. Thus, rules provide for and limit legislative, judicial, and executive authority. Rules also provide for and limit the powers of private persons and entities to enter and enforce contracts, to make wills, and to acquire property. Rules also specify criteria of valid law, define and regulate interpretive method, govern the imposition of sanctions, and more.

Rules are the main legal instruments for authoritative embodiment not merely of essential civic policies such as community peace, order and safety, but of all kinds of problem-specific policies ranging from the reinforcement of the family, to facilitation of traffic flow, to regulation of food and drugs, and so on. Rules are also the principal means of authoritatively incorporating into the system such fundamental political values as legitimate authority, interpersonal justice, and basic freedoms, which include not merely political freedom but freedom to enter contracts, to own property, to make wills, to form associations for business and other purposes, and more. Further, we use rules to incorporate such general legal values as certainty and predictability, the dignity and efficiency of citizen self-direction under law, equality before the law, freedom from official arbitrariness, dispute avoidance, dispute settlement, and various other "rule of law" values. We use rules not merely to authoritatively incorporate all of the foregoing types of policies and values. We also devise and utilize many auxiliary rules to implement the authoritative policies and values so incorporated.[14]

Moreover, when we turn to a legal system as a whole, we find heavy reliance on rules to organize, integrate, and coordinate basic functional elements into general operational techniques for the creation and implementation of state-made law, and of privately-created law such as contracts and wills. Thus, we typically use rules to incorporate basic functional elements into one or more of five general operational techniques for making and implementing law, namely: the penal, the grievance-remedial, the administrative-regulatory, the public-benefit conferral, and the private-ordering (on which, more later). Furthermore, in system-wide perspective, rules figure prominently in the definition and implementation of those principles of legality and the rule of law that we deploy to regulate and police the workings of the foregoing five general operational techniques and the legal system as a whole. Indeed, the rule of law is largely a law of rules.

What are legal rules? There are many varieties of such rules in any functioning legal system. Of most, perhaps of nearly all such rules, we can say the following:

(1) they have content;

(2) are prescriptive rather than hortatory, or merely descriptive;

(3) directly or indirectly prescribe action and thereby prohibit, permit, or require such action (deontic modalities);

14 *See* SUMMERS, *supra* note 4, at 195.

(4) are designed directly or indirectly to serve substantive policy or to serve fundamental political values or general legal values, or rule of law values, or private preferences, or equity (or one or more of these types of ends at the same time);
(5) are based directly or indirectly either on an empirical generalization implying a causal relation between means and ends, or on a theory about how law can organize and facilitate some end such as the election and accountability of political leaders, or on a general moral or social principle, or on a conception of the essential form or the otherwise appropriate form of an institution, process, method, or the like;
(6) are expressed in a form that prescribes content as above, and exhibits a degree of generality, of completeness, and of definiteness;
(7) are simple or complex (or something in between);
(8) are embodied in some authoritative encapsulatory form, be it statutory, an administrative regulation, a common law form, a contractual form, or some other recognized authoritative form;
(9) are usually expressed relatively explicitly and in writing at least if the rule is a state-made rule;
(10) are expressed in a common language of the system;
(11) can usually be found recorded in official books or other sources.

How are rules formal? I propose throughout this Article to use the word "formal" in accord with standard English usage, rather than merely with some personal theory of what might be formal. Thus, I claim that all the concepts of "formal" that I invoke here are well-grounded in English usage (though I do not claim that every application I make of "formal" to legal phenomena is itself established English usage.) It follows that what I designate here as formal is not, conceptually, my own invention. I use "formal" as an adjective in the English language, and as an adjective, it is largely an expression that derives its meanings from the noun forms of the word "form" recognized in English. I will now introduce five such meanings of "formal." I would formulate the first standard meaning of "formal" as follows: "pertaining to the form or constitutive essence of a thing."[15] I call this "essential form." Every thing or idea has to take some relatively constant form to be a thing or idea of that type. Thus, a rule, to be a legal rule, must be prescriptive, as above, and be sufficiently general, complete, and definite. Plato identified all of these features, and singled out definiteness for special emphasis: "[U]nless you are definite, you

[15] 6 OED, *supra* note 13, at 82 (quoting entry for "formal" no. A.1.a). *See* WEBSTER'S, *supra* note 13, at 893 (entry for "formal" no. 1.a.).

must not suppose you are speaking a language that can become law."[16] (A broad grant of discretion can, of course, be law.)

Prescriptiveness, and minimal degrees of generality, completeness, and definiteness, then, are defining features of a rule, and so, formal in the above sense. Each feature is different from the others, is independently significant, and can be analyzed on its own (and in relation to the others) in some depth. Moreover, each serves or can be designed to serve, severally or conjointly, significant policies or values.

Thus, ordinary legal rules are, first of all, formal insofar as their defining features are present, that is, insofar as they take what I call at least the minimum essential form of legal rules. It might be objected that this is only to say that such rules are rules, a mere tautology, empty of all significance. But if this be a tautology (which it is not), then it is one worthy of explicit formulation. A totally formless "rule"—one that fails to prescribe, one that is totally incomplete, or totally indefinite, or totally particular—would not be a rule. An extended analysis here would further our understanding of the essential form of legal rules, of their defining features, of the types of policies and values these features may serve, and of how appropriately formal features shape the form and content of rules in the course of their creation.[17] When I say the formal features of rules shape the form and content of rules, what I mean can be readily understood if we imagine varying formulations of a rule having the same general subject matter, such as the regulation of speed on highways. For example, a higher degree of the formal feature of definiteness in such a rule shapes the form and content of the rule differently from a lower degree. A 65 mph rule shapes form and content differently than a "drive reasonably" rule.

When we say that a given rule is formal, we often mean something more than that it merely conforms to the minimum essential form of a rule, i.e., more than that the rule is just barely over the definitional threshold of "ruleness." Often we mean that the rule is appropriately formal, that is, appropriately prescriptive and appropriately general, complete, and definite, given its subject matter and the policies and values to be served. When we mean by "formal" that the rule is appropriately formal, we are not saying that the rule is formal in a second sense wholly independent of essential form. Appropriate form generally presupposes minimum essential form.

Appropriate form often goes far beyond minimum essential form, and the scope for elaboration and variation to achieve appropriately

[16] 2 THE DIALOGUES OF PLATO 491 (B. Jowett trans., 1937). Aristotle, too, identified all of these formal features. *See, e.g.*, THE BASIC WORKS OF ARISTOTLE 1326 (Richard McKeon trans., 1941).

[17] In my book in process, I have separate chapters on each such feature.

formal features is often considerable, depending on the nature of the form involved, the subject matter, and the policies and values at stake. These elaborations and variations may show themselves in further degrees of generality, completeness, and definiteness that are simply continuous with these defining features. For example, the policy to be served by a rule often requires a much higher degree of generality than merely that which is minimally necessary for it, conceptually, to be a rule at all. Or it may be that a degree of definiteness, a major formal feature itself defining in nature, must go well beyond that minimum merely required for ruleness, if the rule is appropriately tailored to serve its ends.

The features of essential form, and of any extra-essential form continuous with essential form and thus beyond its threshold requirements, are formal in a second sense of the word, well recognized in another commonly used noun variant of "form" in the English language, namely structure. "Formal" in our language thus also has a second meaning that I would formulate as follows: "of or pertaining to structure."[18] I would then formulate the meaning of structure as follows: "the way a part or parts of a whole is organized."[19] Thus, alternative formulations of a rule may display differing prescriptive modalities (duties, prohibitions, powers, etc.), differing degrees of generality, differing degrees of completeness, and differing degrees of definiteness. Definiteness of a given degree, for example, contributes in its own way to how the parts of a whole rule are put together. It is not merely an ingredient or part of the rule (like policy); it is also a way of organizing the parts of the rule. It follows that definiteness in a rule is formal not only because it is a defining feature, i.e., not only because it pertains to the essential form of a rule. Definiteness is also formal because it is structural. It is a feature that contributes to, and so structures, the overall form and content of a rule. Such a feature then, is formal both in the sense of being a defining feature of the essential form of a rule, and formal also in the sense of contributing to the structure of the rule—to how it is organized. Thus, definiteness

18 "The particular character, nature, structure, or constitution of a thing . . . ." 6 OED, *supra* note 13, at 78 (entry for "form" no. I.5.a). "[T]he shape and structure of something as distinguished from the material of which it is composed." WEBSTER'S, *supra* note 13, at 892 (entry for "form" no. 2.a.). In *OED*, both completeness and definiteness are specifically recognized as formal. *See* 6 OED, *supra* note 13, at 82 (entries for "formal" nos. 3.b & 5).

19 "Manner of building or construction; the way in which an edifice, machine, implement, etc. is made or put together." 16 OED, *supra* note 13, at 959 (entry for "structure" no. 2). See also entry no. 3 for "structure." "The mutual relation of the constituent parts or elements of a whole as determining its peculiar nature or character; make, frame." *Id.* In entry no. 3.d for "structure," *OED* notes that this applies to linguistic phenomena, too. *See id.* *Webster's* entry no. 3 for structure is: "the manner of construction: the way in which the parts of something are put together or organized." WEBSTER'S, *supra* note 13, at 2267.

is nonetheless structural for also being defining. When the structural feature of definiteness, though continuous with the minimum definiteness required for essential form, is elaborated beyond that minimum, we should still say that this extra-essential degree of definiteness is also formal in the second sense, i.e., "structurally formal." That is, the degree of definiteness contributes to the structure of the rule—to the way in which the parts of the rule are organized. Generality is thus structural, too. So is completeness. As I have said, there is great scope for elaboration and variation here beyond the definiteness, generality and completeness required for the minimal essential form of a rule. Indeed, the formal features of rules typically go beyond the requirements of minimal essential form. Such features just are, up to their threshold of minimum "essential form," formal in essential form and also formal in how they contribute to the structure of the rule, and beyond that threshold, are formal merely in the sense of structural.

There are still other major varieties of form which are not at all continuous with features of the essential form of rules. For example, all rules exhibit another feature of form and content, namely that of being either simple, not so simple, somewhat complex, or very complex. The appropriate degree of simplicity or complexity of a rule is affected at least by its degrees of generality, completeness, and definiteness, by variations in its subject-matter content and by the policies and values at stake. This feature of simplicity (or complexity) is also structurally formal.[20] For example, a decrease in the complexity of a rule must show itself in content, and may also show itself in effects on other formal features such as definiteness or generality or completeness. It then becomes appropriate to say that the relations between form and content in the rule have changed—its structure has changed. The feature of simplicity (or complexity) is a structural feature. The degree of simplicity or complexity of a rule is not, however, continuous with any defining feature of a rule, and is thus structurally formal quite independently of the defining features of the essential form of a rule.

There is a third major sense of "formal" that is also not continuous with any feature of the essential form of rules. All rules are what I call "expressionally formal" in varying degrees. I formulate this meaning of "formal" as follows: "of or pertaining to mode of expression."[21] The mode of expression of a rule encompasses:

---

20 *See supra* note 19.

21 Thus, *OED* entry no. I.9 for "form" as a noun provides: "Style of expressing the thoughts and ideas in literary or musical composition, including the arrangement and order of the different parts of the whole." 6 OED, *supra* note 13, at 79. *See also id.* at 82 (entries A.1.c & A.5 for "formal"). *Webster's* definition for "form" as a noun includes references to "style," method of expression, and "orderly arrangement." WEBSTER'S, *supra* note 13, at 892 (quoting entries 4.a & 10.a).

(1) the extent of its explicitness;
(2) the extent it is set forth in writing;
(3) the extent it is set forth in a technical or other specialized vocabulary; and
(4) the extent it is formulated with compactness and organizational rigor.

The appropriate mode of expression of a rule may be highly formal or less formal or even informal, depending on the subject matter and the policies and values at stake. Again, the degree of expressional formality of a rule is not a feature that is continuous with prescriptiveness of content, generality, definiteness or completeness. Thus, it is quite independent of the essential form of a rule. It is also not the same as structural form.

Yet a fourth major sense of "formal" is also one that is not continuous with any feature of the essential form of rules. This fourth sense derives from the fact that all legal rules are set forth in some recognized legal form or mould. Thus, all legal rules are set forth either in: constitutional law, or statutory law, or judge-made law, or customary law, etc. I call this familiar concept encapsulatory form. "Formal," in reference to this type of feature, means something like: "of or pertaining to mode of encapsulation."[22]

So far I have considered the formal character of rules in terms of their essential form, of their continuous "extra-essential" form that is structural, their non-continuous extra-essential form that is structural, and of further varieties of form that are expressional and encapsulatory. In this, I have treated the prescriptive nature of the content of

---

22 One *OED* entry for the adjective "formal" provides in part: "pertaining to the form, arrangement, external qualities (*e.g.*, of a work of art, a composition, etc.)." 6 OED *supra* note 13, at 82 (entry no. A.1.c). Another *OED* entry for the adjective "formal" provides in part: "Done or made with the forms recognized as ensuring validity . . . ." *Id.* (entry no. A.5). The *OED* entry for the noun "form" provides "One of the different modes in which a thing exists or manifests itself; a species, kind, or variety." *Id.* at 78 (entry no. 5.b). *Webster's* offers an entry for the adjective "formal" that provides: "relating to, concerned with, or constituting the outward form, superficial qualities, or arrangement of something as distinguished from its content." WEBSTER'S, *supra* note 13, at 893 (entry no. 1.b).

Roscoe Pound, following the practice of E.C. Clark and noting that the expression has come into "more or less general use," refers to the variety of encapsulatory forms in which rules and other legal precepts may exist as "'forms of law.'" 3 ROSCOE POUND, JURISPRUDENCE 382 (1959) (quoting E.C. CLARK, PRACTICAL JURISPRUDENCE 198-99 (1883)). Pound describes these "'forms of law'" as: "the literary shapes in which legal precepts and doctrines are authoritatively expressed, the authoritative forms of expression to which courts are referred in the decision of controversies and to which counselors must resort for the bases of prediction when called on to advise." *Id.* at 383. Pound notes that what I call the encapsulatory forms of legal precepts may be divided generally into three categories: "In general, they may be classified as (1) legislation; (2) case law, i.e., law expressed in the form of judicial decisions of past controversies; and (3) text book law, i.e., law expressed authoritatively in juristic writings." *Id.* at 416. Of course, a more extended typology is possible. (I am indebted to Professor Peter Müller-Graff for suggesting the name "encapsulatory.")

rules as a feature of the essential form of rules. So far, I have not focused on the subject-matter content of rules. There is still a fifth major sense of "formal" recognized in our language that is relevant here and one might formulate it as follows: "of or pertaining to organization, procedure, technique or methodology."[23] I call this "organizational form." In this fifth sense, the subject-matter content of many types of legal rules is formal. Indeed, all the rules that prescribe features of such basic functional elements of a legal system as elections, legislatures, courts, administrative bodies, and methods of interpretation, are formal in subject-matter content. This is also true of all rules that specify the methodical and the unifying features of a legal system and its operations as a whole. Likewise, any rules which prescribe the structural, expressional, or encapsulatory form of other rules are also formal in content. For example, a constitutional rule prescribing a high degree of definiteness in criminal statutes is formal in content.

All the foregoing varieties of form reveal and reflect numerous types of choices of design in the formality of a rule. The policies and values at stake in such choices are varied and significant.

To summarize, all legal rules are formal in that they:

(1) exhibit at least the defining features of the *essential form* of rules, including especially

—prescriptive content,
—minimum generality,
—minimum completeness, and
—minimum definiteness;

(2) exhibit features of *structural form* either within, or beyond, minimum defining prescriptiveness, generality, completeness, and definiteness continuous with those defining features, and exhibit structural form in non-continuous features such as simplicity or complexity;

(3) exhibit features of *expressional form;*

(4) exhibit features of *encapsulatory form;* and

(5) in some rules, exhibit form that prescribes the *organizational form*—organizational formality of content—of basic functional elements such as elections, legislatures, courts, criteria of validity, interpretive methodology, or of organizational aspects of the system as a whole, or prescribe features of structural, expressional, or encapsulatory form.

---

23 The *OED* entry for "form" as a noun provides the following: "Due shape, proper figure; orderly arrangement of parts, regularity, good order . . . ," 6 OED, *supra* note 13, at 79 (entry no. I.8); "Manner method, way, fashion (of doing anything)," *id.* (entry no. I.10); and, "A set, customary, or prescribed way of doing anything; a set method of procedure according to rule (*e.g.*, at law); formal procedure," *id* (entries I.11.a & b). See also the *OED* entry 4.a for "formal": "Regular, having a definite principle, methodical." *Id.* at 82. *Webster's* entry for "form" at 4.b provides: "established method of expression or practice: fixed or formal way of proceeding . . . ." WEBSTER'S, *supra* note 13, at 892.

The foregoing scheme of concepts, distinctions, and nomenclature affords a relatively comprehensive basis for analyzing the formal character of rules, and for identifying significant choices of form in the construction of rules. It also affords a basis for the systematic and stable use of the concept of a "highly formal rule." Indeed, the most formal rule might be analyzed as one that exhibits high degrees of structural features that are defining or continuous with defining features; exhibits a high degree of structural complexity; exhibits a high degree of expressional form; exhibits canonical encapsulatory form; and incorporates subject-matter content that is itself formal, i.e., organizational.

A critic might object that the foregoing varieties of the formal are all my own invention. But the above five senses of formal—essentially formal, structurally formal, expressionally formal, encapsulatorily formal, and organizational formality of content—are all rooted in standard English usage of the words form, formal, and their derivatives. It is true that some of my applications of concepts of form and formal to legal phenomena may not themselves be established uses of these words. For example, we do not ordinarily refer to the mode of encapsulation of legal content as formal (let alone use the word "encapsulatory" in this way). But this does not mean that the relevant legal phenomena do not answer to the relevant concept or concepts of the formal. They do, as I have demonstrated.

A critic might also object that the five senses of formal have "nothing in common." But there is no inconsistency between them, and each coheres with the others. Moreover, it is not necessary that these usages have anything in common. Each except the last (organizational formality of content) applies to all rules. Each except the last is a common "golden thread"—a standard understanding of the word "formal" applicable to all rules. I am not claiming that each of the four types of "golden threads"—each standard meaning of formal—applies to the same facet of each rule. While it is true that essential form and structural form do, to some extent, pertain to the same facet of rules, expressional form, encapsulatory form, and organizational formality of content pertain to their own relatively distinct facets: mode of expression, mode of encapsulation, and any organizational content. In sum, there are always at least four "golden threads" here, running through all rules, and these establish that form pervades rules. It would be an objection to my thesis if some rules were formal only in the sense of essential form, other rules only in the sense of structural form, still other rules only in the sense of encapsulatory form, and so on. If that were so, my thesis would rest on equivocations. But this is not the case.

A critic might also object that my analysis proves too much. It might be said that since my analysis indicates rules are far more formal, in perfectly intelligible and well-recognized senses of the word, than at least American theorists have heretofore generally assumed, the analysis leaves no place at all, or very little place, for the non-formal in rules, and is therefore very largely a vacuous thesis devoid of contrast and rebuttability. But it is not true that my analysis leaves no place for the non-formal in rules. First, any subject-matter content of rules that does not itself prescribe organizational or other formal features is not formal. This means that a great many rules have content that is not formal. Foremost among these are rules with problem-specific policy content. Then there are still other facets of rules that are obviously not formal in any of the senses used here. The particular natural language in which the rules are expressed is not formal in the senses explicated here. Nor are the authoritative books and other repositories in which rules are set forth formal. Moreover, rules are not the whole of the law, and much of the remainder is not formal, though it is intimately concerned with the creation and implementation of rules. Essential social acceptance of law is not. Trained personnel are not. Material resources are not.

Finally, a critic might object that my analysis fatally omits the negative or contrastive meanings that "form" and "formal" have in our language, and that these are the true meanings of these terms. One possible thesis here might be that form and formal are entirely parasitic for their meanings on negative contrasts with the other side of a dichotomy—with whatever they are used to negate or rule out on particular occasions, such as substantive policy content, or justice and equity in a particular case, and so on.[24] Thus, on such a view, the meaning of formal in regard to a rule is essentially negative—is merely whatever is not substantive policy content, for example. But each of the five senses of formal taken here from standard English usage is, on my analysis, affirmative or positive in meaning. A formal feature is affirmative or positive in the sense I intend if it is actually present, as distinguished from merely lacking or failing to express an opposed quality, such as policy content. Whatever is formal in any one of the foregoing five senses exists apart from, and can be characterized independently of, any relation of negation or contrast that it may have with an "opposite" such as substantive policy or the like. Thus, form and formal in the five senses I have identified are not parasitic on any contrast with opposites. They have affirmative or positive meanings of their own. Consider a feature of what I call essential form—a degree of generality. This feature is affirmatively present in a rule. It is not a

[24] It is true that some words are best understood as excluders. *See* J. Austin, Sense and Sensibilia 70-71 (G.J. Warnock ed., 1962).

feature that merely lacks or fails to express the opposed quality of particularity. (The same is true of generality as a structural feature of a rule.) Similarly, the degree to which a rule is set forth in writing, a feature of what I call expressional form, is something actually present. It is not a feature that merely lacks or fails to express the opposed quality of not being in writing. The same is true of encapsulatory form and of organizational form, *mutatis mutandis*.

A closing caveat is in order. When the formal features of a rule are well drafted and are enshrined in written form—even in constitutional or statutory forms, it still does not follow that subsequent practice under these seemingly "fixed" forms cannot effectively alter the degree or level of any of the varieties of form in such rules. Here we know that there may even be considerable divergence between law in books and law in action, especially if there is a highly activist judiciary.

### B. The Formal Character of Basic Functional Elements Within a Legal System

Rules alone are not enough. Plainly, they cannot create themselves. They cannot qualify themselves as authoritative. They cannot apply themselves. They cannot enforce themselves. Nor can they serve in place of rulings, principles, orders, maxims, nor in place of other species of law such as private contracts, wills, and property arrangements not reducible to rules.

As I have indicated, an operational system of law requires authoritative institutions and processes by which representatives of the state may make, apply and enforce law. It also requires authoritative arrangements by which private parties and officials may make and carry out contracts and wills, create and transfer property, and more. A system of law also requires interpretive and other methodologies for applying state-made, and privately created, forms of law to particular states of fact. This list is by no means exhaustive. Such elements of a legal system I call "basic functional elements," and when operational, these elements also utilize official and other personnel, a common language, material resources, and more. An extended categorization of such elements in a modern system of law would include:

(1) electoral processes;
(2) a legislature;
(3) courts and a court system;
(4) administrative hierarchies;
(5) institutions and processes for the creation and administration of law by private parties and entities;
(6) public and private entities such as the state, corporations, partnerships, private persons with legal capacity, etc.;
(7) interpretive methodologies for state-made law and for privately created forms of law;

(8) a body of constitutional law, including criteria for determining the validity of law;
(9) a body of state-made substantive law;
(10) a body of state-made procedural law;
(11) a body of evidentiary law;
(12) a sanctioning system;
(13) mechanisms and devices for recruiting and assigning personnel to roles in the system; and
(14) a legal profession.

Each of the foregoing basic functional elements is more or less discrete in its own way. Each element has a special function, or functions, within the system as a whole. In addition, each is internally organized to fulfill that function or functions. Each presupposes other such elements, and, within an operational system, each is integrated and coordinated with certain other elements in one or more basic ways, as we will see.

Some of the basic functional elements of a legal system are highly complex. Among the most complex are certain legal institutions such as legislatures, courts, and administrative hierarchies. These institutional elements have organized functions. They have organized differentiation, specialization and centralization of roles. They have organized procedures, organized supervisory and other hierarchies, organized selection of personnel, and more. A well-organized legal institution effectively organizes who is to do what, when, where, and how, all in order to discharge the essential functions of that institution. An institution just is an organ that is organ*ized* in a variety of dimensions. Legal rules are the principal social device for designing and organizing a legal institution, and indeed, for designing and organizing any basic functional element of a legal system. Valid legal rules not only specify and prescribe the features and subject matter of such a basic functional element, but most importantly of all, express the initial authoritative understanding of the system as to the specific nature of the element. Thomas Hobbes was among the first to stress the role of rules here: "The skill of making, and maintaining commonwealths, consisteth in certain rules . . . not . . . on practice only . . . ."[25]

Yet, institutions, processes, methodologies, entities, and other basic functional elements of law cannot be reduced to rules. These elements consist of far more than the rules used to organize them. In developed systems, we use rules to organize institutions and other basic functional elements of the system in the first instance. The resulting institution or other element, however, does not itself consist of those rules, and its features and subject matter, as an "up and run-

[25] THOMAS HOBBES, LEVIATHAN 136 (Michael Oakeshott ed., 1960).

ning" element, are not the features and subject matter of the rules organizing it. Institutions and other functional elements have features and subject matter of their own, quite apart from the rules that prescribe such features and subject matter. Also, the features and subject matter of institutions and other basic elements of law, once "up and running," frequently thereafter diverge somewhat from the prescriptions in their organizing rules. This is one type of divergence between law in books and law in action. Such "divergence gaps" may be wide or narrow, depending partly on how effectively the rules and other machinery can be invoked to close such gaps. But the very reality of such gaps is still another reason why institutions and other basic functional elements cannot be reduced to rules. Moreover, institutions and other elements of a system of law require far more than rule-prescribed modes of organization to exist as functional social phenomena. They require general social acceptance for their very existence and operation; trained personnel; specialized knowledge; a common language; material resources; and still more if they are to function at all. And these social assets, too, can hardly be reduced to rules. Yet, without rules systematically organizing the legal uses of these social assets, basic functional elements as we know them simply would not exist.

How are the basic functional elements of a legal system formal? For now, I will treat illustratively, and in abbreviated fashion, how only three types of such elements are formal: namely a legislature, courts, and an interpretive methodology for statutes. Legislatures and courts are institutional in character, whereas methodology is not.

A system of law in a modern Western society would be fundamentally defective without a legislative body as a basic functional element of the system. Some such body must exist with legitimate power to make general written law ordering human relations in advance. Accordingly, the composition, powers, and procedures of a legislature are a focus of natural legal concern in a society to be ruled by law.

A legislature is not formless. It is, first of all, formal in the sense that it conforms in some degree to the minimum essential form of a legislature. This minimal form varies somewhat from society to society.[26] In most developed Western societies, the legislature is:

(1) a representative body;

(2) with power to make general and prospective written law for the whole society (though this may require concurrence of an executive);

(3) with power to make law which takes priority over all other law except constitutional law;

26 Here, "formal" is used in the sense "of or pertaining to essence." *See supra* note 15 and accompanying text.

(4) and which has a procedure generally designed to bring facts, reason, and public opinion to bear on proposed laws;

(5) and has voting and other procedures that enable it to resolve differences over proposed laws.

I do not claim that these are universal defining features of all legislatures—a universal essential legislative form. But for my purposes, the foregoing is sufficient to identify a "noun foundation" of minimal essential form for the corresponding adjectival expression "formal," as applied to legislatures. Any developed society has at least some such minimal conception of the defining features of a legislature—of its essential form, though that conception is not identical for all such societies. When it is said that a legislature is formal, one sense of "formal" that may be meant, then, is simply that what is referred to conforms to the prevailing minimal conception of essential legislative form, whatever that conception for the particular society happens to be.

The accepted appropriate form of a legislature in a given society may, and commonly does, go beyond what is required by the minimal essential form for a legislature. That is, what is accepted as the appropriate form of a legislature commonly includes elaborations and variations that go beyond its minimal defining features. As I will explain, these elaborations and variations in the name of appropriate form are themselves formal in further major senses fully recognized in our language. Of course, these elaborations and variations likewise differ from system to system. Conceptions of the overall appropriate form of a legislature probably differ between Western systems more than do conceptions of minimal essential form. An account of the main ways in which a legislature is formal in Western systems requires that we go beyond "formal" in the sense of "essential form."

Some of the formal elaborations and variations that go beyond the essential form of a legislature are continuous with one or more defining features of the essential form of a legislature as sketched here. That is, they are continuous at least in the sense that they consist of further auxiliary rules and other devices designed to secure these very features. For example, the defining feature of a legislative procedure designed to secure rational deliberation on legislative proposals may be quite elaborate, and may vary significantly from system to system. A given legal system may, for valid enactment of a statute, require merely a majority vote of a single chamber favoring a bill after being through only a single "reading" before the legislature. But another system may go well beyond this, and require not only several "readings" of a proposed law at periodical intervals but also require public hearings, and require a committee report supporting the final version of the bill to be voted on. Whether or not continuous with any defining features, at least some of these elaborations and variations that go beyond minimal essential form are formal in a second major sense also fully recognized in our language. That is, they are formal simply in the sense that they are procedural. They pertain to the well-established noun meaning of form, which we may formulate as: "manner, method, or style of proceeding."[27] I will call this procedural form. Of course, insofar as such procedural features of a legislature are also defining features, they are formal in two senses at the same time: formal in the sense of conforming to minimal essential form, and formal in the sense of procedural.

Some of the defining features and some elaborations and variations on the essential form of a legislature are formal in a third well-recognized sense of the word, namely, "of or pertaining to structure,"[28] where what structure means is itself formulated as follows: "the way a part or parts of a whole is organized."[29] The organizational framework of a legislature is structural. For example, its structure may include one chamber or two chambers. Again, that a legislature must have at least one chamber is also formal in the sense that this feature is a defining feature which pertains to the essential form of a legislature as well. Beyond the number of chambers, there are other features of the organizational framework of a legislature, too, such as differentiation of official roles within the legislature, any committee system, relationships between the legislature and the executive, and the extent to which legislative power overall is centralized in a single body for the whole society instead of "federally" shared.

An institution such as a legislature may also be described in terms of its overall definitiveness. Thus, its composition, structure, and procedures may be tightly organized and operate in a highly regularized fashion. The more so, the more definitive; the less so, the less definitive. The overall definitiveness of the organization and mode of operation of a legislature is a fourth type of formal feature of such an institution. This sense of formal derives from an established usage of "form" which may be phrased as follows: "fixed, orderly, and clear in outline."[30] The factors that most affect the definitiveness of an institution such as a legislature include the precision of its organizational

---

27 *See supra* note 23 and accompanying text.

28 *See supra* note 18 and accompanying text.

29 *See supra* note 19 and accompanying text.

30 *OED* entry no. I.8 for the noun "form," provides: "Due shape, proper figure; orderly arrangements of parts, regularity, good order . . . ." *See supra* note 23. See also *OED* entry no. I.11.a. for "form": "A set, customary, or prescribed way of doing anything . . . ." *See supra* note 23. *Webster's* entry no. 4.b for the noun "form" says: "fixed or formal way of proceeding," WEBSTER'S, *supra* note 13, at 892, and at entry 10.a: "orderly arrangement or method of arrangement," *id.* Under synonyms, *Webster's* states that "Form may suggest an appearance in which both clear outline and also structure and orderly disposition of details are presented or suggested." *Id.*

design; the faithful prescription of that design in rules; and the readiness of legislators, judges, officials, and affected parties to criticize departures from those rules and to take action to remedy or counter such departures.[31]

A fifth meaning of formal as applied to a legislature or other institution is simply arranged or fixed "according to rule."[32] The various dimensions of a legislature are, in varying degrees, arranged or fixed according to rule, and so are what I will call "preceptually" formal. Moreover, these rules are also formal in that they display all of the varieties of formality already addressed here in my discussion of the formality of rules, including their structural, expressional, and encapsulatory formality.

In sum, a legislature is formal (1) in terms of those of its features that are defining, i.e., that pertain to its essential form; (2) in procedural terms; (3) in structural terms; (4) in definitiveness; and (5) in being fixed according to rule. A critic might ask: Is there anything about a functioning legislature that is not formal? My thesis is not vacuous. Many things about a legislature are not formal, including most obviously, its actual acceptance in the society as a law-making institution, the personnel elected to the legislature, the material resources they utilize, the language they utilize, the knowledge and expertise they bring to bear, the substantive policy content of proposed legislation, and more. Of course, such non-formal social assets are duly organized within an operating legislature partly through the use of rules and other formal devices.

I now turn to courts, mainly trial courts, as another basic functional element of a legal system. A system of law without courts would be fundamentally defective. For a variety of reasons, disputes of law and of fact are inevitable in any society. The disputing parties cannot alone resolve all such disputes through negotiation or other means, even when acting in good faith. Courts are needed to resolve some proportion of these disputes. No other institution has the impartiality and objectivity, nor the required procedural apparatus, to resolve such disputes in accord with law and fact. Accordingly, the design of a court is also a focus of natural legal concern.[33]

31 *See* HART, *supra* note 6, at 56-57, 88-90, 102-03, 115-16.

32 *OED* entry no. I.11.a for the noun "form" states: "a set method of procedure according to rule . . . ." *See supra* note 23. The *OED* entry for "formal" no. A.3.a. provides: "That is, according to recognized forms, or to the rules of art or law." 6 OED, *supra* note 13, at 82. *Webster's* entry no. 4.b for the noun "form" says: "procedure according to rule . . . ." *See supra* note 23. *Webster's* entry no. 2.a for "formal" reads: "following or according with established form, custom, or rule." WEBSTER'S, *supra* note 13, at 893. See also entry no. 3.a: "based on forms and rules." *Id.*

33 In Anglo-American law, Lon L. Fuller wrote more perceptively about adjudicative design than anyone else. *See* ROBERT S. SUMMERS, LON L. FULLER 90-100, 164 (1984).

A trial court is not formless. It is, first of all, formal in the sense that it takes the form essential for its existence as a court. That is, it conforms to the minimum essential form of a court. Again, conceptions of what this is vary somewhat from system to system. In most Western systems, the essential form for trial courts includes the following features:

(1) provision for an independent and impartial official decision maker (which may include lay jurors);
(2) provision of some opportunity for each disputing party (with or without a lawyer) to prepare and present evidence and argument to the decision maker, and to respond to the other party in the presence of the decision maker;
(3) provision that the decision maker is to decide largely on the basis of the evidence and argument so presented by the parties;
(4) provision that the decision maker shall have power to enforce any decision made not only against a party who fully participates, as above, but also against any party properly notified who refuses to participate.

The foregoing features of the essential form of a trial court are designed to fulfill the dispute-resolving function of a court, and to do so in accord with law and fact, thereby also serving the policies of the legal rules ultimately applied, general legal values, equitable considerations, any private preferences embodied in a contract or the like, and other values.

As I have said, the notion of minimal essential form of a trial court varies somewhat from system to system. But when it is said that a court is "formal," a primary sense that may be meant is simply that the institution conforms to the prevailing minimal conception of the essential form of a court for that society, whatever that conception. The defining features of the essential form of a court, even with the basic auxiliary rules that secure them to some degree, comprise no more than a minimal conception. As instantiated in practice, this minimal conception could only imperfectly fulfill the function of a court to resolve disputes in accord with law and fact. Further elaboration is required.

As we saw with regard to rules and with regard to a legislature, the accepted appropriate form of a trial court in a given society also usually goes well beyond what is required merely by its defining features of essential form. That is, the appropriate form of a court typically includes significant elaborations and variations on the minimal conception. These elaborations and variations are themselves formal in straightforward ways fully recognized in our language. Again, these further elaborations and variations that do not pertain to the essential form of courts are themselves not uniform across Western systems. Here, conceptions of overall appropriate form probably differ between Western systems even more than conceptions of minimal essential form. A full account of the main ways in which a court may be formal in Western systems requires that we go far beyond the sense of formal which merely means the minimal essential form.

Many of the elaborations and variations going beyond essential form are formal in the further sense that they pertain to procedural form. Consider, for example, the vast elaborations of court procedures for defining and resolving disputed issues of fact that exist in many systems. These procedures for preparation and trial of factual issues are typically extensive and complex. These procedures, though continuous with, typically go far beyond what would be required merely to satisfy the minimal requisites of "essential form." These procedures are formal in the sense that they pertain to the well-established noun meaning of form: "manner, method or style of proceeding."[34] Again, insofar as such procedural features of a court are also defining features, these are formal in two senses at the same time: formal in the sense of conforming to essential form, and formal in the sense of procedural.

Furthermore, the essential form of a court requires an independent adjudicator to secure impartiality. Elaborations and variations here include some that go beyond, yet are continuous with, the essential feature of independence. At least they are continuous in the sense that they consist of further auxiliary devices that secure this very feature. In all developed systems, judicial impartiality is secured at least by rules that prohibit outside political interference with judicial decision-making. But some systems have numerous auxiliary rules here, too. Thus a system may have rules prohibiting the parties from making any contact with the judge except in the presence of the other party. A system may have rules prohibiting judges from deciding disputes between corporations in which they have a financial interest. A system may have rules requiring judges to recuse themselves when a party is a personal acquaintance. Elaborations and variations that thus secure impartiality through independence of the judge from the influence of politicians and of parties are formal in the sense of structural. These structural features organize the whole process so to shield the judge from improper influence. Insofar as these features are also defining features, they too are formal in two senses at the same time: formal in the sense of conforming to essential form and formal in the sense of structural. Still other elaborations and variations of a structural nature are known to Western systems. For example, in American public law litigation,[35] the party structure may go

34 On procedural form, see *supra* note 23.

35 *See generally* Abram Chayes, *The Role of the Judge in Public Law Litigation*, 89 HARV. L. REV. 1281 (1976) (explaining public law litigation).

well beyond simply two opposing parties or sides. Also, within a court system as a whole, important features of structure include the degree of centralization of courts and whether there be one level or two levels of appeal in the hierarchy. All the foregoing are structural and so formal. That is, they pertain to "form" in another of its standard meanings, namely "structure."[36]

As we have also seen, the definitiveness of a legal institution introduces still another formal dimension. Thus, a court, like a legislature, may be tightly organized and operate in a highly regular fashion. Or a court may be loosely organized and operate not so regularly. The more closely organized and the more regularized its operations, the more definitive a court is. Overall definitiveness is partly a function of structural and procedural form, though some varieties of structural and procedural form may have little bearing on definitiveness. The main factors that affect the definitiveness of an institution such as a court are the precision of its organizational design, the faithful prescription of that design in rules, and the readiness of judges, officials and affected parties to criticize departures from those rules and to take action to remedy or counter the departures.[37] The definitiveness of an institution is formal in a fully recognized sense of that word, namely the sense derived from the noun in which "form" means, simply, "fixed, orderly, clear in outline."[38]

Again, a further basic use of formal as applied to an institution means that it is something "fixed . . . according to rule."[39] A court is also formal in this way. As I have already indicated, numerous and elaborate rules define, constitute, and regulate a court. Such institutions, then, may be said to be preceptually formal, that is, significantly dependent on rules for their contours. All such rules also take some encapsulatory form, as we have seen. That is, all are encapsulated either in constitutional, statutory, regulatory, common law, customary, or other form.

In sum, a court is formal in terms of those defining features of form essential to its being a court at all. Beyond that, a court is also an institution that is elaborately organized in a variety of ways, and these are formal procedurally, structurally, definitively, and preceptually. Moreover, the preceptual formality of a court is itself set forth in a recognized encapsulatory form.

---

36 On structural form, see *supra* note 19 and accompanying text.

37 *See supra* note 31.

38 On definitive form, see *supra* note 30 and accompanying text. Definiteness of rule is different from definitiveness of institutions and processes. Definiteness of rule pertains to its meaning, whereas definitiveness of institutions and processes pertains to the operational contours thereof. On definiteness of rule see *supra* note 16 and accompanying text.

39 *See supra* note 32.

With all these ways in which a court is formal, a critic might ask what there is about a functioning court that is not formal? Again, the formality thesis is not vacuous. Many things about a functioning court are not formal, including its general social acceptance as an authoritative body, the official personnel and other persons participating in its processes, the policy content of substantive law that a court applies, the testimonial and other evidence introduced to establish facts, the natural language utilized, the material resources deployed, and still more, all of which are likewise essential to the workings of a court.

All the varieties of form that I have identified here reveal, reflect, and pose countless choices of design in the formality of legislatures, courts and other legal institutions.[40] Of course, at any given time, only a few of these choices will be open. That is, at least the basic choices of design will have already been made. The values at stake in such choices are numerous and often fundamental. Well-designed legislatures serve democracy, rationality in law-making, social policies of many kinds, the rule of law, and more. Well-designed courts and court systems function to resolve disputes in accord with law and fact and thereby serve the policies of the substantive law in issue; rule-of-law values; process values such as procedural fairness; and general legal values such as certainty, freedom from official arbitrariness, and more. Another formal feature that legislatures, courts and other institutions share is this. Legislatures have authority to address proposed law of highly varied content. Courts of law have authority to resolve disputes of highly variable content. Similarly, other legal institutions of public and of private law are set up to deal with matters that are highly variable in content. This generality of institutional scope is methodical, another established meaning of the word formal.[41] Each institution stands ready to apply the same systematic general method or approach not to a single instance but regularly to many relevantly similar instances, though highly varied in content. Of course, institutions are specialized as to scope and method. Some make general written law, some resolve disputes and so on.

I now turn to a third illustrative basic functional element in a legal system, and consider how it is formal. This element consists of the interpretive methodology for statutes, an element that, unlike a legislature and a court, is not institutional in nature. Of course, courts regularly deploy some such methodology, and insofar as it is formal, this is a further respect in which we can say that courts, too,

40 On appropriate form, see *infra* Part III.A.

41 *OED* entry no. A.4.a for "formal" states: "Regular, having a definite principle, methodical." 6 OED, *supra* note 13, at 82. *Webster's* entry no. 3.b for "formal" states: "characterized by punctilious respect for form: exact, methodical, orderly." WEBSTER'S supra note 13, at 893.

are formal. In Western systems, interpretive methodologies for statutes appear to be less formally organized and more variant in features and subject matter than legislatures and courts. Again, a system of law without any interpretive methodology for statutes would be fundamentally defective. Issues of statutory interpretation are inevitable and numerous in any system, all the more so to the extent a system lacks a sound and coherent interpretive methodology. An interpretive methodology has vast scope for operation. It is not merely that courts apply it. Administrative officials apply it. Legislators apply it when creating statutes in the first place. And, above all, citizens apply it outside of court and beyond official settings when they make decisions in daily life and work. Without a sound and coherent interpretive methodology, life under law would certainly be more disputatious and more disharmonious. Also, less legislative policy would be served. Legislators would not know how to draft statutes in the first place. Different, or even the same, judges would resolve the same issues differently. Citizens and others would not be able to rely sufficiently on their interpretations from the inception of statutes, and so would frequently be required to guess until courts speak. The rule of law would flounder. Regularly determinate statutory reasons for action would not be available. Indeed, statutory rules might in practice come to lack all prescriptiveness.

A methodology for interpreting statutes is not formless. As with other basic functional elements such as legislatures and courts, an interpretive methodology is formal in a number of ways. First and foremost, such a methodology is formal in that it conforms to the minimum essential form required to count as an interpretive methodology at all.[42] While there is far from universal agreement in Western systems on what this essential form is, several general features of operative methodologies of interpretation are widely shared.[43] Thus, many such systems explicitly recognize a number of the same basic types of interpretive arguments.[44] Further, many systems tend to accord the argument from ordinary meaning (and its variant, the argument from technical meaning) some special weight or primacy.[45] Nearly all such systems tend to interpret criminal statutes, in certain types of doubtful cases, favorably to defendants.[46] While these defining features fall far short of a developed interpretive methodology, they can be considered to provide at least a minimal "noun" founda-

---

42 *See supra* note 15.

43 *See generally* D. NEIL MACCORMICK & ROBERT S. SUMMERS, INTERPRETING STATUTES—A COMPARATIVE STUDY (1991) (discussing similarities and differences; for summary see Chapter 12).

44 *See id.* at 464-65.

45 *See id.* at 466.

46 *See id.* at 559 (providing index entry citing relevant pages).

tion of "essential form" for the adjectival expression "formal," as applied to interpretive method.

In some Western societies, what is generally accepted as the appropriate form of an interpretive methodology goes far beyond the foregoing minimalist conception, but in other societies, such as the United States, not nearly so far.[47] The further elaborations and variations of appropriate form likewise vary from society to society. It is possible to sketch a model that captures most of the directions which many such further elaborations and variations take, or would conceivably take, though no particular system known to me conforms fully to this model. A sketch of such a model of interpretive methodology would include: (1) a preamble which states that the purpose of the methodology is to define and organize processes of resolving issues of statutory interpretation in the best justified way; (2) definitions and descriptions of the authorized types of interpretive arguments; (3) general procedures for the rational construction of instances of such types of arguments, with inventories of the materials that may be incorporated in such instances; (4) procedures for evaluation of the force of instances of each type of argument, with some focus on the main ways each type can break down; (5) specification of any "top-rung" or other primacy that any general type of argument, e.g., the argument from ordinary meaning, is to have, in competition with other types; (6) any special considerations of relevance to general types of statutes, e.g., criminal statutes may not be extended by analogy; and (7) appropriate methodological maxims for constructing well-justified interpretations for use by judges when writing opinions, and for use by other officials, and lawyers.

We may treat the foregoing, then, as merely general directions in which a legal system might elaborate its own conception of the essential form of an interpretive methodology. Many systems have in fact so elaborated their interpretive methods in some such directions to some extent. As I have said, no single system known to me fully conforms to the foregoing model of the appropriate general form of an interpretive methodology, and systems differ greatly in the degree to which they resemble the model. Moreover, such elaborations and variations on minimal essential form are formal in several further ways fully recognized in our language. All such elaborations and variations are, of course, methodical, and we have seen that this is another established meaning of the word "formal."[48] Additionally, some of these elaborations and variations are also structural, and so formal in that

47 The United States does not have an accepted general interpretive methodology for statutes. For an account of method and its variations in the U.S. Supreme Court, see *id.* at 407-59.

48 *See supra* note 41.

way, as well.[49] Consider, for example, an elaboration which prioritizes one general type of argument over another. Such an elaboration concerns the relations between different elements of the methodology and thus is structural. Furthermore, some elaborations and variations contribute to the definitiveness of the methodology, and so are formal in this sense.[50] For example, those that define types of arguments and specify procedures for their rational construction contribute to the overall definitiveness of the methodology. In addition, the fact that such a methodology is to a large extent prescribed in rules signifies that it is preceptually formal, and therefore in this respect formal in all the ways that rules are formal.

Nevertheless, even an interpretive methodology, which by nature seems formal through and through, is not, in its operation, totally formal. Its general social acceptance as an authoritative methodology is not formal. The "raw materials" that interpreters must deploy to instantiate types of argument are not formal. For example, the resources of ordinary language argumentation that figure in the argument from ordinary meaning are not themselves formal. Nor are committee reports, records of floor debates, and other evidence of legislative history that figure in the argument from legislative history. Nor is extrinsic evidence of legislative purpose that figures in the argument from ultimate purpose. Moreover, citizens, officials, judges and other persons must apply a methodology if it is to be effective. Yet, these requisite types of personnel, of course, are not formal. Nor is the policy content of statutes being interpreted.

Basic functional elements of a modern legal system, then, are all formal in a number of ways. Most fundamentally, all basic functional elements of a legal system, even in their minimalist defining conceptions, are formal in the sense that each conforms to its own essential form. A legislature without, for example, any voting procedure for decisive resolution of conflicting views would not be a legislature. A court that, for example, does not even require judicial impartiality would not be a court. An interpretive methodology that imposes no restrictions on what can count as an interpretation would be formless, and so could not be a methodology. And so on, for each functional element of a legal system. But beyond the minimal defining features of the essential form of these constituent elements, there are, as we have seen, also features, including elaborations and variations, that are formal in still further ways. Here, we have encountered the procedural, structural, definitive, preceptual, and methodical formality of legislatures, courts and of legal institutions generally. With regard to

49 *See supra* notes 18, 19.

50 *See supra* note 30.

interpretive technique for statutes, we have encountered methodical, structural, definitive and preceptual formality.

An analysis of the formal character of law's basic functional elements deepens understanding of those elements. It also heightens awareness of the types of choices that must be made in their design and administration. It likewise sharpens awareness of the distinction between appropriate and inappropriate form. Thus, systematic thought about the formality of a basic functional element can even suggest fundamental ways in which the element may be improved. Systematic thought about the formality of basic functional elements of a given legal system can even uncover major gaps in those elements. The American legal system, for example, lacks an accepted and coherent interpretive methodology for statutes. Nor has the American system ever squarely confronted the problem of justifying judicial amendment of statutes.[51] Indeed, it may even be that American judges depart from statutory rules in the guise of interpretation with some regularity!

C. The Formal Character of the System Viewed as a Whole

The first sense in which a legal system as a whole is formal is, again, that it partakes of at least the minimum "essential form" of a legal system.[52] In Western systems generally, this minimum includes at least:

(1) basic functional elements such as a legislature, a court system, etc., as constituents of the system;
(2) some integration and organization of these elements into general operational techniques, or the like;

---

51 As a result, the U.S. system has no methodology for this. Ordinarily, when our judges depart from statutes, they do so in the guise of interpretation. Here are several illustrative examples: Welsh v. United States, 398 U.S. 333 (1970) (holding that a personal moral code was a religion within the meaning of the statute despite statutory language expressly to the contrary); Markham v. Cabell, 326 U.S. 404 (1945) (permitting claim for debt arising during World War II despite language barring claims after 1917). There are many instances of departures in the highest courts of the states as well. *See, e.g.*, Friends of Mammoth v. Board of Supervisors, 502 P.2d 1049 (Cal. 1972) (holding the California Environmental Quality Act applicable to private development despite clear language to the contrary.) As two scholars have stressed: "[J]udicial departures from the obligation to decide in accordance with the established rules has become a deeply ingrained and characteristic feature of the judicial process, a feature sustained by the milieu in which Judges operate." MORTIMER R. KADISH & SANFORD H. KADISH, DISCRETION TO DISOBEY 91 (1971). I do not argue that no statutory departures are ever justified. I only argue that the U.S. system should have a more formal methodology here in which judicial departures are openly dealt with. The methodology would allow some types of departures but not others. It would not be easy to devise such a methodology, but it would address whether and how far departures would be permissible in such cases as the following: statutory obsolescence, over-inclusion, under-inclusion, "core" inclusion yet in the face of powerful countervailing principle or policy, and so on.

52 *See supra* note 15.

(3) coherent bodies of law ordered in accord with criteria of validity; and

(4) principles of legality ("rule of law").

Not all systems share the foregoing in the same degree, and there is, of course much elaboration and variation from system to system.

The second way in which a legal system considered as a whole is formal is entirely derivative. A legal system is made up largely of various parts, and these parts include rules and other precepts, various basic functional elements including legislatures, courts, and so on. We have already seen how such rules, precepts, and basic functional elements are themselves formal in a variety of senses. Indeed, several varieties of form pervade such rules and elements.

A system of law is formal in still other ways, too. It is not possible for any single basic functional element of a legal system to operate entirely on its own to achieve the ends and values of a legal order. Each such element must be combined with others. At the same time, no basic functional element can be combined with other elements in ad hoc, haphazard, and patternless ways and yet be consistently effective. Each element must be systematically combined, integrated, organized, and coordinated within general operational techniques for creating and implementing law. These general techniques thus structure how law is made and implemented. Because of this structural effect, and because these techniques are essentially methodical, they are formal.[53]

Thus a legal system viewed as a whole is far more than a mere inventory of its basic functional elements. It also consists of general operational techniques which combine, integrate and coordinate these functional elements so to create and implement law. In modern systems, it is possible to identify at least five main types of such general operational techniques:[54]

(1) the penal type of technique in which legislatures and courts prohibit anti-social behavior, and these prohibitions along with police, prosecutors, and systems of punishment operate to punish criminals and deter would-be criminals;

(2) the grievance-remedial type of technique in which legislatures and courts define wrongful behavior, with courts providing remedies therefor, and the technique as a whole operating not only to remedy grievances, but also to reduce their frequency and to induce private settlement of grievance-remedial claims;

(3) the administrative-regulatory type of technique in which legislators, courts, and administrative officials lay down standards regulat-

53 *See supra* notes 18, 19, 41.

54 *See* Robert S. Summers, *The Technique Element in Law*, 59 CAL. L. REV. 733, 736-45 (1971).

ing otherwise wholesome economic or other behavior, administrators take steps, such as licensing, designed to secure compliance with those standards, and administrators impose sanctions on violators (which may require court action too);

(4) the public-benefit conferral type of technique in which legislatures and public bureaucracies define substantive benefits such as education, health care, welfare, public roadways, etc., define the classes of eligible recipients, distribute these benefits, and secure the material means required for such distribution (through taxation and otherwise); and

(5) the private-ordering type of technique in which private parties choose to enter into legally recognized types of consensual arrangements such as marriages, business and other contracts, employment relations, corporate and other associations, property arrangements, religious and social bodies, and more, with the law facilitating the realization of the aims of such arrangements in various ways.

It is through these five types of relatively discrete structural patterns (and readily recognizable variants) that modern legal systems combine, integrate, and coordinate basic functional elements of the system to deter and punish anti-social behavior, deter and remedy grievances, administratively regulate wholesome economic and other activity, distribute public benefits, and facilitate private ordering. It would, of course, be possible to provide, for any given system, a highly detailed account of what roles each major functional element plays within each of the foregoing formal techniques. These roles differ somewhat from technique to technique. For example, the law-making roles of a court vary depending on the technique in which the court is functioning. Also, the relative roles of private citizens and public officials to take initiative to enforce the law or put the law in motion vary from technique to technique. A legal system as a whole, then, is formal not only in its essential form, and is formal not only derivately in the sense that it incorporates functional elements that are themselves formal. A legal system is also formal in its general operational techniques which methodically combine, integrate, and coordinate these elements, and which themselves operate as a whole in methodical fashion.

There is still a further and related way in which modern legal systems viewed as a whole are structurally and methodically formal. Although these systems are far from uniform here, all of them provide, to some degree, for regulation of the law's operations in accord with most or all of the principles of legality, i.e., the "rule of law." These principles regulate how law itself is to be made and applied. These principles generally require that, so far as feasible, the law take the form of general rules; that these rules be clear and intelligible; that any new law be publicly promulgated or otherwise publicly available; that the citizenry generally have advance notice of the effective date of new law and ready access thereto; that such new law generally be prospective rather than retrospective in operation; that the law be free of conflicts with other law; that all law be interpreted or applied in accord with appropriate methodologies generally understood in advance; that prior to significant denials of claimed right, or to adverse grants of remedy, or to imposition of sanctions, the party to be adversely affected have an opportunity to contest such action before an independent and impartial body in accord with due process; and so on. Such principles of legality regulate the operation of law's basic functional elements and of law's general operational techniques, but they are less concerned with efficacy than with the legitimacy and fairness of how law operates. Indeed, total failure of a system to implement merely a single such principle, e.g., prospectivity, may signify that the system is not truly one of law at all.[55] Such principles are formal because they are structural and are methodical.[56] They govern the operation of law's basic functional elements and general techniques, rather than directly determine the content of any law so made and applied.

A legal system considered as a whole is also formal structurally in the degrees to which it centralizes and hierarchically orders the making and implementation of law. It may, for example, centralize all lawmaking power in one legislature with country-wide jurisdiction or it may decentralize this power. Also, it may, for example, centralize all final judicial appeals from lower court cases in one country-wide Supreme Court, or it may decentralize this role.

A modern legal system, viewed as a whole, is formal in still further fundamental ways. The overall content of its bodies of law is relatively unified and consistent, a fourth major sense in which such a system is formal.[57] Thus, in a legal system there are many possible sources of prima facie valid law. Indeed, even within each type of general operational technique, there may be two or more institutions or entities with authority to create prima facie valid law. For example, in a technique of the administrative-regulatory type, legislatures, courts, and administrative agencies may all create prima facie valid regulatory law applicable within the technique and to its addressees. In a technique

55 *See* FULLER, *supra* note 6, at 39.

56 *See supra* note 41.

57 *OED* entry no. I.9 for "form" reads: "method of arranging the ideas in logical reasoning; good or just order (of ideas, etc.), logical sequence." 6 OED, *supra* note 13, at 79. Also, the *OED* entry no. A.4.a for "formal" "Regular, having a definite principle, methodical." *Id.* at 82. *Webster's* entry no. 10.a for "form" reads "manner of co-ordinating elements . . ." WEBSTER'S, *supra* note 13, at 892. *Webster's* entry no. 1.b.1 for "formal" also includes "having a symmetical arrangement of elements . . . ." *Id.* at 893. The foregoing notions at least implicitly rule out inconsistency and incoherence.

of the private ordering type, private parties, corporate and non-corporate, enter consensual arrangements of many kinds that, along with legislative and judge-made law, are also prima facie valid. Indeed a complete inventory of the authorized makers of law within a complex modern system would extend well beyond those identified so far.

Given this multiplicity of authorized lawmakers in modern systems, the potential for conflicts between prima facie valid forms of law emanating from different sources is considerable. The reality is that such conflicts are common in some systems, and that in all systems with which I am familiar, the prevailing criteria of validity provide, to some extent, for the resolution of such conflicts in accord with a systematic hierarchical ranking of the law-making sources, e.g., legislative, judicial, etc. (Such criteria are mainly source-oriented rather than content-oriented, and so are themselves largely formal.) It is familiar that in the United States, constitutional law takes priority over statute law, and over all other conflicting types of law. Statutory law takes priority over conflicting administrative regulations, over non-constitutional judge-made law, and over all other law emanating from sources lower in the hierarchy.[58] Judge-made law generally takes priority over contract law and other privately made law, including custom. Contract law takes priority over custom. Thus, a modern legal system secures system-wide consistency in the content of its bodies of law to a large extent through a hierarchical ranking of law-making sources.[59]

But inconsistencies between laws arise not only from different law-making bodies or sources of law. Inconsistencies also arise between laws made by the same law-making body or source. Thus inconsistencies may emerge as between two statutes or between two rules of judge-made law. Mere hierarchical prioritization of different sources is incapable of purging a system of inconsistencies such as these. Yet the desiderata of systemic unity and consistency apply here, too, and modern systems recognize various ways of securing these ends. For example, statutory coherence is sought through interpretive techniques validating more specific statutes over more general ones, more recent ones over earlier ones, and the like. Statutory coherence is also achieved through model codifications and through ad hoc legislative intervention. Similarly, a unified and coherent case law is secured partly through a centralized judicial hierarchy that enforces adherence to higher court precedents and resolves conflicts in precedents set by the lower courts of the same jurisdiction. Ad hoc legislative intervention occurs here to secure consistency of precedent, too.

58 But American courts not infrequently depart from statutes in the name of interpretation when they are in fact amending statutes. *See supra* note 51.

59 *See* HART, *supra* note 6, at 100-110.

The degree to which a legal system is complete in overall content is still another dimension of formality.[60] A system may be more, or less, complete not only in basic policy content but also in basic organizational elements as well. (But then, too, there may be gaps.) Still another formal systemic dimension is the degree of definitiveness of a legal system as a whole.[61] A system is definitive to the extent that its five general operational techniques, its devices for securing coherence in the content of the system, and its provisions for orderly modes of change are tightly organized and operate in regularized fashion. This, in turn, is partly a function of what is yet another formal dimension, namely, the extent such matters are well-prescribed in rules with citizens and officials ready to condemn departures and to take necessary remedial steps. In many Western systems, many such rules are expressed in the special encapsulatory form of a written constitution.

In sum, a legal system is formal insofar as it conforms to the conception of the essential form of such a system accepted there, formal derivatively in that its constituent functional elements are themselves formal in a number of ways, formal structurally in its organization and coordination of these elements into integrated general operational techniques for making and implementing law, formal structurally and methodically in its functioning in accord with such techniques, formal structurally and methodically in its deployment of principles of legality and the rule of law, formal structurally in the degree it centralizes the making and implementation of law, formal in the unity and consistency of its bodies of substantive and procedural law, formal in the degree of completeness of its basic policy content and its basic organizational content, and formal in its overall definitiveness and in how far its systemic features are preceptually prescribed and also embodied in a written constitution or other law.

## II
## Why Appropriate Form Matters—Some Jurisprudential Implications

The central problem of jurisprudence and the philosophy of law is that of providing an account of the nature of law. One way to cast light on the nature of law is to analyze law's basic characteristics and the relationships between them. One such characteristic is that law is formal. Among law's basic characteristics, form has special primacy.

---

60 *OED* entry no. A.3.b for the adjective "formal" states: "Made in proper form, regular, complete." 6 OED, *supra* note 13, at 82. *Webster's* entry for "formal" includes at 2.b: "characterized by or formal in due order: regular." WEBSTER'S, *supra* note 13, at 893.

61 *See supra* note 30.

### A. Generally Appropriate Form as One Basic Characteristic of Law

Law in a developed society consists of highly complex and varied social phenomena which cannot be reduced to a simple set. The basic characteristics of law are numerous, multi-faceted, and inter-related. These basic characteristics may be succinctly categorized as follows:

(1) Characteristically, a system of law serves human interests, and if it generally fails to do so, it is, as Plato suggested, not truly law.[62]

(2) Where there is law in a modern society, it is characteristic that the society recognizes and accepts as legitimate an authoritative, relatively autonomous, exclusive, and organized methodology for making and implementing legal rules and other legal devices of social facilitation and control.

(3) This recognized and accepted methodology can itself be broken down into a characteristic set of basic functional elements including electoral processes, a legislature, courts, interpretive methods, criteria of validity, bodies of law, and so on, some of which consist of highly complex institutions and other social arrangements.

(4) These basic functional elements are characteristically combined, ordered and integrated by and within various general operational techniques: penal, grievance-remedial, administrative-regulatory, public-benefit conferring, and private-arranging.

(5) Within these basic functional elements, and within these general operational techniques, the state, official personnel, private citizens and other legal entities characteristically fulfill law-making and law-implementing roles in accord with a complex division and specialization of legal labor, itself defined and delimited by law.

(6) Characteristically, most of the law made by state organs is in the form of general rules reduced to some written form, i.e., statute, regulation, judicial opinion, etc., while law created by private parties and entities may or may not be written, and takes more varied forms, e.g., contracts, property arrangements, and wills.

(7) The totality of the bodies of state-made law characteristically has a minimum substantive policy content encompassing at least basic protection of the bodily integrity of human beings, the protection of property and promises, and thus, characteristically serves corresponding values.

(8) The law publicly and privately created is characteristically regarded as generating, in accord with criteria of validity and with prescribed interpretive and other applicational methodologies, authoritative reasons for citizens and other entities, and for officials, to take action or to make decisions accordingly.

(9) The addressees of the law characteristically act or decide voluntarily in accord with the authoritative reasons for action or decision

62 *See* PLATO, *supra* note 16, at 486-87.

so generated by valid law and relevant interpretive or other applicational method, and the system is thus generally efficacious.

(10) The system, however, characteristically has the capacity to coerce or sanction those persons or entities who do not voluntarily act in accord with the authoritative reasons so generated.

(11) The system characteristically provides for orderly modes of change in the content and form of the law, in basic functional elements, and even in features of the system as a whole.

(12) The system characteristically operates, to a large degree, in accord with certain general legal values, in accord with principles of legality and the rule of law, and in accord with various limitations on governmental power, and thus, characteristically serves the corresponding values.

(13) The operations of the system are characteristically dependent for their efficacy on social acceptance and social attitudes, on a common language, on the dissemination of various forms of legal and other knowledge, on trained personnel, and on various other social and material resources.

(14) The system is characteristically formal in rules and related devices, in basic functional elements, and in core features of the system taken as a whole.

The last general characteristic in the foregoing categorization is that law is formal. In Part I of this Article, I have already introduced the concepts required for the perspicuous and synoptic representation of this complex characteristic in its wide-ranging varieties. To recapitulate briefly: rules of law are formal in that they conform to the essential form of rules. Beyond this, all rules are formal structurally, expressionally, and encapsulatorily. Some rules are also formal in that they have organizational content. A similar yet appropriately modified analysis can be deployed to explicate the formality of rulings, principles, maxims, and other species of law. All basic functional elements of a legal system such as the institutions of legislatures, courts, and interpretive methodology for statutes are formal in their conformity to the essential forms of such phenomena accepted in the society, and are formal in their elaborations and variations beyond minimal essential form: procedurally, structurally, methodically, definitively, preceptually, and encapsulatorily. The system as a whole is formal insofar as it conforms to the minimal essential form of a legal system, and is also derivatively formal insofar as its constituent functional elements are formal. The system as a whole is also structurally and methodically formal in its general operational techniques which incorporate, integrate, and coordinate these elements within functioning wholes. Further, the system as a whole is formal in its conformity to systemic rule-of-law principles which regulate how law is made and applied in accord with each general operational technique. The system as a whole is structurally and methodically also formal in its consistency and coherence of content, which is secured mainly (though not only) through formal prioritization of potentially conflicting sources of law.

B. Appropriate Form as a Characteristic Having Special Primacy

The formality of law is not merely one of the basic characteristics of law, in itself and on its own. Generally, appropriate form has special primacy among all of law's characteristics, in five major respects. Appropriate form underlies or figures in each of the other leading characteristics of law. Moreover, appropriate form is required for the very existence of the preceptual, institutional, and other elements of a legal system. As Jhering emphasized, form is grounded in the innermost essence of law ("im innersten Wesen des Rechts begründet").[63] In addition, appropriate form has primacy because it is indispensable to legitimate, civic authority. Also, appropriate form has primacy because it goes to the very identity of a legal system. Further, appropriate form, especially in the institutionalized methodology of the system, distinctively enshrines, symbolizes, radiates and reinforces most of the fundamental values of the system.

First, the formal character of law has primacy among law's characteristics because it underlies or figures in each of the others. Rules figure in all of these other basic characteristics, and rules are formal in several major ways. Indeed, each of the other characteristics is itself internally organized, and rules are the primary instruments of such organization. One or more basic functional elements figures, directly or indirectly, in each of the law's characteristics, and again, we have seen that such elements are formal in several major respects. Further, the formal features of the system as a whole, e.g., its structural, its methodical, and its unifying features, are system-wide in scope and bearing. Moreover, many varieties of form contribute directly and indirectly to the incorporation and organization of non-formal elements within the law and the law's general operational techniques. These non-formal elements include substantive policy content, official personnel, material resources, specialized knowledge, and more. Here, form is a kind of binding that ties all together.

Secondly, the formal character of law has primacy among law's characteristics because it is required for the very existence of the preceptual, institutional, and other elements of any legal system. As I have shown, rules can be formal in at least five major ways, and without rules in appropriate form, a modern system of law could not exist because its essential institutions and processes could not be duly organized in the first place. Also, a system of law depends on basic func-

63 JHERING, GEIST, *supra* note 6, at 479.

tional elements such as a legislature, courts, criteria of validity, bodies of rules, interpretive methodologies, and more. Plainly, such elements could not exist at all if they failed to conform at least to their minimal essential forms, whatever those might be for the society involved. Also, such elements are dependent for their efficacy on elabo rations of their formal features and subject matter, elaborations that, if appropriate to their ends, typically must go beyond their minimal essential forms. Even were such basic functional elements to exist and be duly elaborated beyond their essential forms, we could still not have a system of law in its full sense unless these elements were duly combined, integrated, and coordinated within general operational techniques for making and implementing law: the penal technique, the grievance-remedial technique, the administrative-regulatory technique, the public-benefit-conferral technique, and the private-ordering technique. Such techniques are structural and methodical and so, formal. Similarly, we could not have a system of law if these techniques failed to an appreciable degree to operate relatively systematically in accord with formal principles of legality and the rule of law. A formless regime of political administration, or a formless reign of "state" terror, could not operate in a sufficiently law-like way and so could not count as a system of law, whatever the temporary efficacy of any such "state" force and violence. Nor could we have a system of law without general coherence of content, a further general formal feature.

Thirdly, appropriate form has primacy among law's characteristics because it is indispensable to the very existence of duly constituted, and so legitimate, civic authority. Such authority is foundational. The most fundamental political value is that of securing within a society legitimate political authority to make and implement law. Here, the antithesis is anarchy. Appropriate form is indispensable to organized public decision-making—to the very existence of legitimate authority. Without duly constituted authority, there can be no valid rules or other law, and no authoritative interpretive and other applicational method, and so, no legally authoritative formal reasons for action. Without such reasons, there is no law. In order for authority to make law to exist, the "authors" who make law must be authorized. This authorization cannot exist if "law"-making is ad hoc and haphazard. It must be organized and regularized through the adoption and implementation of formal rules establishing law-making roles and conferring law-making power on occupants of those roles.[64] Moreover, such authority must be similarly established for

---

64 An American judge once put matters this way:

> Those who are impatient with the forms of law ought to reflect that it is through form that all organization is reached. Matter without form is

those who interpret and apply rules in cases of dispute. The very efficacy and legitimacy of the law's methodology for making and applying rules and other law is heavily dependent on form. Appropriate form is indispensable to organized public and private decision-making—to the very existence of effective and legitimate authority. Without such a "set" methodology and operational techniques, and without the established mandatory and exclusionary force of legally authoritative reasons for action that this methodology and these techniques generate, there could be no social objects of sufficient determinateness and constancy through time to which the people of a society could express or imply their assent, acceptance, or acquiescence—the primary sources of legitimacy in modern systems. And without such legitimacy, the levels of voluntary compliance in accord with the formal reasons for action that law generates could not be sustained. Yet because the efficacy of the coercive apparatus of such systems is itself also heavily dependent on such legitimacy, it might well be that this apparatus could not then alone secure sufficient levels of compliance.

Fourth, any basic feature, or general set of features, that goes to the very *identity* of the phenomena in question has a claim to primacy. A primary measure of the very identity of any particular legal system is the nature and extent of its formal character, overall. One way to test this view is to imagine that a number of basic changes in the formality of a given system take place over a discrete period, and then to pose the issue of whether that system might be said to have lost its very identity and to have taken on a new one. Suppose, for example, that the formal constitutional structure of the system is changed in basic ways, as from a cabinet form to a non-cabinet form, from a limited electoral franchise to a fully democratic one, from a system without judicial review of legislation to one with it, or from a system without independence of the judiciary to one with it. And suppose also that the system is changed from one of commonly incomplete rules at inception to largely complete ones; that the system is also changed from one of open-ended rules to highly definite ones; that the system is changed from one in which law is interpreted ad hoc and rather freely in light of substantive ends and means implicated in particular cases to one in which law is interpreted and applied more strictly in light of an interpretive methodology of some formality; that the system is changed from one in which judges have vast power to modify antecedent law at point of application to one in which they have only very restricted power to do so. Now, if even only some of these changes

---

> chaos; power without form is anarchy. The state, were it to disregard forms, would not be a government, but a mob. Its action would not be administration, but violence.

Cochran v. State, 62 Ga. 731, 732 (1879).

were cumulatively to occur, such a system, so changed solely in these *formal* respects with their complementary manifestations in content, would not any longer be considered the *same* legal system. And yet many more such formal changes, major in nature, can be imagined.

Fifth, a system of law in appropriate form not only creates and implements policy. The contours and content of its very institutional and processual architecture, and its daily operations, can distinctively express, enshrine, symbolize, radiate, and reinforce the legal commitments of the society to such fundamental political values as democracy, justice and fairness of process, rationality of decision-making, principles of legality and the rule of law, liberty, limited government, and still more. Appropriate form is indispensable here.

Consider the example of democracy. Appropriate form in the law's institutional architecture and daily functioning is required to express, enshrine, symbolize, radiate, and thus reinforce this fundamental value. Without appropriate form, there can be no electoral process and no elected legislature. Appropriate form here requires not only the minimal essential forms for the existence of an electoral process and of a legislature, but also various elaborations on these basic functional elements if they are to be effective. Many of these elaborations are organizational, structural, methodical, and procedural, and so formal in all these ways. An electoral process is highly rule defined, and it includes such rules as those that prevent ineligible persons from voting, and prevent persons from voting twice. Further, the legislature has to be formally organized so that the results of democratic elections are, in turn, implemented in the law-making process. Moreover, if the fundamental political value of democracy is to be realized, organizational, structural, methodical, procedural, and other formal limits must be imposed on still other institutions of the legal system, and these must take appropriate encapsulatory form. For instance, courts and other authoritative institutions must not have a general power, in the guise of interpretation, to amend and thus undo statutes adopted by the democratically elected legislature. This seems obvious, but in some major Western democracies, judges amend statutes in just this way, a practice that has other adverse secondary effects as well. For example, it imposes an impossible burden on what should be the leading type of argument in any rationally designed methodology of statutory interpretation, namely, the argument from ordinary meaning. This type of argument simply cannot survive the double duty of justifying particular statutory interpretations when it is also purportedly used to "justify" departures from statutes as well.

The foregoing mode of analysis is only one way that the formal character of law can cast light on the very nature of law itself, and this mode of analysis is susceptible of further elaboration. Moreover, the formal character of law bears on still other major problems of jurisprudence and the philosophy of law besides the nature of law. It even reveals in its own way important necessary connections between law and morals. I will consider these and still other theoretical issues in the book I am writing.

## III
## Why Appropriate Form Matters—Some Further Practical Implications

We have already seen how the jurisprudential implications of appropriate form in the law are not merely jurisprudential. They are themselves freighted with practical implications. What could be of more practical relevance than the very existence of such basic functional elements of a legal system as a legislature and courts, and still other types of institutional phenomena heavily dependent for their efficacy on choices of appropriate form? Indeed, one may readily hypothesize the availability of all possible "raw materials" required for a functioning legal order, including embryonic ideas of basic functional elements, mere notions of relevant policy and of other values, potential official personnel, possible citizen willingness to accept duly constituted authority, available physical resources, general knowledge, and more. Yet, all these "raw materials" would be useless without numerous choices of appropriate legal forms and their due implementation. Duly organized and duly formal institutions, processes, methodologies, entities, and more, are required for the incorporation of both formal and non-formal "raw materials" into an effective system of law. Thus, as I have argued, appropriate form is indispensable to the very creation of a system of law and to the very existence of legitimate civic authority. Also, if appropriate form in legal institutions, processes and other basic functional elements incorporates, expresses, enshrines, symbolizes, radiates, and reinforces fundamental values of the society, then this must matter practically, too. Here, the distinction between theory and practice dissolves. Yet appropriate form is of immediate practical significance in still other ways, too.

### A. Appropriateness of Form in the Law Has an Integrity of Its Own, Cannot Be Taken for Granted and Must Be Planned, Designed, and Secured

Although form pervades rules and other precepts, basic functional elements, and the system taken as a whole, it still does not follow that all these varied and wide ranging formal features and subject matter will be *appropriately* formal in any particular system at any particular time. And if form is not appropriate, it may be ineffective as a means to ends. It can even become an instrument of evil. And if form is not appropriate, if wrong choices are made as to form, and if these wrong choices are consequential, it follows that form matters practically and that it requires due attention. The hazards of inappropriate form are all the greater if unsound theories of form abound in a given legal culture. Thus, if many theorists believe that any insistence on formality must be formalistic, then it becomes all the more important to demonstrate the contrary, and to give due attention to appropriateness of form. Alternatively, if some theorists believe that form really has no integrity of its own, and, in application, always collapses into something else, such as "substance," or "material content," or "policy," or the like, then again it becomes all the more urgent to demonstrate the contrary, and to give due attention to appropriateness of form.

I do not believe it is possible usefully to characterize appropriate form in the abstract. What constitutes appropriate form will vary with the type of form involved. For example, appropriate structural form, i.e., an appropriate degree of generality in a rule, is one thing, appropriate encapsulatory form for that same rule something else. What is appropriate form will vary also with the type of legal phenomenon involved. For example, an appropriately formal feature of a rule, such as definiteness, may be one thing, while the appropriate overall definitiveness of an institution such as a court will be quite another. Similarly, the appropriate procedural form for a legislature will be quite different from the appropriate procedural form for a court.

Appropriateness of form depends not only on the type of form, and the type of legal phenomenon involved. It also depends on the type of subject matter involved. In the case of rules, for example, some types of subject matter require, or perhaps even dictate, highly formal rules whereas other subject matter dictates rules that are less formal. The very subject matter of a statute of limitations may be said to dictate high degrees of definiteness and completeness, for example. Otherwise, it could not serve its primary function of repose. The very subject matter of a rule providing for the award of custody of children, however, may be said to require or dictate a less definite and less complete rule. Of course, appropriateness of form also depends on the problem-specific policy or policies to be served, and any general legal values implicated, a subject I will treat at length in Part III.D of this Article.

It may be that at some future time it will be possible, on the basis of accumulated experience and reflection, to articulate what might be called "laws of appropriate form." For example, it *may* be possible to formulate a kind of "law" to the effect that whenever the rights of third parties may be adversely affected, as with the issuance of certain commercial instruments, appropriate form generally requires highly definite and complete rules. Such "laws" could serve as maxims for drafters, and could have still other uses. But whatever the prospects here for the formulation of such "laws" of appropriate form, the very exercise of trying to formulate such laws and of then evaluating them is certainly one way to deepen our grasp of this complex subject. Let us consider another simple example, a more general one. We might imagine the following candidate for status as a "law" of appropriate form: "The more formal, or the more highly formal, the more appropriate." On reflection, however, we should reject any such "law." It is familiar that, for example, some precepts require relatively low degrees or low levels of formal attributes. Awarding custody on the basis of the best interests of the child is an example. A high degree of definiteness and completeness in a rule on custody could, for example, require that the child always be awarded only to one parent, such as the mother, or to the parent with the most material resources. But such a more formal rule could be justly criticized for neglecting other considerations more relevant to the well being of the child, overall. In an important sense the rule would be over-formal, i.e., formalistic (though this is not the only sense of "formalistic"). It is simply a fallacy to conclude that in matters of legal ordering the more formal or the higher formality is always the more appropriate. Likewise, it is a fallacy to conclude that low formality or lesser degrees of formality are always inappropriate.

It follows that form can be appropriate, and yet not be formalistic. Appropriate form, then, is hardly a contradiction in terms. This is not to say that what is truly formalistic can still be appropriate. When form is appropriate, it is not formalistic—is not overformal and thus bad form. But the pathology of form—the systematic study of the major varieties of inappropriate form—would also require that we go beyond the over-formal, i.e., the formalistic. The study of the pathology of legal form requires that we also consider the underformal, and thus the substantivistic (though in the legal academic world in America, some scholars are not especially sensitive to this type of defect). Just as there can be many meanings of formalistic, so there can be various meanings of substantivistic. One of these is simply that the rule is too open-ended, providing little or no firm guidance to its addressees on the front lines of human interaction, and in instances of disputed applicability, inviting an endless canvassing of all possible substantive considerations. An example is a highway "speed limit" (as in Montana) requiring only that drivers drive "reasonably."[65]

The pathology of legal form also includes the study of how rules that are initially well-designed and so appropriately formal become substantivistic in judicial application.[66] In such instances, it might be

65 MONT. CODE ANN. §61-8-303 (1995).

66 I am indebted to Professor DeMott for leading me to think further about this.

said that appropriate form in the rule is swallowed up by (or collapses into) substantive considerations of policy or of justice and equity in the particular case.[67] It cannot be denied that, in the American system, appropriate form in a rule sometimes, perhaps frequently, vanishes in judicial application, especially when the rule seems to over- or under-include. Versions of the parol evidence rule in the American law of contracts provide familiar examples. So many meanings have been given to its terms, and so many exceptions created to it, that in some jurisdictions it has become something of a sieve.[68] But the problem is hardly confined to judge-made law. Even appropriate form in a well-designed statute may be swallowed up in a frenzy of judicial policy making at point of application.

But there is nothing inevitable about the undue collapse of appropriate form into substance, into policy, or into justice and equity in the course of applying a rule to a particular case.. While any legal system might reasonably confer on judges some limited power of dispensation or even power of statutory amendment (duly circumscribed), thereby explicitly enabling judges to disregard appropriate form in certain cases, it would hardly follow that appropriate form in rules would then no longer have any role to play. Appropriate prescriptiveness, generality, definiteness, and completeness in rules, for example, would continue to be general desiderata if for no other reason than that there is much more to rules than substantive policy. Moreover, there is nothing inherent in these formal features that lends them to being so swallowed up. They have an integrity of their own. Indeed, any legal system that regularly tolerates wholesale judicial departures from appropriate form in antecedent rules simply cannot be said to have a genuine rule of law.

The study of the pathology of legal form also requires that we study what might be called the "malformed." An *institutional* example of malformation is an adjudicative process in which the role of zealous complainant-oriented prosecutor is purportedly combined with the important role of an impartial and neutral tribunal finding facts and applying law. Any attempt to combine these inconsistent roles to a significant degree risks the forfeiture of both the reality and the appearance of the impartiality and neutrality of the tribunal. A body that seeks first to approach the evidence in a partisan prosecutorial

---

67 This way of thinking has some respectable antecedents. See, for example, the work of John Stuart Mill: "All action is for the sake of some end, and rules of action, it seems natural to suppose, must take their whole character and color from the end to which they are subservient." JOHN STUART MILL, UTILITARIANISM, LIBERTY, AND REPRESENTATIVE GOVERNMENT 2 (A.D. Lindsay ed., 1951).

68 *See, e.g.*, Pacific Gas & Elec. Co. v. G.W. Thomas Drayage & Rigging Co., 442 P.2d 641 (Cal. 1968). For a different view of the rule see *Trident Center v. Connecticut General Life Insurance*, 847 F.2d 564 (9th Cir. 1988).

spirit is likely in the course of that to prejudge or appear to prejudge when it later comes time to find the facts. Moreover, such a process is likely to be, and to appear, unfair to the adversely affected party. Any such process would be malformed.

But I cite this example not merely to illustrate malformation of an institution. I also wish to contrast this example with its appropriately formal counterpart, an adjudicative process having appropriate role differentiation. Such a process also illustrates how appropriate form in adjudication has an internal integrity of its own which does not collapse into something else such as "substance," or "material content," or "policy," or justice and equity of outcome in the particular case (or whatever the adjudicator takes to be the ultimate end or ends of the process). Indeed, we judge the appropriateness of the design of a basic functional element such as an adjudicative process not only in light of the policy, equity, or other "outcome" ends it may serve through accurate fact-finding and objective application of law. We also judge its appropriateness in terms of whether it is intrinsically fair *as a process*.[69] And we try to design it to differentiate prosecutorial and fact-finding roles, with an eye to the intrinsic fairness of the process as such. Indeed, let us suppose that the policy ends of substantive rules being adjudicated would be served as well or almost as well without such role differentiation. We ought nonetheless to embrace role differentiation on grounds of intrinsic processual fairness. It follows that appropriate adjudicative form, even insofar as designed to serve policy ends, does not in any sense collapse into those extrinsic ends. Its design is informed by internal considerations of processual fairness, too. And, as appropriate form, it has an existence and a stability all its own. It is not to be "appropriated" to something else.

### B. Appropriate Authorizational Form Is Commonly Required Not Only to Validate But Also to Determine the Very Content of Law

The authority to make valid law is always conditioned to a large extent on following appropriate form—on what I will call requirements of "authorizational form." For example, the authority of a legislature to make a valid statute depends on the extent of its law-making power, on the procedures it follows (including voting procedures), and on mode of promulgation. Validity here depends largely on compliance with appropriate authorizational form, and so is largely for-

69 *See* Robert S. Summers, *Evaluating and Improving Legal Processes—A Plea for "Process Values,"* 60 CORNELL L. REV. 1 (1974); *see also* Robert S. Summers, *Professor Fuller's Jurisprudence and America's Dominant Philosophy of Law*, 92 HARV. L. REV. 432, 444-45 (1978).

mal.[70] The only major exception in some Western systems is where validity depends also on compliance with any applicable content-oriented criterion of validity.

A legislature regularly enacts valid statutes. Administrative officials and bodies regularly make valid orders and valid regulations. Courts create precedents that are valid. Private parties make valid contracts and valid wills, and create corporations and the like. But validative effect is not the only effect of actions that conform to appropriate authorizational form. That is, legislative and other law-making is not merely *validative.* Such action is also commonly *determinative* of law's content as well, a major factor that further demonstrates the practical significance of form in the law. When legislatures enact statutes, this very action commonly resolves issues of content as well as validates that content. This occurs because, as St. Thomas Aquinas long ago emphasized, the powers of human reason and persuasion are limited, and so must often be supplemented by the exercise of formal authority in determining the very content of law.[71] It is only through appropriate form that many necessary law-making choices can be made at all. Appropriate authorizational form is, in such instances determinative, as well as validative, of content.

It is true that the power of human reason, and of persuasion, largely or exclusively determines the content of some statutes. For example, a proposed statute may simply incorporate a ready-made, rationally justified, and intrinsically persuasive moral principle such as the principle that contracting parties shall perform in good faith.[72] Here, let us assume that the entire content of the law is determined more or less by the force of human reason and persuasion. In its statutory embodiment, the principle may even remain almost identical in content to its usual formulation in the general critical morality of the society. Here we may say that conformity with appropriate authorizational form, in itself, contributes little or nothing to the determination of the content that is ultimately validated. Conformity merely validates. That is, it merely renders the content legal. There are still other types of cases where the exercise of formal authority merely contributes the stamp of validity, the stamp of appropriate authorizational form, while the weight of human reason (including persuasiveness)

---

70 *OED* entry no. A.5 for "formal" states: "Done or made with the forms recognized as ensuring validity . . . ." 6 OED, *supra* note 13, at 82. *Webster's* entry no. 2.b for "formal" provides: "done in due form." WEBSTER'S, *supra* note 13, at 893.

71 *See, e.g.*, ST. THOMAS ACQUINAS, TREATISE ON LAW 78 (Gateway ed., 1965). *See also* JOHN FINNIS, NATURAL LAW AND NATURAL RIGHTS 284-90 (1980).

72 *See* U.C.C. § 1-203 (1994) ("Every contract or duty within this Act imposes an obligation of good faith in its performance or enforcement."); Robert S. Summers, *"Good Faith" in General Contract Law and the Sales Provisions of the Uniform Commercial Code*, 54 VA. L. REV. 195 (1968).

determines all else. For example, the weight of policy reasoning is sometimes heavily and discernibly on one side, and general legal values such as predictability and equality before the law may unequivocally point the same way, as with, for example, a rule that generally permits citizens of a society to own property. Here, too, reason (including persuasiveness) may be said to be almost entirely determinative of the proposed content of the law, with formal authority merely validating that content.

But there are many other types of examples along a continuum on which the influence of reason (including persuasion) diminishes, and the role of formal authority—of mere authoritative choice—increases in determining the content of law to be validated. Consider a general highway speed limit of, say 65 mph. Here, the weight of policy reasoning heavily favors having some speed limit. Also, the weight of reason by way of general legal values such as predictability, the "learnability" of law, the dignity and efficiency of citizen self-direction, equality before the law, freedom from arbitrary official interference, factual realizability, and dispute avoidance all weigh heavily in favor of a definite speed limit in a precise rule. But even with this powerful convergence of policy reasoning and general legal values, the power of reason alone in this type of example, is still not itself wholly determinative. Why 65 mph? Why not 64? 66? 67? Here, some exercise of formal authority alone is required to determine the specific number. Thus, we may say that, here, choice in the name of the appropriate authorizational form for enactment of a statute not merely validates content, but also plays at least a limited role in the final choice of the very content to be validated.

And, as we move farther out along our continuum, we encounter more examples in which mere authoritative choice in the name of appropriate authorizational form, not merely validates content but increasingly contributes, in itself, to the resolution of issues of content, and thus, is determinative of content as well. Consider, for example, a proposed statute of limitations for breach of warranty. Should it be for two years? Four years? Here, the force of reason strongly favors the policy goal or end of such a statute, but does not so clearly favor one means over another—two years over four. It might be said here that, as to means, the reasons favoring the alternatives are stalemated. This is not uncommon. And stalemate may occur farther along the means-end continuum, more in respect to ends than means. Consider, for example, a proposed statute always awarding custody of a child of divorced parents to the mother. Here, the reasoning favoring such a proposal may be the argument that the maternal relationship is special. But the policy and the equitable considerations generally weighing the other way could, in a given society be equally or almost equally strong in many particular cases. When ends are thus stalemated, yet there is still need for settled law, appropriate authorizational form determines, or goes far to determine, that content. Indeed, in cases far along the continuum, it may, in a sense, even be all there is.

So far, I have stressed the determinative effect on content of mere law-making choice in the name of appropriate authorizational form. The formal criteria of authorized source, of scope, of voting and other procedures, of due enactment, of appropriate promulgation, and the like, not merely ultimately *enable* valid law to be adopted. They also *exert pressure* for determinate resolution of issues with respect to the content of proposed law. These, however, are not the only ways that formality in the law exerts pressure for resolution of issues of content in the law-making processes. Anytime the law to be adopted is also to be embodied in a rule or other precept with formal features that may on their own serve policy and other values in varying degrees, those formal features and the values they implicate will exert their own pressure for the structuring of content. I now turn to this.

### C. Appropriate Form in a Precept Is Required for It to Serve as an Adequate Means to Policy Goals

If law is to serve adequately as a means to policy goals, law must not only have relevant policy content. It must also have appropriate preceptual and other form. As Jhering said: "There can be no content without form."[73] At the law-making stage, various types of choices of preceptual (and other) form are necessary. And each choice might be made appropriately or inappropriately. Consider the example of a legislative proposal to require automobile owners to have periodic inspections for roadworthiness. The proposer of such a law would have to choose an appropriate preceptual form for imposing this duty of inspection, and related duties. Not just any preceptual form would be appropriate. The preceptual form of an order would be too particular. A general principle would be too imprecise. A broad grant of discretion to owners would not be apt, although some cars might not require annual inspection. Clear guidance to citizens out of court is required. Only the preceptual form of a relatively definite rule would be appropriate (and several rules would be required at that). We have seen that the essential form of a rule consists largely of a general prescription that is also complete and definite in some degree.

It is plain that the mere choice of an appropriate preceptual form, i.e., a rule, can not itself guarantee appropriateness of form in all its other varieties. It is even possible to choose an appropriate

73 Jhering, Geist, *supra* note 6, at 473 (translation my own).

preceptual form, such as a rule, yet fail to choose an appropriate degree of generality, definiteness, completeness, or some other structurally formal feature such as simplicity. If, for example, the duty to have vehicle inspections is not made sufficiently definite, the policy of safety will not be well served. Thus, appropriate form requires not only the choice of a suitable type of precept but also choice of formal features which appropriately structure the policy content of the rule. And in our present example, a number of rules with appropriate formal features would be needed, for the law creator would have to address a number of questions if the policy is to be sufficiently refined to be operational, including: What vehicles should be subject to inspections? How frequently? By whom? What should be the scope of an inspection? With what effects? And so on.

Our law creator would also be called upon to consider, if only briefly, still a further type of choice of form, namely, "encapsulatory form." The decision having already been made that such a regulatory matter cannot be left to enlightened evolution of private customary practice, the lawmaker would also be certain to rule out case-by-case common law development. (Of course, the matter does not qualify for constitutional embodiment.) Only the encapsulatory form of statute or regulation would be appropriate here.

Choices of appropriate expressional form would also be on the lawmaker's agenda, though these overlap somewhat with issues of structural form. Thus, how explicit should the law be? Should it be expressed in lay language or in technical vocabulary?[74] And so on.

In sum, choices of appropriate preceptual, structural, encapsulatory, and expressional form are required if law is to implement policy satisfactorily. Choice of policy content is never alone enough. Of course, there will be interactions here between formal features and policy content, in the course of arriving at the final form and content of the rule.

### D. Appropriate Form in Precepts Is Also Required as a Means to General Legal Values, and Such Form Sometimes Justifies Limited Sacrifice of Policy

Whenever law is used to serve policy goals, this also implicates some general legal values, including predictability, "learnability" of law, fair notice, the dignity and efficiency of citizen self-direction under law, equality before the law, freedom from official arbitrariness, and dispute avoidance. The category of general legal values is large and complex, but for present purposes it is not necessary to catalog

74 *See* HARRY W. JONES, THE EFFICACY OF LAW 18-19 (1968) (recounting how the choice of lay terms can be optimal).

these values. Roughly, general legal values differ from policies in two major ways. Policies are problem-specific in scope, whereas general legal values are not. That is, some (perhaps many) general legal values come into play whenever law is used to implement any policy, whatever its problem-specific content. Second, only uses of law bring most general legal values into play. Many policies pursued through law, however, may be or are concurrently pursued through non-legal means as well.

Rules should be designed and administered so far as feasible not only to serve policy goals but also to serve general legal values. But will choice of the same form in a rule or other law that is appropriate as means to policy also be appropriate as means to the realization of general legal values?

Consider this example, again from a familiar context. We may imagine two candidates for a highway speed limit rule: Rule *A* imposes a speed limit of 65 mph (possibly subject to limited modification through enforcement practice) and Rule *B* specifies no precise limit and requires only that drivers drive at reasonable speeds. Both rules have policy content and formal features. We might also say that Rule *A* and Rule *B* have the same degree of the formal feature of generality. Yet Rule *A* is simpler, more definite, and more complete at inception, and thus differs from Rule *B* in these formal features, and so in corresponding content. If we focus merely on appropriate preceptual and structural formality, the question arises: which rule has the form (with corresponding content) that is more appropriate as the means to the policies of highway safety and efficient traffic flow?

In my view, the form of Rule *A* is the more appropriate means to these policies. Its formal features of simplicity, definiteness, and completeness generate more determinate guidance and thus, clearer formal reasons for action by drivers. The conceptual content of the rule is specific and immediately intelligible. The facts on which the rule turns are easily and readily determinable. Hence, the rule is factually realizable. Also, the rule and the formal reasons it generates exclude other substantive considerations that could operate at point of application. Drivers can better self-administer this simpler, more definite, and more complete rule than they can the "drive reasonably" rule. They can also coordinate their driving with the driving of others more effectively. Assuming that a 65 mph speed limit is itself empirically justified, the form of Rule *A* will therefore serve the policies of safety and efficient traffic flow more effectively than the form of Rule *B*. This is true even though Rule *A* over-includes (some roads may be safe above 65) and under-includes (some roads may be unsafe even at less than 65), whereas Rule *B*, on its face, neither over-includes nor under-includes. Under Rule *B*, however, drivers will be called upon to make far more judgments on their own as to what speeds are safe, and will probably err more often as to what is reasonable (e.g., judge a road safe at a given speed when it is not), a major factor that may well offset any policy losses from the over- and under-inclusion of Rule *B*.[75]

In this example, the choice of form that is more appropriate as the means to policy—here, the simpler, more definite, and more complete 65 mph rule—is, at the same time, also the more appropriate form to serve nearly all general legal values. Thus, the two types of effects of form as means are here concordant. The form of the simpler, more definite and more complete 65 mph rule—Rule *A*—serves general legal values more fully than the form of the "drive reasonably" rule—Rule *B*, and so is the more appropriate form overall. Consider several such general legal values. Rule *A* provides more certainty, more predictability, and fairer notice to drivers than Rule *B* because Rule *A* affords drivers better access to the operative content of the law when driving (including any modifications arising from enforcement practice). Rule *A* also accords drivers the dignity and efficiency of self-direction without official intervention far more than Rule *B* (at least in American conditions). Indeed, Rule *B* may induce police, out of role-borne zeal (or other motives), regularly to second-guess drivers, thereby substituting their own ad hoc substantive judgment for that of drivers. Such official interventions under Rule *B* would diminish scope for responsible and effective choices and so diminish the dignity and efficiency of citizen self-direction under law. At the same time, Rule *A* promises more equality before the law and still more freedom from official arbitrariness, for it vastly reduces the opportunities for officials to treat similar cases differently, as compared to the open-ended Rule *B*. Further, and as already indicated, Rule *A* will generate far less dispute than Rule *B*, for Rule *B* is conceptually less determinate, and a more fecund source of factual dispute.

As the foregoing example indicates, the same formal features that serve policy well may also serve general legal values well. We might call this phenomenon in legal ordering the "CONCORDANT EFFECTS OF APPROPRIATE FORMS." Here appropriate formality, problem-specific policy, and general legal values are in unison. This highly fortunate convergence, though perhaps only an accident of fate, is, I believe, quite common in legal ordering.

But such "concordant effects" of a choice of appropriate form are far from universal. Sometimes the formal features of law that are appropriate for the realization of certain general legal values serve those values only at the expense of at least some sacrifice of policy efficacy. When that is so, we may encounter what might be called the "DIS-

75 *See* SCHAUER, *supra* note 6, at 149-55 (1991).

CORDANT EFFECTS OF APPROPRIATE FORMS." The form more appropriate as the means to fuller policy realization should not necessarily take primacy. Rather, the choice of form more appropriate as means to general legal values may, in light of those values, justify some level of sacrifice of policy realization. When that is so, we may call this the "GLV PRIORITAL EFFECT" (an effect of General Legal Values that enthusiasts of "law is policy" tend to overlook).

I will now provide one example of the discordant effects of form that also illustrates how the "GLV PRIORITAL EFFECT" may justify some level of sacrifice of policy realization. Consider another prosaic yet highly important problem of legal policy, namely, when and how to retire and replace aging police officers on the beat. Let us assume that a rule requiring police supervisors to make an ad hoc annual inquiry into the fitness of an officer in each case after an appointed age, say age 55, would in fact be the most effective means of identifying fit and unfit officers, and thereby of serving the policy of having a fit force. Through full-fledged inquiries into fitness, itself a multi-faceted concept, the unfit would be sorted out, case by case, and retired. Such a rule, however, would not be very definite, and it might turn out to be not at all simple. A rule with these formal features would not serve general legal values well compared to an alternative rule requiring all officers in active police work to retire, say, at age 60. This is so in several ways, but I will suggest only four. First, compared to a "fitness" rule, an "age 60" rule would be more certain and predictable in operation and would thus afford officers and their families a more reliable basis on which to plan retirement. It would also afford police supervisors a more reliable basis on which to plan replacements.

Second, the enforced retirement of officers in accord with the "age 60" rule would maximize the freedom of officers and their families from administrative irregularity. The rule would leave little or no scope for official arbitrariness or inconsistency of treatment, and thus would also serve equality before the law. The open-endedness of the fitness rule, on the other hand, would afford administrators opportunities to adjust or even manipulate the concept of fitness or any relevant findings of fact, with consequent decreases in objective and fair administration, and in the appearance thereof.

Third, the officers and others affected under an "age 60" rule would be able to see readily that particular retirement decisions are made solely on the basis of clear antecedent law applicable to their cases, and thus would perceive these decisions to be fully authorized and legitimate. This would be significantly less certain under a fitness rule, which would be far more disputatious, and would provoke calls for a costly appeals procedure inside the administration.

Fourth, the "age 60" rule would be much cheaper to administer. It would not require case by case inquiries into fitness on an individual basis.

The far greater furtherance of general legal values under the "age 60" retirement rule, would, in my opinion, justify a choice of this rule as the more appropriately formal rule over the alternative "fitness" rule, at least assuming there is a close enough general correlation in the first place between age 60 and unfitness.[76] I believe this choice would be justifiable even though the "age 60" rule plainly over-includes and under-includes, that is, even though it would retire some officers still in their prime at 60 and fail to retire some no longer in their prime prior to 60. As I have earlier suggested, even under an ad hoc fitness rule, mistake or bias would be likely to enter into some decisions, and this, along with the greater realization of general legal values under an age 60 rule, would counterbalance the over- and under-inclusion of such a rule. In the end, perhaps we could say that the "age 60" rule does not over-include or under-include at all. This is because it incorporates, as part of its content, the limited priority of general legal values over the fitness policy as such.

Here, then, the choice of form appropriate as a means to general legal values would justifiably triumph to an extent over what would otherwise be the substantive policy content of a rule. As I have said, we might call this the "GLV PRIORITAL EFFECT" on appropriate form in the content of a rule. Here, the formal demands of general legal values diverge from the formal demands of problem-specific policy, and the former take priority to an extent in the adoption of a rule. This is only one of the major ways that a choice of appropriate form affects content in legal ordering, but it takes place in rule-making, and is one of the most dramatic of all types of effects of form on substantive content. Observe that in this and in many similar examples, this dramatic effect occurs not only by way of incorporating the more appropriately formal "age 60" feature of form and content, but also necessarily by way of excluding other substantive content, i.e., excluding a direct and full-fledged inquiry into substantive fitness, case-by-case. This type of exclusionary effect is, of course, a typical normative effect of form in the law. Thus, we must heed not only what form incorporates, but also what it excludes. This effect might be called the "SUBSTANTIVE EXCLUSIONARY EFFECT OF APPROPRIATE FORM."

We may conclude that some problem-specific policies require lower degrees of definiteness for their most effective implementation.

---

76 The question of when a sufficiently close general connection exists, in light of policies and values at stake, is a complex question which I will address in detail in my forthcoming book. Legislative drafting manuals almost universally ignore this and other questions of appropriate form as such.

But most such policies are ones that already depend for their effectiveness not mainly on citizen self-application of rule out on the front lines of human interaction (as in the periodic vehicle inspection example, and in the speed limit example), but rather on official or judicial administration of rule in the usual case. This is true, for example, of various substantive standards for the official issuance by health authorities of licenses to public restaurants, to the "best interest of the child" standard in custody disputes before welfare agencies and courts, and to various sentencing guidelines in criminal cases before judges. In all three of these examples, there is not a "front line of human interaction" where citizens must have "pre-administrative" or "pre-judicial" guidance in the fashion required by citizens in my vehicle inspection example and my speed limit example. All three of these examples require official or judicial application of the law to specially found facts, and depend on this for policy effectiveness, rather than on citizen self-application in the usual case. But even where the policies are thus officially or judicially administered in the usual case, sometimes the highly definite rule will still be preferable, as in my police retirement example.

In concluding this Section, I will add that a choice of form and the general legal values it independently serves may have an even more fundamental kind of legal significance, too. If general legal values are not sufficiently served in an actual or projected use of law, this may be a sign that the use of law may not really be law-like, may lack legitimacy, and so may at least be presumptively unwarranted in its entirety. This is all the more true if fundamental political values such as legitimacy and freedom are adversely implicated as well.

### E. Appropriate Form as a Desideratum in the Creation of a Rule or Other Precept Tends to Beget Good Content Therein

When responsible legislators and other lawmakers create rules and other legal precepts, they also strive for good content. Insofar as they also strive for appropriate form, this tends to beget good content. "Good content" in a rule includes content that serves well as a means to policy goals. Suitability as a means to policy is not merely a matter of relying on relevant causal generalizations such as that annual vehicle inspections reduce accidents. We saw in Sections C and D above how formal features of a proposed rule such as degree of definiteness may also be more suitable than others as means to the relevant policy. Indeed, such features manifest themselves in content. When a lawmaker formulates the formal features of a rule so that the rule is more suitable as means to policy, this is one way that attention to appropriate form may tend to beget good content in the precept as a whole.

But "good content" in a rule also includes its suitability as a means to the realization of general legal values, too. We saw in Section D above how some formal features of a proposed rule may be more suitable than others as a means to general legal values. "Good content" in a rule may refer to this. When a lawmaker formulates the formal features of a rule so that the rule is more suitable as a means to general legal values, this is still another way that attention to appropriate form tends to beget good content in the precept overall. When the form required for efficacious policy and the form required for efficacious realization of general legal values are discordant, as illustrated in the police retirement example, and the lawmaker goes on to make the more justified choice, this is a further way that due attention to appropriate form tends to beget good content overall in the precept finally created.

Yet the proposition that due attention to appropriate form in the creation of precepts tends to beget good content overall can be developed still further. Those who create legal rules must choose appropriate degrees of formal features, including appropriate degrees of generality, definiteness, and completeness. Assume the drafter of a statutory rule is one who rigorously considers the appropriate degree of generality in the rule under consideration. Such a drafter will be more likely to identify and incorporate into the rule those general categories of things, persons, actions, circumstances, etc., to which the rule should apply if it is to serve effectively as a means to the problem-specific policy at hand. For example, given the ends of safety and traffic flow, a rule with content specifying a speed limit should be highly general in scope, and thus should apply to all drivers of all types of vehicles. Here, at least some of the resulting "fit" of means to ends should be attributed to the thoughtful consideration given to the appropriate degree of the formal feature of generality. Of course, in this example so far, I assume that the appropriate degree of the formal feature of generality is driven primarily, if not entirely, by the problem-specific policy at stake.

But generality may be rationally driven by general legal values, too. One such value is that of treating like cases alike, and another is the related value of minimizing arbitrariness in lawmaking. A proposed law that would confer benefits on persons may unjustifiably fail to extend those benefits to all who are similarly situated. For example, a local ordinance providing generally for the grant of licenses to supermarkets might include an exception denying such licenses to WalMart. This would not only fail to implement the relevant policy, but unfairly discriminate as well, and thus fail to secure equality before the law, a general legal value. The law would also be unjustifiably under-inclusive in its conferral of benefits and so not appropriately general. The desideratum of appropriate generality may be said to exert special force of its own that distinctively favors more inclusive content, a force attributable to the general legal value at stake. When this wins out, we may say that good form—appropriate generality—is one of the factors begetting good content. And here, the appropriate form of generality is not merely a means to something else, i.e., some policy or policies. We treat similarly situated persons the same before the law also because that is worth doing in itself. (We do not universalize merely in order to do justice. We universalize, and in that, do justice.)

Similarly, the generality of a proposed law that would impose burdens is rationally driven not only by the policy behind the burden, but also by the general legal values of treating like cases alike and the related value of minimizing arbitrariness in lawmaking. Yet a proposed law might, solely because of the excessive political influence of its proponents, fail to impose a burden on all those who are similarly situated. Indeed, it might even create an exception for a favored class. Such a law would be unjustifiably under-inclusive and so not appropriately general. Here, too, the desideratum of generality would exert justificatory force of its own favoring the more inclusive content, force attributable to the general legal values at stake. And when this desideratum wins out, we may again say that good form—appropriate generality—is one of the factors begetting good content in the final version of the rule that is adopted.

Definiteness and completeness are still other formal features of rules that serve not only problem-specific policies but general legal values as well. Thus, among other things, these features provide fair notice and contribute to the determinateness and so, citizen self-administrability of rules. These features exert force that (along with generality) resolves and refines the content of a proposed rule in the course of its rational construction. Without appropriate definiteness and completeness, a rule could not be satisfactorily operational. In resolving and refining the content of a rule, definiteness and completeness (along with generality) express, prescribe, structure, constrain, and delimit content. And the tendency is to beget good content, or at least better content than would otherwise result. Per contra, bad form tends to beget bad content, as Roscoe Pound noted when he said "irrationality of form continually breeds irrationality of substance."[77]

77 3 POUND, *supra* note 22, at 735-36.

### F. Appropriate Form in Basic Functional Elements of the System Tends to Beget Good Content, and Good Processes

We have seen how basic functional elements of a legal system such as a legislature, courts, and interpretive methodologies exhibit minimal essential form, and we have seen how these elements are also structurally formal, procedurally formal, formal in degree of definitiveness, and formal in still other ways. When these varieties of formality are also appropriately designed, they tend, in operation, to beget good legal content and good processes. David Hume once put this even more strongly:

> So great is the force of laws, and of particular forms of government, and so little dependence have they on the humors and tempers of men, that consequences almost as general and certain may sometimes be deduced from them as any which the mathematical sciences afford us.[78]

For now, it is enough to provide a few examples that will remind us of Hume's general truth that good form in basic functional elements tends to beget good content and good processes. When a legislature consists of persons who must at periodic intervals be re-elected to continue in office they will, as John Locke also stressed, tend to make better laws.[79] Yet the mode of composition of a legislature is a matter of organizational and structural form. Similarly, when the mode of operation of a legislature requires that proposed laws be publicized and subjected to scrutiny in committee hearings and in legislative debates, these procedurally formal features will tend to beget good content in the laws finally adopted. At the same time, good form in the design of procedures also tends to beget good processes in actual operation. This is important not merely because such processes tend to yield laws better in content, i.e., better outcomes. It is also important because the form of such a process in actual operation may also be good in itself, as when a formally well-designed process operates fairly, and in a procedurally rational fashion that elicits relevant general facts and brings reason to bear.

The same is plainly true of a court, *mutatis mutandis*. When a court is appropriately formal in structural and procedural terms, it will operate independently of political influence on the decision of particular cases, and of improper litigant influence, and will, in light of the evidence and argument, decide cases more in accord with applicable law and fact. That is, these formal features will tend to beget outcomes that are good in content. At the same time, such good form

[78] David Hume, Political Writings 102 (Stuart D. Warner & Donald W. Livingston eds., 1994).

[79] John Locke, The Second Treatise of Government 79 (Thomas P. Peardon ed., 1976).

also begets good processes. This, too, is important not merely because such processes beget better outcomes and so better content, but also because an adjudicative process may, in actual operation, be good in itself, as when a formally well designed process operates fairly and in a procedurally rational fashion.[80] In fact, good processes are probably even more a function of good formal design than are good outcomes.

### G. Appropriate Form in Precepts, in Basic Functional Elements, and in the System as a Whole, Extends and Enriches the Possible Goals and Means of Social and Civic Life

We have seen how appropriate form in the law is required for law to serve as an effective means to policy goals, to general legal values, to fundamental political values and more. I will consider one familiar example of the use of law to serve policy goals. The exhaust from automobiles causes air pollution in cities. For the legislature, let us assume that this causal generalization itself generates a legal "means-goal" hypothesis: if auto drivers are required by legal rules to use lead-free gasoline, this will substantially reduce pollution and thus contribute to the goal of securing cleaner air. Accordingly, the legislature adopts rules requiring that new cars utilize only lead-free gasoline. Now, such rules require not only necessary policy content, but appropriate form as well. They must be appropriately general, definite, complete, and simple. They must also be appropriately expressed, encapsulated, and promulgated, all features of form.

Now, in this example, and in many others like it, the goal (cleaner air), the means (lead-free gas), and the cause-effect relationship on which the rule is based, are all antecedently identifiable, definable, and describable on their own prior to any incorporation in legal rules, or, indeed, prior to the existence of any law. Moreover, in examples of this nature, means, goal, and causality have a reality all their own quite independently of the law. We may assume that the law contributes nothing to this reality as such. It is true that the use of law to prohibit leaded gas serves the goal of improved air quality, and that law itself here may be credited with adding importantly to our social means. But apart from this, it cannot be said that such a use of law extends and enriches the total range of possible goals and means that citizens might pursue in social and civic life.

Yet in modern societies, law is typically used in many ways that can be said to extend and enrich the range of possible goals and means of social and civic life. As a result, citizens constantly entertain and pursue goals and means that would not otherwise be available to them. Indeed, it might even be said that the law creates, or contrib-

80 *See supra* note 69.

utes to the creation of new varieties of social and civic life.[81] And in this, appropriate legal form plays indispensable roles. Indeed, it is not even possible to identify, define, and describe the goals and means that the law itself thus makes possible without at least implicit reference to law and to its appropriate form.

Consider, for example, the goal that many citizens have of effectively leaving their property to certain of their descendants on death, and consider the means of doing so by making a will. Such a goal and such a means cannot be identified, defined, and described without at least implicit reference to law and the appropriate legal forms for leaving property by will. Indeed, such a goal and such a means cannot be pursued apart from law and its appropriate form. In these respects, "leaving property by will" is quite unlike "improving the air by reducing the use of leaded gasoline." Not only are the latter goal and the latter means wholly intelligible entirely apart from law; citizens might even voluntarily seek to improve the air this way with considerable effectiveness entirely without resort to any law or to any legal motivation at all. But this is simply not possible with respect to "leaving property by will," a type of goal and a type of means constituted and defined by law itself. Thus, when the law provides for such things as the making and implementation of wills, it extends and enriches the menu of possible goals and possible means that citizens may pursue in society. It makes new varieties of human activity and of social and civic life possible.

Now, so far I have not merely recounted the familiar Hobbesian story that without law there would be no order or social peace, and therefore no commerce, no industry, no productive labor, no architecture, no arts, no letters and no culture at all.[82] Rather, what I wish to stress here is that the affirmative (rather than merely restraining) contribution of legal form to social and civic life here goes far beyond the securing of order or social peace, important though these are. Moreover, what I have recounted so far gives far more credit to law and to its appropriate form than contemporary philosophical accounts such as those of John Searle.[83]

We might call law's contribution here the "INVENTIVE EFFECT OF APPROPRIATE FORM IN LAW." Thus, the law invents and provides for new modes of human activity such as the disposition of property by will. Appropriate legal form is indispensable to such inventive effects. In the case of leaving property by will, the law must define the legally essential form of a valid will. The law must set this forth in

81 *See* B.J. Diggs, *Rules and Utilitarianism*, *in* CONTEMPORARY UTILITARIANISM 203 *passim* (Michael D. Bayles ed., 1968).

82 *See* HOBBES, *supra* note 25, at 80-84.

83 *See* JOHN R. SEARLE, THE CONSTRUCTION OF SOCIAL REALITY *passim* (1995).

prescriptive rules with appropriately formal attributes of generality, definiteness, and completeness. There must also be rules with content specifying who has power to make a will, how, and with what effects. Such content is largely organizational in nature, and is in that respect also formal. All these rules require appropriate expressional and encapsulatory form, too.

The law and its appropriate form can, and does, extend and enrich the range of possible goals and means of social and civic life far beyond the familiar case of "leaving property by will." It invents and so provides for the recognized ownership and protection of property in the first place, a highly complex cluster of legal constructs. It invents and provides for the creation of property interests to secure loans of money. It invents and provides for entry into contractual relations. It invents and provides for the creation and operation of corporations, business associations, and still other organizations. It invents and provides for marriage. It invents and provides for money. And much more.

Nor is the inventiveness of appropriate form in law and through law confined to new varieties of social and civic life and new goals and means solely for persons acting as individuals, i.e., solely through individual "acts in the law" such as the making of a will. The law extends and enriches the range of possible collective goals and means as well. Consider for example, the collective goal of democracy as pursued through such means as the public election of lawmakers. Within a particular society this goal and this means cannot be defined, described, and pursued apart from the legally constituted structures and processes for the election of lawmakers in that society. Indeed, such legal means just are very largely constituents of the goal of democracy in that society, and so are not merely means, but part of the end itself. Appropriate legal form is indispensable here. Thus, just as valid wills and contracts (and all other such "private facilities") are inventions of law, so, too are authoritative elections. The law defines, constitutes, and so invents the essential form of elections. Through appropriate legal form, a system expresses, enshrines, symbolizes, radiates, and enforces commitment to fundamental political values, including democracy. Democratic election of officials is simply a social invention that is necessarily constituted partly by rules and other formal legal devices. Formal rules and other law are required to specify and structure the organizational content of electoral processes. The same is true of legislatures. Here, the appropriate legal forms may be said to create the very possibility of a valued and fundamental form of social and civic life. The social reality in which "elected legislators" exist and carry out their duties presupposes formal electoral processes defined and structured by law, and a legislature defined and structured by law.

Such law has appropriate organizational content, and is formal in this and other ways. There can be no place here for formlessness if these processes are to serve democracy. Appropriate legal form thus makes possible whole new modes of civic thought and action. With this, it becomes meaningful to say, for example, "Edith and Joe want to run for the House of Representatives. It has been their ambition to be members of the majority party, to draft several major bills, especially on fiscal matters, and to see them passed and signed into law."

Of course, the inventiveness of law for collective social life is hardly limited to democratic elections and legislatures. The menu of possible collective "acts in the law" extends far beyond electing and legislating to official administering, adjudicating, interpreting, sanctioning, military defense, and much more. All of these are law-dependent goals and means. The menu includes all the goals and means of government through law. And appropriate form is essential for all of these. The extension and enrichment of possible individual and collective goals and means that appropriate legal form and the law bring to social life must be counted as one of the most fundamental of all contributions to modern civilization from any source.

## Conclusion

In the literature of Western jurisprudence and legal philosophy, appropriate form is the most neglected of law's general characteristics. Yet once it is duly conceptualized in all of its major varieties and seen to be a relatively discrete general subject, and once a uniform and stable nomenclature is introduced to identify and articulate the formal features and subject matter of law, and once it can be seen to have an existence and integrity all its own that does not collapse into something else (such as substance or policy), it becomes possible to give form its due. We can then see it for what it is, grasp its pervasiveness, identify the types of choices of design and implementation it reflects and poses, differentiate its appropriateness from its inappropriateness, and determine its general jurisprudential and practical implications overall. In the end, it also becomes possible to put form in its proper place in relation to other ingredients of law. Much more remains that I will say about form in my forthcoming book, and my views continue to be in the process of alteration and development. For me, form is one of law's most important characteristics, though, of course, there is far more to law than appropriate form. By now all this may seem obvious, if not also banal, at least to some. Perhaps I may be allowed to close, by way of analogy, with another passage from Wittgenstein:

> Philosophical problems can be compared to locks on safes, which can be opened by dialling a certain word or number, so that no

force can open the door until just this word has been hit upon, and once it is hit upon any child can open it.[84]

84 Ludwig Wittgenstein, Philosophical Occasions (1912-1951) 175 (James C. Klagge & Alfred Nordmann eds., 1993).

# [3]
# Evaluating and Improving Legal Process – A Plea for 'Process Values'

## I

## Introduction

Neglected topics sometimes call for lengthy introduction. So it is here. Legal systems operate through various legal processes, including processes for designating officials, for creating law, for applying it, for enforcing remedies, and for imposing sanctions. It is possible to evaluate not only the *results* of a process, but the *process*, too. Consider this example:

> Example (1): Bodea was a small society with a democratic legislature. An organized crime syndicate assumed control of the

* My work in this area has gone slowly. For the record, I wish to recount the following: I treated part of the topic in a lecture at the University of Aberdeen, Scotland in April, 1965. I later published a much-revised version of the lecture as *Law, Adjudicative Processes, and Civil Justice*, in LAW, REASON AND JUSTICE 169, (G. Hughes ed. 1969). During 1968-1969, I taught Civil Procedure at Cornell Law School, an experience which gave more concrete focus to my thinking about process values. During 1970-1971, I revised my teaching materials for undergraduate courses about law and included five sections on "Process Values". *See* R. SUMMERS & C. HOWARD, LAW, ITS NATURE, FUNCTIONS AND LIMITS 98-102, 168-85, 265-68, 351-57, 426-32 (2d ed. 1972). During 1973-1974, I co-authored a booklet of public school teaching materials entitled: PROCESS VALUES—HOW OUR LAW DOES ITS JOBS ALSO COUNTS, in R. SUMMERS, A. CAMPBELL & J. BOZZONE, JUSTICE AND ORDER THROUGH LAW (1974).

† Professor of Law, Cornell University. B.S. 1955, University of Oregon; LL.B. 1959, Harvard University; on leave, 1974-1975 at Oxford University, Oxford, England.

The author is especially grateful to Professor David Lyons of the Department of Philosophy, Cornell University, for his many helpful suggestions in the preparation of this Essay. The author is also indebted to colleagues who, as participants in the Cornell Law School Faculty Research Seminar, offered valuable criticisms of an early draft. In addition, the author wants to record his appreciation for encouragement and suggestions provided by other persons who either read the manuscript or reacted orally to its central thesis: Professors Rudolph B. Schlesinger, Kurt L. Hanslowe, A. H. Campbell, John C. McCoid, Herbert W. Titus, Harry Pratter, and Mr. Geoffrey Marshall. The author is also grateful for the helpful reactions of former students, too numerous to identify by name. Finally, the author wishes to thank Ms. Pamela Cummings for prolonged and highly proficient secretarial work on the Essay, cheerfully done.

legislature and secured enactment of a law that for a time abolished police forces. This disrupted the peace of Bodea and left its people insecure.[1]

It will be apparent that in Example (1) both the lawmaking process and its results were bad. Its *results* were bad partly because they disrupted peace and security, high values in any legal system. The process itself was bad, *as a process,* at least because lawmaking processes controlled by self-serving minorities are unlikely to yield results good for all. Such processes lack efficacy as means to good results—"good result efficacy." Democratic legislatures, on the other hand, have significant "good result efficacy," for they are far more likely to yield results good for all. (This is not to say, however, that they *guarantee* such results.)

Example (2): Bodea had a constitution with a bill of rights similar to that of the United States. However, the Bodean police lost confidence both in prosecutors and in the courts. As a result, the police became vigilantes and undertook not merely to identify and apprehend suspects, but also to "convict" and "punish" them. Police invaded the homes of suspects and even tortured them. By mistake, the police frequently "convicted and punished" persons who were not guilty.[2]

It should be apparent that in Example (2) both the law-applying process and its results were bad. Its *results* were bad partly because they were unjust: punishment of the innocent is a form of injustice. The process itself was bad, *as a process,* at least because law-applying processes that fail to provide for impartial and deliberative fact-finding run a high risk of error. Again, such processes lack efficacy as means to good results—"good result efficacy."

My remarks on Examples (1) and (2) indicate how we can evaluate process results, *as results,* in light of such standards as peace, security, and justice. The evaluation of results is an important social practice. However, it is not my objective to explore it in this Essay.

My remarks on Examples (1) and (2) also reveal how the process itself, *as a process,* can be evaluated in terms of what I call good result efficacy. If a process is a significant means of achieving good results, it is in that respect good *as a process.* The evaluation of

[1] The example is not wholly fanciful. Some societies have even sought to dispense with criminal law. *See, e.g.*, I. Lapenna, Soviet Penal Policy 28-39 (1968) (recounting post-revolution efforts in Russia to dispense with traditional criminal law).

[2] Again, the example is far from fanciful. *See* R. Summers & C. Howard, Law, Its Nature, Functions and Limits 184-85 (2d ed. 1972) (describing São Paulo, Brazil, Death Squads—off duty police who formed vigilante groups to administer criminal law).

a process in terms of "good result efficacy" is also an important social practice. Although it is not my main objective here to explore this variety of evaluation in depth, I will offer some account of it.

Is good result efficacy the only kind of value that a process can have *as a process*? Return to Example (1) and assume that the syndicate-controlled legislature happened to make laws good for all.

In my view, this legislative process would still be bad *as a process* because it displaces democratic rule. Put in affirmative terms, a legislative process that is democratic is good in that respect *as a process*, quite apart from whether it is also an efficacious means to good results in the form of beneficial laws. For a process of this kind serves participatory governance, a "process value." Similarly, in regard to Example (2), it is my view that a vigilante law-applying process would be bad *as a process* even if its "good result efficacy" were high, because it is procedurally irrational (*e.g.*, it is partial rather than impartial), inhumane (people are tortured), and is undignified and invades privacy. Put in affirmative terms, a law-applying process that is procedurally rational, humane, and respectful of individual dignity and personal privacy is good in those respects *as a process*, quite apart from whether it is also an efficacious means to good results (just convictions, just acquittals, etc.). For procedural rationality, humanity, and regard for dignity and privacy are "process values."

I use the phrase "process values" to refer to standards of value by which we may judge a legal process to be good *as a process*, apart from any "good result efficacy" it may have. I use "process value efficacy" to refer to the capacity of a process to implement or serve process values, as distinguished from its capacity to yield good results ("good result efficacy").[3] From the examples I have cited, it should already be evident that, of those values that can qualify as process values in my scheme of analysis, some are generically familiar (and uncontroversial): But how these values qualify as process values is not so familiar. And not all process values are generically familiar in the first place.

[3] Some philosophers might here prefer that I use their own terminology of "intrinsic value" and "extrinsic" or "consequential value" to mark the distinction I am drawing between "process value efficacy" and "good result efficacy." See generally, W. FRANKENA, ETHICS 79-94 (2d ed. 1973). However, I have chosen not to do so. Philosophers themselves do not always use their terminology to mark the same distinction. In addition, the terminology itself has some implications that I do not intend. For example, I do not intend "process value efficacy" to exclude "good result efficacy." That is, a feature of a process that has the former may also have the latter, yet to designate the former in terms of "intrinsic value" implies the contrary for some philosophers.

My principal thesis in this Essay is that a legal process can be good, *as a process,* in two possible ways, not just one: It can be good not only as a means to good results, but also as a means of implementing or serving process values such as participatory governance, procedural rationality, and humaneness. Although the first kind of goodness is "result-oriented," it is nonetheless a form of process-related goodness, for one process is generally preferable to another, *as a process,* to the extent that it is a more efficacious means to good results. The second variety of goodness—the extent to which a process implements or serves process values—*is exclusively* "process oriented," and in this Essay I will concentrate on it.[4] Why do I choose to concentrate on evaluating and improving legal processes rather than process results, and on process value efficacy rather than good result efficacy?

First, modern societies give far less evaluative emphasis to processes than to results. Both in the world of thought and in the world of action, process values fail to get their due. Thus our own scholarly literature on process values is in a primitive state.[5] Although we have many books and articles on such important social values as participatory governance, fairness, and rationality, there is not yet a single systematic essay on how these familiar and uncontroversial values can qualify as process values in a legal order. In the world of action, too, process values are not only neglected but often ignored altogether. We are ready to assume that unless the results of our legal processes turn out bad, then "no harm done." But if my thesis is valid, "harm" can be done merely by disregarding process values.[6] Surely it is bad to neglect or

[4] Of course, from what has been said so far in the text, a legal process may not only be good—have value in the two ways I have indicated, but may also be bad—have disvalue—in two corresponding ways. It may both lack good result efficacy *and* ignore or infringe a process value. I will usually refrain from stating these negative possibilities in the text. They can be inferred when appropriate. Occasionally I will call them "disvalues."

[5] In 1970, after an extensive search, I found only one article that even seemed to recognize the topic as a unitary subject for study. See the brilliant article by Kadish, *Methodology and Criteria in Due Process Adjudication—A Survey and Criticism,* 66 YALE L.J. 319, 346-63 (1957). As its title implies, however, its orientation is different from that of the present Essay. As an incidental part of his article, Professor Kadish does identify and split off one process value: "respect for the dignity of the individual." *Id.* at 346-47. It is some indication of the primitive state of the literature on process values that another distinguished law professor immediately hailed Professor Kadish's feat as a "major contribution." Newman, *The Process of Prescribing Due Process,* 49 CALIF. L. REV. 215, 219 (1961). All this was over a decade ago. As far as I can determine, there has been little since. *See* note 75 *infra.* Of course, I do not contend that the legal literature is devoid of concern for all aspects of legal processes as such. There are many essays on legal processes *as means to desired outcomes.*

[6] Even Shakespeare sometimes seemed to think that only that is bad which ends bad, or

ignore such values as participation, fairness and rationality when embodied in legal processes. Even when these values are recognized and consciously weighed, they are typically overridden. But it can hardly be true that it is always justified to override them. Process values are not weightless. And it is especially important to give process values their due in those circumstances, often frequent, in which the standards for evaluating process results are not clear or are not agreed upon, or the facts required for applying agreed-upon standards are not ascertainable. In these circumstances, the entire "process-result" aggregate can be judged only in terms of the quality of the process itself, and thus largely in terms of the process values it implements or serves.[7]

Second, an analysis of process values and their role in the evaluation of legal processes should help clarify some distinctive forms of social criticism. Thus it should enable us to understand more fully what social critics frequently mean—but often fail to articulate—when they invoke the maxim, "The end does not justify the means," or when they condemn action as too "result-oriented." For what such critics frequently seem to mean is that the course of action being judged unjustifiably sacrifices process values, or worse yet, ignores them altogether.[8] This analysis should also render explicit much of what lawyers, jurists, and elected officials intend to convey when they stress the "morality of process"[9] or otherwise emphasize "legal process."[10] Similarly, it should further our under-

---

well that ends well. Shakespeare, *All's Well That Ends Well*, in THE COMPLETE WORKS OF SHAKESPEARE 861 (Cambridge ed. 1936). This, of course, is the only respect in which he ever erred.

[7] *Cf.* J. RAWLS, A THEORY OF JUSTICE, 83-90 (1971).

[8] For example, see the perceptive piece by William F. Baxter, addressed to the then Assistant Attorney General William H. Rehnquist, *Faculty and Government Roles in Campus Unrest*, in 50 EDUCATION RECORD 411 (1969), in which the "ends-means" maxim is frequently invoked. *See generally*, Gomperz, *When Does the End Justify the Means?*, 53 ETHICS, 173 (1942-43). Admittedly, criticism that behavior is too "result oriented" may mean something other than that the behavior sacrifices or ignores process values. For example, it may be a criticism of those who espouse a given rationale only when it happens to serve the result they want at the moment. *See, e.g.*, Wechsler, *Toward Neutral Principles of Constitutional Law*, 73 HARV. L. REV. 1, 10-35 (1959).

[9] *See, e.g.*, Bickel, *Watergate and the Legal Order*, 57 COMMENTARY 19, 25 (1974) (using phrase "morality of process" attributed to Professor Freund).

[10] *See, e.g.*, United States v. UMW, 330 U.S. 258, 307 (1947) (Frankfurter, J., concurring) ("Legal process is an essential part of the democratic process.") And, for a statement by an elected official, consider this recent example: "[T]he values of democracy are in large part the processes of democracy, the way in which we administer justice, the way in which Government deals with individuals." Address by Senator William Fulbright, University of Arkansas at Fayetteville, April 13, 1974, in N.Y. Times, May 25, 1974 § 6 (Magazine), at 35.

standing of the broad phrase "the rule of law," as invoked in criticism of social action.[11]

Third, this Essay might contribute to our understanding of the nature of law, at least in Western democracies. Some jurisprudential theorists have sought to characterize law in terms of "salient" elements including a "value" element. Yet they have neglected the "process value" element in legal systems. Instead, they have stressed the values typically embodied in the non-procedural law of a society, such as security of person and property, freedom of contract and movement, and substantive justice.[12]

Fourth, the ideas presented here might qualify as a modest contribution to contemporary moral theory, for most moral theorists are preoccupied with utilitarian or result-oriented evaluation.[13] Similarly, this Essay can serve as a reminder to those many social scientists who focus their studies on processes merely as means to good results, to the neglect of process values as such.[14]

Finally, this analysis might even contribute to the improvement of actual legal processes. It might arouse conscious interest in designing legal processes to implement or serve process values or even make some officials more conscious of process values and less disposed to "short-circuit" prescribed processes to secure desired results (when this is unjustified). And it might help citizens more effectively to discharge their democratic "watchdog" functions, for to perform these functions at all well, citizens must be conscious of the relevant values and capable of articulate criticism in their name.[15]

One thing is certain: The topic is timely, at least in the United States. The status of process values is now at low ebb here. The excesses of the civil rights movement testify to this. The works of the "Watergaters" are also illustrative. So, too, are student takeovers of campus buildings. The "law-administering" and "law-

---

[11] *See, e.g.*, Cox, *Civil Rights, The Constitution and the Courts*, 40 N.Y.S.B. BULL. 161 (1968).

[12] *See, e.g.*, H.L.A. HART, THE CONCEPT OF LAW 189-95 (1961).

[13] On this dominant form of evaluation, *see* Smart, *Utilitarianism*, in 8 ENCYCLOPEDIA OF PHILOSOPHY 206-11 (P. Edwards, ed. 1967).

[14] *See, e.g.*, Arrow, *The Organization of Economic Activity: Issues Pertinent to the Choice of Market Versus Non-Market Allocation*, in STAFF OF JOINT ECONOMIC COMM., 91ST CONG., 1ST SESS., THE ANALYSIS AND EVALUATION OF PUBLIC EXPENDITURES: THE PPB SYSTEM, pt. 1, at 47-67 (Comm. Print 1969); Stigler, *The Law and Economics of Public Policy: A Plea to the Scholars*, 1 J. LEGAL STUDIES 1 (1972).

[15] When President Nixon refused to hand over the Watergate tapes sought by then special prosecutor, Archibald Cox, the public rose up in articulate anger, and the President capitulated. If citizens are to be good watchdogs, this kind of articulateness is vital.

creating" activities involved in such forms of behavior sacrifice or ignore process values of high importance, including participatory governance and procedural rationality.[16]

Now for some disclaimers and caveats: My purpose in this Essay is not to undertake an analysis of the positive law of any society. In particular, it is not my intent to survey our own constitutional doctrines of due process, to treat such phenomena as the Warren Court's exaltation of process over outcome in criminal cases.[17] My aims are jurisprudential and therefore more general. Furthermore, I am not claiming in this Essay to have discovered a whole new class of values called "process values." Indeed, I have acknowledged that many of the values I call process values are already generically familiar to us in some form or another—*e.g.*, participatory governance, fairness, rationality, etc. Once we recognize how such values can qualify as process values, we can readily see some evidence of their espousal, *as process values,* all about us—in legal precepts, in official pronouncements, in books and journals on law, and even in newspapers and popular periodicals.[18] Of course, some of the ideas presented here are not yet fully worked out. I nevertheless offer them now, for I believe they may stimulate useful reaction.

## II

## Legal Processes as Separate Objects of Evaluation Distinct from Related Phenomena

In complex societies, many occasions arise to evaluate legal processes, for those processes are both important and numerous. In the United States, there are many varieties of processes for designating officials, for creating various forms of law, for dis-

[16] *See* Part V *infra.*

[17] *See generally,* Wright, *Must the Criminal Go Free if the Constable Blunders?*, 50 Texas L. Rev. 736 (1972); Oaks, *Studying the Exclusionary Rule in Search and Seizure,* 37 U. Chi. L. Rev. 665 (1970).

[18] "Once we identify legal principles as separate sorts of standards, different from legal rules, we are suddenly aware of them all around us. Law teachers teach them, lawbooks cite them, legal historians celebrate them." Dworkin, *Is Law a System of Rules?*, in Essays in Legal Philosophy 41 ( R. Summers ed. 1968). But the independent status of most process values is not nearly so evident in our legal practices as that of legal principles to which Professor Dworkin refers. One would think that judges, above all, would be sensitive to process values as such. But one can find only scattered instances of *explicit* judicial recognition of process values as such. *See, e.g.,* Benton v. Maryland, 395 U.S. 784, 796 (1969); Baker v. Carr, 369 U.S. 186, 208-09 (1962); Rochin v. California, 342 U.S. 165, 172-73 (1952); Lisenba v. California, 314 U.S. 219, 236 (1941).

seminating, enforcing, or otherwise implementing the law, and even for creating and modifying these processes themselves.

The overall goodness or badness of a process is a function of specific evaluations of the various features of that process. Those features can be found in the rules and other prescriptive legal norms that constitute and regulate the process.[19] Thus, for example, important process features are specified in rules which provide:

1. How the process is to be commenced and who is entitled to commence it;
2. What stages the process is to go through;[20]
3. The various activities that are to occur at each stage;[21]
4. Who is to participate at each stage and what activities the participants are to perform;
5. Whether there is to be any "review" of the workings of the process, or any "veto" on its outcomes or the like;
6. By what means the process is to be made efficacious or "sanctioned";
7. How the process is to be terminated, and by whom;
8. How process personnel are to be designated.

To illustrate the notion of "process features," we may briefly consider a process for revoking a driver's license. The rules that constitute and regulate such a process might specify features as follows: commencement via service of notice on the driver of a proposed revocation; provision for an impartial hearing in which the driver may have the aid of a lawyer; a requirement that any revocation decision be made only by a three member board; an opportunity for review; and final order.

When a legal process is evaluated, the focus may be: (*1*) on a specific feature which, in turn, may be either (*a*) regular or (*b*) irregular in the particular case; or (*2*) on the process as a whole. The distinction between regular and irregular features can be readily illustrated: In our judicial processes, usually only litigants present evidence and argument. Accordingly, this activity is what I

[19] Those interested in a philosophical account of how processes are constituted should consult J. SEARLE, SPEECH ACTS 3-54 (1969); MacCormick, *Law as Institutional Fact*, 90 LAW Q. REV. 102 (1974).

[20] *E.g.*, a judicial process may have a pleading stage, a preparation stage, a trial stage, and so on.

[21] *E.g.*, the activities in the "preparation" stage of a judicial process include discovery, stipulation, preparation of witnesses, etc.

call a "regular" feature of a judicial process. But if a judge should cross-examine witnesses or otherwise engage in fact-finding in a particular case, this would be what I call an "irregular" feature. A legal process may be evaluated not only for its "positive" features (regular and irregular) but also for what it is not—its "negative" features. For instance, an evaluator might criticize a process for *failure* to afford a right to a hearing in a certain type of case.

Before evaluating a legal process it is often necessary to do some preliminary study. It might be necessary to determine what the regular features of a process are and how they work. Or it might be necessary to determine what causal impacts the process has in terms of results. And to assess the workings of a process in a particular case, facts concerning those workings must be ascertained. Sometimes it will be difficult to determine relevant facts about a legal process. For example, confidentiality, as in the case of juries, may be an obstacle to effective fact-finding. Inadequacies of social science methods may create difficulties in, for example, determining cause and effect in penal processes.[22]

Legal processes should be distinguished from other closely related phenomena that are often objects of evaluation as well. Thus, for evaluative purposes, a legal process must be differentiated from process results. These results include immediate outcomes, side effects, and collateral consequences. Of these, immediate outcomes are most important and include designations of officials, specific laws, applications of laws, court judgments, and administrative orders.[23] Such results can be evaluated on their own

[22] But some important empirical work on the operations of certain types of legal processes is now under way. *See, e.g.*, Thibaut, Walker & Lind, *Adversary Presentation and Bias in Legal Decision Making*, 86 HARV. L. REV. 386 (1972).

[23] I offer the following more or less comprehensive table of types of processes from which their corresponding "immediate" outcomes must be distinguished for evaluative purposes:

| Legal Processes | General Types of Immediate Outcomes |
| --- | --- |
| A. Processes for selection of officials elective and appointive | A. Designation of officials |
| B. Processes for creating law | B. "Creation" outcomes |
| 1. Legislative | 1. Statutes |
| 2. Judicial | 2. Precedents |
| 3. Administrative (regulatory and executive) | 3. Regulations, rulings, etc., formal and informal treaties; international agreements, etc. |
| 4. Referenda | 4. Popular enactments |
| 5. Contracts, wills, trusts, etc. | 5. Particular contracts, wills, trusts, etc. |
| C. Processes for publicizing and disseminating law | C. "Publication" and "dissemination" of law |

(Cont. on p. 10)

terms apart from the legal processes from which they emanate. (An evaluator may not only wish to evaluate a particular outcome, but a series of outcomes as well.)

Side effects and collateral consequences of a process are separable objects of evaluation, too. They include the extent to which the process generates public confidence and respect for law and authority, the extent to which its results are acceptable to the parties involved, and so on.[24]

For evaluative purposes it is also important to differentiate a legal process from the non-procedural law applicable within the process. Even in law-creating processes there might be applicable non-procedural law. For instance, a constitutional provision may impose a duty on participants in a legislative process to enact a certain kind of law, or to refrain from enacting a certain kind of law.[25] Of course, in a law-applying process, the very substantive law to be applied can usually be distinguished from the process itself. Imagine, for example, a binding substantive statute providing that Puerto Ricans, but not blacks, can recover damages in court for employment discrimination. If a court should apply this law to

| Legal Processes | General Types of Immediate Outcomes |
|---|---|
| D. Processes for applying law | D. "Application" outcomes |
| 1. Negotiation | 1. Settlements; plea bargains; etc. |
| 2. Judicial—civil | 2. Judgments; orders |
| 3. Judicial—criminal | 3. Convictions; acquittals |
| 4. Administrative (executive and regulatory) | 4. Rulings, orders, etc. |
| 5. Self-application by private citizens and organizations | 5. Decisions consistent with law (or not) |
| E. Processes for enforcing law | E. "Enforcement" outcomes |
| 1. Civil—"common law" | 1. Payment of proceeds from sheriff's sales to judgment creditor (and the like) |
| 2. Civil—"equity" | 2. Fines or imprisonment for contempt, etc. |
| 3. Criminal | 3. Fines or imprisonment, etc. |
| 4. Administrative | 4. License revocation and the like |
| 5. Use of militia | 5. Military detention and related enforcement mechanisms |
| 6. Enforcement by private citizens and organizations | 6. Various "self-help" outcomes |
| F. Processes for creating and modifying processes | F. Creation and modification of processes |

[24] On acceptability and associated values in adjudicative processes, see L. FULLER, THE PROBLEMS OF JURISPRUDENCE 706-7 (1949); *Alternatives to Administrative Trial-Type Hearings for Resolving Complex Scientific, Economic and Social Issues*, 71 MICH. L. REV. 111, 146 (1972).

[25] An example of the former is the New York constitutional provision that requires the legislature to maintain a system of public schools. N.Y. CONST. art. IX, § 1. An example of a constitutional provision that proscribes certain kinds of unwise laws is, of course, the first amendment to United States Constitution.

deny relief to a black claimant, the outcome would be bad, but this would be traceable to the non-procedural statute, not to the judicial process. Further, in many legal systems there is another body of non-procedural law called the law of "evidence." This law might obstruct the discovery of truth and therefore contribute to injustice, but, again, the process would not necessarily be to blame. In sum, there are several varieties of non-procedural law that can be evaluated on their own terms, distinct from the processes within which and to which these laws apply.

Finally, to the extent that officials have broad discretion to perform process activities in diverse ways or to exercise ultimate discretionary judgments in the process, it is often wise to single out those discretionary activities and judgments as distinct objects of evaluation, even though they are not wholly separable from the process. For example, in adjudicative processes there arise "hard" cases and "close" cases that call for the exercise of the art of judging, an art which some judges perform well, others not so well. This art of judging can be evaluated by its own distinctive standards.[26] Votes of legislators in legislative processes are analogously illustrative. These votes are often "judgment calls," and deserve evaluation on their own terms distinct from (though in conjunction with) the legislative process involved.[27]

I am not, however, claiming that the features of legal processes have no bearing whatsoever on the quality of discretionary exercises of judgment. On the contrary, some kinds of abuse of discretion can be traced directly or indirectly to deficiencies in process design. For example, a judge might abuse his discretion because he lacks impartiality, and this, in turn, might be attributable to a deficiency in the process which fails to secure impartial judges.[28]

## III

## Standards for Evaluating Legal Processes *as Processes*: "Good Result Efficacy"

Once the features of a legal process are laid bare, and once other related objects of evaluation are identified and put aside, the

[26] Many judges have written on various aspects of the "art of judging." *See, e.g.*, B. Cardozo, The Nature of the Judicial Process (1921); C. Wyzanski, A Trial Judge's Freedom and Responsibility (1952).

[27] Legislators have sometimes written perceptively about the art of legislative judgment. *See, e.g.*, T. Smith, The Legislative Way of Life (1940). On the art of judgment in policy making generally, see the interesting essay by G. Vickers, The Art of Judgment (1965). *See* L. Wade & R. Curry, A Logic of Public Policy (1970).

[28] *See* Fuller, *The Adversary System*, in Talks on American Law 30 (H. Berman ed. 1961).

standards for evaluating the process, *as a process*, can be considered. These standards are: (*1*) the efficacy of the process as a means to good results—its "good result efficacy"; and (*2*) the process values that the process serves, including the degree of efficacy of the process in serving those values. Although my primary focus will be on the latter, it is necessary to offer some account of the former, if only to clarify my views.

In the phrase, "good result efficacy," I use "result" to include the immediate outcomes of the process, *e.g.*, designations of officials, laws made, court judgments, and the like, and also the side effects and collateral consequences of the process. As mentioned previously, outcomes can usually be assessed on their own terms without reference to the processes from which they emanate.[29] Consider, for example, the election of a public official. His election can be judged good or bad in light of his intelligence, his capacity for work, and the quality of his judgment. Or consider newly enacted statutes. They can ordinarily be judged on the basis of their contribution to public peace, to liberty, to welfare, or to justice. Particular court decisions, too, can be judged by such standards quite apart from the nature of the process from which they emanate. The same is true of side effects and collateral consequences of legal processes.

If process results, as judged on their own terms by appropriate standards, are good, this will often be traceable *partly* to the process from which they emanate. When this is so, the process is good in that respect, as a process, for it demonstrates good result efficacy.[30] Of course, the good result efficacy of a process will usually not be the only factor contributing to the results. The quality of non-procedural law, and of any discretionary judgment, will usually contribute to the results, also. Indeed, these other factors will often be equally, if not more, important than the process itself in accounting for such results.[31]

When the causal issues are resolved and it is determined that the process did contribute to the results, then the process may be said to have some measure of good result efficacy. It is one thing for a process to have this quality in a particular case, and another for it to have it in the usual case. Obviously, it is more desirable for a process to have general good result efficacy than for it to be only an occasional and therefore unreliable contributor to good results.

[29] *See* notes 23-24 and accompanying text *supra*.

[30] *See* notes 2-3 and accompanying text *supra*.

[31] Sometimes it will not be possible to tell whether the process contributed at all, or it will only be possible to speculate that it did.

It is important to note that a process might generally contribute to given results, but those results might be bad. In that event, the process would not be good as a process insofar as its result efficacy is concerned. The good result efficacy of a process is therefore an inherently derivative kind of value. It derives from the goodness of process results, as results, and is in that respect "result-oriented."[32]

A legal process, then, may be good as a process insofar as it contributes to good process results. And a process that generally contributes to good results is preferred, as a process, to one that so contributes only irregularly and unreliably. Processes are commonly judged exclusively by such criteria. That is, insofar as a process is considered good as a process, this is commonly by virtue of its good result efficacy, or its efficacy in bringing about such side effects or collateral consequences as public confidence, acceptability of process outcome, and the like.

## IV

## Standards for Evaluating Legal Processes *as Processes*: "Process Values" and "Process Value Efficacy"

Good result efficacy is not the only kind of value a process can have *as a process*. I have already indicated that a process may also be good insofar as it implements or serves[33] "process values" such as participatory governance and humaneness.[34] These forms of goodness are attributable to what occurs, or does not occur, in the

[32] The illustrative table below shows various process features in the left hand column and the corresponding good result efficacy of the feature in the right hand column:

| Process Feature | Good Result Efficacy |
|---|---|
| 1. Participation by party to a law-applying process | Better informed decision, factually and legally |
| 2. Prohibition of torture in a criminal process | More reliable verdicts |
| 3. Use of committees in a legislature to study proposed laws | Better laws |
| 4. Requirement that an official grant (or deny) a welfare application within 30 days after receipt | Early provision of benefit where need shown |

[33] When a process feature is intentionally designed to further a process value, it is appropriate to say that it "implements" that value. Many process features, however, have evolved over time so that it is not appropriate to say they were intentionally designed to further a process value, even though they do. Here it is not appropriate to use the word "implement," with its "intentional" overtones. Instead, the word "serve" is used.

[34] *See* Part I *supra*.

course of a process. They are thus process-oriented, rather than result-oriented. For example, a feature of a process allowing for participation by interested parties is generally good for that reason, apart from whether in the end it also contributes to good results. Similarly, a feature of a process that prohibits torture is generally good for that reason, apart from results. These process features implement or serve, respectively, the process values of participatory governance and humaneness. Features of processes that implement or serve what I call process values are prizable whether or not they contribute to good results, though they may, of course, be justifiably overridden.

A skeptic may quarrel with various aspects of my "process values" thesis, or even deny the reality of process values altogether. But I invite him to suspend judgment until the end of this section. I will stop at that juncture and confront several skeptical attacks.

A. *A Procedure for Compiling a Catalogue of Process Values*

Since, in my view, features of legal processes are good insofar as they implement or serve what I call process values, it is important to compile a catalogue of such values for use as evaluative standards. I have already cited several examples of process values.[35] I will now outline a general procedure for identifying them, and will follow with the beginnings of such a catalogue.

My relatively simple procedure for identifying process values calls for a "case by case" approach at this primitive stage of the art, at least. Under this approach, legal processes are to be singled out one by one and examined to determine whether their features implement or serve values that qualify as process values. Of course, even with this kind of "common law" approach,[36] it is necessary to know in advance what one is seeking to identify. In my analysis, a value qualifies as a process value if (*1*) it is a value that can be implemented through, or served by, features of a legal process, (*2*) it is a value that can be "realized" in the course of the workings of a legal process rather than merely in its end results, and (*3*) it is a value that can render a feature of a legal process prizable regardless of its effect, if any, on results. These are closely related requirements for process value status. However, I do not assert that there are two totally independent classes of values—process

[35] *See id.*

[36] I call it a "common law" approach because it resorts to "cases" of legal processes as sources of standards for evaluation in a fashion somewhat comparable to that by which courts extract law from cases.

values and, for example, "substantive" values—with the former inherently applicable only to processes and the latter only to results. Thus, I do not claim that every value that qualifies as a process value is *inherently* process-oriented in its scope and therefore can never properly apply to evaluate process results, as well.[37]

My "common law" procedure for identifying process values consists of ten principal steps. Briefly, they may be summarized as follows:

STEP ONE—*Single out a legal process.*

Usually, it will be relatively easy to single out a legal process as a separate object of evaluation.[38] Of course, it is not necessary that the process singled out be an actual one. It may be purely hypothetical, yet still serve as a "source" of process values. But to guarantee realism it seems best, at this primitive stage of the subject, to single out actual processes and focus on selected instances of their operation.

STEP TWO—*Determine the operational features of the process.*

The operational features of a legal process can be found in the constitutive and regulative rules (and other norms) that define the process. These may be written or unwritten. Of course, the law in books is not necessarily the same as the law in action. A sophisticated observer should, however, be able to compile a list of the rules and other norms that define the process at hand, and from these the operational features can be readily gleaned.[39]

STEP THREE—*Identify results of the process.*

The relevant results to which a process contributes in a selected instance or instances can usually be identified without undue difficulty. As discussed previously, these results consist of immediate outcomes, side effects, and collateral consequences.[40]

Before specific process results can be evaluated, however, they must be specified in sufficient detail. To characterize them by type, such as "elected official," or "law," will not be enough. Such entities would be too insubstantial to be satisfactorily evaluated.

[37] Fortunately, it is not necessary to address some of the hoarier questions in value theory. Thus, for example, I need not explore the *general* criteria for deciding whether a value is truly a value. Nor do I need to offer a theory of what values are "supreme" or "ultimate." And, of course, it is not necessary for me to show "where the values come from" or that they are in some sense "universal."

[38] Although difficult problems of "individuating" legal processes can arise, it is not necessary to go into them for present purposes.

[39] For several illustrative examples of process features see note 32 *supra*.

[40] *See* notes 23-24 *supra*.

STEP FOUR—*Evaluate the process results.*

Once selected process results are specified in sufficient detail, the standards appropriate to their evaluation will usually be apparent. Thus, legislation abolishing police would, under ordinary circumstances, be bad, for it would disturb peace and security. But legislation creating a police force would be good. Similarly, enforcement of criminal law by vigilantes would be bad, for its results, we may assume, would regularly include punishing the innocent. But prohibition of vigilantism would be good, for it would ensure against such injustice. Peace, security, and justice are among the values appropriate to evaluating process results. Of course, the evaluation of results as such is naturally and appropriately result-oriented rather than process-oriented.

STEP FIVE—*Determine which process features, if any, contributed to good results.*

Bear in mind that various factors other than the process itself may contribute to good results. Indeed, these other factors may be exclusive causes. Sometimes it will be difficult to tell if a process feature contributes at all. But if a process feature contributes in significant measure to good results, it will have good result efficacy. The good result efficacy of a process feature makes the process good in that respect as a process. But this variety of process goodness must not be confused with process values. The goodness of good result efficacy derives from the goodness of process results. But process values are not result-oriented at all.

STEP SIX—*Determine whether any process features that have good result efficacy are also good for other non-result-oriented reasons.*

With this step, it becomes possible to identify process *values*. Consider this example: Assume that an adjudicative process for trying criminal defendants has the feature that indigents shall be entitled to free counsel.[41] Assume this feature is good because counsel will inform the adjudicators better and thus the relevant outcomes—*i.e.*, convictions or acquittals—will be more accurate and just. This feature would have good result efficacy. But might this feature also be good for other non-result-oriented reasons?[42] In

[41] *Cf.* Argersinger v. Hamlin, 407 U.S. 25 (1972); Gideon v. Wainwright, 372 U.S. 335 (1963).

[42] There are at least two relevant non-result-oriented reasons. First, a process feature may be valuable for its own sake as a form of some process value. A feature securing participatory governance is an example. Second, a process feature may be valuable as a means to some other process value. For example, orderliness serves the process value of procedural rationality.

my view, the answer is "yes." It is good also because it furthers a form of participatory governance. It makes the accused's participation all the more meaningful (although it will be more vicarious). Such participatory governance is therefore good for what it is, apart from results, and qualifies as a process value. Thus, putting good result efficacy to one side, a "process-result aggregate" can be good on at least two distinct counts, both traceable in part to the same process feature: the result can be good in light of standards for judging results (here, justice), and the process can be good in light of relevant process values (here, participatory governance). Note well that the goodness of the process feature (here, provision of free counsel) does not, however, depend only on the goodness of particular process results (here, just conviction or acquittal). The result might happen to go awry in particular cases, and yet the relevant process feature remain valuable for what it is, namely a form of participatory governance.

A process feature that implements or serves a process value may be said to have "process value efficacy." Often the same feature will have both kinds of efficacy and imaginative and careful analysis will be required to disentangle the two.[43]

STEP SEVEN—*Determine whether any process features that have bad result efficacy are nevertheless good in other ways.*

This step, too, can enable us to identify process values. Some process features may actually have *bad* result efficacy. For example, processes for apprehending, convicting, and punishing criminals may have the feature of prohibiting involuntary stomach pumping of persons suspected of drug offenses.[44] In some cases, guilt or

[43] This is a possibility often overlooked. Even those who go so far as to denominate certain procedural rules as "rules of natural justice" tend to view these rules solely as means to good outcomes. *See, e.g.*, H. Marshall, Natural Justice (1959). One might add a third column to the table in note 32 *supra* to further illustrate this phenomenon:

| Process Feature | Good Result Efficacy | Process Value Efficacy |
|---|---|---|
| 1. Participation by party to a law-applying process | Better informed decision, factually and legally | Realization of participatory governance |
| 2. Prohibition of torture in a criminal process | More reliable verdicts | Humaneness |
| 3. Use of committees in a legislature to study proposed laws | Better laws | Procedural rationality |
| 4. Requirement that an official grant (or deny) a welfare application within 30 days after receipt | Early provision of benefit where need shown | Timeliness |

[44] *Cf.* Rochin v. California, 342 U.S. 165 (1952).

innocence might depend *exclusively* on the fruits of such stomach pumping. Yet a flat prohibition of stomach pumping precludes access to this evidence and thus has *bad* result efficacy. Does it have any redeeming virtues? In particular, does it serve any process values? I believe it does, for a prohibition against involuntary stomach pumping respects individual dignity. A process feature that respects individual dignity is good for that reason alone, regardless of results, and thus qualifies as a process value.

Consider a second example: Many law creating bodies are popularly elected and operate by majority rule. But it is arguable that these features have almost as much bad result efficacy as they have good. It is at least true that democratic legislatures create their share of bad laws. Yet the participatory features of democratic legislatures are nevertheless good for what they are, apart from results. They comprise a form of participatory governance which is good for its own sake and therefore qualifies as a process value.

STEP EIGHT—*Where it is not possible to say whether process features affect results or to tell whether affected results are good or bad, determine whether any such features are good for non-result-oriented reasons.*

Sometimes it will not be possible to say whether process features affect results for good or for ill. And sometimes it will not be possible to tell whether results partly traceable to process features are good or bad, either for lack of facts or for lack of agreed standards. Thus, we may imagine certain designations of officials the goodness or badness of which cannot be determined. The officials may be politically unknown, for example. Yet the features of the electoral process that designated the officials may provide for a form of participatory governance—a process value.

Or, to cite another common case, a legislature may hold hearings, deliberate, and finally enact a statute, yet it may be quite unclear whether this law is good or bad. But the features of the process that call for reasoned reflection and deliberation remain good as forms of procedural rationality. Although these features are good as a means to good results, they are also good apart from results. Unlike random or arbitrary, or nakedly coercive process features, procedurally rational ones are intelligible to us as applications of human reason.

STEP NINE—*Compare any process value identified by the foregoing procedure with others already catalogued, and enter it either as a variety of some process value already entered or as a distinct value.*

As part of this step, it will be desirable to elaborate on the value significance or "content" of at least the less familiar entries. Also, when different features of a single process or of different processes implement or serve the same value, it will be useful to note this with illustrations.

STEP TEN—*Move on to another legal process (or to other operations of the process at hand) and repeat the foregoing procedure.*

By repeating this relatively simple procedure with respect to a variety of processes, it should be possible to compile an extended catalogue of "process values" for use in evaluating legal processes. I have said that these values are values that *(1)* can be implemented through, or served by, features of legal processes, (2) have a kind of value significance that is realizable in the course of the workings of legal processes rather than merely in their end results, and *(3)* can render the features of those processes valuable whether or not they contribute to good process results. I concede that the foregoing procedure for identifying such values is not foolproof, nor is it without other limitations. A process singled out pursuant to this procedure might not be one that implements or serves process values. In that event, the procedure would bear no fruit. Also, some persons who use the procedure may simply miss process values that the process does implement or serve. And two different persons will not always identify the same values by applying the procedure to a given process. This should not be surprising, for fruitful use of the procedure calls for fact-finding about processes, for value sensitivity, for imaginative reflection, and for articulateness. But it is not just that these capacities are unequally distributed in our "natural lottery." Sometimes there is room for reasonable disagreement over whether a process does serve a process value. And until we understand ourselves better, some process values may elude even the most sensitive, imaginative, and articulate among us.

But for now, the foregoing procedure and the beginnings of a catalogue (about to be presented) are all I have to offer. I hope that others can improve on the procedure, or perhaps even fashion an altogether different and less circuitous strategy for identifying process values.

B. *The Beginnings of a Catalogue of Process Values*

If I am right about process values, then it follows that it would be valuable to have a catalogue of these values for use in evaluating legal processes. My own efforts to apply the procedure for identifying process values outlined in the preceding section have borne some fruit (although of varying degrees of ripeness). Accordingly, I now offer sketches of several possible catalogue entries to indicate how the beginnings of the catalogue might look. The names I have given to some of the values listed are inevitably somewhat arbitrary, but I hope they are not misleading. They are names for *values,* not names for general process *features* that implement or serve these values. However, I will include within each entry illustrative examples of process features that do implement or serve the relevant process value. It should be clear that some very familiar values can readily qualify for entry as process values. Participation and fairness are examples. But for some values, it is not easy to articulate "value content." On this score, some of what I say will seem sketchy and question-begging—at least initially. But I hope that on reflection, it will seem intuitively plausible if still not wholly convincing.[45] It should be kept in mind that the "catalogue entries" listed below are but beginnings. I do not claim that the values listed are universally valid, although I do want to leave open the possibility that some may be. I concede that some are widely espoused only in Western democracies. And even in those societies, it would not be sound to design *every* legal process to implement or serve every one of the values listed. Nor are these values "absolutes." In some cases they may be justifiably overridden.

1. Participatory Governance. One of the most common features of legal processes in democracies is that they assign various participatory roles to citizens, and to citizens elected by citizens (or appointed by those elected). Voting is such a role, and so is electoral office holding. But citizens also have roles in non-electoral processes too. In legislatures they may testify, lobby, advise, etc. And in law-applying processes, they are often the "prime movers." Usually, participatory roles are assigned at least to secure good result efficacy. If people elect the legislators, they are more likely to

[45] The number of possible strategies here is limited. But I can identify at least the following: (*1*) using suggestive examples of values, (*2*) contrasting values with their "opposites," (*3*) analogizing to other closely related and indisputable values, (*4*) imagining unfavorable responses to hypothetical situations in which the values are not present, and (*5*) pointing out conflicts in which we would still prize the value even if this meant giving up something else.

make laws for the good of all; if litigants present evidence and argument in a law-applying process, it is more likely that the truth will "out" and the right law be applied, thereby yielding good results (assuming the law itself is good), and so on.

But whether or not participatory governance helps secure good results, it is also good for another reason and thus qualifies as a process value: it is an approximation to autonomous self-determination of varying degrees of directness. It is likely that most citizens in democracies would prefer to manage themselves and do somewhat less well, in terms of results, than have others manage them and do somewhat better. Among the "opposites" of participatory governance are slavery, political subjugation, and martial law. In Western history, at least, there is evidence that slaves and the politically or militarily oppressed have objected not only to the results of such a rule (when bad) but to its nature as well, even when results were good. They have wanted a voice in governing themselves, too. It is not merely that they wanted freedom; they wanted a measure of self-determination. In varying degrees, the participatory roles provided for in legal processes have afforded this.[46]

2. Process Legitimacy. A process may *(1)* lack legal legitimacy because it is legally unauthorized, or *(2)* lack political legitimacy because it does not have the assent or acquiescence of citizens in a democracy, or *(3)* lack moral legitimacy, that is, not be worthy of moral respect because its decisions are morally bad. A process can have features designed to secure all three forms of legitimacy: rules of jurisdiction can help ensure that a process is legally authorized; rules requiring public accountability can help secure assent and acquiescence; rules providing for vetoes, for bicameralism, and for review by another body, can, in very general but often effective ways, help secure morally acceptable decisions. But for now, I will not contend that the first or the third forms of legitimacy qualify as process values.

The second form of legitimacy, public assent to, or acquiescence in, a mode of governance in democracies, also helps secure good results. It at least signals that the immediate outcomes of the process are more likely to be acceptable to the public at large, and

[46] *Cf.* COHEN, DEMOCRACY 268-74 (1971) (discussing "intrinsic values" of democracy). Professor David Lyons has suggested to me that participation in official processes may be good as such, apart from whatever goodness it may have as an approximation to self-rule. However plausible this may be, I do not explore it further here, for my analysis does not require it.

this, in turn, signals that these outcomes are more likely to achieve their purposes. But in my view, this form of legitimacy is also prizable, at least in a democracy, whether or not its implementation improves results. People prefer being ruled through a process they assent to, or acquiesce in, rather than by one imposed on them. The first kind regards them as human beings, the second as objects or common pawns. Like participatory governance, assent or acquiescence is a democratic value. It is not itself a form of actual participatory governance, but rather a kind of "condition" upon which a share of the ruling task is turned over to others.

That legitimacy as such is conceptually distinct from participatory governance can be readily seen by reflecting on the nature of legitimacy in many non-democratic societies. There, legitimacy derives not from anything that smacks of participatory governance, but rather from such sources as divine right, blood succession, superior force, or the like. In non-democratic societies there would be little temptation to confuse legitimacy with participatory governance.[47] Similarly, legitimacy in those societies cannot have the same value significance as democratic legitimacy.

3. Process Peacefulness. Most people in Western societies take this process value for granted. The general criminal law and special "rules of order" applicable to specific legal processes help secure this value. For example, duelling is forbidden as a process for settling disputes. Vigilantism and lynching are outlawed as processes for enforcing criminal law. Revolution is proscribed as a process for deciding whether there is to be private property. War as a process for conducting foreign policy is usually considered a drastic alternative and special procedures may be required before war can be officially declared.

Generally, well-ordered societies have elections, legislatures, courts, and the like. One rationale for this is that results are likely to be better. Justice is not identical with the interests of the stronger, the more violent, or the "peaceless." But even if unpeaceful methods should regularly secure good results, we ought to object to those methods. Indeed, a peaceful process is generally preferable even when its results are somewhat less good than those realizable through less peaceful methods. This is true not only because in violent or disorderly processes people frequently suffer physical harm; people understandably dislike strife and tension

[47] *See generally*, Sternberger, *Legitimacy*, in 9 INT'L ENCYCLOPEDIA OF THE SOC. SCIENCES 244 (D. Sills ed. 1968). For an interesting analysis in relation to the United States, see Hurst, *Problems of Legitimacy in the Contemporary Legal Order*, 24 OKLA. L. REV. 224 (1971).

even when no one is physically harmed and the risk of harm is not high. Other things being more or less equal, peace and repose are simply preferable to strife and tension. Of course, as with all process values, people may choose to sacrifice peace and repose for some desired result even in well-ordered societies. The point is that this would be a sacrifice, not that it would always be unjustified.

4. Humaneness and Respect for Individual Dignity. The constitutive and regulative rules of a legal process may safeguard persons against inhumane actions. For example, rules for investigating crime may prohibit torture. Such rules might be defended solely on the ground that "tortured evidence" is not reliable.[48] In other words, torture is bad because it impairs the good result efficacy of a process. But again, there is more to it. The use of torture in a fact-finding process is bad in itself. It is inhumane, brutal, and barbarous, although it may in particular cases actually yield reliable evidence. Even when it would yield reliable evidence, however, we ought not to approve torturing procedures, unless the circumstances are most extraordinary.

Even though a process is not inhumane, it may fail to respect individual dignity. The use of a stomach pump (even if painless) to extract evidence of drug use against the will of a suspect is an example. The practice degrades, and except in the most extraordinary circumstances, is unjustified. But again, this is not because the evidentiary fruits of the practice are necessarily unreliable, but because respect for human dignity qualifies as a process value.

The dictates of respect for individual dignity are not exhausted in proscriptions against undignified fact-finding processes. Lynching, vigilantism and other similar processes also offend human dignity. Moreover, denial of fair access to legal processes on grounds of race, color, or creed offend human dignity. *Official* discrimination of this kind invidiously brands or degrades individuals. The victims are not treated as equally worthy of respect before the law. They are treated as inferior beings or at best second class citizens deprived of important grounds for self respect.

Denial of participatory governance, as in the cases of slavery and political subjugation, is also degrading. The dictates of respect for individual dignity range far and wide.[49]

---

[48] Bentham would not have defended them in this way. *See* Twining & Twining, *Bentham on Torture*, 24 N. Ir. L.Q. 305 (1973).

[49] *See generally* Pritchard, *Human Dignity and Justice*, 82 Ethics 299 (1972); Spiegelberg, *Human Dignity: A Challenge to Contemporary Philosophy*, 9 Philosophy Forum 39-64 (1971).

5. Personal Privacy. The investigative function of law-making processes and the fact-finding function of law-applying processes may infringe upon personal privacy. Officials may force individuals to reveal their personal beliefs or personal history. Officials may invade homes and places of work. Various features of our own legal processes serve as safeguards against such infringements. Again, features of this nature are not to be rationalized solely on the basis that they help secure good process results. On the contrary, these features can be obstacles to truthful fact-finding. Yet in those very instances we should value these safeguards as protecting personal privacy, for privacy is valuable in itself whether or not its protection yields good process results. Safeguards of privacy bar unjustified intrusions and thus implement a right to be "let alone." Of course, this right serves many other ends, too.[50]

6. Consensualism. Features of legal processes, at least in many Western democracies, permit prospective participants to *decline* to participate. Thus, it is generally not a crime to refrain from voting in an election. And administrative law-making via regulations and rulings generally does not require affected parties to participate. Even a criminal suspect can refuse to participate in his trial, and a civil litigant can decline to respond to a claim. Moreover, the laws generally do not require that citizens exercise their legal rights to invoke a legal process. These and other examples illustrate a bias against coercion and in favor of voluntarist values.[51] It is difficult to explain this state of affairs solely on the basis that process results might be better this way. On the contrary, compelled voting, for example, might yield better results, usually in the form of better officials. Coerced public participation in administrative lawmaking might yield better rulings and regulations, and so on. I contend that consensualism is a process value—a value we should espouse apart from any good result efficacy it may have. In the absence of special circumstances, and other things being equal, consensual participation is preferable to coerced participation simply because choice is left to the individual.[52]

7. Procedural Fairness. The features of legal processes that secure fairness differ from process to process. Often what is fair

The growing literature in moral philosophy on "respect for persons" is relevant here, too. *See, e.g.*, R. Downie & E. Telfer, Respect for Persons (1969).

[50] *Cf.* C. Fried, An Anatomy of Values 125-32, 137-55 (1970).

[51] For a very brief account that accords with the spirit of the text, see Wolff, *Is Coercion Ethically Neutral?*, in NOMOS XIV—Coercion 144-48 (J. Pennock & J. Chapman eds. 1972).

[52] Of course, this is not to say that a legal system can dispense with coercion entirely.

can be understood only in contrast to what is unfair.[53] Consider briefly two examples: unfair allocation of procedural advantages within a process and unfair access to a process. In an adjudicative process, the adjudicator might grant advantages to one side and thereby deny the other a "fair shake." For example, an adjudicator might choose to hear only one side of the case, or to hear one side via both oral and written briefs, but the other via only written briefs. This would be unfair. But would it be unfair only because it is likely to bias the results in favor of the advantaged party? I think not. Whether the advantaged party wins or loses, the procedure itself is unfair, for the adjudicator does not accord equal procedural rights to parties similarly situated in relevant respects.

Many legal systems have process features designed to secure fair process access. For example, a rule may provide that indigent suspects shall be given free counsel in criminal proceedings. Or a statute may limit campaign expenditures in electoral processes and thus make offices more accessible to the poor. Or a constitutional provision may specify that access to a process must not depend on race, color, or creed. In some processes, fair equality of access may only irregularly improve process results. In others, it may regularly improve them—as in criminal cases where indigents are given free counsel (rather than no counsel at all).

However, regardless of whether fair equality of access improves process results, the features that secure this equality are valuable. To deny access for irrelevant "reasons" of wealth, race, color, or creed is arbitrary and therefore unfair. Except in very special circumstances, "reasons" of this nature cannot justify differences in access.[54]

8. The Procedural Rule of Law: "Procedural Legality." A legal process may lack procedural legality in either of two basic ways: (*1*) it may simply lack rules and thus leave officials with too much discretion, or (2) it may fail to provide mechanisms for keeping officials within the rules. Procedural legality is valuable whether or not it improves process results. It provides for procedural governance "by law instead of men." Other things being equal, rule by law is generally preferable to rule by officials acting in a legal vacuum, even in procedural matters. We may imagine two processes that yield similar results with only one being law-

---

[53] This is true of many expressions. *Cf.* Summers, *"Good Faith" in General Contract Law and the Sales Provisions of the Uniform Commercial Code,* 54 VA. L. REV. 195 (1968).

[54] Those denied fair equality of access are also denied the opportunity for participatory governance. Equality of access is also a dictate of procedural fairness.

governed. We should generally prefer the law-governed one, for its operations would be more certain and predictable. Of course, these qualities can serve good results, too, for they enable process participants to make intelligent procedural choices that may lead to good results. But certainty and predictability are valuable in their own right, as well, for they simply enable people to know where they stand before official authority.[55]

9. Procedural Rationality. As Aristotle and others have observed, man is a rational animal.[56] Accordingly, humans generally prefer to order their affairs through reason rather than through random or arbitrary action, or through naked force. This value I call *procedural* rationality. For many legal processes, its dictates (expressed as maxims) include the following: (*1*) "carefully ascertain relevant evidence and carefully canvas relevant argument," (*2*) "carefully weigh that evidence and argument," (*3*) "deliberate calmly and carefully," (*4*) "resolve issues impartially and therefore solely on the basis of their merits," (*5*) "be prepared to give reasons for what is decided." Legal rules that constitute and regulate legal processes typically incorporate these dictates.[57]

Obviously, these dictates may serve good result efficacy. For example, their pursuit in electoral processes is more likely to yield better officials. And their pursuit in law-applying processes is a necessity if law is to be "applied." Further, in lawmaking the results are more likely to be better if the process is rational. But procedural rationality is valuable as such, apart from any good result efficacy it has. Absent extraordinary circumstances, it is preferable to random or arbitrary or exclusively coercive methods. Thus, of two legal processes yielding more or less the same results, only one of which is a rational process, we should generally prefer the rational one. This is because it involves scrutinizable effort to use human reason and is therefore *intelligible* to us in a way that the other kinds of processes are not. Those who participate in, or are affected by, rational processes generally have a better chance of

[55] *Cf.* Beinart, *The Rule of Law*, 1962 ACTA JURIDICA 99; Burin, *The Theory of the Rule of Law and the Structure of the Constitutional State*, 15 AM. U.L. REV. 313 (1966). The procedural rule of law can serve other process values, too, including rationality.

[56] Woman, too. *See* ARISTOTLE, ETHICS 38 (Penguin Classics ed. 1953).

[57] Professor Fuller has emphasized that various features of legal processes secure "guarantees of deliberateness" which express "more profoundly than does the principle of majority rule itself the role Western culture has historically assigned to reason." Fuller, *Jurisprudence*, in XIII ENCYCLOPEDIA BRITANNICA 152 (1965). On impartiality see especially Eckoff, *Impartiality, Separation of Powers, and Judicial Independence*, 9 SCANDINAVIAN STUDIES IN LAW 9 (1965).

knowing "what is going on"—of knowing what is happening to them and why. This knowledge, in itself, is worth having.

10. Timeliness and Finality. When it is said that a process operates with dispatch, or that it is dilatory, it is the "timeliness" of the process that is being evaluated.[58] In our own system, for instance, electoral processes typically operate in a timely fashion, but our legislative and law-applying processes often do not, and are often condemned for this. Their failure to operate in a timely fashion can significantly affect results. For example, when a legislature delays, the problems may worsen to such an extent that it can no longer deal with them. If a judicial proceeding is delayed, witnesses may die, move out of the area, or become forgetful, thus making a fact determination difficult.

Regardless of whether or not processes improve results by disposing of issues in a timely fashion, timeliness is itself valuable and thus qualifies as a process value. Timeliness is, on the one hand, the "opposite" of dilatoriness, and on the other hand the "opposite" of haste. Dilatoriness is objectionable even if it does not affect results. Persons to be affected by a process ought not be kept "up in the air" for no reason. And haste is objectionable if only because it disserves procedural rationality.

Lack of process finality and dilatoriness are related. That is, lack of a *final* result may unduly draw out the proceedings. In adjudicative processes where finality is of prime importance it secures repose and freedom from harassment. A dispute-settling process that is always subject to "reruns" of the same issues is deficient as a process.[59]

The preceding ten items are but sketches for entries in a projected catalogue of process values. Doubtless these entries can be expanded and otherwise improved upon. Indeed, whole books have been written on some of the listed values. Still other entries are needed if the catalogue is to be at all complete.[60]

## C. *"Process Value Efficacy"—Notes for a Special Catalogue Entry*

The catalogue of values for evaluating processes should include a special entry on process value efficacy just as it should

---

[58] For an insightful discussion of the value of time that has bearing in legal contexts, see Brown, *The Value of Time,* 80 ETHICS 173 (1970).

[59] Of course, this deficiency may impair the quality of ultimate process results and be objectionable on that ground too.

[60] Among the many other possible candidates for process value status are: truth telling, tolerance for dissent, official integrity, and public openness.

include a special entry on good result efficacy.[61] It is important to distinguish between *particular* process value efficacy and what I will call *general* process value efficacy. A process may or may not regularly or generally implement or serve a process value. General "reliability" in implementing or serving a process value is preferable. Consider, for example, the process value of participatory governance in criminal processes. A criminal process that merely permits an indigent-accused to participate without also providing him with a lawyer cannot reliably serve participatory governance. The participatory role of an indigent in his defense cannot be as meaningful as if he were represented by a lawyer (in what is, after all, a technical process). Accordingly, to secure *general* efficacy in implementing the relevant participatory value, the government must provide free counsel to indigents.

The general efficacy of a process in implementing a process value depends on two factors: (*1*) the efficacy of the legal rules that prescribe the features of the process which implement or serve the process value (*e.g.*, rules providing for assigned counsel in the above example), and (*2*) the efficacy of "implementive mechanisms"—any corrective procedures, sanctions, or the like—to be utilized or imposed if the foregoing rules are not followed in the particular case (*e.g.*, if assigned counsel is not provided).

The first of these factors embodies a means-end hypothesis—*e.g.*, that meaningful participation (the "end") by an indigent accused requires competent counsel (the "means"). The means-end hypothesis may not be soundly conceived. If unsound, implementive effort will fail for that reason. But even if sound, it may fail for want of corrective or sanctioning mechanisms to be resorted to, if the legal rules embodying the hypothesis are not followed.

"General process value efficacy" should be distinguished from "general good result efficacy" discussed previously.[62] Recall that the goodness of general good result efficacy ultimately depends on the goodness of the results as judged by appropriate standards. But the goodness of general process value efficacy does not depend on the goodness of results. Instead, it depends merely on the relevant process value being *truly* a process value.

Of course, the efficacy of a process to implement or serve a process value may conflict with the efficacy of that process to yield a good result. For example, police investigations may pose this

[61] *See* part III *supra*.

[62] *See id.*

conflict. To solve a crime (good result efficacy) it may be necessary to detain and interrogate a person against his will in circumstances in which the suspect is put in fear and feels helpless, thereby infringing the process value of respect for individual dignity. Or, an administrative-regulatory process, for example, may pose a "process vs. result" conflict. Thus, to reduce drunken driving (good result efficacy), drivers may be required to submit to blood tests against their will, thereby infringing respect for individual dignity and personal privacy (both process values). Numerous other examples could be cited.

D. *An Addendum on the Relations Between Process Values and the Values for Evaluating Process Results*

Of the various kinds of process results, what I have called "immediate outcomes" are most commonly evaluated. These outcomes include laws, applications of law, court orders, and the like. Among the familiar values often used to evaluate such outcomes, the following may be listed:

1. Liberty. This value includes both "daily life" liberties such as freedom of worship and movement, and political liberties such as freedom of expression.
2. Substantive justice. This value encompasses the justice of deserved reparations and compensation, the justice of punishments, the justice of inter-personal transactions, and the justice of state distributions of benefits and burdens.
3. Income and wealth.
4. Formal and substantial equality of opportunity. Included here are equality of access to education and the absence of restrictions on access to significant social roles.
5. Security of person and property.
6. Community peace.
7. Human dignity.

Although the foregoing list overlaps the list of process values discussed previously,[63] I believe that some values are *generally* appropriate only to evaluating processes as processes while others are appropriate only to evaluating process results. I will not, however, try to establish this, for my principal thesis does not depend on it. My principal thesis is that there are values which, when implemented in an appropriate process, are prizable whether or not their implementation improves process results. To sustain this thesis, it is not necessary to show that values for judging

[63] *See* text accompanying notes 45-60 *supra.*

processes and values for judging results are different. These values could all be the same and the thesis still hold. Consider this example: Assume that a lawmaking process is peaceful. Assume also that it yields laws that help secure community peace. This "process and result aggregate" is valuable on two counts, not one: the process itself is peaceful, and its results contribute to community peace. Now, assume that although the lawmaking process is itself peaceful, it fails to yield laws that help secure community peace. The process is still good *as a process* in that it is peaceful. Process peacefulness, then, qualifies as a process value, for it is prized whether or not its implementation also improves results. Yet the standards of value for judging both process and result in this example are the same.

In any event, this much is undeniably true: *In a particular case,* the values appropriate to evaluating a given process will *not necessarily be the same* as the values for evaluating its results. Indeed, the values will often be different. For example, a lawmaking process may be judged good *as a process* because it provides for participatory governance, is peaceful, and operates in a fashion that is procedurally rational and fair. But its results—statutes—might be judged good because, for example, they contribute to the general safety by requiring that cars not be capable of going faster than fifty miles an hour. How the values relevant to judging processes and to judging results may vary can be indicated schematically as follows:

1. A process might be judged good because it has V1, V2, and V3, but its outcomes good because they have V4 and V5.
2. A process might be judged good because it has V1, V2, and V3, but some of its outcomes bad because they lack V4 and V5.
3. A process might be judged bad because it lacks V1, V2, and V3, yet some of its outcomes good because they have V4 and V5.
4. A process might be judged bad because it lacks V1, V2, and V3, and its outcomes bad because they lack V4 and V5.
5. A process might be judged bad because it lacks V1 and V2, and it might be unclear whether its outcomes are good or bad. (A common kind of case.)
6. A process might be judged good because it has V1 and V2, and it might be unclear whether its outcomes are good or bad. (A common kind of case.)

Many other permutations are, of course, possible.

In summary, then, at least some values *generally* appropriate to judging results are also *generally* appropriate to judging processes. But *in particular cases*, the values appropriate to judging the one and the other will not necessarily be the same, and, in fact, will often be very different. Process values, then, at least have this kind of independent significance.

### E. *Process Values Reconsidered—Five Skeptical Attacks*

A skeptic may quarrel with various aspects of my process values thesis, or even deny the reality of process values altogether. Therefore, I shall address various skeptical attacks.[64] My responses are not absolutely decisive, but they are all I can now offer.

#### 1. *"Ideal Results" Skepticism*

I have contended that features of processes that implement or serve process values are good regardless of any good results to which these features may contribute. Imagine an "ideal results" skeptic who counters as follows:

> Suppose an ideal world ruled by a philosopher queen (P.Q.) who by her own *direct action* always makes ideal laws, always applies them correctly, and always achieves the correct result. In such a society there would be no legal processes. Consequently, there could be no process values. And if we lived in this society, we would not object to P.Q.'s governance, for the results would be ideal. This shows that process features are valuable only because in our own world legal processes are necessary to provide good results with regularity. Accordingly, there are no "process values."

In response to the "ideal results" skeptic, I offer three points. First, I deny that even in such an ideal world, people would not object to P.Q.'s rule. I believe that if those people were like us, they would prefer at least some measure of participatory governance.

Second, P.Q.'s world is simply not our world. *We* need legal processes to maximize good results.

Third, in any event, the conclusion of the "ideal results" skeptic does not follow from his premise. Even if in his ideal world

[64] For my purposes it is fortunately not necessary to go into every source of value skepticism here. For instance, I do not undertake to treat the sophisticated arguments of those philosophers who stress the disanalogies between facts and values and deny that value judgments can be rationally defended. *See, e.g.*, A. AYER, LANGUAGE, TRUTH AND LOGIC (2d ed. 1946). Nor do I treat commonplace sources of value skepticism more characteristic of the laity—*e.g.*, the view that any phenomenon (whether a value or not) which is abstract, general, nebulous, and somewhat imprecisely articulable is more or less unreal.

legal processes are not needed, and therefore citizens have no occasion to espouse process values, it would not follow that in a society where legal processes are needed, their features are prized only for their good result efficacy. Why should not these processes be good as processes, too? Although process values are "parasitic" on processes, it does not follow that process features that serve those values are valuable only because they further good results desired by those who set up the process.

2. *"Future Results" Skepticism*

In arguing for process values, I have sometimes cited examples in which a process is bad because it ignores or infringes a process value, but its result in the particular instance nonetheless is good.[65] I have then concluded that the badness of the process cannot derive from badness of result, because the results are good. Imagine a "future results" skeptic who responds as follows:

> Where the process is bad but the results good, the badness of the process is still result-dependent, for while badness of process has no adverse effect on results in the case or cases at hand, its regular reoccurrence would necessarily affect results adversely. Hence, *any* criticism of process badness is really result-oriented, even if those results are hypothetical future ones.

I offer these responses: First, any force the skeptic's argument may have diminishes insofar as the causal relation between badness of process and badness of result is tenuous. The causal relation between some process features that in my view implement or serve process values, and the corresponding process results, is tenuous indeed. Participatory governance, for example, finds expression as a process value in majority vote of an elective legislative body. Yet failure to abide by majority rule, for example, is far from any *guarantee* that the result will be bad in future cases, let alone the case at hand. But we nonetheless espouse majority rule as a prizable feature of lawmaking processes. It therefore seems highly unlikely that our espousal is solely attributable to whatever good result efficacy majority rule may have in future cases.

Second, even if people should come to think like the "future results" skeptic, I contend that they ought not to do so. Instead they *ought* to recognize process values for what they are—values that make process features prizable in their own right, independent of result. These values are realizable *in the course* of the workings of a process rather than merely in its *end* results. Why

[65] *See* text accompanying notes 2-3 *supra*.

should not the inner workings of processes be recognized as a possible "realm of value realization," too, independently of end results? The future results skeptic seems blind to this possibility.

3. *"Skeptical Behindism"*

I have contended that process features can be good solely for the sake of the process values they implement or serve. The skeptic who insists on what I will call "behindism" might argue as follows:

> It won't do just to give a name to, describe, or elaborate on what an alleged process value is, and then *assert* that a process feature is good for the sake of this process value. Moreover, to say that an alleged process value, such as participatory governance, is good for its own sake is to stop the analysis at an arbitrary point. If we will only *go behind* alleged process values, we will always discover relevant "outcome" values. Thus, it will always turn out that the goodness of a process, "as a process," depends on its contribution to the goodness of process results as judged by "outcome" values.

First, I do not deny that many process features, *in addition* to being good for the sake of the process values they implement or serve, are also good for the sake of any good results that they contribute to. Second, "behindism" carried to extremes would land us in an infinite regress. There must be a stopping point somewhere.[66] The "behindism" skeptic might concede as much but assert that this point is reached only when, in going behind a so-called process value, we identify a higher value appropriate to judging process results. In my view, it is dogmatic to insist on this. Third, it is simply not arbitrary to halt the regress with a process value. Admittedly, in my listing and analysis of process values I sometimes rested merely with suggestive or intuitively plausible sketches of how it is that they render process features valuable. But some process values are so taken for granted in our own society —even though they are not necessarily implemented—that it ought to be sufficient merely to call attention to them. I invite the skeptic to review in this light such examples as participatory governance, humaneness, process peacefulness, procedural fairness, and legitimacy. Fourth, I readily admit to less than perfect understanding of some process values. Their value significance is difficult to articulate. I believe, however, that I have done more than merely give names to possible values. In regard to each value I have said at

[66] Or so many believe. This issue is discussed in C. Wellman, Challenge and Response—Justification in Ethics ch. 6 (1971) ("Infinite Regresses").

least enough to rebut any charge that I am merely labeling phenomena as valuable. It therefore seems fair to shift the burden of proof to the "behindism" skeptic.

4. *"Ultimate Values" Skepticism*

It might be possible to formulate a satisfactory theory about the "ultimate value grounding" of process values. For instance, one might try to "ground" these values in generalities about human nature, or in some all-encompassing theory of rationality, or in an ideal conception of society. Since I have not attempted this, a skeptic might contend:

> In order for the process values thesis to be convincing, proponents of the thesis must show in ultimate terms *why* claimed process values are *valuable*, and this would require that they be grounded in some comprehensive and justified axiological theory.

I concede that, if I could show some such "ultimate value grounding" for each process value, this might strengthen the justificatory force of my thesis. But the very possibility of executing such a project is itself the subject of philosophical debate.[67] And the project is beyond the purposes and scope of this Essay. To sustain my principal thesis, it is only necessary to cite some process values which, *as values*, are familiar and uncontroversial, and which render process features prizable regardless of results. I believe that most of my catalogue entries fall in this category.

5. *"Experiential Effects" Skepticism*

I have claimed that process features that implement or serve process values are valuable for the sake of those process values. Imagine an "experiential effects" skeptic who argues as follows:

> Process features that implement or serve process values are not valuable for the sake of those process values. They are valuable only if those involved in or affected by the process actually experience certain psychological reactions or sensations. These experiences are one type of process result. Hence process values are result-dependent values.

Before responding to this argument, I will state it more fully. Consider the following two tables:

[67] *See generally* P. TAYLOR, NORMATIVE DISCOURSE 68-188 (1961); Feigl, *Validation and Vindication–An Analysis of the Nature and Limits of Ethical Arguments*, in READINGS IN ETHICAL THEORY 667 (W. Sellars & J. Hospers eds. 1952).

TABLE A

| Process Feature Implementing a Process Value | Experiential Effects |
|---|---|
| 1. Accused's unimpaired participation in his own defense (Process value: Participatory Governance) | Feeling of accused that he has had his full "day in court" |
| 2. Accused's freedom from torture to get a confession (Process value: Humaneness) | Avoidance of fear and physical harm to accused |
| 3. Plaintiff's equal opportunity to present his side of his case (Process value: Procedural Fairness) | Feeling of plaintiff that he has been treated fairly |
| 4. Administrator's statement of findings of fact and reasons for denying an application for welfare benefits (Process value: Procedural Rationality) | Feeling of applicant that he has been treated in a rational, non-arbitrary way |

TABLE B

| Process Feature Infringing a Process Value | Experiential Effects |
|---|---|
| 1. Denial to accused of any participation in his defense | Accused's anger, bitterness |
| 2. Torture of accused | Fear, physical harm, anger, bitterness |
| 3. Denial to plaintiff of right to present his case to civil court | Plaintiff's anger, bitterness |
| 4. Arbitrary denial of application without reviewing facts | Anger and bitter feelings of applicant |

The "experiential effects" skeptic argues that values such as participatory governance, humaneness, procedural fairness, and procedural rationality are valuable only for the experiential effects that accompany their implementation through features of processes. Thus, they derive their value from other "things" (right column, Table A), and also their disvalue (right column, Table B), and these other things are classifiable in my own scheme as process results—side effects or consequences collateral to immediate outcomes.[68] Accordingly, the skeptic concludes that the very concept of process values is logically incoherent. There simply cannot be any values which make process features valuable without regard to whether these features contribute to good process results. The experiential effects required for process values to render process features valuable are themselves one variety of process "result," as that term is used in this Essay.

In my view, however, the process value served by a process feature is not *dependent* for its value on occurrences of feelings and other experiences, at least not in particular cases. Suppose, for

[68] *See* notes 23-24 and accompanying text *supra*.

example, that a litigant is actually given a full and fair opportunity in court. That very litigant may still go away dissatisfied and embittered. The experiential effects skeptic would say that the process therefore did not accord the litigant either an opportunity for participatory governance, or procedural fairness. But if this is so, we will be plunged into subjectivism. The same feature of a process would or would not be regarded as having process value, depending on the subjective experiences of those involved or affected. Yet various factors may explain why the persons involved or affected may not be satisfied when, on objective analysis, the process features do serve relevant process values. These persons might have been mistaken about facts. They might have misunderstood an official. They might have been unreasonable. Their expectations might have been unrealistic in the first place. Or they may be so dissatisfied with the immediate outcome that they are unable to perceive anything good in the process. Similarly, process disvalue is not dependent on the occurrence of feelings of anger or bitterness.[69]

An "experiential effects" skeptic might espouse a less radical view, namely, that although process features that serve process values are not dependent for their value on the occurrence of "value experiences" *in particular cases,* they do *generally* depend for their value on the more or less regular occurrence of such experiences. It is not possible for me to respond satisfactorily to this view here. But even if the view is correct, at the very least it would remain open to me to revise my theory as follows: A process value is a value which makes features of a process good, whether or not those features also contribute to good *outcomes* (as opposed to such outcomes *plus* side effects and collateral consequences). Thus, process values would still constitute standards for evaluating a process *as a process.* And these standards would be distinct from "good outcome efficacy." They would not necessarily be the same as the standards appropriate to judging process outcomes, *as outcomes,* in particular cases. Thus, my principal thesis would remain largely intact.

### F. *A Summary Diagram*

It may now be useful to summarize the specific ways in which an illustrative process feature might contribute to the total goodness of a process *as a process.* In the diagram below, I have used the process feature of "party participation" in an adjudicative process as an illustration.

[69] *Cf.* Baylis, Grading, Values, and Choice, LXVII Mind 485, 495-96 (1958).

DIAGRAM

WAYS AN ILLUSTRATIVE PROCESS FEATURE MAY HAVE VALUE THAT CONTRIBUTES TO THE OVERALL GOODNESS OF A PROCESS *AS A PROCESS*

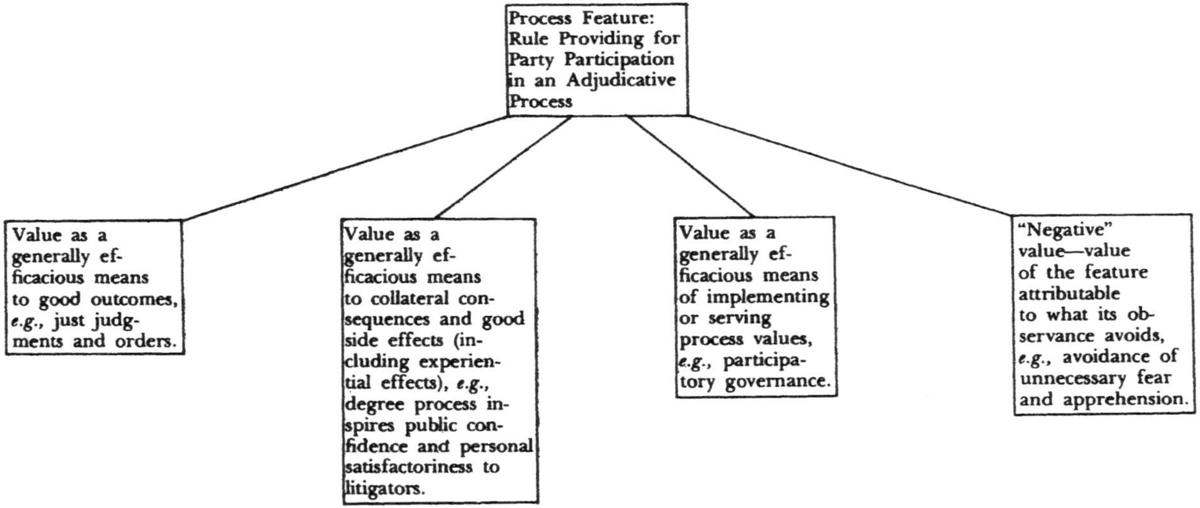

## V

## The Nonuse and Misuse of Process Values in Actual Practice—an Inventory

Process values are relevant in evaluating and in choosing between legal processes, actual or proposed. I will identify several different ways in which these values may be ignored or misused. My examples will be drawn from our own society. In this way, the reader may judge whether a "plea for process values" is appropriate.

### A. *Evaluations and Choices That Ignore Process Values—"Result Orientation" Par Excellence*

A review of the scholarly literature will dismay believers in process values. Many "policy scientists," moral philosophers, and students of decisional strategies in government ignore process values.[70] Thus, when economists and others theorize about government benefits and "public goods," only rarely do they count process values as benefits or goods.[71] Some political scientists, especially behaviorists, seem to ignore evaluative questions altogether.[72] "Systems analysts" commonly leave process values out of account.[73] Many moral philosophers—particularly those of utilitarian persuasion—stress quality of result (consequences)[74] and ignore process values. Even law professors regularly neglect process values,[75] although they insist on "due process" as a means to good outcomes.

Do the myopias of social theorists ever afflict social actors? It would be strange if they did not. Presidents in our time have ignored the most elemental process values. So, too, legislators. Indeed, even judges as sophisticated as Holmes,[76] and more re-

[70] Proving "negatives" is almost always impossible, strictly speaking. Here I will rest with references to what I take to be representative figures.

[71] Even the most important thinkers say little or nothing of process values. *See, e.g.*, Arrow, *supra* note 14; Stigler, *supra* note 14.

[72] This is an oft-noted and oft-discussed fact. *See, e.g.*, Berns, *Law and Behavioral Science*, 28 Law and Contemp. Prob. 185, 203 (1964). But there are signs of change.

[73] *See, e.g.*, Systems Thinking (F. Emery ed. 1969).

[74] *See generally*, J. Smart & B. Williams, Utilitarianism For and Against (1973); Brock, *Recent Work in Utilitarianism*, 10 Am. Phil. Q. 241, 249-65 (1973).

[75] But there are rare exceptions. Two notable ones are Professors Laurence Tribe and Charles Fried of Harvard. *See* C. Fried, An Anatomy of Values 105-15 (1970); Tribe, *Policy Science: Analysis or Ideology?*, 2 Phil. & Pub. Affairs 66 (1972).

[76] For example, see Holmes's opinion in McDonald v. Mabee, 243 U.S. 90, 92 (1917), in which he justified giving the defendant an opportunity to be heard solely as a means of doing "substantial justice" in terms of outcome.

cently, Fortas,[77] sometimes have failed to perceive process values under their very noses. Then, too, lay ignorance of process values is widespread. Consider how often laymen seem ready to dismiss procedural rules as "mere technicalities" even though these are the very rules which must secure most process values.

B. *Evaluations and Choices in Which Process Values Are Only Dimly Appreciated*

It is one thing to ignore process values altogether. It is another to fail to grasp the significance of relevant process values. Doubtless one reason some process values are ignored is because they are inherently elusive and vague. They would be less often ignored if they were more easily perceived. The value significance, for instance, of legitimacy, procedural legality, and procedural rationality lack instant intelligibility. Moreover, even when such values are readily understood, their practical dictates in the context at hand may not be perceived. Of course, not all process values are elusive to the understanding. For example, participatory governance and procedural fairness can be grasped more or less readily.

Evaluations and choices, then, may sometimes be made with only a *dim appreciation* of relevant process values. And although this will not necessarily lead, in particular cases, to determinations that undesirably sacrifice process values, it presumably inclines decision makers to accord less weight to process values than they otherwise would.

C. *Evaluations and Choices that Unjustifiably Sacrifice Process Values: A Further Form of "Result Orientation"*

Values inevitably conflict. And in order to achieve desired results, it will sometimes even be necessary to sacrifice process values. But particular sacrifices may be quite unjustified. For example, some "men of action" might prefer the election of one presidential candidate over another. Consequently, they might clandestinely sabotage electoral processes in order to secure the outcome they desire. In so doing, they would be sacrificing at least the process values of participatory governance, of legitimacy, and of fairness of process. Many observers believe this is exactly what occurred during the Nixon reelection campaign for the Presidency in 1972. Certainly some of Nixon's supporters interfered with

---

[77] An example is provided by his opinion in *In re* Gault, 387 U.S. 1, 19-20 (1967), where, after only an oblique reference to fairness, he proceeds to justify according "due process" to juveniles on the ground that it yields better outcomes.

Democratic primaries and with the Democratic general election campaign. Part of their strategy was to facilitate the nomination of an arguably "weak" opponent. Some of former President Nixon's supporters presumably felt that he must be reelected at any cost,[78] process values be damned.

Similarly, when President Nixon offered a federal district judge the directorship of the FBI during the course of a criminal trial over which the judge was presiding, and in which the President's own appointees were prosecuting a celebrated anti-Nixonite (Daniel Ellsberg), the President apparently evinced a willingness to sacrifice impartiality for the sake of influencing the trial's outcome.[79] Impartiality is a dictate of procedural rationality: It helps to assure that only factors relevant to the merits influence the outcome. President Nixon similarly sacrificed impartiality and legitimacy when he refused to permit the first Watergate special prosecutor to function independently, and dismissed him for refusing to limit a prosecutorial investigation to which the President himself was subject.[80]

Activists of the left have also sacrificed process values in circumstances in which the sacrifice was dubious. It is now almost trite to cite in this context the excesses of the civil rights movement in the late 1950's and early 1960's.[81] But consider the "building takeovers" on university campuses in the late 1960's and early 1970's, too. Frequently these were not mere "protests," but efforts to "negotiate" campus lawmaking and other decisions, in which the building occupants frequently refused to vacate until their demands were met (or until they had sufficient assurances that their demands would be met).[82] These activists sacrificed, for the sake of

---

[78] *See Hearings on Presidential Campaign Activities of 1972 Before the Senate Select Committee on Presidential Campaign Activities*, 93d Cong., 1st Sess., bk. 2, at 814 (1973) (testimony of Jeb Stuart Magruder).

[79] At the President's direction, John Ehrlichman met twice with Judge Matthew Byrne, and the Judge met once with the President. *See generally id.*, bk. 6, at 2617-22 (testimony of John Ehrlichman).

[80] For relevant reflections of the former special prosecutor, see Cox, *Ends*, N.Y. Times, May 19, 1974, § 6 (Magazine), at 27. Professor Cox observed that the Watergate affair illustrates the erosion of process values in public life, though he did not use this terminology. *Id.* at 66, 68, 72.

What many of those involved in Watergate did also constituted violations of personal moral standards recognized in our society. But process values must not be confused with such standards, although there is some overlap.

[81] But for an exceptional account, see Bickel, *Watergate and the Legal Order*, 57 COMMENTARY 19 (1974).

[82] *See generally* R. SUMMERS & C. HOWARD, *supra* note 2, at 533-95 (1972). As might be expected, the literature on "political direct action" of this period is generally devoid of

outcomes, such process values as legitimacy (the campus building takeover is not a legitimate decisional process), participatory self-rule (only the self-appointed occupants participate "for the students"), and procedural rationality (seldom do such permit rational deliberation, fact-finding, and the like).[83]

Of all branches of our positive law, it is in the criminal field that process values and desired outcomes regularly conflict most dramatically. Since conviction of the guilty is a desired outcome of high priority, it should not be surprising that officials have occasionally subordinated process values to this outcome. For example, until recently police not uncommonly infringed the process values of humaneness, of respect for individual dignity, and of personal privacy, all in the name of convicting the guilty via warrantless intrusions and "third degree" methods.[84] The courts have now interpreted the Constitution to prohibit most such infringements and have extended the "exclusionary rule" to put teeth in these prohibitions.[85] But it has not always been so, and it is not always so in practice even now. Indeed, in many places plea bargaining accounts for a high proportion of our criminal convictions, yet it offends many process values, including some of the very ones protected by these recent constitutional interpretations. Thus, when police and prosecutor induce an accused to "bargain away" rights guaranteeing him protection from a lawless police intrusion or coerced confession, in exchange for a guilty plea to a charge carrying a lighter sentence, the so-called "exclusionary rule" loses a measure of its efficacy as a means of protecting process values.

I do not contend that sacrifices of process values are never justified. It is always possible to postulate overriding considerations. In some circumstantial patterns, sacrifices of process values may even be regularly justified. In internal security employee

---

concern for process values, even as authored by sophisticated college professors. *See, e.g.*, M. WALZER, POLITICAL ACTION—A PRACTICAL GUIDE TO MOVEMENT POLITICS (1971).

[83] Of course, this is not necessarily to say that what the campus activists did was as objectionable as what the "Watergaters" did. *Official* misbehavior is especially objectionable and dangerous. *See* J. LIEBERMAN, HOW THE GOVERNMENT BREAKS THE LAW (1972).

I want to stress that in this Essay I have striven for an analysis that is politically neutral as between liberals and conservatives. Whether I have succeeded is for the reader to judge. But I do plead guilty to advocating a thesis that conserves process values, many of which are liberal in character. Is a thesis which conserves liberal values conservative? If so, so be it.

[84] *See, e.g.*, Paulsen, *The Fourteenth Amendment and the Third Degree*, 6 STAN. L. REV. 411 (1954).

[85] The main developments are recounted in admirably concise fashion by two scholars of the subject in J. ISRAEL & W. LAFAVE, CRIMINAL PROCEDURE IN A NUTSHELL 85-179, 210-56, 280-335 (1971).

dismissals, for example, it may be justifiable to accord an employee less than a full public hearing for the sake of safeguarding state secrets. Here the process value of participatory governance, among others, is sacrificed to some egree. Or, in order to remove risks from the roadways more efficiently, allegedly drunken drivers might be denied a right to cross-examine those who perform blood tests. Here, too, there may be justifiable sacrifice of a participatory value.

I believe, however, that many officials are inclined, as a matter of course, to sacrifice process values in return for desired outcomes, whether or not the sacrifice is justified. And I believe that unjustified sacrifices would occur less often if more officials were alert to process values and if a workable calculus could be devised for weighing process values against other values. The late Learned Hand and others have noted that such a calculus would be extraordinarily difficult to devise.[86]

It may be useful to try to explain why process values tend to be sacrificed to outcomes when the two come into conflict. First, of course, the value of the outcome served may simply outweigh, or be thought to outweigh, process values. Second, insofar as process values are difficult to articulate and hard to measure, decision makers probably accord less weight to them. Third, the legal precepts that purport to secure process values seldom wear their rationales on their faces;[87] accordingly, the protected values are somewhat hidden from view and have to be "unearthed" for consideration. Fourth, there is a widespread tendency merely to view procedures as technicalities or rules of thumb. Any values they protect are therefore assumed to be inconsequential.

D. *Evaluations and Choices Which Unjustifiably Sacrifice One Process Value to Another*

There are many examples of the phenomenon whereby one process value is sacrificed to another. For instance, speed of decision (timeliness) is a process value (as contrasted with dilatoriness). Yet unhurried deliberation and careful fact-finding are dictates of quite another process value too: procedural rationality. Sometimes these values conflict. The majority of the Supreme Court in the "Pentagon Papers" case hurried to an early decision

[86] L. Hand, The Spirit of Liberty 261 (1952). *See also* B. Cardozo, Paradoxes of Legal Science 56-57 (1928).

[87] *See* Part VI (C) *infra*.

even though this involved, according to Justice Harlan, an unjustified sacrifice of procedural rationality.[88]

Thus, officials may sacrifice a process value not merely for the sake of an outcome they desire, but also to achieve that outcome quickly. To cite a further clash of process values: Full participation by both sides in an adjudicative process may conflict with the process value of finality. This can occur when one party later learns of new evidence and seeks to have a case reopened.

### E. *Evaluations and Choices Which "Overvalue" Process Values*

Although in my opinion, the overwhelming tendency in our society is to undervalue most process values, they may sometimes be overvalued too. Participatory governance, for instance, is commonly overvalued. It is simply not possible in a society like ours for persons to participate in every significant stage of every significant decisional process that might significantly affect them. And even where possible, it would not necessarily be appropriate, given such other desiderata as expertise and confidentiality. Where participation is both possible and appropriate, the specific form of proposed participation might be inappropriate. For example, it would hardly be appropriate to decide on the tenure of a teacher solely by majority vote of students, or on the content of a public school curriculum solely by majority vote of parents. Yet our law carries some participatory roles to excess. For example, in many states, laws give teachers' *unions*—as distinguished from teachers—a large say in formulating basic educational policy in our public schools.[89] And it is notorious that our laws generally permit vested economic interests a large say in legislative processes through lobbying, campaign contributions, and the like.

### F. *Evaluations and Choices Which Neglect General Process Value Efficacy*

The evaluator (or "chooser") neglects still another important evaluative dimension when he fails to consider how a process might be *better* designed in order to implement the process values it is supposed to implement. This is not a rare occurrence. For example, it took American courts over a hundred years to see that our criminal processes were poorly designed to secure meaningful

---

[88] New York Times Co. v. United States, 403 U.S. 713 (1971) (Harlan, J., dissenting). Of course, this is not to say that the only values at stake were process values.

[89] *See e.g.*, N.Y. CIV. SERV. LAW §§ 200-214 (McKinney Supp. 1973) ("Taylor Act").

participation by indigent defendants. In the end, the courts required free counsel.[90]

## VI

## Implementing Process Values Through Law—General Requirements

A people that seeks to implement values through law as *process values* will (*1*) stand ready to criticize infringements upon or departures from these values for *special* reasons—reasons that are not exclusively result oriented; and (*2*) see to the legal implementation of these values, even though this does not necessarily enhance the quality of process results. Thus, *even when results are good,* the people will be concerned about departures from and infringements upon process values.

In order to implement process values through law, a legal system must provide:

1. Means of designing process features to "embody" process values in the first place.
2. Corrective mechanisms, sanctioning devices, and the like which may come into play when "built-in" process values are infringed, regardless of outcome.
3. Means by which process administrators and persons affected by processes can tell whether specific processes are in fact intended to secure process values (or ought to be so regarded).
4. Means by which process administrators (official and other) can tell whether a process value that a process has been designed to implement has been infringed in a particular case.

I will now discuss each of these requirements.[91]

### A. *Means of Designing Process Features to "Embody" Process Values in the First Place*

This is a relatively unproblematic requirement. Through the use of procedural norms—rules, principles, maxims, rulings, and

[90] *See* Argersinger v. Hamlin, 407 U.S. 25 (1972); Gideon v. Wainwright, 372 U.S. 335 (1963).

[91] It should be recalled that more effective implementation of process values is but one way of improving legal processes. *See generally* Rosenberg, *Devising Procedures That Are Civil To Promote Justice That Is Civilized,* 69 Mich. L. Rev. 797 (1971).

the like—the features of a process can be designed to "embody" a value. For example, rules and other norms can provide for a hearing to implement the process value of participatory governance. As already indicated, whether one value rather than another is secured can affect the shape of a process in terms of the stages of the process, who is assigned what participatory roles in the process, what steps are specified in these roles, and so on.[92]

In some legal systems, specific constitutional provisions require that certain processes have specified features.[93] And in some systems there may be a generalized "due process" requirement applicable to all legal processes.[94] Requirements of this nature may operate to implement process values, too.

B. *Corrective Mechanisms and Sanctioning Devices*

Even though the law prescribes a process feature (*e.g.*, right to a hearing), in order to implement a process value (*e.g.*, participation), that feature might be unlawfully ignored or bypassed in particular cases. Corrective mechanisms and sanctioning devices are therefore needed as well.

Corrective mechanisms include provisions for vetoes, for review by another body, for invalidation of an outcome as unauthorized, for optional or required "reruns" of the process (including reruns without use of the same facts as used in the first "run"), and so on. Sanctioning devices include ordinary penalties like those imposed under the criminal law, administrative sanctions, private remedies against officials, and whatever sanctions there may be in internal codes of ethics applicable to officials.

The main types of occasions for invoking corrective mechanisms and sanctioning devices when process values embodied in a process are ignored or bypassed (contrary to law) are three-fold:

(A) The "bad process," "bad outcome"[95] cases.
(B) The "bad process" cases in which it is unclear whether the outcome itself is good or bad (a large class of cases), and
(C) The "bad process," "good outcome" cases.

A legal system may choose to use different mechanisms or devices in these cases. If the case is of type (C). the system might choose

[92] *See* Part II *supra*.

[93] *See, e.g.*, U.S. CONST. amend. V. *See generally* M. MOSKOWITZ, HUMAN RIGHTS AND WORLD ORDER (1958).

[94] *Id.*

[95] "Outcome" is used here to refer to "immediate outcomes" of the types listed in note 23 *supra*.

not to "rerun" the process, for the outcome was good by the relevant *outcome* standards of value. Instead, in cases of type (C), the system might only provide for sanctions against anyone *culpably* responsible for the "bad process." But even in some kinds of type (C) cases, the social desirability of emphatically vindicating the desired process value might call for a rerun of the process as prescribed in the first place. For example, we might require that a legislative process yielding a good law (good outcome) without a majority vote (bad process) nevertheless be repeated. Or a criminal conviction based partly on conclusive evidence (good outcome) secured through involuntary stomach pumping (bad process) might be overturned with the proviso that the case be retried without the use of any "pumped out" evidence.[96]

In cases of type (A) it will often not be possible to tell whether the process deficiency contributed to the outcome. Yet there will be cases where it plainly did contribute. In both of these situations, a rerun will often be appropriate for two purposes: to secure the desired outcome and to vindicate the relevant process value. But what if the case is one in which the process deficiency plainly did not contribute to the bad outcome? Here, it may be enough to impose some sanction on the infringing party without any kind of rerun. But again, the value involved might be of such significance that a rerun would be called for either alone or in addition to the sanction.

All cases of type (B) can be treated analogously to those of type (A).

### C. *Means of Determining Whether a Process Value is to be Implemented*

It would do little good to design processes to implement process values, and to provide for corrective mechanisms and sanctioning devices, if it would be impossible for anyone reliably to tell when a process feature had been designed to implement a value *as a process value* rather than designed *merely* as a means to certain outcomes or types of outcomes.

Identification is an acute problem because most process features capable of implementing process values are at the same time capable of serving as means to certain outcomes. A right to participate in a hearing is an apt example. As I have noted, this right might be built into a process *merely* to facilitate fact-finding re-

[96] Rochin v. California, 342 U.S. 165 (1952).

quired for certain outcomes and not because participatory governance is in itself considered desirable. Or this right might be built into the process *both* to secure the participatory process value *and* to serve the outcome value of truthful fact-finding. At least when such a right is intended to secure a process value, officials should generally take appropriate corrective or sanctioning steps to implement that value whenever (*1*) both process and outcome are bad, and (*2*) process is bad but quality of outcome unclear. But how can officials tell when a process feature is designed to implement a process value (at least in part)? Of course, simple cases can be imagined in which those responsible for a process are quite explicit about why its features are as they are, and an official record of these reasons might even be kept.

However, the designers and others responsible for legal processes in particular societies are rarely so explicit. Consequently, those who wish to bring corrective mechanisms and sanctioning devices into play will often be called upon to argue for the proposition that a given feature is intended to implement a process value and that its infringement calls for repetition of the process or some other form of corrective or sanctioning action.

I know of no formula for the required arguments. I offer only an illustrative case to show the general character of such argumentation. Much of this argumentation is essentially evidentiary but some of it is more speculative and rationalistic.[97]

We may imagine a society, Bodea, that has the following somewhat extreme legal principle (A): "Whenever the administrators of a legal process infringe a prescribed process value, the process itself shall be repeated without the infringement, even though the outcome is good." We may imagine further that the Bodeans have adopted another legal principle (B): "Statute laws are to be enacted by a majority vote of the democratically constituted Bodean legislature." Assume the Bodeans do not leave any evidence as to their reasons for adopting (B).

Assume also that forty percent of the legislature assembles and "passes" a law against religious discrimination in employment, formerly a problem in Bodea. All Bodeans applaud this law as a good outcome. But some Bodeans—let us call them the PV Bodeans—claim that the actions of the legislators violate principle (B), and that a majority vote is a process feature designed to secure the process value of participatory governance *within the meaning of*

[97] *Cf.* Kadish, *Methodology and Criteria in Due Process Adjudication—A Survey and Criticism*, 66 YALE L.J. 319, 328-34, 339 n.125 (1957).

*principle (A)*, and that the process must therefore be repeated to "vindicate majority vote," and to validate the law.

Did the people of Bodea, in adopting (B), intend it, among other things, to be a means of implementing a participatory process value as such, or did they intend it only as a way of securing good outcomes or as a safeguard against bad outcomes? How might the PV Bodeans, assuming Bodea is very much like America, argue for the former? At the outset, they would need to establish that majority vote is indeed susceptible of being espoused for reasons in addition to, or wholly apart from, desired outcomes. This the PV Bodeans could readily do. For example, they could urge persuasively that majority vote not merely guarantees better outcomes, but also that it is *possible* for Bodeans to believe in majority vote for reasons apart from outcomes, such as the desire for participatory governance. Once having shown that a given process feature is susceptible of having process value (and not merely instrumental value as a means to outcomes), the PV Bodeans would then have to argue that the relevant Bodeans did *in fact* incorporate majority vote in their legislative process at least partly because of its approximation to self-governance. Assuming that there is no indisputable or substantially convincing direct evidence of this espousal, we might expect the PV Bodeans to try to make arguments of the following types.

First, it would be helpful for the PV Bodeans to try to establish a presumption that any process features susceptible of having process value shall, in the absence of contrary evidence, be viewed as intended to secure the relevant process value. This would be a presumption as to the likely intent of those responsible for the process (assuming, as we are, that there is no convincing direct evidence of this intent). The strength of any such presumption would vary from society to society. For example, such a presumption would be exceedingly weak in any society in which process designers rarely sought to implement process values through law. But the contrary would be true in societies in which process designers frequently designed process features not merely as means to certain process outcomes, but also as means to secure process values.

The presumption would be strengthened all the more if it could be shown that the society is one *generally* infused with regard for process values. Indications of this might take a variety of forms. For example, explicit signs might be found throughout the general law and relevant forms of legislative and other lawmaking history of the society. But one should also look at the standards of criticism that social critics invoke to judge the behavior of process designers. Such standards would be found in the various media, journals, books, and so forth. Further, one should look to oft-repeated slogans from everyday life, provided they reflect more than lip service. Two examples readily come to mind: "The end does not justify the means" and "It is not whether you win or lose, but how you play the game that counts."

Second, it may be possible to show that the value in question is one that the society generally espouses in a variety of other contexts, apart from the one at hand, *for reasons that are relevant to its characterization as a process value.* In the case of majority rule, one would try to show that the society generally espouses majority rule. Obviously, if one can show that the society not only generally espouses process values, but also generally espouses the particular process value at hand, the case for concluding that the process is intended to secure this value is greatly strengthened.

Third, it may be possible to cite evidence that members of the society regularly criticize departures from or infringements upon the value in question, even when the process outcome is good. Various explanations of such critical behavior are possible. It could be that the process is prized as securing a process value and not merely as a means to desired outcomes. An alternative explanation might be that the critics prize the process merely as a means to desired outcomes and object to the infringement simply because of a fear that the general quality of outcomes in the future will decline. At least in the case of some process values, the force of this alternative explanation will be inherently weak. Thus, where the process features securing the value are ones which fall far short of constituting any kind of guarantee of good outcome, it is not very plausible to say that the criticism is merely outcome oriented. Criticism of departure from majority rule happens to be a good example, since majority rule is not itself much of a guarantor of good outcomes.[98]

As a corollary to this third type of argument, it may be possible to cite evidence that relevant members of society regularly criticize *twice, not once,* when officials depart from or ignore a process value and bad outcomes occur at the same time. The fact that two criticisms—and not one—are typically heard, may indicate that the

[98] Consider the discussion of "future results" skepticism at text accompanying note 65 *supra.*

critics espouse the process not merely as a means to desired outcomes but as securing a process value, too.

Fourth, it may be possible to construct strong analogical arguments to show that the process in question is intended to serve a process value. If, for example, majority rule is intended to secure a process value in a legal process closely analogous to the one in question, it can be argued with some force that process designers probably intended the same in the instant situation.

Fifth, it is always possible to convert the issue from an "is" question to an "ought to be" question. That is, the process designers *ought to be* viewed as intending that the process implement relevant process values, even though the evidence is at best ambiguous. A great many legal arguments purportedly of the form, "A is B" are, realistically viewed, arguments that "A ought to be considered a B and therefore is a B." And on one view of the nature of law itself, this is as it ought to be.[99]

D. *Means of Determining Whether a Process Value Has Been Infringed in a Particular Instance*

Assuming that given features are designed to secure a process value, it generally should not be difficult to tell whether or not the value has been infringed in particular cases. Usually this factual issue will simply call for an inquiry into whether a particular legal rule or other legal precept securing the value has been broken.

It is important to recognize, however, that process values may be disregarded even though no legal rule or precept is infringed. Process designers may simply ignore a relevant process value in designing the features of the process. For example, a driver's license revocation process might be set up without providing the licensee any right to a hearing. It would be appropriate to condemn such a process as one that disregards an important process value.

There should be no need to set up a separate body called the "Board for Determining Particular Process Value Infringements." Rather, the very processes involved can provide their own "adjunct" procedures for determining (*1*) whether features of a process are designed to secure a process value, and (*2*) whether that value has been infringed in the particular case. For example, the parties to an adjudicative proceeding could also raise "process

[99] *See* L. FULLER, THE LAW IN QUEST OF ITSELF (1940); Hart, *Holmes' Positivism—An Addendum*, 64 HARV. L. REV. 929, 930 (1951).

value" issues (in both their factual and legal aspects) for adjudication in the ordinary way.

Are process values, at least in theory, easier to secure through law than good results? It would appear so since their implementation only calls for rules and other norms prescribing that they shall be implemented, and for corrective mechanisms, sanctioning devices, and the like. Generally it should not be as difficult to design these as it is to design ways of securing good results as such. We often do not know how to secure good results. Indeed, we often cannot even agree on what results are good.

By way of summary, it may be useful to list the possible respects in which we may be critical of a process from the "process value point of view":

1. The process fails to prescribe the implementation of appropriate process values.
2. The process prescribes inappropriate (or inappropriate forms of) process values.
3. The process values prescribed by the process are left highly ambiguous.
4. The process only imperfectly (*e.g.*, sketchily) prescribes process values.
5. The process does not embody the right means-end hypothesis for prescribing appropriate process values (*e.g.*, participation of the accused is prescribed, but no provision is made for free counsel to indigents, or an impartial tribunal is specified, but no institutional provision is made to secure suspension of judgment until both sides are heard).
6. The process fails to provide corrective mechanisms, sanctioning devices, or the like.
7. The process fails to provide for recruitment of administrative personnel sensitive to process values.

## Conclusion

In this Essay, I have sought to identify process values for what they are. In legal ordering, man does not live by results alone. Yet we often fail to recognize process values, and even when we do, we tend to neglect or override them almost as if they were weightless. Accordingly, I have entered a *plea* for process values. But in closing, I am mindful that there is much more to be said than I have been able to say. In particular, I have no fear that there will be wanting thinkers who can improve upon my articulations of the "value content" of process values, or formulate better responses to the various forms of process value skepticism, or perhaps even develop ways of assigning weights to process values. Indeed, it may be that my basic approach to the entire topic can be shown to be misconceived. Whatever the course of any future developments, it will, for me, be gratifying if this Essay at least serves to sharpen our awareness of process values.

# [4]

# Two Types of Substantative Reasons: The Core of a Theory of Common-Law Justification

> It is on the question of what shall amount to a justification, and more especially on the *nature of the considerations* which really determine or ought to determine the answer to that question, that judicial reasoning seems . . . often to be inadequate.
>
> —*O. W. Holmes, Jr.*[1]

---

This Article consists of modified (and tentative) versions of several chapters of a book in progress. While working on this subject, I profited from discussions with judges in seminars I conducted for members of the Washington appellate judiciary at Olympia, Washington, on April 19-20, 1977; for members of the Tennessee judiciary at Nashville on October 14-15, 1977; for New England judges at Durham, New Hampshire, on January 14-15, 1978; and for judges participating in the A.B.A. Appellate Judge's Seminar at Tucson, Arizona, on March 23, 1978.

I also benefited from discussions of the thesis of the Article while teaching at a Law for Economists Institute sponsored by the University of Miami on June 21-25, 1977.

I am indebted as well to colleagues of the Cornell law faculty who participated in a Faculty Research Seminar on this subject on September 11, 1977. I have also lectured on the subject of this Article at a number of institutions: University of Sydney, Australia National University, Monash University, MacQuarie University, University of Queensland, all in Australia; University of Auckland in New Zealand; University of Hamburg, West Germany; University of Leuven, Belgium; and the University of Tennessee, Mansfield College, and Cornell University in the United States. In each instance I profited from discussions that followed.

I am most grateful to Professor David Lyons for numerous discussions and extensive commentary. Other members of the Cornell philosophy department who kindly discussed

TABLE OF CONTENTS



the subject of the Article with me are Richard Boyd, Carl Ginet, Richard Miller, Robert Stalnaker, and Nicholas Sturgeon.

Others to whom I am indebted for written or other extended reactions at various stages over the past three years are Professors Christopher Arnold, Patrick Atiyah, Stanley Benn, Jan Broekman, David Cass, Roger Cramton, Ronald Dworkin, Torstein Eckhoff, Michael Fisher, George Fletcher, Alan Fogg, Oscar Garibaldi, Kent Greenawalt, Peter Hacker, George Hay, Les Holborow, Ian Macneil, Geoffrey Marshall, Thomas Morgan, Kenneth Pinegar, Samuel Stojar, Brian Tierney, William Twining, and Robin Williams.

In addition, I wish to acknowledge indebtedness to the students in my course at Cornell Law School on Jurisprudence and the Legal Process for the years 1976 and 1977. The theory I offer here is the better for discussions I had with those students.

I am indebted to Mr. Leigh Kelley, a second-year Cornell law student, for valuable aid in the final stages of this Article, and to Mr. Kenneth A. Thomas, J.D. 1978, Cornell University, for valuable research assistance.

Finally, I wish to record my appreciation to Mr. Dan Coenen, Editor-in-Chief, and Mr. Stuart Altschuler, Managing Editor, of the *Cornell Law Review*, for numerous helpful editorial and substantive suggestions.

[1] Vegelahn v. Guntner, 167 Mass. 92, 105-06, 44 N.E. 1077, 1080 (1896) (dissenting opinion) (emphasis added). Holmes displayed extraordinary methodological self-consciousness in justificatory matters.

## INTRODUCTION

Reasons are the tools of judging, for with reasons judges resolve issues and justify decisions. My topic will be reasons in common-law cases. Although I will address appellate judges, this Article should also interest theorists of judging, and of justification in general. And if of value to judges, practitioners should find it useful, too. While I will focus on the common law (including equity), I believe my central theses have wider bearing.

Appellate judges strive not only to reach the best decisions in common-law cases, but also to justify them in written opinions. Good reasons necessarily figure in justified decisions. They ordinarily figure in processes of arriving at the best decisions, too, for judges usually consider reasons supporting each alternative before reaching a decision.

But, at least in nonroutine cases, judges do not invariably reach the best decision. And even when they do, the reasons they give are not infrequently wanting.[2] When judges appeal to precedent—

[2] A familiar point. *See, e.g.*, Pound, *The Theory of Judicial Decision* (pt. 3), 36 HARV. L.

give "authority reasons"—the cited cases may be distinguishable or otherwise without rational bearing. When judges appeal to moral, economic, political, institutional, or other social considerations—give "substantive reasons"—these may be question-begging, insufficiently strong, or otherwise inadequate.[3]

Of course, society cannot expect perfection from mortals. Constructing reasons is not easy. Moreover, a judge often encounters special difficulties. He might have to hurry, and counsel might provide little help. But a judge might also lack the capacity to identify and deploy good authority reasons. Likewise, he might not be well equipped to give good substantive reasons.[4]

Even if a judge is good at giving substantive reasons, he might be uneasy about resorting to them. Solicitous of stare decisis, he might feel that only authority reasons are legitimate. Or he might think that to give substantive reasons is to "legislate" (retroactively at that) and thus to encroach on other agencies of government. In addition, he might believe that such reasons call for personal and subjective value judgments and are therefore inherently suspect. Yet, as I will show, a judge in our system must give substantive reasons and must make law. Indeed, the most important attributes of a judge are his value system and his capacity for evaluative judgment. Only through the mediating phenomena of reasons, especially substantive reasons, can a judge articulately bring his values to bear.[5]

---

REV. 940, 951 (1923). *See generally* Leflar, *Some Observations Concerning Judicial Opinions,* 61 COLUM. L. REV. 810 (1961).

[3] This is not intended as a formal definition of the phrase "substantive reasons." Rather, it is meant to reflect generally and informally an important distinction between authority reasons and substantive reasons. Although a more precise definition could be formulated, there is no need to do so here. Judges already have a working familiarity with the notion of a substantive reason as distinguished from a reason based on prior legal authority.

[4] There may be various explanations for this. For example, judging is, as I will show, complex in its own ways, and when lawyers ascend to the bench they receive almost no formal instruction in these complexities. Most educational programs for new judges focus on administrative and related matters and on recent developments in specific fields of substantive or procedural law.

[5] For a different formulation, consider these remarks:

> Much of law is designed to avoid the necessity for the judge to reach what Holmes called his "can't helps," his ultimate convictions or values. The force of precedent, the close applicability of statute law, the separation of powers, legal presumptions, statutes of limitations, rules of pleading and evidence, and above all the pragmatic assessments of fact that point to one result whichever ultimate values be assumed, all enable the judge in most cases to stop short of a resort to his personal standards. When these prove unavailing, as is more likely in the case of

In my view, a comprehensive and integrated theory of justification should be highly valuable to judges, if adequate to the complexities and presented in teachable form. In this, the theorists of judging have let the judges down. It is true that there are writings on authority reasons—on precedent—a subject that necessarily figures in any theory of common-law justification.[6] There are also essays on whether courts can and should make law.[7] But, until late, theorists have done little work on substantive reasons—on their varieties, their internal complexities, the differences among them, and the significance of these differences.[8] There are virtually no writings on the capacities required to identify, construct, and evaluate substantive reasons. Essays on the general nature and ends of common-law justification are also rare. And we have no unifying theories purporting to tie all these aspects of reasons and reason-giving together.[9]

---

> courts of last resort at the frontiers of the law, and most likely in a supreme constitutional court, the judge necessarily resorts to his own scheme of values. It may therefore be said that the most important thing about a judge is his philosophy; and if it be dangerous for him to have one, it is at all events less dangerous than the self-deception of having none.

Freund, *Social Justice and the Law*, in SOCIAL JUSTICE 93, 110 (R. Brandt ed. 1962).

[6] *See, e.g.*, R. CROSS, PRECEDENT IN ENGLISH LAW (1961); R. WASSERSTROM, THE JUDICIAL DECISION chs. 3-4 (1961); APPELLATE JUDICIAL OPINIONS ch. 2 (R. Leflar ed. 1974); Schaefer, *Precedent and Policy*, 34 U. CHI. L. REV. 3 (1966); Sprecher, *The Development of the Doctrine of Stare Decisis and the Extent to Which It Should Be Applied*, 31 A.B.A. J. 501 (1945).

[7] On the creative roles of judges in common-law cases, see generally R. KEETON, VENTURING TO DO JUSTICE (1969); K. LLEWELLYN, THE COMMON LAW TRADITION (1960).

[8] Perhaps the most significant recent work has been done by Dworkin, Eckhoff, Greenawalt, Hughes, and Wellington. For some of their writings, see note 27 *infra*. Wellington's effort, for example, is illuminating. Nevertheless, he does not discern that the values underlying what I call "goal reasons" may be noninstrumental. Nor does he consider the internal complexity of substantive reasons. Consequently, he misses some of the important differences between various reason types. Yet, in these respects, he is not alone.

[9] The work of the late Roscoe Pound is an exception. Pound saw the importance of general justificatory theory, and offered judges a "theory of interests" (drawn mainly from German thinkers). For a summary of his theory, see 3 R. POUND, JURISPRUDENCE chs. 14-15 (1959). In my view, Pound's theory is fundamentally misconceived; it gives controlling importance to the concept of an interest, whereas any justificatory theory must focus on the concept of a good reason. Furthermore, Pound's fundamental "decision rule"—namely, that judges should reach the decision, among the alternatives, that secures the most interests with the least friction—is deficient in at least three ways: (1) it is vacuous and hence indeterminate; (2) judges cannot possibly know enough to apply it; and (3) it incorporates a minimal theory of the good.

Pound also stressed that judges should evaluate alternative decisions in terms of their likely social effects. He thus neglected an important subset of substantive reasons—those having to do not with predicted decisional effects, but with how the case *came about*. Yet many common-law decisions are based mainly, and properly, on such reasons, which I will call "rightness reasons."

A legal periodical can provide neither space nor format for presentation of a full-scale theory of common-law justification. Here my focus must be far narrower. I will concentrate on only one facet of the theory I have underway, namely, substantive reasons.[10] As I will show, this facet must constitute the core of any comprehensive theory.[11] Yet I cannot even treat all of it here. And, because of the complexity and novelty of the topic,[12] some of my treatment will have to be schematic and tentative at that. Nonetheless, I believe that my theory of substantive reasons is sufficiently developed to invite useful criticism—it has sufficient "body" that proposed modifications need not appear arbitrary, and their consistency with the theory can be more or less readily determined. Also, the theory is now sufficiently detailed to be tested against the realities of common-law justification.[13]

Although relatively new, the theory of substantive reasons I will offer is not a personal contrivance, let alone some utopian ideal. While my effort is not exclusively descriptive, it is in large measure so. Thus, I open with a general survey of the varieties of good reasons and of the complexities of justificatory structures actually found in common-law opinions. Judges at their best actu-

The general lack of "reasons theory," apart from Pound's work and that of a few others, may be one of the unhappy influences of legal realism. Indeed, in their more extreme moments, some realists suggested that giving justified answers to legal issues is simply impossible. Professor Dworkin's insistence that there is almost always one right answer might be interpreted in part as a salutary overreaction to realist extremism. *See* Dworkin, *No Right Answer?*, in LAW, MORALITY, AND SOCIETY 58 (P. Hacker & J. Raz eds. 1977). For two quite different critiques of Dworkin, see Greenawalt, *Policy, Rights, and Judicial Decision*, 11 GA. L. REV. 991 (1977); Soper, *Metaphors and Models of Law: The Judge as Priest*, 75 MICH. L. REV. 1196 (1977).

[10] I will not treat here the following other facets of the theory I am developing:

(1) the nature and ends of common-law justification;

(2) the nature of the concept of "justificatory force," and how it differs from mere persuasiveness on the one hand, and logical validity on the other;

(3) the theory of precedent and its rationales, and how reasons of substance are transmuted into legal doctrine;

(4) the nature and scope of institutional reasons, including those arising from the relations among courts, legislatures, administrative agencies, and private parties as creators and appliers of law; and

(5) a decision procedure for choosing between conflicting sets of reasons, substantive and otherwise.

[11] See Part III *infra* on the primacy of substantive reasons.

[12] *See generally* Bodenheimer, *A Neglected Theory of Legal Reasoning*, 21 J. LEGAL EDUC. 373 (1969). This type of theory has not been so neglected on the continent. See, for example, C. PERELMAN, THE IDEA OF JUSTICE AND THE PROBLEM OF ARGUMENT (1963); T. VIEHWEG, TOPIK UND JURISPRUDENZ (1963).

[13] To clothe the theory it has been necessary to devise some special terminology. I have kept this to a minimum, however, and have not invented any new words.

ally work with implicit models of good substantive reasons. Many judges will, if the matter is put to them, agree on what the general features of these models are, and on the extent to which particular reasons conform to them.[14] It does not follow, however, that judges are generally self-conscious about their formulation and deployment of reasons. Of course, it is possible for a judge who is not self-conscious to give good substantive reasons. Just as an inhabitant of a city may regularly find his way about without being able to draw an adequate map of it, a judge may be generally good at giving substantive reasons without being able to describe precisely "what is going on."

It falls to the theorists and other students of judging to discover and articulate the relevant structures and models. Much of my Article will therefore be an exercise in what philosophers sometimes call "rational reconstruction."[15] I will, particularly in Parts IV and V, strive to formulate important aspects of what must be going on (justificatorily, not psychologically)[16] when judges successfully identify, construct, and evaluate substantive reasons.

To the extent my analysis is right, the theory of substantive reasons I offer here should beget better decisions and better justifications. Precisely how, and why, I will explain en route. The importance of reaching the best judicial decisions cannot be gainsaid. When a judge fails to reach the best decision, he may sacrifice justice, liberty, security, or any of a host of other significant values.

It is also important that a judge construct the best justifications. Ideally, he should construct the justification available for each alternative decision, compare these, and then choose the decision supported by the best justification. A judge who goes through this process will more likely reach the best decision.

Even when sure he is arriving at the best decision, a judge may usefully expend additional effort constructing and deploying reasons. In so doing, he may guide other judges to better decisions in future cases. And he may serve still other ends, too. He may

[14] I base this statement on extensive discussion with a number of judges over the course of several years.

[15] *See* Strawson, *Construction and Analysis*, in THE REVOLUTION IN PHILOSOPHY 97 (1957).

[16] For a brilliant discussion of the distinction between justification and possible accompanying psychological processes, see R. WASSERSTROM, *supra* note 6, ch. 2. Professor Wasserstrom explains how the failure to draw this distinction has badly flawed much of the literature on judicial reasoning. It may be added that the literature is deficient in other ways, too. Theorists have imported irrelevant models from formal logic, and, most important, have failed to consider a wide range of actual examples of judicial reasoning.

render the result more acceptable to the parties, thereby reducing the need for coercive enforcement (with attendant friction, waste, and loss of liberty); and he may render the resulting state of the law (1) more "law-like" and therefore consistent with "rule of law" values (including predictability), (2) more respectworthy and consequently capable of motivating higher levels of conformity generally, and (3) more readily appraisable and thus susceptible of rational revision as conditions and values change.[17]

I turn now to my theory of substantive reasons. In Part I, I will identify substantive reasons as one of several types of reasons that judges give in common-law cases. I will, in Part II, summarize the complexities of common-law justification in which substantive reasons figure. That such reasons are the most important type in the common law will be the thesis of Part III. In Parts IV and V, I will treat the construction and evaluation of the two main types of substantive reasons—what I call "goal reasons" and "rightness reasons." In Parts VI and VII, I will identify the differences between these two types of reasons and consider whether rightness reasons are inevitably reducible to goal reasons. In Part VIII, I will explain the importance of this duality of substantive reasons.

The Article as a whole outlines the core of my general theory of common-law justification. I believe that if the theory is right, it will be of significant value to judges in common-law cases. With an increased consciousness of the nature and role of substantive reasons, and with an enhanced capacity to construct and evaluate such reasons, judges should give better reasons for what they do. Better reasons should in turn beget better results and better law.

## I

## The Variety of Good Reasons

Common-law justification is varied and complex. Here and in Part II, I will provide an overview of the justificatory landscape. It is important to locate substantive reasons within this broader picture before focusing on their construction and evaluation. Judges who acquire a commanding view of this terrain, and of the place of

[17] The preceding two paragraphs do not purport to be an exhaustive specification of the ends of common-law justification, a separate topic beyond the scope of this Article. I believe that the adequacy of any particular justification cannot be determined without reference to such ends. For a different view, see T. Perry, Moral Reasoning and Truth ch. 4 (1976).

substantive reasons within it, will be better equipped to do their work.

A typology of potentially relevant reasons can help a judge in several ways. He might miss a relevant reason altogether, a less likely occurrence if he keeps an exhaustive typology of reasons in mind. In particular, it is not uncommon for judges to miss substantive reasons.[18] Missed substantive reasons frequently account for the criticism: "Right result, wrong reason."[19] Moreover, an overlooked reason might prove decisive, at least when opposing reasons are evenly balanced. Even if not determinative, the reason might strengthen the justification and provide valuable guidance in future cases. Of course, when a judge does reach the right result solely for a wrong reason, his failure to give the right reasons leaves the decision entirely without stated justification.

A judge sometimes fails to disentangle different reasons—even reasons of different types. He might run them together as if they were one.[20] Again, a judge will be less likely to make this error if he keeps a typology of good reasons in mind. Running reasons together usually makes their exact nature more difficult to grasp. This analytic confusion may obscure the force (or lack of force) of reasons and even lead judges to apply inapposite standards of evaluation.[21] It may also lead to misapplication of precedent in later cases.

A judge mindful of the typology will be more fully aware of the differences and relations between substantive reasons and authority reasons, and should thus become better at deploying authority reasons. Authority reasons can easily be misformulated and mistakenly brought to bear. It is therefore all the more important that judges take care when resorting to them. In particular, a judge

---

[18] *See, e.g.*, Boomer v. Atlantic Cement Co., 26 N.Y.2d 219, 257 N.E.2d 870, 309 N.Y.S.2d 312 (1970) (although it notes in footnote that defendant's plant employs over 300 people, court fails to articulate this as goal reason supporting denial of injunction that would shut down plant and reduce local employment).

[19] *See, e.g.*, Escola v. Coca Cola Bottling Co., 24 Cal. 2d 453, 461, 150 P.2d 436, 440 (1944) (concurring opinion, Traynor, J.) (in products liability case, majority's decision should have rested not on manufacturer's negligence, but on policies favoring absolute liability).

[20] *See, e.g.*, Groves v. John Wunder Co., 205 Minn. 163, 168, 286 N.W. 235, 237 (1939) (judge fails to set forth distinctly a rightness reason—*i.e.*, decision for defendant would favor contractual bad faith—and a goal reason—*i.e.*, decision for defendant would undermine ability to plan for future).

[21] *See, e.g.*, McConnell v. Commonwealth Pictures Corp., 7 N.Y.2d 465, 475, 166 N.E.2d 494, 500, 199 N.Y.S.2d 483, 490-91 (1960) (in attacking majority's rightness reason for denying recovery (plaintiff committed bribery in performing contract) dissenter resorts to goal reason (denial of recovery will encourage breaches of contract)).

should not invoke an authority reason without identifying and interpreting the substantive reasons "behind" the precedent or rationally attributable to it.[22]

Most judges are mindful that reasons of different types figure in their opinions. For example, a judge might claim that "reason and authority"[23] support his decision or remark that "both utility and justice" require a result.[24] But such cryptic remarks, however suggestive, cannot serve as a typology.

In my view, the typology that follows includes all basic types of good reasons found in common-law cases. Of course, not all that judges say to support their decisions can qualify as reasons. Thus, question-begging "reasons" and emotive appeals do not appear in the typology. It includes only genuine reason types: "substantive reasons," "authority reasons," "factual reasons," "interpretational reasons," and "critical reasons."

A. *Substantive Reasons*

A good substantive reason is a reason that derives its justificatory force[25] from a moral, economic, political, institutional, or other social consideration.[26] There are three main types of substantive reasons: goal reasons, rightness reasons, and institutional reasons.[27]

---

[22] *See* notes 78-84 and accompanying text *infra*.

[23] *See, e.g.*, Garrison v. Warner Bros. Pictures, Inc., 226 F.2d 354, 355 (9th Cir. 1955) (defendant's contention "not supported by any authority or reason"); Mier v. Hadden, 148 Mich. 488, 495, 111 N.W. 1040, 1043 (1907) (concurring opinion) (majority's holding supported by "reason and precedent").

[24] *See, e.g.*, Bowles v. Mahoney, 202 F.2d 320, 327 (D.C. Cir. 1952) (dissenting opinion, Bazelon, J.) ("the rule operates to defeat the interests of utility and justice").

[25] The concept of justificatory force, as I use it here, is roughly equivalent to the "essential strength of a reason." The degree of a reason's justificatory force is the reason's most important attribute. In forthcoming work, I will offer an extended analysis of this concept. Among other things, I will argue that the relevant metaphor is not "following" but "supporting." In other words, justificatory force arises not from a deductively valid derivation, but from a reason's supporting relationship to a decision.

[26] The rational bearing of such a consideration does not depend on its recognition in a precedent or other legal authority. Indeed, I contend that for almost any noninstitutional substantive reason given by a court, it is possible to identify a counterpart reason (with almost identical elements) likely to be given in parallel circumstances in daily life.

[27] Others have sought to articulate differences between types of substantive reasons, although no one, so far as I know, has differentiated them in the fashion I do here. For some of these efforts and resulting criticisms, see T. Eckhoff, Justice 19-25 (1974); E. Freund, Standards of American Legislation ch. 2 (1917); Dickinson, *The Law Behind Law* (pts. 1 & 2), 29 Colum. L. Rev. 113, 285 (1929); Dworkin, *Seven Critics*, 11 Ga. L. Rev. 1201 (1977); Dworkin, *Hard Cases*, 88 Harv. L. Rev. 1057 (1975); Dworkin, *Judicial Discre-*

1. *Goal Reasons*

A goal reason derives its force from the fact that, at the time it is given, the decision it supports can be predicted to have effects that serve a good social goal. The goal may or may not have been previously recognized in the law. Below are some examples of goal reasons drawn from actual cases:[28]

(a) *"General safety"*: Because the defendant railroad is financially hard-pressed and *will* improve general safety with the money it saves from not having to perform its contract with the plaintiff, the plaintiff will be denied specific performance.[29]

(b) *"Community welfare"*: Because judicial refusal to recognize the defense of retaliatory eviction *will* make it difficult to maintain decent housing standards, this defense will be recognized.[30]

(c) *"Facilitation of democracy"*: Because the flow of information about candidates for public office *will* facilitate democracy, a newspaper that publishes falsehoods may not be held liable unless the newspaper acted in bad faith.[31]

(d) *"Public health"*: Because a utility's gas reservoir *will* adversely affect the health of people living near it, the utility may be ordered to relocate it.[32]

(e) *"Promotion of family harmony"*: Because allowing this kind of intrafamily lawsuit *will* disrupt family harmony generally, the suit will not be allowed.[33]

All goal reasons are future-regarding. They derive their force from predicted decisional effects that purportedly serve social goals

---

*tion*, 60 J. PHIL. 624 (1963); Dworkin, *The Model of Rules*, 35 U. CHI. L. REV. 14 (1967), *reprinted in* ESSAYS IN LEGAL PHILOSOPHY 25 (R. Summers ed. 1968); Greenawalt, *Discretion and Judicial Decision: The Elusive Quest for the Fetters That Bind Judges*, 75 COLUM. L. REV. 359 (1975); Greenawalt, *supra* note 9; Hughes, *Rules, Policy and Decision Making*, 77 YALE L.J. 411 (1968); Lefroy, *The Basis of Case-Law* (pts. 1 & 2), 22 L.Q. REV. 293, 416 (1906); Linde, *Judges, Critics, and the Realist Tradition*, 82 YALE L.J. 227 (1972); Wellington, *Common Law Rules and Constitutional Double Standards: Some Notes on Adjudication*, 83 YALE L.J. 221 (1973); Winfield, *Ethics in English Case Law*, 45 HARV. L. REV. 112 (1931); Winfield, *Public Policy in the English Common Law*, 42 HARV. L. REV. 76 (1928). It is interesting to note that nearly all of the earlier writers cited here have had little or no influence on their successors.

[28] Professor Dworkin has suggested that courts do not "characteristically" give some of the reasons I call goal reasons. *See* Dworkin, *Hard Cases*, *supra* note 27, at 1060. The case law, however, does not seem to bear him out.

[29] Seaboard Air Line Ry. v. Atlanta, B. & C. R.R., 35 F.2d 609, 610 (5th Cir. 1929).

[30] Dickhut v. Norton, 45 Wis. 389, 397, 173 N.W.2d 297, 301 (1970).

[31] Coleman v. MacLennan, 78 Kan. 711, 741, 98 P. 281, 292 (1908).

[32] Romano v. Birmingham Ry., Light & Power Co., 182 Ala. 335, 340-41, 62 So. 677, 678-79 (1913).

[33] Campbell v. Gruttemeyer, 222 Tenn. 133, 137-40, 432 S.W.2d 894, 896-97 (1968).

*in the future*. While most goal reasons incorporate general welfare values (as in all of the above examples), some goal reasons are concerned with bringing about more rightness—with rightness values. The parol evidence rule, for example, rests on a goal reason rooted in such values. Consistent application of the rule, which bars the plaintiff from introducing parol evidence of alleged contract terms, supposedly induces more people to commit entire agreements to writing; this, in turn, minimizes the possibility that fraudulent oral "terms" will be enforced.[34] If this particular reason were a good one, it would qualify as a goal reason even though it concerns the achievement of more rightness.

Presently, I will identify a special class of reasons which I call "concomitant parasitic goal reasons"—goal reasons generated by decisions based on rightness reasons. But it is first necessary to introduce and exemplify the notion of a "rightness reason."

2. *Rightness Reasons*

A good rightness reason does not derive its justificatory force from predicted goal-serving effects of the decision it supports. Rather, a rightness reason draws its force from the way in which the decision accords with a sociomoral norm of rightness as applied to a party's actions or to a state of affairs resulting from those actions. The applicability of most such norms cannot be determined without reference to how the case *came about*. (Later, I will elaborate the differences between goal reasons and rightness reasons at length.[35])

Below are some examples of rightness reasons drawn from actual cases:

(a) *"Conscionability"*: Since the seller knowingly took advantage

[34] *See, e.g.*, Mitchill v. Lath, 247 N.Y. 377, 160 N.E. 646 (1928).

[35] *See* Part VII *infra*. Because some goal reasons are concerned with bringing about more rightness and so may incorporate concepts and norms of right action, the terms "goal reasons" and "rightness reasons" may mislead: they suggest that the former may never concern rightness. Nonetheless, I have used the term "rightness reasons" because such reasons *always* turn on the accordance of a decision with applicable norms of right action. What I call "goal reasons," on the other hand, *always* involve a prediction of future decisional effects. Thus, my terminology is appropriate in at least these important respects. Other pairs of terms I considered but discarded include "forward-looking" vs. "backward-looking," "consequentialist" vs. "nonconsequentialist," and "morality-regarding" vs. "welfare-regarding." These labels are less satisfactory than the terms employed here. Note that what I seek is descriptively felicitous terminology rather than abstractions such as "A-type" and "B-type" reasons. It is almost certain, however, that no single pair of ordinary terms will include and exclude with total accuracy.

of the buyer's illiteracy, ignorance, and limited bargaining capability, the price charged to the buyer must be reduced.[36]

(b) *"Punitive desert"*: Since the seller deliberately misrepresented the mileage on a used car (by turning the odometer back), the buyer may recover punitive damages.[37]

(c) *"Justified reliance"*: Since the builder reasonably relied on the owner's untrue representation of fact and thereby suffered a foreseeable loss, the owner must compensate the builder.[38]

(d) *"Restitution for unjust enrichment"*: Since the owner of a boat has been unjustly enriched by the plaintiff, who found the boat adrift and, at his own expense, took care of it for the owner, the owner must compensate the plaintiff.[39]

(e) *"Comparative blame"*: Since the plaintiff promoted a distinctively named theatrical act by deceitful means, an injunction will not be granted against another who deliberately used the act's name for gain.[40]

(f) *"Due care"*: Since the decedent was negligent, his estate may not recover for his injuries.[41]

(g) *"Relational duty"*: Since the parent brought the dependent child into the world, the parent has a duty to support it.[42]

(h) *"Fittingness or proportionality of remedy"*: Since an injunction would impose a grave burden on the polluting defendant, and the plaintiff would receive only a slight benefit in comparison, the injunction will be denied.[43]

It should be evident that rightness reasons play important roles in common-law justification. Consider, for example, the prominence of justified reliance in contract, blameworthiness in tort, unjust enrichment in the law of restitution, and interpersonal fairness in the various fields of equity.[44]

Among the variety of rightness reasons, two main types stand

---

[36] Frostifresh Corp. v. Reynoso, 52 Misc. 2d 26, 27-28, 274 N.Y.S.2d 757, 758-59 (Dist. Ct. 1966), *rev'd on other grounds*, 54 Misc. 2d 119, 281 N.Y.S.2d 964 (App. Term, 2d Dep't 1967).

[37] Boise Dodge, Inc. v. Clark, 92 Idaho 902, 907, 453 P.2d 551, 556 (1969).

[38] Mercanti v. Persson, 160 Conn. 468, 478, 280 A.2d 137, 142 (1971).

[39] Chase v. Corcoran, 106 Mass. 286, 288 (1871).

[40] Howard v. Lovett, 198 Mich. 710, 717, 165 N.W. 634, 636 (1917).

[41] Maki v. Frelk, 40 Ill. 2d 193, 195-96, 239 N.E.2d 445, 447 (1968).

[42] Commonwealth v. Ribikauskas, 68 Pa. D. & C. 336, 337-38 (Phil. Mun. Ct. 1949).

[43] Boomer v. Atlantic Cement Co., 26 N.Y.2d 219, 223, 257 N.E.2d 870, 871-72, 309 N.Y.S.2d 312, 315 (1970).

[44] For the nearest thing to a general discussion of the use of rightness reasons throughout the common law, see P. DEVLIN, THE ENFORCEMENT OF MORALS (1951).

out: "culpability" reasons and "mere fairness" reasons. The force of a culpability reason turns on the culpability of the past action of one of the parties to the case. Cases (a) and (b) above are illustrative. In those cases, the actions are culpable in light of relevant sociomoral norms of right action, and these norms require the culpable party to "make amends" for the loss or other adversity he has caused. A culpability reason might also serve to justify denial of a claim, as in cases (e) and (f).

The force of a "mere fairness" reason does not turn on the culpability of a party's past action—indeed, that action might be neutral or even meritorious. Rather, a reason of this kind depends for its force on the fairness or unfairness of leaving the resulting state of affairs between the parties "as is." Cases (c) and (d) are illustrative. According to sociomoral norms of right action (requiring compensation for justified reliance and for unjust enrichment, respectively), the resulting state of affairs between the parties in each case is unfair unless amends are made. Yet the action of each defendant might not be culpable.[45]

Case (g) illustrates another type of rightness reason—one that turns on the past occurrence of what may be characterized as a "relational" undertaking. Indeed, there is a further type of rightness reason—one that turns, as in case (h), on the fittingness or appropriate proportionality of remedy. There may be still other types, but "culpability" and "mere fairness" reasons are the most important, and there is no need to go into others here.

A judge may bring a sociomoral norm to bear through a rightness reason even though the norm has not yet found its way into a common-law decision. Today, many forms of culpability and unfairness are legally recognized, but it does not follow that basic sociomoral norms exist only by virtue of such legal recognition, or that judges have given all the rightness reasons they might give in the name of norms already recognized in the law.

All rightness reasons are either primarily past-regarding or primarily present-regarding. *Most* are primarily past-regarding; they derive their force from how the case *came about*. Cases (a) through (g) fall into this category. Case (h), on the other hand,

[45] Of course, under appropriate circumstances, a claim of justified reliance or unjust enrichment might also rest partly on a culpability reason. But culpability is not required for such a claim to find support in a "mere fairness" rightness reason. Note that in case (c) I am assuming that the falsity of the representation was not blameworthy.

illustrates a present-regarding rightness reason—contemporaneous equity or fairness in fashioning relief.[46]

I have said only that rightness reasons are *primarily* past-regarding or present-regarding. Actually, a rightness reason may bear on the future by generating a special type of goal reason in two ways. First, insofar as a decision based on a rightness reason is publicized beyond the immediate parties, it constitutes a symbolic, public affirmation of the relevant rightness norm and the values that norm reflects. This affirmation may have desirable socializing effects. Second, a decision based on a rightness reason constitutes a precedent; the decision may influence judges and other actors to decide or act in accordance with the relevant rightness norm in the future. The prediction that a decision will have either of these sorts of beneficial effects (symbolic-affirmational or precedential) generates a future-regarding reason that may be characterized as a "concomitant parasitic goal reason." In our system, this kind of goal reason is a potential concomitant of every rightness reason. The concomitant parasitic goal reason is not itself a rightness reason, although it envisions a resulting state of more rightness. Rather, it is a goal reason, for it contemplates a future state of affairs brought about through decisional effects. It is, nevertheless, only a *parasitic* goal reason—a reason that depends for its force on the antecedent force of the rightness reason on which the affirmation or precedent is based.

If a proposed rightness reason lacks all force, so will its concomitant goal reason. And if a rightness reason is weak, its concomitant goal reason will be weak as well. But a parasitic goal reason might also be weak because of factors unrelated to the rightness reason from which it draws force. In the particular case or realm of human activity, the affirmation or precedent might not make a real difference to future actors, especially actors other than judges. Few might learn of the case prior to acting. Those who learn of it might not understand its bearing. Others might have no incentive to follow it.[47]

---

[46] The force of a present-regarding fairness reason does not depend on how the case came about, but on what would be fair treatment of the parties now before the court. The administration of procedural rules affords many examples. That the judge should administer these rules evenhandedly is a present-regarding fairness reason.

[47] *See generally* J. GRAY, THE NATURE AND SOURCES OF THE LAW 100 (1909). Consider also Judge Jerome Frank's skepticism about the extent of actual reliance on precedent expressed in Aero Spark Plug Co. v. B.G. Corp., 130 F.2d 290, 297-98 (2d Cir. 1942) (concurring opinion).

Note that a concomitant parasitic goal reason is distinguishable from the type of goal reason that furthers rightness but which is independent of, rather than parasitic on, the antecedent force of any rightness reason. The parol evidence example given earlier is illustrative. There, a judge sacrificed rightness in the particular case, purportedly to further the social goal of bringing about more rightness (through the predicted effects of a decision adhering to the parol evidence rule).[48]

It is now possible to offer a tabular summary of the most significant varieties of substantive reasons:

SUBSTANTIVE REASONS

| Goal Reasons | Rightness Reasons |
|---|---|
| (1) Nonrightness-regarding—*e.g.*, health, economic productivity, facilitation of democracy | (1) Culpability |
| | (2) Mere Fairness |
| | (3) Other |
| (2) Rightness-regarding<br>(a) autonomous (*i.e.*, independent of any accompanying rightness reason)<br>(b) concomitantly parasitic | |

3. *Institutional Reasons*

An institutional reason is a goal reason or a rightness reason that is "tied" to a specific institutional role or process. It derives its force from the way in which the projected decision would serve goals or accord with norms of rightness applicable to the actions of participants (including officials) in institutional roles and processes. Below are some examples of institutional reasons drawn from actual cases:

(a) Because recognition of the plaintiff's novel claim would necessarily launch the court upon a voyage of arbitrary distinc-

[48] *See* text accompanying note 34 *supra*.

tion-drawing, and because courts, above all institutions, should only decide in accord with principle, the claim will be denied.[49]

(b) Because the plaintiff's claim requires a major change in the common law, a change that the legislature may wish to consider as part of a comprehensive reform of this entire field of the law, the court should abstain and leave the decision to the legislature.[50]

(c) Because the plaintiff's claim calls for a change in the law that cannot justifiably be made without access to "general social facts" that only a legislature can adequately investigate, the court ought not to make the change, but should leave it to the legislature.[51]

(d) Because the issue is now moot, the court should not decide it.[52]

(e) Because the trial judge did not give the claimant a full and fair hearing, the decision must be reversed.[53]

(f) Because it would be impossible to measure damages reliably in cases of this kind, the court ought not to recognize the proposed new cause of action.[54]

(g) Because a court could not supervise the decree, an injunction will be denied.[55]

Even this partial list amply illustrates the diversity of institutional reasons. The values they incorporate, although often hidden from view, are intrinsically no less significant than most values that figure in other substantive reasons. Institutional reasons relate to such important matters as the rational division of legal labor, the efficient workings of judicial machinery, the practicability of remedies, "process values" such as full and fair participation,[56] and even the limits of law's overall efficacy.

I have chosen to isolate institutional reasons as a separate type of substantive reason. As I will later explain, some institutional

---

[49] Tobin v. Grossman, 24 N.Y.2d 609, 618-19, 249 N.E.2d 419, 424, 301 N.Y.S.2d 554, 561 (1969).

[50] Johnson v. Oman Constr. Co., 519 S.W.2d 782, 786 (Tenn. 1975).

[51] O'Callaghan v. Waller & Beckwith Realty Co., 15 Ill. 2d 436, 440-41, 155 N.E.2d 545, 547 (1959).

[52] Excellent Laundry Co. v. Szekeres, 382 Pa. 23, 114 A.2d 176 (1955).

[53] Whitehead v. Mutual Life Ins. Co., 264 App. Div. 647, 37 N.Y.S.2d 261 (3d Dep't 1942).

[54] Zepeda v. Zepeda, 41 Ill. App. 2d 240, 260-62, 190 N.E.2d 849, 858-59 (1963).

[55] Edelen v. W.B. Samuels & Co., 126 Ky. 295, 307-09, 103 S.W. 360, 363-64 (1907).

[56] *See generally* Summers, *Evaluating and Improving Legal Processes—A Plea for "Process Values,"* 60 CORNELL L. REV. 1 (1974).

reasons figure intimately in the force of *noninstitutional* goal or rightness reasons. These reasons might therefore be incorporated into the analysis of noninstitutional reasons rather than classified separately as institutional. But, as I will explain, there are good reasons to classify them separately.

B. *Authority Reasons*

Common-law authority reasons consist primarily of appeals to precedent. In addition, judges sometimes appeal to statutes and regulations by analogy, and to restatements, treatises, and other "authorities."[57] But judges seldom resort to statutory analogy as a source of common law, and the "authority" of restatements and experts usually depends on the force of supporting reasons of substance. For purposes of this typology, it will be enough merely to indicate the major varieties of authority reasons that take the form of appeals to precedent.

First, judges sometimes appeal directly to a nondistinguishable precedent or "line of authority" that is binding on the court.[58] This kind of authority reason derives its justificatory force from two main sources: (1) the substantive reasons behind the precedent itself, and (2) the applicability of further substantive reasons that support the doctrine of precedent.

Second, a precedent might be in point but not binding because of the status or locale of the deciding court. Generally, such authority is cited solely for the intrinsic force of the substantive reasons behind it, or because of the extrinsic consideration of "uniformity."[59] Such reasons derive no force from the doctrine of *binding* precedent.

Third, judges sometimes justify decisions on the basis of analogy to or harmony with prior decisions. The precedent cited might, in light of the substantive reasons behind it, have force by analogy. Or, though not closely analogous, it might have force by virtue of its coherence and harmony with existing authority. For example, once a court has decided that acceptance of an offer by post is

---

[57] Judges sometimes even cite law review articles!

[58] Of course, theories and practices differ on what within a precedent is binding. *See generally* Bodenheimer, *supra* note 12, at 374; Simpson, *The Ratio Decidendi of a Case and the Doctrine of Binding Precedent*, in OXFORD ESSAYS IN JURISPRUDENCE 148 (A. Guest ed. 1961); Stone, *The Ratio of the Ratio Decidendi*, 22 MOD. L. REV. 597 (1959); Comment, *Diverse Views of What Constitutes the Principle of Law of a Case*, 36 U. COLO. L. REV. 377 (1964).

[59] For useful discussion of what one theorist calls "trend reasoning," see Bodenheimer, *supra* note 12, at 386-87.

effective on dispatch, it becomes more harmonious to hold that a revocation is effective only on receipt.[60]

A fourth and familiar type of authority reason consists of the formal elaboration of concepts already recognized by the common law. Without appealing to substantive reasons, a judge might argue that the internal logic or content of concepts requires a specific result. For example, he might argue in a given case that no contract could have arisen because one of the parties to the purported contract, a corporation, was not formed at the time the contract was allegedly entered into, and the existence of the relevant parties at the time of contracting is a requirement of our contract law.[61] Here the justificatory appeal is to an existing authoritative state of affairs (built up through precedent), namely, our concept of contract. Such an appeal might or might not ultimately be to binding precedent, and it might even be to precedent that is merely analogous.[62]

C. *Factual Reasons*

Factual reasons are reasons that support findings of fact. A judge in a common-law case may have to justify findings of either "adjudicative" or "legislative" fact.[63] When reviewing rulings on the admissibility of evidence or on motions for a directed verdict, for example, appellate judges pass on findings of adjudicative fact. The force of reasons that support such findings turns partly on whether sufficiently probative relations exist between evidentiary fact and ultimate fact.[64] Such reasoning is often far from "purely factual." It is also rationally influenced in complex ways by goals, norms of rightness, the law's limited machinery for ascertaining truth, and other factors.[65]

---

[60] Byrne & Co. v. Leon Van Tienhoven & Co., 5 C.P.D. 344, 348-49 (1880). *See generally* D. HODGSON, CONSEQUENCES OF UTILITARIANISM ch. 5 (1967).

[61] *See* Cramer v. Burnham, 107 Conn. 216, 219, 140 A. 477, 479 (1928) (absent ratification, contract with inchoate corporation unenforceable).

[62] Langdell may have given this kind of reasoning a bad name. *See, e.g.*, C. LANGDELL, A SUMMARY OF THE LAW OF CONTRACTS § 178 (2d ed. 1880). But not all such reasoning is unsound.

[63] On the distinction between legislative and adjudicative facts, see generally 2 K. DAVIS, ADMINISTRATIVE LAW TREATISE § 15.03 (1958); Davis, *An Approach to Problems of Evidence in the Administrative Process*, 55 HARV. L. REV. 364, 402-10 (1942); Hart & McNaughton, *Some Aspects of Evidence and Inference in the Law*, in EVIDENCE AND INFERENCE 48 (D. Lerner ed. 1958).

[64] For a classic treatment, see J. WIGMORE, THE PRINCIPLES OF JUDICIAL PROOF (1913).

[65] *See generally* R. SUMMERS, TEACHING MATERIALS ON JURISPRUDENCE AND THE LEGAL PROCESS ch. 25 (1977) (unpublished manuscript). The usual theory is that trial judges (and juries) engage in fact-finding while appellate judges engage in fact review. When reviewing

An appellate judge may also have to justify his own conclusions of "legislative" fact.[66] Both ordinary factual reasoning and substantive considerations may figure in this type of fact-finding, too.

D. *Interpretational Reasons*

In many common-law cases judges must justify one interpretation of the text of a private arrangement over alternative interpretations. Such texts include contract language, the language of corporate, partnership, and other articles of association, and the language of wills and trusts.

All of the main types of reasons so far considered—substantive, authority, and factual—may figure in interpretational reasons. But such reasons are in some ways distinctive, too.[67]

E. *Critical Reasons*

The various types of reasons so far listed—substantive, authority, factual, and interpretational—can all be characterized as autonomous reason types. "Critical reasons" are not of this character. Rather, a critical reason merely formulates a criticism of some element or aspect of a given autonomous reason. Critical reasons appear not only in dissents and concurring opinions, but in majority opinions as well. Examples of critical reasons (with references to their corresponding "targets") include:

(a) The proposed goal reason is unsound because it does not involve a good goal.

(b) This rightness reason is unsound because the defendant's action should not be characterized as right.

(c) This rightness reason is unsound because the underlying norm of rightness is unsound.

---

rulings on such issues as relevance and weight, appellate judges should bear in mind the extent to which such issues in the law are not purely factual, but are also to be resolved by reference to goal reasons and rightness reasons, and to purely institutional considerations such as the limited efficacy of the law's fact-finding apparatus.

[66] *Cf.* Doe v. Bolton, 410 U.S. 179, 208 (1973) (concurring opinion, Burger, C.J.) (though troubled by majority's notice of scientific data, concedes that Court did not exceed bounds of judicial notice).

[67] Distinguishing features of interpretational reasons include the importance accorded to the intention of the author of the text, and the role played by the language of the text in determining intention. For discussion of the distinctive importance of interpretational reasons, see generally Farnsworth, *"Meaning" in the Law of Contracts*, 76 YALE L. J. 939 (1967); Halbach, *Stare Decisis and Rules of Construction in Wills and Trusts*, 52 CALIF. L. REV. 921, 922 (1964).

A critical reason derives its character from the element of an autonomous reason to which it is addressed. Thus, to identify the types of critical reasons, it is necessary to isolate the various elements of autonomous reasons—a task I undertake in regard to substantive reasons in Parts V and VI.

## II

## The Complexity of Justificatory Structures

The structure of the justification in even a seemingly simple common-law case may be complex in several ways. Judges who understand this complexity will not be as likely to misinterpret or misapply precedent. They will also have a better grasp of available justificatory avenues.

Consider first the justificatory structure in the simplest possible case. To the extent that any law is applicable in this case, it is common law. There is only one issue—an issue of law. One reason "lines up" on each side of the issue. The two reasons are readily separable, and easily classified in terms of the foregoing typology. The reasons are of the same type and flatly contradict each other. The issue is resolvable, and the judge resolves it in all-or-nothing fashion. He does not seek to accommodate opposing reasons; one prevails and the other is sacrificed entirely. The prevailing reason bears immediately and directly upon the decision it supports, and since there is only one reason on each side of the issue, the judge need not consider the aggregate force of mutually supporting reasons.

But the usual case is more complex, and some cases are far more complex. Although there are "pure" common-law cases, many cases also involve statutes and other forms of authority that complicate their justificatory structure. Further, while there are "pure" issues of law, many issues are more complex; "mixed" questions of law and fact are illustrative.

Moreover, common-law cases often pose more than one significant issue. In many cases, the problem is not simply whether to affirm or reverse, but how to decide each of several issues in the course of deciding whether to affirm or reverse. And these issues will not always be wholly independent. For example, it is often assumed that so-called liability and remedial issues are completely unrelated. This is false. Some judges treat these issues as interdependent, and properly so. Thus, the drastic consequences of a remedy might rationally influence the court to decide for a defendant on the issue of liability.[68]

Several reasons—sometimes as many as a half-dozen significant ones—may line up on either side of each issue. Frequently, a single reason will not suffice to justify resolving the issue one way or another. Instead, the cumulative or aggregate force of several reasons will tip the balance toward a particular decision.[69]

When evaluating the bearing of a precedent, a judge often must determine the types of reasons that appear in the cited opinion. Sometimes it will be possible to construe the previous judge's formulation as either a goal reason or a rightness reason. Consider, for example, a case in which the judge dismissed the plaintiff's action because damages would impose a "crushing burden" on the defendant. Such a statement might be construed as a rightness reason—namely, that liability would impose an unfair or disproportionate burden on the defendant as judged in relation to his prior actions (or in relation to the benefit the plaintiff would realize). Alternatively, the reference to a "crushing burden" might be construed as a goal reason to the effect that courts should seek to preserve existing, ongoing economic units rather than throw them into bankruptcy. Sometimes a close look at the facts and the opinion will enable one to determine which type of reason the judge intended to employ. But, regardless of the judge's intent, *both* reasons may properly support the result.

Nor will reasons, whether mutually supporting or opposed, always be of the same type. Reasons of several varieties and subclasses will sometimes line up on each side of an issue or of several issues. In these circumstances, the judge must commensurate different reasons and aggregate the force of reasons of different types.

In addition, a conflict between reasons will not always take the form of straightforward opposition, in which one reason *counterbalances, overrides,* or *outweighs* another. The relation of reason "not-*A*" to reason "*A*" may instead be *cancellative*. For example, the defendant may have intentionally harmed the plaintiff (thus giving rise to a culpability-based rightness reason), but the plaintiff may have assented to the harm, thereby cancelling the entire force of

---

[68] *See generally* Keeton, *Rights of Disappointed Purchasers*, 32 TEX. L. REV. 1 (1953).

[69] For a general discussion of cumulative reasons, see Smith, *Cumulative Reasons and Legal Method*, 27 TEX. L. REV. 454 (1949).

the reason.[70] Or the relation of reason not-*A* to reason *A* may be *discountive*. That is, if reason not-*A* is a critical reason rather than an autonomous reason, it may reduce the force of reason *A* in some respect without cancelling it entirely. For example, the goal reason that giving priority to upstream water users "will more fully develop the region" might be criticized as resting on an improbable prediction.[71] This critical reason discounts the force of the relevant reason on the other side of the issue. The foregoing does not purport to be an exhaustive account of the possible relations between conflicting reasons, but it indicates the complexities that may arise, especially when relations between conflicting reasons vary.

Mutually supporting reasons, like conflicting reasons, give rise to complexities. The justificatory bearing of reasons may be intermediate and indirect. Thus, just as some reasons bear on a decision (the "chair") in the fashion of direct supports (the "legs"), other reasons may be one level removed and thus support the direct supports (the "platform" for the legs of the chair).[72]

The complex relationships among reasons often produce complicated results. For example, a judge might not resolve an issue or cluster of related issues in all-or-nothing terms. Instead, he might fashion a compromise in which reasons cutting one way show up in a *general doctrine*, while countervailing reasons shape *exceptions* or *provisos*.[73]

I have not sought to explore exhaustively the justificatory structures found in common-law cases.[74] I believe, however, that I have identified all but one of the principal forms of complexity—the *internal* complexities of substantive reasons. Before turning to these, and to the construction and evaluation of substantive reasons, I will argue for the justificatory primacy of such reasons.

[70] *See, e.g.*, Ford v. Ford, 143 Mass. 577, 10 N.E. 474 (1887).

[71] *See, e.g.*, Irwin v. Phillips, 5 Cal. 140 (1855). For a general criticism of goal reasoning as too speculative, see Aero Spark Plug Co. v. B.G. Corp., 130 F.2d 290, 295-96 (2d Cir. 1942) (concurring opinion, Frank, J.)

[72] *See, e.g.*, Gerhard v. Stephens, 68 Cal. 2d 804, 442 P.2d 692, 69 Cal. Rptr. 612 (1968).

[73] For a perceptive discussion of how reasons show up in and shape doctrinal formulations, see R. Keeton, *supra* note 7, at 65-69.

[74] The following cases are illustrative of substantial complexity in justificatory structures: Kline v. 1500 Mass. Ave. Apt. Corp., 439 F.2d 477 (D.C. Cir. 1970); Meeker v. City of East Orange, 77 N.J.L. 623, 74 A. 379 (1909); Shelley v. Shelley, 223 Or. 328, 354 P.2d 282 (1960).

## III

## The Primacy of Substantive Reasons

A specific theory of the nature and role of substantive reasons must form the core of a comprehensive theory of common-law justification. Substantive reasons, more than authority reasons, determine which decisions and justifications are best.

Why might a judge insist on or assume the primacy of authority reasons—or at least adhere to a method in which he merely matches facts and cites precedent? Today there are more than three million reported cases.[75] In almost every case that arises, one precedent will at least be relevant. Moreover, there are strong substantive rationales for following precedent. These include predictability, evenhandedness, efficiency, and the "rule of law" itself.[76] Further, the power of substantive reasons is not unlimited. There may be no strong substantive reasons on either side of an issue, or the substantive reasons on each side may stalemate each other. If so, only authority reasons can tip the balance. Nevertheless, the case for the decisional and justificatory primacy of authority reasons pales when compared with the parallel case for reasons of substance.[77]

### A. *Substantive Reasons and the Intelligibility and Scope of Precedent*

A judge cannot apply a precedent wisely without determining which proposed application is most consistent with the substantive reasons behind the precedent.[78] This familiar fact, too frequently forgotten,[79] extends to both routine and difficult cases. Thus, to construct the usual authority reason, a judge must identify and interpret the determinative substantive reasons set forth in the pre-

[75] M. Cohen, Legal Research in a Nutshell 64-65 (3d ed. 1978).

[76] For discussion of these rationales, see authorities cited in note 6 *supra*.

[77] Thus, the reader will find relatively little in this Article about "reasoning by analogy," an authority-oriented maneuver that has received far more attention in the literature than it merits.

[78] Courts are sometimes quite self-conscious about this approach to determining the scope of a precedent. *See, e.g.*, Brown v. Merlo, 8 Cal. 3d 855, 506 P.2d 212, 106 Cal. Rptr. 388 (1973). For general discussion of the wisdom of this approach, see R. Keeton, *supra* note 7, at 64-69; W. Twining & D. Miers, How to Do Things with Rules 113-18 (1976).

[79] The author of a useful student note persuasively contends that the draftsmen of the Uniform Commercial Code plainly intended its provisions to be applied in light of "their reasons," yet courts have repeatedly failed to do so. *See* Note, *How Appellate Judges Should Justify Decisions Made Under the U.C.C.*, 29 Stan. L. Rev. 1245 (1977). Similarly, common-law cases abound in which judges have applied doctrine and precedent without regard to their underlying substantive reasons.

cedent. If no reasons are stated, the judge must go back to prior precedents in the line of authority and dig them out. If even this fails, he must imaginatively construct reasons that are faithful to the materials. The usual precedent ultimately consists of nothing less than facts, issues, rulings, and substantive reasons for those rulings. It is impossible to comprehend a precedent without grasping these elements. It is especially hazardous to try to analyze and interpret precedent without a sure grip on substantive reasons.[80] Of course, when judges simply lay down a rule, one can, within limits, understand its content. But this sort of understanding is significantly incomplete. Without an appreciation of the reasons for the rule, one will usually be unable to determine its justified scope.[81]

In one respect, then, the distinction between a substantive reason and the usual authority reason is misleading, for the usual authority reason cannot be launched without resort to its underlying substantive reasons. Once launched, authority reasons move under their own power, even though partly "made up of" substantive reasons.

I do not claim that the reasons originally given to support a precedent must always determine its scope. Such reasons might be weak or poorly stated. Our traditions, however, provide for this possibility by allowing judges (within limits) to "follow" precedents in light of new or different substantive reasons rationally imputable to those precedents.[82]

Substantive considerations delimit the range of authority reasons. Moreover, judges justifiably advert to the rationales that underlie the doctrine of precedent itself in deciding how far to extend a particular precedent.[83] Although these rationales govern authority reasons, they are substantive in nature, too.

---

[80] Limitations of space prohibit the extended discussion necessary to establish this truth. I will explore the question in forthcoming work.

[81] For a perceptive discussion of why the common law cannot be reduced merely to rules, see Simpson, *The Common Law and Legal Theory*, in OXFORD ESSAYS IN JURISPRUDENCE 77 (A. Simpson ed. 1973).

[82] For example, Chase v. Corcoran, 106 Mass. 286 (1871), was fictionally based on a contractual authority reason, but later came to be cited as a leading unjust enrichment case. In Gerhard v. Stephens, 68 Cal. 2d 864, 442 P.2d 692, 69 Cal. Rptr. 612 (1968), the court referred to the special nature of oil and gas deposits and associated drilling operations as a reason to follow the common-law view that perpetual *profits a prendre* are analogous to perpetual easements and, like easements, may be abandoned through nonuse.

[83] *See, e.g.*, Barnes v. Walker, 191 Tenn. 364, 234 S.W.2d 648 (1950). *See generally* Aero Spark Plug Co. v. B.G. Corp., 130 F.2d 290, 298 (2d Cir. 1942) (concurring opinion, Frank, J.).

An authority-minded judge fails to recognize the primacy of substantive reasons. He is therefore more likely to apply precedent mechanically, in light of the literal meaning of sentences or phrases, rather than in light of underlying substantive reasons.[84] As a result, he may miss relevant precedents, or may rely on precedents not in point.

In sum, judges cannot apply a precedent soundly or consistently if they do not resort to the substantive reasons behind it, and behind the doctrine of precedent itself.

B. *Substantive Reasons and the Paucity or Plethora of Precedent*

To note without more that there are more than three million precedents is to exaggerate the extent of viable case authority. Not all decisions are in common-law fields, and many common-law cases have little precedential value because they involve unique or rarely recurring issues. The precedential significance of other cases is diminished by procedural and similar factors.[85] Change, too, takes its toll on the stock of useful precedent. In short, the conditions for the rational application of precedent are satisfied less frequently than many suppose.

Even at this late date in the history of the common law, a significant number of cases of first impression arise every year.[86] Although they take many forms, cases of first impression by definition cannot be decided solely by reference to precedent. To decide such cases, judges must construct, evaluate, and choose between conflicting reasons of substance.[87]

Cases also arise in which precedents point in opposite directions.[88] Here, too, judges cannot rationally decide without compar-

[84] *See, e.g.*, Courteen Seed Co. v. Abraham, 129 Or. 427, 275 P. 684 (1929).

[85] For general discussion of factors that may weaken the force of a precedent, see R. Cross, *supra* note 6, ch. 4; Aigler, *Law Reform by Rejection of Stare Decisis*, 5 Ariz. L. Rev. 155 (1964).

[86] Of course, whether a given case is truly a case of first impression will itself often be contested. At least one party will usually claim that there is a controlling precedent. For a sophisticated argument that there can be no genuine cases of first impression, see Dworkin, *supra* note 9.

[87] The "statutory" common law also generates cases of first impression. Legislatures sometimes block out areas or topics and leave it to the courts to evolve common law within the specified bounds. *See, e.g.*, U.C.C. § 2-302.

[88] Countless examples might be cited to illustrate conflicts of precedent, and these conflicts take a variety of forms. *See, e.g.*, Crenshaw v. Williams, 191 Ky. 559, 231 S.W. 45 (1921). Note also: "The foremost criticism heard today and early voiced by Kent is that the great mass of extant case law often makes it impossible or a task of considerable magnitude to discover precedents, and as often makes it possible to find precedents on both sides of a

ing substantive reasons supporting alternative results. (Of course, judges *could* decide such cases by reference to the comparative stature of the deciding courts, the ages of the precedents, or similar extrinsic factors.)

An authority-minded judge who rejects or remains oblivious to the primacy of substantive reasons will feel more comfortable with cases of conflicting precedent than with cases of first impression. In the former, he will at least have some "law" to apply, and often he will conveniently find that one of the two precedents can be distinguished away,[89] a course not open in a case of first impression.[90]

In cases of first impression, an authority-minded judge may confront a genuine crisis. For him, the law consists solely of authority, yet in such cases there is none. Rather than create a new precedent out of substantive reasons, as has been necessary since the beginning of the common law,[91] the authority-minded judge might rest his decision on precedent not truly controlling. Or he might bend or fictionalize relevant doctrine and thereby dim the lights for future judges.[92]

The vitality of a precedential system (to say nothing of the sound resolution of particular issues) requires that judges understand how important classes of cases arise in which precedents provide no answers, and why in those cases substantive reasons must control. Of course, courts should not proceed to a decision on the merits in all such cases. In some it will be appropriate to defer to the legislature.

### C. *Substantive Reasons and the Failure of Predecent: Original Error and Obsolescence*

Although precedents may provide answers, those answers may be wrong. Ours purports to be not only a rule of law, but also a rule of just and good law. Tensions between these two ideals are inevitable.

---

given question." Sprecher, *supra* note 6, at 506 (footnotes omitted). *See also* Gilmore, *Legal Realism: Its Cause and Cure*, 70 YALE L.J. 1037 (1961).

[89] *See, e.g.*, White Showers, Inc. v. Fischer, 278 Mich. 32, 270 N.W. 205 (1936).

[90] I certainly do not mean to deny that there are many judges who feel a deep moral obligation to ground every decision in precedent. Although I do not think that this sweeping view is sound, I do not wish to cast doubt on the sincerity of the judges who hold it.

[91] *See* Lefroy, *supra* note 27.

[92] *See, e.g.*, Courteen Seed Co. v. Abraham, 129 Or. 427, 275 P. 684 (1929). Many examples of legal fictions are cited and discussed in Fuller, *Legal Fictions* (pts. 1-3), 25 ILL. L. REV. 363, 513, 865 (1930-1931).

Despite the long history of the common law, no one has discovered a way to prevent judges from making mistakes. Thus, at any given time there will be "originally" bad precedents. Further, given the inevitability of change, some precedents are certain to become outmoded. For similar reasons, cases will regularly arise in which judges must consider whether an exception to a precedent should be created, whether the precedent should be extended, or whether several precedents should be synthesized into a new body of doctrine.

Although a legal system might provide that only the legislature may revise precedent, that is not our system. Early on, judges undertook to overrule or otherwise revise case law.[93] The authority-minded judge who is unwilling to construct, evaluate, and choose between reasons of substance cannot perform this work. The rational revision of precedent must proceed in the name of improving the law, and this effort requires that judges give substantive reasons to justify their revisions.[94]

The authority-minded judge takes a more conservative attitude than our system calls for. He will often resist proposed changes when counsel or fellow judges argue that precedent should be overruled. In a fundamental sense, he *might not really understand* what bad or obsolete precedent is. A precedent can be bad or obsolete only in light of substantive reasons; yet an authority-minded judge might refuse to recognize such reasons, or fail to accord them sufficient weight. And even if willing to invoke reasons of substance, he might refuse to acknowledge their primacy. This, in turn, may keep him from seeing how the substantive reasons behind the challenged precedent might have originally lacked sufficient force, or how reasons initially strong might have lost their force through change.[95]

---

[93] For a perceptive study of recent judge-made changes in the common law, see R. Keeton, *supra* note 7.

[94] This is not to say, however, that a judge should never cite cases to help justify overruling a precedent.

[95] Technological change, growth in moral enlightenment, social and political developments, or other factors may explain why precedents become obsolete.

Judges have sometimes explicitly recognized the need to identify and revise erroneous or obsolete precedents. *See, e.g.*, Thurston v. Fritz, 91 Kan. 468, 138 P. 625 (1914):

"[W]ith the death of the reason for it every legal doctrine dies."

. . . .

. . . The fact that the reason for a given rule perished long ago is no just excuse for refusing now to declare the rule itself abrogated, but rather the greater justification for so declaring; and if no reason ever existed, that fact furnishes

It is one thing to grasp the primacy of substantive reasons in a healthy common-law system; it is another to comprehend their internal complexity, and to know how to construct and evaluate them systematically. In what follows, I will first take up goal reasons, then rightness reasons. I will explore their internal complexities and their construction and evaluation. Thereafter, I will consider the differences between the two types of reasons and explain the significance of these differences. My sequence of presentation reflects these simple considerations: To appreciate the significance of the differences, one must first understand the differences; and to understand these differences, one must grasp the essential nature of each reason type.

## IV

## Construction, Evaluation, and Legitimacy of Goal Reasons

I define a goal reason as a reason that derives its force from the fact that, at the time it is given, the decision it supports can be predicted to have effects that serve a good social goal. Goal reasons constitute one of the main types of substantive reasons appearing in common-law opinions.

### A. *Construction*

Goal reasons are internally complex, far more so than commonly supposed. Without reference to these internal complexities, judges cannot construct good goal reasons in a systematic and methodologically self-conscious fashion.[96]

There is evidence that judges need to improve their proficiency in constructing goal reasons. For example, a judge might vaguely sense the relevance of a goal reason, yet fail to formulate it *as a reason*.[97] Or he might run together a goal reason and another

---

additional justification.

*Id.* at 474-75, 138 P. at 627 (quoting Harrington v. Lowe, 73 Kan. 1, 21, 84 P. 570, 578 (1906)).

[96] Holmes, it will be recalled, stressed that judges must understand the "nature of the considerations" on which the adequacy of a justification depends. Vegelahn v. Guntner, 167 Mass. 92, 105-06, 44 N.E. 1077, 1080 (1896) (dissenting opinion), *quoted in* text accompanying note 1 *supra*.

[97] *See, e.g.*, Boomer v. Atlantic Cement Co., 26 N.Y.2d 219, 257 N.E.2d 870, 309 N.Y.S.2d 312 (1970) (although it notes in footnote that defendant's plant employs over 300 people, court fails to articulate this as goal reason supporting denial of injunction that would shut down plant and reduce local employment).

reason and thereby fail to set forth the two as *distinct* reasons.[98] He might mingle foreign elements in his formulation of the reason.[99] He might give a goal reason in which the posited means will fail to serve the relevant goal.[100] He might misstate a goal reason by couching it in unduly conclusory or question-begging terms.[101] Or he might give a goal reason in which the goal is simply undesirable.[102]

To construct a good goal reason a judge must take a number of steps to combine a variety of related internal elements. I will illustrate these elements and steps by using an actual case.[103] Assume that the plaintiff office-holder claims that the defendant newspaper libeled him during his campaign for reelection. At the

---

[98] *See, e.g.*, Hadley v. Baxendale, 156 Eng. Rep. 145 (Ex. 1854) (court fails to separate goal of facilitating contract planning from rationale of safeguarding defendants against liability greatly disproportionate in light of quid pro quo).

[99] *See, e.g.*, Cornpropst v. Sloan, 528 S.W.2d 188, 199 (Tenn. 1975) (dissenting opinion) (reference to irrelevant adverse effect—impact on inner cities—mingled with statement of reason in personal injury action).

[100] *See, e.g.*, Mitchill v. Lath, 247 N.Y. 377, 160 N.E. 646 (1928) (to further goal of preventing future fraud, court purports to adhere strictly to parol evidence rule although evidence overwhelmingly established extrinsic term and underlying means-goal hypothesis seems highly questionable).

It is odd that while jurisprudential literature abounds on the lawyer's prediction of judicial decisions, there is relatively little on the judge's prediction of the effects of his decisions.

[101] *See, e.g.*, Horsley v. Hrenchir, 146 Kan. 767, 73 P.2d 1010 (1937) (in denying plaintiff recovery, majority uses goal reason that allowing recovery would undermine security and certainty of title provided by written deeds; but, in concurring judge's view, majority fails to consider soundness or strength of reason's internal elements).

Note that the time and effort a judge spends in articulating a reason will often depend on the extent to which he believes that others take for granted the values implicit in the reason.

[102] Bad goals espoused by courts are often simply goals that courts have failed to specify in sufficiently narrow terms or with the necessary qualifications. For example, "promoting limited freedom of contract" is a good goal—its pursuit is rational as long as conflicting goals and rightness factors are properly taken into account. But "promoting *unlimited* freedom of contract" is a bad goal, since its pursuit would rule out the relevance of other goals and rightness considerations that may in fact be relevant. Many goals traditionally pursued by common-law courts, if described very broadly, would be universally condemned. We generally accept, for example, the goal of securing rights in private property; we reject, however, the goal of facilitating slavery, which many antebellum courts pursued under an overly broad, illegitimate definition of "property." A contemporary example of a bad general goal that some common-law courts have adopted is the goal of recognizing and facilitating unionization in public employment. *See, e.g.*, Chicago Div. of Ill. Educ. Ass'n v. Board of Educ., 76 Ill. App. 2d 456, 222 N.E.2d 243 (1966). For the arguments that this goal is, indeed, bad, see R. SUMMERS, COLLECTIVE BARGAINING AND PUBLIC BENEFIT CONFERRAL: A JURISPRUDENTIAL CRITIQUE (1976).

[103] Coleman v. MacLennan, 78 Kan. 711, 98 P. 281 (1908). I am not unmindful that there is post-1908 law on the issues posed in this case.

close of the trial, the evidence supported a finding that the defendant libeled the plaintiff, but only negligently, not recklessly or deliberately. The trial judge instructed the jurors that if they reached this finding, they should return a verdict for the defendant. The plaintiff duly excepted, the jury found for the defendant, and the plaintiff appeals. Assume that this is a case of first impression. The appellate court is now thinking about what substantive reasons support affirmance or reversal.

The following outline sets forth the steps (though not necessarily in prescribed sequence) that a methodologically self-conscious judge might take to construct a good goal reason bearing on this decision. At each step I will identify the relevant internal element of the reason.

(1) The judge must determine from the proceedings below and the general decisional context all facts relevant to the goal-serving potential of alternative decisions: Who did what to whom? With what results? Why? In what context? For example, was the defendant newspaper carrying news of political campaigns? Does it usually? Do newspapers generally?[104]

(2) The judge must then predict the effects that alternative decisions will have on the parties to the case, on at least those third parties within the zone of immediate effects, and on parties in similar situations in the future. For example, if courts impose liability on newspapers for merely negligent libel, what will be the added expense to newspapers of continuing their business? Will newspapers be able to pass on this added expense to readers and advertisers through increased prices? If not, will newspapers choose to provide less information about candidates? Will this, in turn, lead to a decrease in the number of voters going to the polls?

Alternatively, will a refusal to impose liability deter potential candidates from seeking office for fear of being negligently maligned?

Finally, what is the degree of likelihood of any of these predictions?

[104] Of course, in one sense, a judge cannot identify facts relevant to a particular goal without first identifying or positing that goal; otherwise, all facts would have to be considered relevant. Still, a judge can survey the facts and decisional context of a case to determine which alternative goals are at least in the ballpark—*i.e.*, which goals might conceivably be served or disserved by a particular decision in the case. In a sale-of-goods case, for example, one possibly relevant goal would be furthering certainty in commercial transactions. Furthering exploration of outer space, on the other hand, would probably not be relevant.

Note that rules imposing liability for negligent libel might apply in other jurisdictions, and that the resulting states of affairs might shed light on the foregoing questions.

(3) Next, the judge must characterize the resulting states of affairs predicted for each alternative. In the present example, is it appropriate to say that a decision leading to a decrease in voter participation (or leading to an increase in the number of political candidacies) diminishes or enhances "democracy"? What is the essential nature of democracy anyway? It is one thing to predict the "brute facts" of a state of affairs, and quite another to characterize that future state of affairs in appropriate conceptual (perhaps even evaluative) terms. Thus, predicting that a reduced flow of information about candidates will decrease voter turnout is not necessarily the same as concluding that democracy will be diminished.

(4) The judge must next determine whether any of the alternative predicted states of affairs either affect public interests or represent particular instances of such interests, and therefore qualify as *social* goals. As I will explain, merely personal goals of a party or of the judge that neither affect nor instantiate public interests cannot qualify as social goals. The interest must be fairly attributable to the relevant community as a whole or to a significant segment thereof.[105]

In giving a reason that serves a social goal, a judge may think of at least one of the parties to the case as a kind of "social agent" whose actions affect relevant public interests. For example, a newspaper's political coverage may affect public interests by informing citizens of the quality of candidates for public office, or by deterring good candidates from running for fear of being maligned.

In other cases, predicted states of affairs will merely constitute instances of public interests. While such decisions might have substantial impact on a party and perhaps on a few related persons as well (*e.g.*, his family, neighbors, or business associates), they might not otherwise have significant community effects. For example, protecting the personal health of several families in a neighborhood might count as an instance of a public interest, even though it will not significantly affect the community as a whole. Because the community *does* have an interest in the health of its members, however, it has an interest in the health of these individual families. Similarly, an individual's desire to engage in a particular business,

[105] I do not postulate a solidarity of interests; interests commonly conflict.

although likely to have limited impact on the community, still qualifies as an instance of a public interest; the community has an interest in allowing people to determine the course of their own lives and careers within the limits of social tolerance.

Certain types of merely personal ends, however, neither affect nor instantiate public interests. A judge's desire to be reelected, for example, cannot qualify as a valid reason for deciding a case one way or the other. Likewise, providing one business with an advantage over competitors usually cannot qualify as affecting or instantiating a public interest, although desired by a party to the case. Society has no interest in seeing a particular judge reelected, *especially* if he decides cases on the basis of his political ambitions. Nor does society ordinarily have an interest in merely giving one business a competitive advantage over others. These interests are merely personal. They cannot qualify as *social* interests and, therefore, cannot figure in goal-serving reasons.[106]

(5) If the predicted results of a decision affect or instantiate a public interest and thus qualify as *social*, further questions arise. Which of the effects, if any, are *generally good*? Which are *generally bad*? Only effects that serve a good social goal can qualify as generally good.[107] Thus, if imposing liability on newspapers for negligent libel will encourage more good candidates to run for office by reducing their fears of negligent malignment, the state of affairs resulting from a decision to impose liability might be independently appraised as good (on the ground that it facilitates democracy, a good thing). As such, the state of affairs qualifies as a good social goal, and may generate a "positive" goal reason—one favoring liability in our example.

[106] I am indebted to Mr. Leigh Kelley for assistance in the formulation of the distinction between social and nonsocial goals. This distinction is particularly elusive and I welcome suggestions. In fact, an alternative approach could be taken here: Eliminate step (4) and collapse it into step (5) on the general goodness or badness of the goal. Some factors or considerations relevant to step (4) and not fully reflected in step (5) might generate institutional reasons bearing on whether a *court* ought to adopt the particular goal in question. The nature, variety, and interrelatedness of the goals that figure in goal reasons are themselves complex topics that call for considerable research. *See generally* Summers, *Naive Instrumentalism and the Law*, in LAW, MORALITY, AND SOCIETY 119, 120-24 (P. Hacker & J. Raz eds. 1977).

[107] Note that the same effects that constitute the brute facts of a predicted state of affairs may be susceptible to characterization in terms of more than one goal. For example, the same state of affairs that will result from imposing liability in our illustrative case might be characterized in terms of increased information, more voting, or greater social solidarity resulting from a wider dispersal of information.

But some predicted effects of a decision might disserve a good social goal. For example, imposing liability might cause newspapers to reduce their campaign coverage; this might lead to a decrease in the flow of information about candidates and a decline in voter turnout. These effects might be viewed as inconsistent with the goal of facilitating democracy and therefore characterized as bad. As such, they could only generate a "negative" goal reason—one opposing liability in our example.

In this fifth step, the judge must appraise predicted decisional effects and determine, in light of independent values, whether the effects serve or disserve good social goals. Even if the judge has appropriately characterized the brute facts of a predicted state of affairs (in step (3)) and has properly concluded that the state of affairs affects or instantiates a public interest (in step (4)), it does not necessarily follow that producing that state of affairs will serve or disserve a good social goal. Furthermore, even if the goal purportedly served by the predicted state of affairs is widely accepted in the community, the judge must, in this fifth step, appraise the goal in light of independent values.[108] If he constructs a reason in which the goal, although widely shared, is bad in light of these values, the justificatory force of the reason cannot be fully genuine, but must to a large extent be merely conventional. In our example, of course, facilitating democracy is not merely a conventional goal, but is also independently appraisable as good.

(6) Moreover, the judge must consider not only whether the predicted effects of alternative decisions *generally* serve or disserve a good social goal, but also whether any predicted increase in goal subservience is really needed, or whether any predicted reduction in goal subservience is really prejudicial. He must inquire more particularly into the desired level of goal subservience and the impact of projected decisions on that level.

A "positive" goal reason—for example, a reason that favors imposing liability in our case because this would reduce potential candidates' fears of negligent malignment and encourage more of them to run—is not a good goal reason if this additional encouragement is unnecessary. That is, if enough good candidates will run regardless of whether newspapers are subject to liability for negligent libel, the further encouragement attributable to imposing

[108] For another discussion of the need to evaluate goals, see Bodenheimer, *supra* note 12, at 394.

liability is not desirable, despite the goodness of the *general* goal of facilitating democracy by encouraging qualified persons to run.

Similarly, a "negative" goal reason—for example, a reason opposing liability in our case because such liability would cause newspapers to cut back on their campaign coverage and thus lead to a diminished flow of information and decreased voter turnout—is not a good goal reason if diminished information and reduced voter turnout are not really prejudicial. That is, if enough information will still be provided and enough voting will still occur regardless of whether newspapers are subject to liability for negligent libel, the decrease in information or voting attributable to imposing liability will not be undesirable. This holds true despite the goodness of the *general* social goal of facilitating democracy by publishing political information and stimulating voter turnout.

In sum, judges must not only consider whether the goals served or disserved by alternative decisions are generally good in themselves; judges must also consider what levels of goal subservience are desirable, and what impact changes in legal rights and duties (with their attendant costs) will have on those levels. Note that this inquiry reintroduces in part the predictive element of step (2). But here the judge predicts not just the decision's effects as such, but the extent to which those effects serve or disserve a desired level of goal realization.

(7) Finally, the judge must formulate the reason clearly, and in appropriate general terms.[109] For example: "Defendant should not be held liable for merely negligent libel because such liability would cause this newspaper and other newspapers to become unduly cautious in providing information about candidates for public office, and this in turn would reduce voting and thus significantly diminish democratic governance. Judgment affirmed."[110]

---

[109] On the appropriate generality of reasons, see the exchange between Dean Edward Levi and Professor Herbert Wechsler: Levi, *The Nature of Judicial Reasoning*, and Wechsler, *The Nature of Judicial Reasoning*, in LAW & PHILOSOPHY 263, 290 (S. Hook ed. 1964). See also the perceptive essay by MacCormick, *Formal Justice and the Form of Legal Arguments*, 6 ETUDES DE LOGIQUE JURIDIQUE 103 (C. Perelman ed. 1976).

[110] In the foregoing illustration, the judge proceeds from the construction and articulation of one available goal reason directly to his conclusion, namely, affirmance of the judgment below. While this fulfills my illustrative aim, the judge in an actual case must usually go much further. He must also (1) formulate any opposing goal reasons, again using the procedure I have just outlined in the text; (2) formulate any opposing rightness reasons, using the procedure outlined in Part V *infra*; (3) formulate any other supporting goal reasons and rightness reasons; and (4) resolve the conflicts between opposing reasons

The foregoing account of the steps and the elements involved in the construction of a good goal reason is necessarily schematic. I have not stopped to describe any of the elements in detail. Nor have I considered where they come from or how they are related. I have not explored the complexities and difficulties of each step (including the ways in which each might go awry). Nor have I discussed the value sensitivities, skills, and capacities required of a judge in performing each step (including the capacity for sound judgment). Although I will eventually treat all of these topics, the foregoing must suffice for purposes of this Article.

Although schematic, the account I have given qualifies as a general analysis of the anatomy and physiology of a goal reason. As such, it represents an effort to unpack "public policy," a phrase judges often use, yet rarely analyze. Furthermore, the analysis explains how and why a good goal reason has justificatory force. In terms of suggestive metaphors, it identifies those "organs" of a goal reason that make it "function"; the "internal mechanisms" of a goal reason that make it "fire"; the "blueprint" and the "materials" from which a goal reason is successfully "constructed."[111]

A judge need not consciously go through each step in the analysis to come up with every goal reason relevant to a case. Some goal reasons are easier to construct than others, and even a judge who is not methodologically self-conscious may get such reasons right. Moreover, counsel will often construct relevant goal reasons for the judge. Even here, however, the judge must evaluate proffered reasons, and this will frequently require reviewing at least some of the relevant steps.

On the other hand, the judge who does go through all the steps consciously and systematically will not necessarily come up with any or all relevant goal reasons. Other things might go amiss. Certain value sensitivities, skills, and capacities are called for, and no judge always commands them all, no matter how qualified. Furthermore, the justificatory resources might simply fail to provide

to reach a final decision. This fourth step is especially important, but I have chosen not to address it in this already extended Article.

[111] I do not claim that the justificatory resources afforded by the facts and decisional context of a case may only generate one good goal reason. They may generate more than one, and these may be mutually supporting or in conflict. If in conflict, the reasons may incorporate the same goal or two different goals. In the libel illustration, for example, it might be argued that liability for merely negligent libel would facilitate democracy more than nonliability, since nonliability discourages worthy potential candidates who wish to avoid exposing themselves even to negligent malignment.

the materials needed to construct a good goal reason. Nonetheless, I claim that, given the necessary resources, the judge who conducts the analysis I have outlined above will, in general, construct and articulate reasons more successfully than judges who do not so proceed.

Whether the process of constructing goal reasons of the kind found in common-law cases is equivalent or reducible to what economists call "cost-benefit analysis" is an interesting and important question, but I cannot explore it here.[112]

B. *Evaluation*

Of course, in performing their decisional and justificatory tasks judges must not only construct goal reasons but evaluate and grade them as well. In fact, construction and evaluation are intimately related, for judges must evaluate each element of a potential reason *in the course of constructing it*. Judges must also evaluate the reasons presented by their brethren in chambers, in conference, and in draft opinions. They must evaluate reasons given by judges in prior cases cited by counsel. And they must evaluate reasons proposed by counsel and by law clerks.[113]

There is evidence that judges need to improve their proficiency in evaluating goal reasons. For example, a judge might purport to give a good goal reason when he lacks the required facts or some other element necessary to construct the reason.[114] Or a judge might discard or deemphasize a goal reason that should figure prominently in his opinion.[115] Indeed, he might fail to select and stress the best reason of all supporting his decision. He might

---

[112] For articles and bibliography on cost-benefit analysis as used by economists, see JOINT ECONOMIC COMM., 91ST CONG., 1ST SESS., THE ANALYSIS AND EVALUATION OF PUBLIC EXPENDITURES: THE PPB SYSTEM (Comm. Print 1969). For an effort to apply such analysis to common-law issues, see R. POSNER, ECONOMIC ANALYSIS OF LAW (2d ed. 1977). The *Journal of Legal Studies* and the *Journal of Law and Economics* often publish studies that apply cost-benefit analysis of one form or another to resolve legal questions or to explain and justify those resolutions. For an interesting discussion of one of Posner's main theses, see Rubin, *Why Is the Common Law Efficient?*, 6 J. LEGAL STUD. 51 (1977).

[113] Evaluation of a reason offered by someone else calls for recognition and appraisal of the elements that would have been used in its construction.

[114] *See, e.g.*, Irwin v. Phillips, 5 Cal. 140 (1855) (decision to allow miners' construction of dams justified by court as furthering development of public mineral lands; court evidently failed to consider that decision might have opposite result, since dams might render downstream areas unworkable by conventional mining methods).

[115] *See, e.g.*, Mercanti v. Persson, 160 Conn. 468, 280 A.2d 137 (1971) (court neglects goal of efficient protection of property against fire loss).

give a weak goal reason or even a nonreason.[116] Or he might give a goal reason likely to grow into a legal weed.[117]

I believe my analysis of the "building-blocks" of a good goal reason identifies all relevant focal points of evaluation—all respects in which a goal reason might be strong or weak. The fusion of these elements accounts for the force of a good goal reason. If a required element is missing, construction of a good goal reason will not be possible. And if a required element is weak—such as an improbable effect or an uncertain fact—the strength of the reason will diminish. Thus, to evaluate a goal reason systematically, the judge must both identify and assess the various elements that figure in its construction.

To illustrate, let us hypothesize a judge, Judge Endz, who in our libel example proposes to hold the defendant newspaper not liable for merely negligent libel. His draft opinion reads: "Because imposing liability for merely negligent libel would cause this newspaper and other newspapers to become unduly cautious in providing information about candidates for public office, and this in turn would reduce voting and thus significantly diminish democratic governance, the defendant is not liable."

Let us also imagine a dissenting judge who attempts to formulate a comprehensive set of criticisms of the proposed goal reason —a criticism for each element. Perhaps no proposed reason would ever have to undergo such an all-out attack, but hypothesizing a point-by-point critique will sharpen the illustration. Some of the specific criticisms formulated by the dissenter will be unconvincing, but they will serve to illustrate the relevant types of criticism a judge might convincingly offer with respect to other goal reasons. Note, too, that the following arguments are not autonomous substantive reasons, but are criticisms of one or more elements of the autonomous goal reason offered by Judge Endz.

(1) The evidence supplied by the record and other permissible sources might fail to establish that the party whose activity supposedly serves a social goal was in fact engaging in this activity when the case arose, or even that the party stands as a representa-

[116] *See, e.g.*, Monge v. Beebe Rubber Co., 115 N.H. 130, 133, 316 A.2d, 549, 551 (1974) (court concludes that employers' malicious or bad-faith dismissals will adversely affect "economic system," although result appears highly improbable).

[117] *See, e.g.*, Rowland v. Christian, 69 Cal. 2d 108, 120-21, 443 P.2d 561, 569, 70 Cal. Rptr. 97, 105 (1968) (dissenting opinion) (majority's "enhanced safety" reason for abolishing common-law distinction between tort liabilities to trespassers and to invitees will open door to unlimited liability and generate uncertainty).

tive of those who engage in such activity. Thus, the dissenter might be warranted in saying: "This newspaper was not carrying campaign news, and it almost never does. In fact, newspapers generally do not. Thus, we do not have before us the public goal-serving 'agent' that Judge Endz requires if his goal reason is to have the force he envisions."

This kind of criticism is fundamental. It questions the facts upon which the challenged reason rests, including the very facts that apparently generated the case.

(2) Even if the proposed reason survives criticism (1), there might be no reliable basis for predicting the relevant effects of the decision it supports. For example, the dissenter might be able to argue: "Judge Endz predicts that newspapers will refrain from covering campaigns if they are subject to liability in cases of this sort. No evidence supports this conclusion; it is mere conjecture. On the contrary, in other states that have imposed liability for negligent libel, newspaper coverage of campaigns continues to be extensive and vigorous. But even if imposing liability will reduce the coverage of campaigns, this might still enhance democracy. The threat of liability might induce newspapers to focus on the issues rather than on personalities, and might encourage qualified persons to run for office who would otherwise refrain from doing so for fear of negligent malignment."

Or the dissenting judge might be in a position to argue: "Although Judge Endz's prediction is more probable than not, it is only barely so. His reason, although not devoid of force, is therefore extremely weak."

(3) Even if the reason survives criticism of types (1) and (2), it might incorporate a mischaracterization of some significant aspect of the predicted state of affairs. It is one thing to predict that a decision will bring about a new and different state of affairs; it is quite another to be sure of the *essential character* of that state of affairs. For example, our dissenting judge might say: "Judge Endz characterizes the predicted state of affairs inaccurately. He argues that imposing liability on newspapers for negligent libel will reduce the flow of information about candidates, and this in turn will reduce voter participation in the electoral process. This, Judge Endz says, should be characterized as diminished democratic governance. I do not agree. Factors other than mere numbers, such as the education of our voters, may be more important to democracy. After all, we don't let children vote."

(4) Even if none of the preceding criticisms is valid, analysis

might still show that the contemplated goal fails to qualify as a *social* goal, because it does not affect or instantiate a public interest. Our dissenter therefore might say: "The purportedly democratic goal cited by Judge Endz is not a social goal, but rather a personal goal of those who own newspapers. Successful pursuit of this goal will simply give publishers more interesting items to write about and thus more to sell, thereby merely furthering their own economic ends. Democracy so conceived simply cannot be a *social* goal."

This criticism obviously lacks "bite" because the reason tendered by Judge Endz incorporates a goal that inherently bears on public interests rather than on merely personal concerns. Nevertheless, not all purported goal reasons involve goals that are immune to this type of criticism.

(5) Even if the proposed goal affects or instantiates a public interest, the purported reason might still fail because the goal it incorporates proves undesirable in light of independent values. Just because pursuit of a goal is appropriately characterized and bears upon a public interest, it does not follow that the goal is good. Thus, our dissenting judge might take a dim view of democracy and argue that, although pursuit of the goal of democratic governance cited by Judge Endz affects a public interest, it still does not qualify as a good goal, because democracy is bad for society. Again, this criticism is unconvincing as formulated for the present context, but this general type of criticism might, in a particular case, easily apply.

The pursuit of a goal, then, might affect a public interest, yet the goal itself might not be good. Indeed, a goal might be intrinsically bad, or its pursuit might lead to undesirable effects.

(6) Assuming that the proposed goal reason survives up to this point, it might still fail or lose considerable force because, for example, the community already has enough subservience of the goal, either from the means envisioned in the reason or from other means. Our dissenting judge might argue: "Even if newspapers stop covering political campaigns altogether, other news media will not stop, and their coverage will be sufficient." Regardless of the probability of this particular prediction, this type of criticism will sometimes undermine proposed goal reasons.

(7) Finally, if a proposed goal reason is not well stated, whatever force it has might not be apparent and, on this basis alone, the reason might fail to support the decision.

In sum, a proposed goal reason might fail or lack force in any of the foregoing respects. But if it withstands the attack of every type of criticism outlined above—even to the slightest degree—the reason necessarily has some force.

A judge who is proficient in evaluating goal reasons will understand, at least intuitively, how each of its constituent elements may be strong or weak, depending on relevant factors.[118] A judge must also be able to evaluate a goal reason overall—as strong or weak, or something in between. This general evaluation will take the form of a two-stage process.[119] Of course, some goal reasons will not call for such elaborate evaluation.

First, the judge must evaluate each *internal* element of the reason as strong, weak, or something in between. For every type of element (except perhaps the last), the judge might imagine a continuum from the strongest element of that type at one end (*e.g.*, highest probability of the prediction), to the weakest element of that type at the other (*e.g.*, lowest probability of the prediction). Thus, the judge might readily imagine cases in which a prediction would be quite strong, quite weak, or something in between, depending on the circumstances. At this first stage of evaluation, the judge would place each element of the reason in the appropriate place on its own special continuum. At the end of this stage, the judge will have characterized each of the reason's elements as relatively strong, relatively weak, or something in between.

With these rough characterizations in mind, the judge would then turn to the second evaluational stage. First, he would imagine a "summary" continuum stretching from the strongest possible goal reason (all elements combined) to the weakest (all elements combined). He would then summarize his specific judgments arrived at in the first stage, and place the reason, evaluated as a whole, at the appropriate point on the summary continuum. The judge would thus arrive at a judgment about the overall strength of the proposed goal reason.

This overall judgment would not be comparative. It would not lead to the conclusion that the reason is stronger or weaker than some other goal reason. An extremely strong goal reason might

---

[118] Discharge of the evaluative task with respect to most elements calls for still further analysis, which cannot be attempted here.

[119] I do not claim that my account of this process is entirely a rational reconstruction of actual practice; but I believe it is consistent with that practice and accurately reveals it in many significant respects. Holmes, for example, consciously practiced something similar to the "continuum" evaluation I reconstruct here. *See, e.g.*, Noble State Bank v. Haskell, 219 U.S. 104, 112 (1911); Haddock v. Haddock, 201 U.S. 562, 631-32 (1906) (dissenting opinion); Commonwealth v. Rogers, 181 Mass. 184, 186, 63 N.E. 421, 423 (1902).

still be weaker than a competing goal reason; the latter, for example, might incorporate a goal of more importance to the community, or might promise more long-term goal realization.

Implicit in this analysis is a general model of the ideal goal reason. The features of this ideal reason can now be meaningfully rendered explicit:

(1) All facts relevant to the construction and evaluation of the reason are indisputably true.

(2) The judge has an unquestionably reliable basis for predicting decisional effects, and the prediction itself is highly certain.

(3) The judge accurately characterizes the predicted state of affairs in all relevant respects.

(4) The predicted state of affairs affects or instantiates public interests—not merely the personal interests of the parties or of the judge; thus, the future state of affairs clearly serves (or disserves) a possible *social* goal.

(5) The predicted state of affairs serves (or disserves) a social goal that is without doubt generally good in light of all relevant values.

(6) The predicted increase in goal subservience is plainly needed in the community (or the predicted decrease in goal subservience is plainly prejudicial to the community).

(7) The reason is well formulated.

Although it is abstract and idealized, this model is not a personal or utopian contrivance that I have conjured up without reference to the realities of common-law decisionmaking. Most aspects of the model are derived from the goal-reasoning practices of common-law judges. In this respect, the model represents a rational reconstruction of actual judicial practice. I do not say that judges are methodologically self-conscious about this process. Indeed, their general lack of self-consciousness makes it necessary to *reconstruct* the steps in their reasoning and the elements that correspond to each of those steps. Nevertheless, most judges are to some extent aware of most features of the model. This is especially evident from the types of critical reasons found in dissents and concurring opinions.[120]

The model is also ideologically neutral, except insofar as any form of goal rationality might be considered ideological. It can

[120] *See generally* Appellate Judicial Opinions, *supra* note 6, ch. 8; Stephens, *The Function of Concurring and Dissenting Opinions in Courts of Last Resort*, 5 U. Fla. L. Rev. 394 (1952).

therefore accommodate both a wide variety of goals and evolutionary changes in goals. Judges of earlier times and different places could and may have used it.

I believe that judges would perform their evaluational work more successfully if they consciously followed this model and evaluated each element of a proposed goal reason, and each reason as a whole, in terms of its proper place on a continuum—at least when the nature of the particular reason calls for such systematic evaluation. Judges who proceed in this manner should be taken in less often by a bad goal reason, and should more often recognize when one reason is stronger than another.

The process, however, cannot be mechanically employed. Several evaluative steps are complex and often controversial. This is true, for example, of prediction and goal evaluation. Moreover, adherence to the procedure cannot guarantee that a judge will always evaluate a reason well. But, at minimum, the model provides a way to structure the exercise of judgment systematically, pointedly, and comprehensively. Many evaluations made by judges who follow the procedure will inevitably be rough, but they are likely to be more refined than those arrived at by judges who follow no systematic method at all.

It may be objected that judges who strive to structure their judgment in this way will become so self-conscious that they will end up unable to give any good goal reasons at all; just as the proverbial centipede lost all capacity for forward motion when he started watching his legs, the judge might lose his capacity for reasoning and deciding. Justificatory activities, however, are quite different from bodily movements, the coordination of which may be diminished by too much self-conscious attention. Unlike walking, which becomes completely second nature, the construction of a legal justification must remain to a great extent a formal and deliberative process—something that cannot be done well without reflection and the conscious exercise of judgment.[121]

### C. *The Bearing of Institutional Reasons*

I have so far said nothing about the bearing of institutional reasons on the construction and evaluation of goal reasons. Institutional reasons are goal reasons or rightness reasons that relate to how judicial roles and processes bear on the decisional and jus-

[121] On thinking about thinking, see A. FLEW, THINKING ABOUT THINKING (1975).

tificatory jobs of judges. Examples include: "This is not the kind of goal that courts ought to adopt and implement without legislative approval"; or, "Since courts cannot readily measure the damages resulting from this type of alleged wrong, we will not recognize it as a wrong."

Some types of institutional reasons might be conceptualized either as internal elements of goal reasons or as autonomous institutional reasons. Suppose, to take an extreme example, that our newspaper libel case arises during a labor shortage that is seriously affecting the city's economy. One judge might argue in support of imposing liability that the decision would force the newspaper into bankruptcy, and would thus free its employees to make needed repairs on an important bridge. Other judges would certainly object that this reason does not embody the kind of goal that a court ought to adopt. Courts, they will argue, are not in the business of managing the economy generally, let alone the local labor market.[122] These judges might readily concede that the reason would qualify as a good goal reason "if we were a legislature." But courts are not legislatures; they are institutionally limited in function.[123]

Perhaps we should conceptualize the foregoing criticism as an attack on an internal, institutional element of the proposed goal reason, which weakens or annihilates the reason *on its own terms*. If so, we might add to my earlier account of the various elements of a goal reason a further element—namely, the goal incorporated in the reason must be one that a court may properly adopt. On the other hand, the objection might be conceptualized not as an attack on an internal element of the goal reason, but rather as an independent reason going to the institutional propriety of proposed judicial action. Regardless of how it is conceptualized, however, the force of this institutional consideration as an argument against exclusively judicial adoption of the proposed goal should be apparent.

Why, then, do I treat all considerations of institutional propriety as a separate type of reason? Such treatment is, I think, more faithful to current judicial practice. On the whole, judges appear to categorize institutional reasons separately. Moreover, this approach

[122] *Cf.* Muskopf v. Corning Hosp. Dist., 55 Cal. 2d 211, 224, 359 P.2d 457, 464, 11 Cal. Rptr. 89, 96 (1961) (dissenter argues that court should leave abolition of governmental tort immunity to state legislature).

[123] In addition, the objecting judges might argue that the proposed goal reason incorporates a faulty means-end hypothesis: even though the newspaper's demise will free its employees to work elsewhere, it is highly unlikely that they will have the desire or the qualifications to work on the bridge.

avoids the intermingling of institutional and noninstitutional concerns, and thus increases the likelihood that each type of concern will receive due consideration. After judges construct and evaluate goal reasons on their own terms (as I have now narrowly conceptualized them), they should always go on to consider the institutional appropriateness of giving them. In pursuing this strategy, judges may bring to bear autonomous institutional reasons that weaken or nullify proposed goal reasons.

D. *The Legitimacy of Goal Reasons*

A skeptic might argue that goal reasons are not really reasons at all because they do not bring genuine values into play. Judges rarely challenge the legitimacy of goal reasons on this ground, however, presumably because goal reasons so often implicate such tangible, "real-life" values as safety, health, peace and quiet, clean air, and voter participation.

Nevertheless, judges and others do sometimes question the legitimacy of goal reasons on the ground that they necessarily sacrifice the individual to the common good.[124] It might be argued, for example, that the refusal to impose liability for negligent libel in the name of preserving sources of information and voter participation, in effect, sacrifices the claim of an injured party to the perceived good of the community. In my view, however, this is not a decisive objection to the legitimacy of goal reasons as such. How much force they have in particular cases is one thing; whether they have any force at all is quite another. Perhaps some courts accord them too much force. In a given case, a goal reason with some force might still justifiably give way to a conflicting rightness reason that favors the individual's interests.

Furthermore, some judges and commentators argue that goal reasons are inappropriate bases for common-law decisionmaking because resort to such reasons always calls for an exercise of the democratic will—solely a legislative function.[125] But judges regularly give goal reasons in common-law cases, and, in my view, this practice is legitimate. Not all goal reasons call for an exercise of the democratic will. Of course, judicial reliance on a particular goal reason in a given case might be institutionally inappropriate.

---

[124] Judges have argued this in conversation with me. *See also* Fletcher, *Fairness and Utility in Tort Theory*, 85 HARV. L. REV. 537, 567 (1972).

[125] *See, e.g.*, Dworkin, *Hard Cases*, *supra* note 27; Winfield, *Public Policy in the English Common Law*, *supra* note 27.

Note, finally, that goal reasons also play important justificatory roles in daily life. It might be thought that, while judges must always decide with society's interests in mind, the goal reasoning of individuals outside the law is inherently egoistic and self-regarding. But this is clearly untrue; some private goal reasoning is purely altruistic, and much is both altruistic and egoistic at the same time. If we abandoned goal reasons entirely, we would drastically diminish our justificatory resources both inside and outside the law.

## V

## Construction, Evaluation, and Legitimacy of Rightness Reasons

Rightness reasons constitute the second basic variety of substantive reasons found in common-law cases. A rightness reason derives its justificatory force not from predicted goal-serving effects of the decision it supports, but from the applicability of a sound sociomoral norm to a party's actions or to the state of affairs resulting from those actions. Reasons of this type do not derive their force from what the future will bring. Rather, most rightness reasons derive their force from how the past came about.[126]

The facts and decisional context of a case might generate only a rightness reason or only a goal reason. On the other hand, reasons of both types might be available, and these might conflict or be mutually supporting.

I now turn to the construction and evaluation of rightness reasons. I will treat these reasons in the same basic fashion as I treated goal reasons. This will call for some restatement. But there will be significant variations, too, which reflect the fundamental differences between these two types of reasons.

As I have already explained, there are two main subspecies of rightness reasons: (1) those that depend for their force on the culpability or nonculpability of a party's past actions; and (2) those that depend for their force on the fairness or unfairness of leaving the parties "as is" in light of their past interaction.

### A. *Construction*

Rightness reasons are internally complex, far more so than commonly supposed. Judges cannot construct rightness reasons in

[126] For discussion of rightness reasons that are not past-regarding, see note 46 and accompanying text *supra*.

a systematic and methodologically self-conscious fashion without reference to these complexities. There is evidence that judges need to improve their capacity to construct good rightness reasons. For example, a judge might overlook a rightness reason entirely, even though the facts and decisional context make it readily available.[127] Or he might undertake to construct a rightness reason as if it were a goal reason.[128] Or he might fail to incorporate all the necessary elements of a rightness reason, by failing, for example, to bring the relevant rightness concept to bear.[129] Or he might formulate a potentially good rightness reason in conclusory terms.[130]

There are indications that some judges and lawyers do not understand rightness reasons as well as they understand goal reasons. Indeed, even some of the most thoughtful scholars only dimly understand the internal complexities of rightness reasons.[131] And I fear that my own efforts have not unraveled all knots. Thus, the analysis I offer is only tentative.

To construct a rightness reason a judge must take a series of steps to combine a variety of elements. Once again, I will use an actual case to illustrate this process.[132] Assume that the plaintiff contracts to build a mast for the defendant's boat on the plaintiff's premises. Before he finishes, the plaintiff becomes worried about the possibility of fire and proposes to buy insurance. The defendant,

---

[127] *See, e.g.*, Oscar Schlegel Mfg. Co. v. Peter Cooper's Glue Factory, 231 N.Y. 459, 132 N.E. 148 (1921) (court neglects to formulate and stress following rightness reason: where price of glue rose sharply during period covered by requirements contract and plaintiff's purchase orders rose by 2500%, granting plaintiff damages for nondelivery of larger orders would be unfair, since increased requirements were neither expected nor foreseeable by defendant).

[128] *See, e.g.*, Cornpropst v. Sloan, 528 S.W.2d 188, 199-200 (Tenn. 1975) (dissenting judge begins to construct rightness reason based on fairness of imposing tort duty on shopping centers, but ultimately formulates goal reason that imposition of duty would serve "best interests of the consuming public," without fully articulating original and independent rightness reason).

[129] *See, e.g.*, International Milling Co. v. Hachmeister, Inc., 380 Pa. 407, 414, 110 A.2d 186, 189 (1955) (court uses fraud concept where bad-faith concept more appropriate).

[130] *See, e.g.*, Groves v. John Wunder Co., 205 Minn. 163, 168, 286 N.W. 235, 237 (1939) (in choosing "cost of completion" over "difference in value" as measure of damages in construction-contract case, court states as rightness reason merely that plaintiff should have benefit of "lost" bargain).

[131] *Compare* Rosenberg, *Methods of Reasoning and Justification in Social Science and Law: Comments*, 23 J. LEGAL EDUC. 199, 202 (1970) (brilliant law professor analyzes rightness reason as "position based on value preferences"), *with* Miller & Barron, *The Supreme Court, the Adversary System, and the Flow of Information to the Justices: A Preliminary Inquiry*, 61 VA. L. REV. 1187, 1199 (1975) (almost as brilliant professor quoted in survey analyzes rightness reasons as requiring "very little data—only a strong ethical idea").

[132] Mercanti v. Persson, 160 Conn. 468, 280 A.2d 137 (1971).

after carelessly checking his own policy, says to the plaintiff: "I'm sure I have coverage already." The plaintiff relies on the defendant's careless representation and does not procure insurance. A fire for which neither party is responsible destroys the boat and mast when the work is nearly completed, and the defendant's policy does not cover the loss. The defendant refuses to pay for the pile of ashes, and the plaintiff sues for the contract price.

Assume that the Uniform Commercial Code would impose the loss on the plaintiff, subject to section 1-103 which authorizes judges to resort to any "general equitable principles."[133] Let us suppose, too, that the plaintiff introduced evidence of the foregoing facts, and the trial judge instructed the jury that if they found the facts as the plaintiff had alleged, they must, under section 1-103, find for the plaintiff on a theory of "estoppel by negligence." The defendant excepts to this instruction, the jury returns a verdict for the plaintiff, and the defendant appeals. The case is one of first impression, and the appellate court must now decide whether to affirm or reverse.

I will now sketch (though not necessarily in sequence) the steps that a methodologically self-conscious judge might take in constructing a "culpability" rightness reason that supports the trial judge's instruction. I will also identify the internal element of the reason that figures in each step.

(1) First, the judge must determine from the proceedings below and the general decisional context all facts relevant to the culpability of the defendant's action: Who did what to whom? With what results?[134] Why? In what type of situation? In the present case, for example, did the defendant make a representation? What facts bear on the ease with which the defendant could have determined the actual extent of his insurance coverage? Did the defendant's statement cause a loss to the plaintiff? Did the plaintiff rely? What circumstances bear on the possible foreseeability to the defendant of the plaintiff's reliance? (Note that such questions might necessitate inquiry into the parties' states of mind.[135])

---

[133] For a general discussion of this section, see Summers, *General Equitable Principles Under Section 1-103 of the Uniform Commercial Code*, 72 Nw. L. Rev. 906 (1978).

[134] Note that concepts of causality play important roles in both goal reasons and rightness reasons. In goal reasons, however, *decisional* effects play a distinctive role.

[135] In contrast, a judge might also inquire into state of mind when he formulates a goal reason, but not for the purpose of determining culpability. Instead, the judge will typically seek to determine the likely effects of the decision on persons acting subsequently with the same state of mind.

(2) In light of the facts ascertained in step (1), and in light of an inventory of *possibly* relevant concepts of culpability (provisionally identifiable also in step (1)), the judge must determine, intuitively or otherwise, which concepts of culpability are in fact relevant to characterizing the defendant's action. This will often require sensitive analysis of the potentially relevant concepts and their careful particularization. Thus, in our example, concepts of negligence and responsibility for one's careless statements would seem to be most relevant in characterizing the defendant's action.

(3) The judge must then determine, in light of relevant rightness values, whether it is possible to formulate a sociomoral norm of rightness that incorporates the concepts identified in step (2), and would, if applicable to the facts, require (or not require) the party who caused the loss to make amends. Thus, a judge in our case might tentatively formulate the relevant norm (including an "amends-making" aspect) as follows:

> A person should not carelessly induce another to rely on a false representation when the representor can readily ascertain the falsity of his representation and can reasonably foresee the other party's reliance. One who does so, without more, should bear the foreseeable loss caused to the relying party.[136]

(4) Having formulated the norm, the judge must go on to evaluate its soundness in light of independent rightness values. The norm formulated in step (3), for example, might or might not be widely shared in society. If it is widely shared, but in light of independent values the court ought not to recognize it, then the justificatory force of any rightness reason that incorporates the norm cannot be fully genuine; much of this force must be merely conventional.[137] Evaluation of a norm must be distinguished from

---

[136] Norms formulated at this step might warrant injunctive relief as well. In such cases, the judge would consider whether the projected action against which the relief is sought *would be* culpable.

Although I focus in this Article on damages and injunctions, the remedial apparatus of the common law extends beyond these devices. Furthermore, while I concentrate on cases involving past interaction of the parties, not all common-law cases involve such interaction.

[137] I do not claim that when the law recognizes a culpability concept embedded in a rightness norm (through a court's reasons for decisions and doctrinal formulations), the concept or the norm never undergoes alteration. Indeed, the culpability concept employed by the law may differ significantly from the concept that a moral spectator would employ in judging the same action in a nonlegal setting for a nonlegal purpose. *See generally* W. Prosser, Handbook of the Law of Torts § 1, at 6 (4th ed. 1971); *id.* § 4, at 18. Nor do I claim that social morality is monolithic; on some issues it is clearly pluralistic.

its formulation, if only because judges (and others) tend to take the soundness of a formulated norm for granted if it is widely shared in the community.[138]

The rightness reason now taking shape in our example might be stated as follows: "Since the plaintiff relied on the defendant's careless misrepresentation and the defendant could reasonably have foreseen this reliance, the defendant should bear the resulting loss." In my view, the rightness norm generating this reason is not only widely shared in our society, but is also worthy of judicial recognition in light of rightness values that are independent of community acceptance. Thus, if the reason holds up through the remaining steps, it will have genuine justificatory force.[139]

(5) Next, the judge must evaluatively characterize the relevant facts—here the action of the party against whom relief is sought—in light of the concepts of culpability identified as relevant in step (2) and embodied in the norm formulated in step (3). In the present case, for example, the judge must ask: Did the defendant actually exercise due care in determining the extent of his coverage? Could the defendant have reasonably foreseen the plaintiff's reliance?

Note how this step differs from steps (2) and (3). It is one thing to survey the facts in order to identify which concepts of culpability are relevant and to determine whether a norm can be formulated that incorporates these concepts. It is another to evaluatively characterize the facts by applying the relevant culpability concepts (itself often a complex act of judgment).[140]

(6) The judge must then apply the rightness norm formulated in step (3) to the facts as characterized in step (5), and decide which disposition of the legal issue *most accords* with the norm as applied to the facts. Thus, in our example, if the defendant through lack of

---

[138] *See* H. L. A. HART, LAW, LIBERTY AND MORALITY 17-24 (1963).

[139] Norms themselves may be highly complex, but I will not consider this here. For the growing literature on norms, see, for example, H. KELSEN, ESSAYS IN LEGAL AND MORAL PHILOSOPHY 83-94 (O. Weinberger ed. 1973); J. RAZ, PRACTICAL REASON AND NORMS (1975); A. ROSS, DIRECTIVES AND NORMS 78-138 (1968); R. SARTORIUS, INDIVIDUAL CONDUCT AND SOCIAL NORMS (1975); E. ULLMANN-MARGALIT, THE EMERGENCE OF NORMS (1977).

[140] Appellate judges sometimes confront a clean slate, and have the opportunity to formulate every element in the construction of a reason. *See, e.g.*, Pavesich v. New England Life Ins. Co., 122 Ga. 190, 50 S.E. 68 (1905). At other times, they must share this work with the trial judge or jury in accordance with a division of functions specified in the law. For example, a factfinder may, when the law considers a question to be one of fact, perform a characterization function (as in negligence cases), and the appellate judge may lack the authority to recharacterize the relevant facts.

due care induced foreseeable detrimental reliance, then, without more, we might conclude that the instruction of the trial judge in the illustrative case should be upheld and the judgment affirmed.

(7) Finally, the judge must formulate the reason clearly, and in appropriately general terms. For example: "Since the plaintiff relied on the defendant's careless misrepresentation and the defendant could have reasonably foreseen this reliance, the defendant should pay damages for the loss he caused. Judgment affirmed."[141]

In the foregoing account, the reason ultimately given will have force if elements (1) through (7) are appropriately combined. I cannot treat here the various elements in detail, or explore the distinctive capacities required of a judge who sets out to construct a rightness reason. I must omit subtleties and complexities. Whole books and articles have been devoted to the culpability concepts that figure in rightness reasons; these include such wide-ranging and complex notions as due care, desert, and good faith.[142] To identify and particularize these concepts, specify their content, and apply them to the facts, judges must rely on moral intuition and exercise sensitive judgment. The very question of whether a court ought to recognize a particular rightness norm may be highly controversial. What types of argument and evidence are relevant to the recognition of a norm has not yet been the subject of extended study, although judges regularly engage in such argument and marshall such evidence. My account also omits discussion of the capacities required for the faithful evaluative characterization of facts and states of affairs.[143] For purposes of this Article, what I have already said must suffice.

I have so far illustrated only the construction of a culpability-based rightness reason. The foregoing analysis applies equally, however, to rightness reasons based on mere fairness. Thus, even if the defendant did not carelessly misrepresent the facts, he might still be held responsible if it would be unfair to leave the resulting loss on the relying plaintiff. Construction of this reason would fol-

[141] As I noted with respect to my outline of the construction of a goal reason (*see* note 110 *supra*), my aim here is simply to illustrate the construction of one available rightness reason. Before reaching a final decision in an actual case, the judge must usually proceed to formulate any other supporting or opposing rightness reasons and goal reasons and then resolve the conflicts.

[142] *See, e.g.*, Summers, *"Good Faith" in General Contract Law and the Sales Provisions of the Uniform Commercial Code*, 54 VA. L. REV. 195 (1968).

[143] For a perceptive discussion, see J. FRANK, COURTS ON TRIAL 37-61 (1966).

low the same seven steps, except that the judge would formulate and apply a rightness norm embodying a particular concept of unfairness. In legalistic terms, "estoppel by negligence" is not the only rationally recognizable form of estoppel. Here, mere "estoppel in pais" might suffice, even if the defendant was not negligent.[144]

Analysis of rightness reasons merely in terms of "justice and equity between the parties" is really no analysis at all. Yet judges and others frequently offer little more than this familiar phrase.[145] My account of rightness reasons qualifies as an analysis of their anatomy and physiology. Moreover, because my analysis breaks rightness reasons down into elements that provide subjects for reasoned argument, the analysis can be used to rebut the charge that rightness reasons are merely "conclusory" and thus without legitimacy.[146]

The seven steps and their corresponding elements also provide a schematic "blueprint," with specifications of required materials, that a methodologically self-conscious judge might follow to construct a good rightness reason. The analysis enables us to see just how a rightness reason has force—in metaphorical terms, how it "fires," "functions," or "goes through." Of course, step-by-step adherence to the blueprint will not always generate a good rightness reason. The required resources might be unavailable, or the judge might lack the necessary skills and judgment.[147]

Rightness reasons should not be equated with what some theorists call "rights" reasons—reasons based upon moral rights.[148] Similarly, rightness reasons should not be identified with "natural law." Nor does the distinction between goal reasons and rightness reasons closely parallel the distinction between so-called teleological and deontological reasons.[149] Rightness reasons are also different

---

[144] *See generally* M. BIGELOW, A TREATISE ON THE LAW OF ESTOPPEL ch. 18 (6th ed. J. Carter rev. 1913); Jackson, *Estoppel As a Sword*, 81 L.Q. REV. 84 (1965).

[145] *See, e.g*, Mercanti v. Persson, 160 Conn. 468, 479, 280 A.2d 137, 142 (1971).

[146] *See* text accompanying notes 169-70 *infra*.

[147] I do not claim that the facts and decisional context of a case can generate only one rightness reason. In the illustrative case, there might have been a further rightness reason flatly contrary to the decisive one—namely, that the plaintiff did not justifiably rely, and therefore really brought the loss on himself. Formulation of this reason would again involve following the seven-step procedure outlined above. But this would not necessarily require formulating a further and distinct rightness norm from scratch. The norm already stated in step (3) could be explicitly revised to allow for the possibility that a competing reason of this sort might arise in a particular case.

[148] *See, e.g.*, Dworkin, *Hard Cases, supra* note 27.

[149] Discussions of teleological and deontological theories can be found in almost any elementary text. *See, e.g.*, W. FRANKENA, ETHICS 15-17 (2d ed. 1973).

from most reasons of "equity" that interest economists.[150] These topics, although of great importance, lie beyond the scope of this Article.

B. *Evaluation*

Judges must not only construct rightness reasons but also evaluate and grade them, and judges do not always perform these tasks well. For example, a judge might purport to give a good rightness reason when he lacks the required facts or some other necessary element.[151] Or a judge might discard or deemphasize a rightness reason that should figure prominently in his opinion.[152] Indeed, he might fail to select and stress the best reason of all supporting his decision.[153] Or he might evaluate a rightness reason as if it were a goal reason, and so employ inappropriate standards.[154] Or he might give a rightness reason likely to grow into a legal weed.[155]

A judge should bear in mind that the internal complexities and the potential strengths and weaknesses of rightness reasons differ

[150] In various contexts, economists use the term "equity" to refer to a property interest, to equality of income distribution, to a fair distribution of costs, and to a variety of other concepts.

[151] Failure to recognize that a purported rightness reason lacks the necessary factual foundation is perhaps the most egregious form of misevaluation. *See, e.g.*, Gerhard v. Stephens, 68 Cal. 2d 864, 892-95, 442 P.2d 692, 714-16, 69 Cal. Rptr. 612, 634-36 (1968) (one element of court's rightness reason was reasonableness of party's expectation that unused mineral rights might someday prove valuable, but party apparently lacked any basis for expectation). A more subtle form of misevaluation takes place when the judge mischaracterizes the facts and as a result applies an inappropriate rightness norm. *See, e.g.*, Marks v. Gates, 154 F. 481, 483 (9th Cir. 1907) (in suit for specific performance of "grubstake" contract, court characterizes parties' transaction as simple quid pro quo exchange, rather than as investment in uncertain venture; consequently, court applies inappropriate fairness norm of gross inadequacy of consideration and denies relief).

[152] *See, e.g.*, Mitchill v. Lath, 247 N.Y. 377, 160 N.E. 646 (1928) (court fails to appreciate fully that decision will result in patent injustice to losing party).

[153] *See, e.g.*, Monge v. Beebe Rubber Co., 114 N.H. 130, 316 A.2d 549 (1974) (court gives dubious goal reason—promotion of economic system—yet fails to articulate robustly independent and conclusive rightness reason—employer's gross bad faith and overreaching).

[154] *See, e.g.*, McConnell v. Commonwealth Pictures Corp., 7 N.Y.2d 465, 475, 166 N.E.2d 494, 500, 199 N.Y.S.2d 483, 490-91 (1960) (dissenting judge appears to attack rightness reason given by majority on ground that decision will have bad consequences).

[155] *See, e.g.*, Greenspan v. Slate, 12 N.J. 426, 439, 97 A.2d 390, 396-97 (1953) (court holds that "normal instincts of humanity and plain common honesty" require that parents compensate others for "necessaries" furnished their children in emergency even in absence of express or implied contract, but court fails to provide clear guidelines for determining, *e.g.*, what counts as "emergency" and what notice must be given, thus opening door to undesirable forms of intermeddling by third persons).

from those of goal reasons. Thus, the evaluation of rightness reasons requires a different analysis, and calls for the exercise of different skills and sensibilities. To evaluate a proposed rightness reason systematically, a judge must advert to each of the various elements that figure in its construction and consider their interrelation. To illustrate, suppose that a judge in our boat-mast case, Judge Normz, proposes to hold the boat owner liable to the builder for the contract price. In support of this decision, he offers the following reason: "The plaintiff foreseeably relied on the defendant's careless misrepresentation as to insurance coverage."

Now, let us imagine a dissenting judge who attempts to formulate a comprehensive set of criticisms of the proposed rightness reason—a criticism for each element. Although some of the imagined criticisms will be unsound with respect to the specific reason offered by Judge Normz, they nonetheless illustrate the relevant types of criticism that might figure prominently in other cases.

(1) The evidence supplied by the record and the decisional context might fail to establish that the defendant acted under the circumstances and with the state of mind (if any) required for the reason. For example, the dissenting judge might be in a position to say: "Judge Normz does not have the facts straight. The defendant never really made a representation about insurance coverage. In fact, the statement attributed to him was not a representation—it was only a guess." The critic thus challenges the brute facts of the episode, and seeks to show that the proposed reason lacks the factual basis upon which its force depends. Rightness reasons, it must be remembered, are generated by applying sociomoral norms to facts, and norms of this nature have their own discrete ranges of factual application.

(2) Even if the necessary facts are established, the rightness concept brought to bear might be irrelevant or misparticularized. For example, the dissenting judge might say: "The relevant concept here is that of ill desert or nondesert, not want of due care, as Judge Normz would have it."

(3) Although the rightness concept might be relevant and appropriately particularized, it might be impossible to formulate a norm that incorporates the concept *and* calls for the making of amends (or the recognition of a defense) in the type of case at hand. In our hypothetical case, for example, Judge Normz formulated the following norm:

> A person should not carelessly induce another to rely on a false representation when the representor can readily ascertain the

falsity of his representation and can reasonably foresee the other party's reliance. One who does so, without more, should bear the foreseeable loss caused to the relying party.

Our dissenter might concede that the norm aptly embodies the relevant rightness concept, but argue that the formulation is too broad and authorizes relief in cases where relief would be unjustified (or supports a defense in cases where the defense should not be recognized). Although this criticism appears unconvincing in the context of the present case, it illustrates a type of criticism that may have force in other cases.[156]

(4) Even if the norm is aptly formulated to authorize relief (or the recognition of a defense) in the type of case at hand, the norm might not be one that, in light of relevant values, the court ought to recognize.[157] For example, in opposition to the norm formulated by Judge Normz, our dissenter might argue for a "caveat relier" principle—*i.e.*, a person should be allowed to represent whatever he wants, and those who intend to rely on his representations should bear the burden of determining their accuracy.

(5) Although the proposed reason survives the first four types of criticism, the action of the party against whom relief is sought might not be susceptible to the evaluative characterization required to bring the rightness norm into play. For example, the dissenting judge might say: "Judge Normz evaluatively mischaracterizes what happened here. The defendant boat owner was not really careless, for the reasonable man cannot be expected to understand an insurance policy. Such policies use ordinary words in very odd ways. As a matter of law, the defendant cannot have failed to exercise due care."[158]

(6) Even if the proposed reason survives to this point, it might still lose force because the decision it purportedly supports is not the decision, among the alternatives, that *most accords* with the

[156] For a case in which the majority agreed that the rightness concept embodied in a norm was infringed but did not agree that the infringement warranted relief, see Zepeda v. Zepeda, 41 Ill. App. 2d 240, 190 N.E.2d 849 (1963).

[157] For an example of a controversial rightness norm, see *id.* (couple should not bring illegitimate child into world). *See also* Meinhard v. Salmon, 249 N.Y. 458, 164 N.E. 545 (1928) (Cardozo, C.J., speaking for majority, and Andrews, J., dissenting, disagree on whether joint venturer ought to bear absolute duty to inform coventurer of any offers made by third persons regarding property involved in joint-venture agreement, even though offer concerns development of property after agreement expires and clearly falls beyond agreement's scope). For a discussion of the necessity to evaluate such norms, see Bodenheimer, *supra* note 12, at 394.

[158] *See generally* note 140 *supra*.

applicable norm. Thus, the dissenter might argue: "Judge Normz has failed to see what his reason is a reason *for*. He says it best supports a decision holding the owner fully liable to the builder, but I say it best supports a decision apportioning the loss between the parties."

This criticism might seem to be aimed more directly at the use of a reason than at the reason itself. The justificatory force of a rightness reason, however, depends partly on the degree of accordance between decision and norm (as applied to the actions of the parties). Reasons for decisions cannot have force in a void. They have force only in relation to decisions, and have more force in relation to some decisions than to others.

(7) Finally, if the proposed reason is not well stated, whatever force it has might not be apparent and, on this basis alone, might fail to support the decision.

A proposed rightness reason might be evaluated in each of the foregoing respects. But a judge must also evaluate reasons as a whole—as strong or weak, or something in between. Again, using the tentative analysis I propose in this Article, a judge might systematically evaluate a rightness reason as a whole in a two-stage process. Of course, many rightness reasons will not call for such elaborate evaluation.

At the first stage, the judge must evaluate each of the seven elements as strong, weak, or something in between. For each type of element (except perhaps the last), he might imagine a continuum from the strongest element of that type at one end (*e.g.*, an appropriate evaluative characterization of a clearly careless misrepresentation), to the weakest element of that type at the other (*e.g.*, a highly questionable characterization of a statement as a careless misrepresentation). Thus, the judge might readily imagine cases in which an evaluative characterization would be highly appropriate, not appropriate at all, or something in between. At this first stage of evaluation, the judge would place each element of the reason in the appropriate place on its own special continuum. At the end of this stage, the judge will have characterized each of the reason's elements as relatively strong, relatively weak, or something in between.

The judge would then turn to the second evaluational stage. He would begin by imagining a "summary" continuum stretching from the strongest possible rightness reason (all elements combined) to the weakest (all elements combined). He would then summarize his specific judgments arrived at in the first stage, and place the reason, evaluated as a whole, at the appropriate point on the summary continuum. The judge would thus arrive at a judgment about the overall strength of the proposed rightness reason.

This overall judgment would not be comparative. It would not lead to the conclusion that the reason is stronger or weaker than some other reason. An extremely strong rightness reason might still be weaker than a competing rightness reason which, for example, incorporates a rightness concept that is more significant.

Implicit in the foregoing analysis is a general model of the ideal rightness reason. The features of this ideal reason are:

(1) All facts relevant to the construction and evaluation of the reason are indisputably true.

(2) The rightness concepts brought into play are indisputably relevant and appropriately particularized.

(3) A rightness norm can be formulated that clearly embodies the relevant rightness concepts *and* authorizes relief (or the recognition of a defense).

(4) The rightness norm is one that the court plainly ought to recognize in light of relevant values.

(5) The evaluative characterizations that apply the concepts embodied in the norm to the facts are indisputably appropriate.

(6) The decision supported by the reason is the one most clearly in accordance with the applicable norm.

(7) The reason is well formulated.

Note that this model is "norm-neutral"; it can accommodate both a wide variety of norms and evolutionary changes in norms.[159] Thus, judges of earlier times and different social outlooks could and may have used the model.

I believe that judges who systematically follow the model to construct and evaluate rightness reasons will generally do their work better than judges who do not. Certainly judges must exercise judgment; they cannot apply the model mechanically, or expect that step-by-step adherence will guarantee the best results. At minimum, however, the model provides a blueprint for structuring the exercise of judgment systematically, pointedly, and comprehensively. Although many of the judgments reached by judges who follow the model will inevitably be rough, they are likely to be more refined than those arrived at by judges who follow no systematic method at all.

159 For an example of an evolving norm, see Florida Publishing Co. v. Fletcher, 340 So.2d 914 (Fla. 1976), *cert. denied*, 431 U.S. 930 (1977).

C. *The Bearing of Institutional Reasons*

My approach in this Article is to treat institutional reasons distinctly. An institutional reason, it will be recalled, is a goal reason or a rightness reason that relates to the bearing of judicial roles and processes on judicial decisions and justifications. For example, a judge might say: "A decision for the plaintiff would require us to recognize a wholly new rightness norm so controversial that we should leave it to the legislature to enact a statute that incorporates it." Or a judge might say: "In particular cases, courts will be unable to ascertain the adjudicative facts necessary to determine whether the proposed rightness reason applies; thus, a decision based on this reason would be unsound because it would introduce a rudderless precedent."[160]

As already noted with respect to institutional reasons and goal reasons, we might conceptualize some types of institutional reasons as internal elements of rightness reasons. But the considerations that militated against incorporating institutional reasons into goal reasons[161] militate against their incorporation into rightness reasons as well. Thus kept distinct, a rightness reason may be good on its own terms, yet an institutional reason may come into play to override, diminish, or nullify it. Moreover, an institutional reason may independently influence the way in which a court implements or gives legal effect to a rightness reason and its underlying sociomoral norm; as a result, the *legal* embodiment of the norm may differ significantly from corresponding manifestations in moral or other nonlegal contexts. For example, institutional considerations account in large part for the law's definition of negligence in objective rather than subjective terms, although the values and norms of daily life in which the legal concept of negligence is rooted often take subjective factors into account.[162]

D. *The Legitimacy of Rightness Reasons*

Judges and others sometimes challenge rightness reasons as illegitimate. Although most judges do not appear to be generally

---

[160] *See, e.g.*, Li v. Yellow Cab Co., 13 Cal. 3d 804, 823-24, 532 P.2d 1226, 1240, 119 Cal. Rptr. 858, 872 (1975) (court notes that adjudicative facts required for allocation of fault are frequently indeterminable).

[161] *See* text accompanying notes 122-23 *supra*.

[162] Thus, for various institutional reasons, a court might adopt an objective test of negligence that does not recognize subjective differences in skill or intelligence, although these might be highly relevant in determining an actor's degree of *moral* fault. The difficulties that would arise if courts gave full recognition to such differences are readily apparent. *See generally* O.W. Holmes, The Common Law 107-11 (1938).

skeptical of rightness reasons, those who have expressed such skepticism include some luminaries.[163] Of course, a judge who is skeptical of rightness reasons because, for example, he considers them conclusory, and who is also skeptical of goal reasons because he thinks only legislators may resort to them, is likely to suffer paralysis in a case of first impression.

What are the sources of skepticism about rightness reasons, and what should be said in response? These questions merit consideration,[164] but they also lead into waters turbulent with philosophical controversy, which I cannot enter here. Instead, I will follow, and at times even intermingle, several strategies. I will propose explanations for the skeptic's stance—explanations designed not to refute him, but to liberate him. I will offer some counterarguments. I will appeal to the usual willingness even of skeptics to embrace goal reasons. (Judges, lawyers, and law professors who are skeptical of rightness reasons are rarely skeptical of *all* substantive reasons.) Finally, I will let the burden of proof with respect to the legitimacy of rightness reasons fall where it should —on the skeptic. In the following discussion I address each of a variety of skeptical positions.

1. *"Rightness Reasons Are Not 'Real' Reasons"*

Some who are skeptical of rightness reasons not only favor goal reasons, but apparently think that goal reasons are the only *real* reasons.[165]

Some might think that a real reason must somehow involve the court in *doing* something. On this view, goal reasons clearly qualify as real reasons because they hypothesize decisional effects. Since rightness reasons do not contemplate such effects, they cannot be real reasons.

Similarly, some will argue that a goal reason qualifies as a real

[163] Several passages in Holmes's most famous essay strongly suggest a bias in favor of "considerations of social advantage," which I take to mean goal reasons. *See* Holmes, *The Path of the Law*, 10 HARV. L. REV. 457, 467-69, 474 (1897). Similarly, in Vegelahn v. Guntner, 167 Mass. 92, 105-06, 44 N.E. 1077, 1080 (1896) (dissenting opinion), Holmes stated that the "true grounds of decision are considerations of policy and of social advantage"—again an apparent reference to goal reasons.

[164] It is important to confront skepticism about rightness reasons if only because it might sometimes adversely affect judges in the performance of their regular tasks. Although such skepticism rarely appears in judicial opinions, judges occasionally voice it in other settings.

[165] *See* note 163 *supra*. Roscoe Pound, who was himself a judge for a time, evolved his theory of interests without according an appropriately distinctive place to rightness reasons. *See* note 9 *supra*.

reason because it is instrumentalist in character. A goal reason "operates" through an intervening mechanism—a decision that produces effects. Thinkers brought up in our technological age as "social engineers" and "instrumentalists" naturally sense the genuineness of goal reasons, because such reasons envision future effects. Rightness reasons, on the other hand, cannot qualify as real reasons because they are noninstrumentalist—they look only to the past or to the present.

In this scientific age, the goal-minded individual is also likely to be an "empiricist." For him, a reason must turn on facts—not just the facts of a particular case, but general facts of social causality. Rightness reasons are not real to the empiricist, since they typically do not turn on such general facts. Rather, they depend on facts about the actions of the parties, or states of affairs resulting from those actions—facts of the particular case.

Further, a skeptic might think that a real reason, or at least one that a public official may appropriately give, must concern the "public interest." Goal reasons meet this test because they serve social goals—goals that affect or instantiate the interests of the community. Because rightness reasons regard only what is right between the parties, they cannot be real reasons.

Finally, to some skeptics at least, goal reasons seem to involve something like what economists call cost-benefit analysis, a kind of calculational rationality that eminently qualifies them as reasons. Since rightness reasons involve nothing of the sort, they cannot, on this view, be real.

Some of these forms of skepticism rest on invalid factual assumptions. It is untrue, for example, that the recognition of rightness reasons only has significance as between the parties.[166] But even if all of the foregoing skeptical propositions are true, none of them counts as an *argument* for the thesis that only goal reasons are legitimate. They boil down to little more than the bare assertion that nothing can be a reason unless it has the essential attributes of a goal reason. As such, they beg the question or merely express a prejudice.

As between the skeptic and the true believer in rightness reasons, who ought to bear the burden of persuasion? Who ought to produce arguments denying or affirming that reasons other than goal reasons have justificatory force? For several reasons the

[166] *See* text following note 46 *supra*.

burden should fall on the skeptic. First, the skeptic has to explain away far more than the true believer. He must explain away: (1) the fact that many common-law cases rest partly or primarily on rightness reasons; (2) the apparent assumption of many judges that, even though a given goal reason sufficiently justifies a proposed decision, a further rightness reason reinforces the justification; and (3) the sense of sacrifice that many judges feel when they let a goal reason override a rightness reason.

Furthermore, the skeptic must explain away not only many features of the common law, but also many corresponding features of daily life, since judges often resort in common-law cases to rightness reasons that people give regularly in nonlegal contexts. Genuine rightness reasons are not just ritualistic or technical justifications conjured up by a priesthood clad in judicial robes. Wholesale abandonment of rightness reasons would vastly diminish our justificatory resources outside, as well as inside, the law. It would rule out, at least in giving reasons, such familiar concepts as desert, good faith, fair reliance, fault, and inequity. Dispensing with such concepts would, in fact, make us quite different people, for concepts so fundamental help to define our very nature.

With the burden of persuasion cast upon his shoulders, the skeptic must produce genuine arguments that rightness reasons cannot serve as justifications of common-law decisions. I now turn to what some of those arguments might be.

### 2. *"Rightness Reasons Are Too Personal and Subjective To Count as Legal Reasons"*

This form of skepticism is of ancient lineage. And it is not unusual to encounter it today. Decisions explicitly based on rightness reasons in the old Court of Chancery sometimes drew the criticism that they varied with the "length of the lord chancellor's foot."[167] More modern versions of this skepticism are usually expressed in less colorful terms: "The judge based his decision on personal preferences," or "The judge relied on subjective value judgments." Note that the skeptic does not deny the genuineness of relevant values. He merely asserts that invoking these values to

---

[167] TABLE TALK OF JOHN SELDEN 43 (F. Pollock ed. 1927). For a recent allusion to the chancellor's foot in a skeptical vein, see Stream v. CBK Agronomics, Inc., 79 Misc. 2d 607, 608, 361 N.Y.S.2d 110, 112 (Sup. Ct. 1974) ("But, as has oft been seen, there is little room for the Chancellor's foot to rotate in the law of bills and notes."), *modified on other grounds*, 48 App. Div. 2d 637, 368 N.Y.S.2d 20 (1st Dep't 1975).

decide cases is a matter of subjective preference.[168] This subjectivist form of skepticism may be subdivided into several strands.

One strand might be called the "value plurality" thesis. On this view, judges who rely on rightness reasons bring into play a nearly infinite variety of rightness values in judging actions or states of affairs, and decisions in given cases will differ depending on which values the particular judges prefer. Hence, any decision is "subjective" to the extent that it rests on rightness reasons. Two aspects of this thesis are questionable. First, it is simply untrue that an infinite variety of values will be relevant to the decision of every case. The potentially significant values are usually quite limited. It is impossible to prove this without inordinately extended discussion of a wide range of cases, and I cannot enter upon that here. I will rest instead on a familiar truth—namely, that *facts govern and circumscribe the relevance of values*. Not just any value will be relevant to any set of facts; every value has a limited factual "range." Furthermore, it is simply untrue that judges cannot agree on which values are relevant to given actions and states of affairs. Judges commonly agree at least on the legal issue, and such agreement also narrows the set of potentially relevant values. For example, most judges "know" when a case involves unjust enrichment rather than justified reliance. The existence of ready agreement in most cases is something the "value pluralist" must explain away.

A second strand of subjectivist skepticism might be called the "no-shared-values" thesis. This view can be stated as follows: "Even if rightness values are not infinitely plural, and even if judges can at least generally agree on which values are relevant to particular actions or states of affairs, the resulting decisions must still be highly subjective because judges simply do not agree on which values should control." This form of skepticism vastly overstates the extent of disagreement among judges; it probably springs from a preoccupation with difficult or borderline cases that present close questions of conflicting values. But not all or even most cases, actual and imaginable, fall into this category. It is possible to pose a wide range of cases that virtually all would agree should be decided in the same way on rightness grounds. Clear cases of deserving conduct, clear cases of want of due care, clear cases of justified reliance, clear cases of unjust enrichment, and so on, are not difficult to imagine. Indeed, they constantly arise.

[168] Thus, the skeptic might concede the intrinsic goodness or desirability of values, and deny only their legitimacy as bases for judicial decisions.

A related strand of subjectivist thought might be characterized as the "value indeterminacy" thesis: "Even if rightness values are not infinitely plural and judges can generally agree on their relevance, and judges share such values and weigh them similarly, the choice of reasons (and the resulting decisions) must still be highly subjective because the relevant values are inherently indeterminate." Stated a bit differently, this thesis holds that value concepts such as "desert," "justified reliance," and "inequitable overreaching" are so extraordinarily vague, ambiguous, essentially contested, or otherwise indeterminate, that judges who apply them to characterize actions or states of affairs will inevitably make highly subjective judgments. But again, it appears that judges *do* commonly agree on the evaluative characterization of particular actions and states of affairs. This at least indicates that such concepts are susceptible of determinate application.

Admittedly, when judges give rightness reasons they rely on the values they have personally come to hold. But this does not necessarily render their decisions unreasonably subjective. Judges cannot give *any* type of substantive reason without bringing values into play. Where should judges get those values? They cannot conduct public referenda; to do so would be to abdicate the office of judging as we know it, and to risk exalting merely conventional over genuine values. In their own daily lives judges participate in society's shared stock of values; indeed, individuals are selected to be judges partly because their values are thought to coincide with those of many in the community. Some values, of course, may be appropriately characterized as "merely personal." But conscientious judges take care not to bring such values into play, and the multijudge character of our appellate courts limits the effect of purely personal notions of rightness.

Skeptics who dismiss rightness reasons are usually quick to embrace goal reasons, since goal reasons clearly qualify as "policy" reasons. Presumably, skeptics simply cannot imagine that reasons of policy might also be subjective. Of course, most of these skeptics realize that judges must frequently give substantive reasons to reach a decision in a case, and that it is therefore important that some such reasons count. Yet most, if not all, subjectivist theses can also be directed against goal reasons. Consider, for example, the claim that rightness reasons are unreasonably subjective because the judge who gives them consults only his own personal values. Does a judge giving goal reasons proceed any differently? In setting goals, judges can sometimes consult legislative or other official pronouncements, but these guideposts will not always point the way. Judges must then appraise purported goals as good or bad, or as better or worse than conflicting goals to be served by alternative decisions. How are they to do this? Again, they cannot hold public referenda, nor should they. Instead, judges must consult their own values and debate those values with counsel and other members of the court.

3. *"Rightness Reasons Are Conclusory or Question-Begging"*

One form of skepticism about rightness reasons apparently rests on the view that such reasons are inevitably conclusory or question-begging.[169] Of course, a conclusory or question-begging "reason" is no reason at all, and therefore cannot justify decisions. A genuine reason must appeal to something independent of the decision to be justified.[170] In contrast, a conclusory or question-begging reason merely characterizes the decision to be justified, or restates some point in issue along the way to the decision.

A good rightness reason appeals to a number of elements independent of the decision to be reached. A rightness reason must appeal to an applicable norm of right action. Thus, to justify a decision for the plaintiff boat-mast builder in our earlier case, a judge might appeal to what lawyers call estoppel—a rightness norm. But the content and soundness of such norms are independent of particular rulings or decisions. Moreover, the justificatory force of a rightness reason depends on the combination and strength of the reason's internal elements. These factors cannot be characterized as a "mere restatement" of the legal conclusion that the reason supports.

4. *"Rightness Reasons, Even If Not Immediately Conclusory or Question-Begging, Are Ultimately So"*

The rightness skeptic might also deploy a kind of "normative regress" argument. Consider this imaginary dialogue:

True Believer: Let's take a hypothetical case. Suppose Edgar

---

[169] Such skepticism is of ancient lineage, too. *See, e.g.*, Millar v. Taylor, 98 Eng. Rep. 201 (K.B. 1769). A colleague, Professor Alan Gunn, has suggested to me that one reason some tort theorists so vigorously pursue economic analysis today may be that they think all rightness reasons are merely conclusory. But see the important writings of Richard Epstein and George Fletcher, tort theorists who are not skeptical of rightness reasons. *E.g.*, Epstein, *Intentional Harms*, 4 J. LEGAL STUD. 391 (1975); Fletcher, *supra* note 124.

[170] "[J]ustification consists in appealing to something independent." L. WITTGENSTEIN, PHILOSOPHICAL INVESTIGATIONS § 265 (G. Anscombe trans. 1953).

knows his dog will bite, yet he carelessly lets the dog loose and it bites Betsy, an innocent victim. I think Edgar deserves to compensate Betsy. Stated in these terms, this is a rightness reason.

Skeptic: I see. But isn't your reference to the concept of desert *immediately* conclusory or question-begging?

True Believer: No. In stating a reason, one typically dispenses with a full exposition of all that goes into its formulation. In my example, I implicitly appealed to an independent norm calling for reparation whenever it is said that a person deserves to be held responsible.

Skeptic: I think I follow you, and perhaps agree up to this point. But at some *ultimate* point your reasoning becomes conclusory or question-begging, doesn't it?

True Believer: How so?

Skeptic: Well, why is it a reason to decide that Edgar deserves to pay Betsy, even assuming that he was at fault and she was an innocent victim?

True Believer: Because this would give Betsy her just due.

Skeptic: So what?

True Believer: Well, interpersonal decency is worth having in itself.

Skeptic: Why?

True Believer: It won't do for you to stand there and keep asking "so what?" or "why?"; you doubtless subscribe to some values yourself, don't you?

Skeptic: Well, yes, I do.

True Believer: Name one.

Skeptic: Well, I've decided some pollution cases on the ground that my decision would bring more health to the community. Now there's a *real* value for you.

True Believer: Human health?

Skeptic: Yes.

True Believer: But so what?

Skeptic: What do you mean "so what?" Can't you see that health is valuable?

True Believer: Oh, I see! So you *do* think there must be some stopping point? But if so—if there must be some stopping point in this kind of exercise—then, provided it is not merely arbitrary, our arrival at that point in regard to a given reason should not make that reason "ultimately" conclusory or question-begging, should it?

Skeptic: Well . . . .

This exchange shows that the skeptic's "normative regress" argument is a two-edged sword; it can be effectively turned against him. Any such regress must stop somewhere. Thus, if no reason can be a "real" reason unless it is always possible to give a satisfactory "reason behind the reason," then nothing will ever count as a reason. Admittedly, the true believer would be expected to say a great deal more about the nature of interpersonal decency in the foregoing dialogue. But the skeptic would be subject to the same demand in asserting that human health is a value.

#### 5. *"Rightness Reasons Are Moralistic or Judgmental, and Involve 'Playing God'"*

Some judges seem reluctant to give rightness reasons because they view those who give such reasons as moralistic or judgmental and thus willing to impose their moral code on others. The solution to this problem (to the extent that it *is* a problem) is to avoid giving bad rightness reasons. It is sobering to recall that goal reasons, too, can be badly formulated, misconstrued, or misapplied. Yet, presumably, the skeptic would not consider this an argument against resorting to goal reasons.

In this secular age, some judges probably approach rightness reasons cautiously or even skeptically because they associate some of these reasons with specific religious origins. Judges who take this attitude, however, fall victim to the genetic fallacy. Even if all rightness reasons could be traced to specific religious teachings, this should not taint those reasons, even for the nonreligious. Reasons must be judged by their intrinsic worth, not by their origins.

In summary, the skeptics have yet to prove their case against rightness reasons.[171] At the very least, enough has been said to take some wind out of their sails. Judges who feel uneasy about rightness reasons should put aside many of their misgivings. By doing so, judges can bring more tools to their work. This should make for better decisions and better justifications.

### E. *The Need for Rightness Reasons*

Some skeptics might concede the legitimacy of rightness reasons, yet claim that they are unnecessary. These skeptics might

---

[171] A further complex source of skepticism about rightness reasons is the view that when a rightness reason apparently has force, this is really because a goal reason has also been set forth or is lurking in the background. This "reducibility" thesis is discussed in Part VII *infra*.

think that judges can always give sufficient goal reasons for a decision, since every decision has effects which will always serve, directly or indirectly, some social goal. Only the unimaginative judge, such skeptics will argue, cannot "harness" causal relations to the framework of goal reasons that are sufficient to decide a case.

But is this so? It is true that both a goal reason and a rightness reason may be available to justify a decision. Thus, a decision might subserve a good end *and* accord with a sound rightness norm. In the boat-mast illustration, for example, a decision for the relying plaintiff would facilitate future economic exchange by encouraging people to participate in relationships in which they cannot obtain perfect information and must rely on the representations of others. At the same time, such a decision would compensate the party who justifiably relied upon another's carelessly chosen words.

In some cases, however, a good goal reason will be unavailable. There might be no relevant social goal, or the causality might be far too speculative, or the community might already have enough fulfillment of the goal. Indeed, any of a goal reason's necessary elements might be lacking. When a judge reaches the bottom of the goal-reason barrel, however, he has not necessarily run out of reasons.[172] One or more rightness reasons may still be available.

Even when the justificatory resources of a case generate both a goal reason and a rightness reason and both support the same decision, it still does not necessarily follow that the rightness reason lacks justificatory significance. Standing alone, the goal reason might be too weak to provide sufficient justification for the proposed decision; the judge must then add the force of the rightness reason. The rightness reason, if well articulated, will not only strengthen the justification, but also make the precedent more intelligible, and thus easier to interpret and follow in future cases. In the latter respect, the rightness reason will not be superfluous even when the goal reason alone suffices to justify the decision.

Furthermore, the justificatory resources might generate conflicting goal reasons, and the judge might need a rightness reason to break the resulting stalemate. Similarly, the case might generate a goal reason and a countervailing rightness reason. Here the judge might resolve the conflict by resorting to differences in

[172] There are numerous cases in which judges give only rightness reasons. *See, e.g.*, Goodman v. Dicker, 169 F.2d 684 (D.C. Cir. 1948); Sidis v. F-R Publishing Corp., 113 F.2d 806 (2d Cir. 1940).

the strength of the reasons or by invoking further rightness reasons.[173]

## VI

## Differences Between Goal Reasons and Rightness Reasons

It is possible and worthwhile to study goal reasons and rightness reasons separately, each on their own terms. Judges must regularly construct and evaluate both types of reasons, and they are likely to do this better if they understand the internal complexities of each reason type. There are, however, important differences between these two types of reasons. I have yet to confront these differences directly and draw them together in one place. But it is important that judges grasp these differences. A judge cannot fully understand the internal workings of each type unless he understands what sets one apart from the other. In addition, the judge who grasps these differences will be less likely to confuse the two types of reasons in his decisional and justificatory labors.[174] The differences are important in other ways, too, which I will indicate en route. But the significance of many of the differences will be best understood only after setting forth what they are, and after considering whether rightness reasons are ultimately "reducible" to goal reasons.[175]

### A. *Inherent Differences*

Some differences between goal reasons and rightness reasons are more or less "inherent." These contrast with "contingent" differences, which I will treat in the following section. Several inherent differences are related, some rather closely.

[173] Of course, goal reasons and rightness reasons frequently conflict. In forthcoming work, I will consider the possibility of devising a systematic decision procedure for resolving such conflicts.

[174] Even sophisticated judges who have thought and written about justification have confused the reason types. For example, it has been suggested that all judicial reasoning is a matter of pragmatic "trial and error," a characterization that does not felicitously apply to rightness reasons. *See generally* B. Cardozo, The Nature of the Judicial Process 98-99 (1921). See also Dewey, *Logical Method and Law*, 10 Cornell L.Q. 17, 26-27 (1924), in which all reasons are characterized as consequentialist.

[175] I am indebted to Mr. Leigh Kelley for discussion and assistance in preparing this Part and Part VII *infra*.

1. *Sources of Justificatory Force*

A goal reason derives its force from the fact that, at the time it is given, the decision it supports can be predicted to serve a good social goal. A rightness reason, however, derives its force from the fact that the decision it supports accords with a sound rightness norm applicable to a party's past action or to the state of affairs resulting from that action.

A goal reason thus requires an appropriate prediction—a causal relation between the supported decision and desired social effects. A rightness reason, on the other hand, requires an accordance between the supported decision and an applicable socio-moral norm—a noncausal relation. A goal reason involves a means-goal hypothesis. Theoretically, this hypothesis can be verified; in time, the predicted decisional effects—effects entirely *external* to the decision—either will or will not have occurred. Rightness reasons are fundamentally different. The reason-giver does not purport to predict the future effects of a decision that implements the reason. Rather, the essential relation of accordance between decision and norm either exists or does not exist at the time of decision. Any prediction that a state of affairs will result from the decision is irrelevant to the force of a rightness reason.[176] If a judge sets out to construct a rightness reason but then raises the prospect of desirable decisional effects, he is in fact undertaking to construct a goal reason, and his labors must take on a different character.

If the prediction on which a particular goal reason rests proves erroneous, it does not necessarily follow that the reason had no force at the time of decision. Of course, if a prediction fails repeatedly, this would bear on the force of the goal reason when given in future decisions. Similarly, events subsequent to a decision based on a rightness reason—*e.g.*, newly discovered evidence or a growth in moral enlightenment—might also lead the judge to revise his earlier judgment that his decision accorded with an applicable norm. But this has nothing to do with the failure of a prediction.

Hence, proficiency in constructing and evaluating the two

[176] Admittedly, judicial authorization of some process for implementing the decision in the future must figure in a rightness reason. (This may involve, for example, a money judgment, an injunction, or a judgment denying both.) But authorization of such process is simply part of what is meant by a judicial decision in the first place. Hence, nothing specific to a rightness reason itself qualifies as a goal external to the decision.

types of reasons calls for different knowledge and capacities. For example, a judge might be skillful in making the predictions required for goal reasoning, but lack the moral intuition, the conceptual sophistication, or the sensitivity to the meaning and significance of norms necessary for rightness reasoning.

2. *Objects of Evaluation*

The construction of a substantive reason requires evaluation of its internal elements. Since these elements differ, the objects of evaluation in the two types of reasons will differ as well. The construction of goal reasons requires a determination of whether posited goals are good, and whether predicted decisional effects serve the posited goals. The construction of rightness reasons, on the other hand, requires the evaluative characterization of past actions or the states of affairs resulting from those actions. This in turn calls for the exercise of the intuitive and conceptual skills needed to select, particularize, and apply relevant evaluative concepts. A judge engaged in this process must also evaluate the accordance between alternative decisions (including the methods of their implementation) and applicable rightness norms. Often he will have to evaluate the soundness of rightness norms themselves. Of course, this last form of evaluation is not limited to rightness reasons, since some goal reasons contemplate more rightness. In the construction of rightness reasons, however, it is *always* required.

3. *Effectiveness of Implementation—Its Bearing on Justificatory Force*

A good rightness reason that favors a decision for the plaintiff does not lose its force even though, at the time of decision, the defendant has no money to pay damages or will be unable to comply with an injunction. A rightness reason will always have force, regardless of whether an effective remedy is available, if a decision for the wronged party accords with the applicable rightness norm —a relation of accordance unrelated to cause and effect. If a judge knew at the time he gave a goal reason, however, that the decision it supported could not be implemented, this would nullify or reduce the force of the reason, since the essential prediction of decisional effects would fail, at least in the particular case.

B. *Contingent Differences*

Some features only "contingently" differentiate goal reasons and rightness reasons. These differences emerge only when specific instances of goal reasons and rightness reasons are compared.

1. *Nature of Values*

The values that figure in specific instances of the two types of reasons do not necessarily differ in character. Most goal reasons look to the realization of welfare values or "public goods"—*e.g.*, more productive uses of resources, more economic exchange, more health, more peace and quiet, more safety, more clean air. Other goal reasons, however, look to the realization of more rightness.

Rightness reasons, on the other hand, necessarily regard rightness—specific conceptions of what is just, equitable, fair, deserving, faithful, etc. It follows that *most* goal reasons differ from *all* rightness reasons in that most goal reasons look to the realization of values other than rightness in and of itself.

2. *"Achievability"*

Although it rarely happens in practice that a goal is fully achieved, in principle most goals that look to the realization of welfare values or "public goods" are achievable. If a goal has been sufficiently achieved, it is no longer appropriate to give a reason in the name of that goal. Thus, judges sometimes abandon a goal and refuse to decide in its name because "we have had enough fulfillment of that goal."[177] The same is not true of norms. That judges should at some point stop giving a particular type of rightness reason "because we have had enough fulfillment of the relevant norm" smacks of the absurd, since rightness norms, unlike most goals, are incapable of such fulfillment.

3. *Factual Requirements*

Judges can usually give rightness reasons without inquiring into facts outside the record. But goal reasons call for predictions, and thus frequently take judges into the realm of general social facts, including the causes and cures of social ills. Frequently such facts will not appear in the trial transcript, which contains "adjudicative facts"—for the most part, facts of the specific case.[178]

Occasionally, however, a judge giving a rightness reason must also go beyond the adjudicative facts. For example, equality of

---

[177] *See, e.g.*, Siragusa v. Swedish Hosp., 60 Wash. 2d 310, 318, 373 P.2d 767, 773 (1962) (court abandons goal of protecting fledgling industry).

[178] For the distinction between adjudicative and legislative facts, see authorities cited in note 63 *supra*.

access to the media might be a rightness consideration bearing on the decision in a libel case, and general social facts relevant to media access might not appear in the record.[179] The judge in this case would have to undertake an inquiry similar to that called for by most goal reasons.

#### 4. *Necessity of Reference to the Past*

Since rightness reasons call for an evaluative characterization of past actions or the states of affairs resulting from past actions, some might think that only rightness reasons look to the past. Goal reasons, however, also direct a judge's attention to past facts: those that make up our accumulated knowledge of social causation.

Even so, the past plays significantly different roles in the construction of the two types of reasons. In giving a goal reason the judge looks back merely to "draw a bead on the future"—to "line up his sights" on what lies ahead. In contrast, the judge who gives a past-regarding rightness reason *must* look back to identify and apply the relevant rightness norms. He is not concerned with the past for the light it may shed on the future; instead, the past provides the essential reference point for bringing his values to bear. Thus, in giving rightness reasons a judge cannot dismiss the past as "sunk costs" or "spilled milk."

In sum, particular instances of the two types of reasons may differ in a substantial number of respects. There is no one, simple "distinction" between the two types, but a variety of differences.

## VII

## Reducibility of Rightness Reasons to Goal Reasons

In previous sections I have discussed the two basic types of substantive reasons, their internal elements, the manner in which these elements are combined, and a variety of important respects in which goal reasons and rightness reasons differ. I have also responded to arguments challenging the need for and legitimacy of rightness reasons. If I am right, the differentiation of the two types of reasons cannot be merely formal—*i.e.*, merely a matter of whether a judge chooses to formulate a reason as one type or the other. Instead, the two types must be substantively distinct and mutually exclusive.[180]

---

[179] *See, e.g.*, Taskett v. King Broadcasting Co., 86 Wash. 2d 439, 546 P.2d 81 (1976).

[180] Nevertheless, a few judges, lawyers, and two law professors have insisted in discussions with me that "the distinction" is "merely formal."

Yet the claim is made, occasionally by judges and more often by law professors, that the justificatory force of a rightness reason is always "reducible to" or "derivable from" the justificatory force of an available goal reason.[181] If some version of this reducibility thesis is true, judges should recognize it, for only then would they fully understand the complex justificatory practices in which they participate. Furthermore, judges who thus came to understand these practices could, once they constructed a relevant rightness reason, always go on to identify and articulate the goal reason on which it "rests." Having thus laid bare the true basis of justification, judges would be better able to reach the best results and better able to justify them.

I cannot thoroughly explore here the complex issue of reducibility. I will identify and rebut only two forms of the reducibility thesis. I will then briefly explain why, even if some version of the thesis is true, my theory of substantive reasons survives almost unscathed.

A. *Reducibility of Rightness Reasons to "Parasitic" Goal Reasons*

A parasitic goal reason derives its justificatory force primarily from the conjunction of two factors: the rightness reason that justifies an original, precedent-setting decision, and the doctrine of precedent itself.[182] For example, a decision based primarily on a "good faith" rightness reason generates, in a precedent system, a further goal reason: it is predictable (or so it is said) that similarly situated parties will follow the precedent and act in good faith. Thus, because precedential consequences qualify as goal-serving effects of the precedent, its underlying rightness reason becomes ultimately goal-serving, however rightness-oriented it might originally be.

This form of the reducibility thesis is unpersuasive. Even if precedential consequences are goal-serving in this way, they only *add* to the justification for the decision. This added force stems from the doctrine of precedent, not from any goal-subservience of the decision itself. Furthermore, whether a precedent-setting decision will produce more rightness in the future depends on whether the decision accords with rightness in the first place. Thus, even if an original rightness-based decision always gives rise, through the doctrine of precedent, to a further goal-serving reason ("bring about more such rightness"), if the original decision rested on a

[181] Again, such claims have been made to me in discussion.

[182] *See* text accompanying notes 46-48 *supra*.

rightness reason that had no justificatory force, the corresponding goal reason would itself lack force, since it could not involve bringing about *more rightness*.

Moreover, without a system of precedent, a rightness reason would still have force in the particular case. At least there is no reason to suppose that its force necessarily depends on projected precedential effects. On the contrary, if the theory of rightness reasons I offer is correct, the force of such reasons derives from the applicability of rightness norms that are primarily past-regarding or present-regarding.

Even under a system of precedent, it is often predictable that a decision based on a rightness reason will influence few, if any, parties in the future. Indeed, there might be no relevant "future," for the decided case might be the last one in the pipeline before the effective date of a statutory reform. Or the decided case might involve factual peculiarities that make it virtually impossible that a similar case will ever occur. But even if the decision does have a "future," many if not most persons whose activities fall within its scope might fail to learn of the decision or grasp its bearing. They might fail to act on the decision because they lack sufficient incentives, because they disagree with it, because the law itself provides that compliance is optional, or for a host of other reasons. Yet even if such factors limit or nullify the future impact of a decision, this does not mean that the decision is poorly justified. Our reducibility proponent, however, would have to say as much.

### B. *Reducibility of Rightness Reasons to Independent Goal Reasons*

Below are several illustrative claims that a reductionist might make when confronted with cases in which the judge explicitly set forth only a rightness reason. In responding to each example, the reductionist might assert that a goal reason is available either in the particular case or generally in such cases.[183]

(1) "Behind justified reliance (concededly a rightness reason) I see the facilitation of economic exchange."

(2) "Behind punitive desert (concededly a rightness reason) I see the deterrence of socially undesirable conduct."

(3) "Behind due care (concededly a rightness reason if confined to basic respect for persons and property) I see community safety for persons and property."

[183] Although a goal reason might be unavailable in a particular case, it does not necessarily follow that goal reasons are generally unavailable for cases of the same general sort.

(4) "Behind doing equity as between the parties (concededly a rightness reason) I see the prevention of disorderly self-help."

In the foregoing examples, the reductionist does not claim that the rightness reason derives whatever force it has from the decision's precedential effects of bringing about more rightness. Rather, he claims that whatever force the rightness reason has derives from an implicit yet independent goal reason available in that very case or generally available in such cases. This type of reductionist views the implicit goal reason not as a parasitic reason concerned with bringing about more rightness (through stare decisis), but as an independent goal reason purportedly securing values wholly apart from rightness—values such as increased productivity, deterrence of dangerous actions, protection of persons and property against inadvertent hazards, and fostering peaceful settlement of disputes.

Two considerations cast doubt on this view. First, it seems odd, or at least incongruous, that different pairs of reasons in which such different values figure could be reducible, one to another. How can "protection of justified reliance" be reduced to "facilitation of economic exchange"? How can "punitive desert" be reduced to "deterrence of socially undesirable conduct"? How can "respect for persons and property" be reduced to "general safety," or "equity" to "prevention of disorderly self-help"? Yet the reducibility thesis calls for the assimilation of such disparate values, and for the anomalous equation of reasons that turn on such disparate concerns. Each of the rightness reasons listed above apparently incorporates all of the required elements of a rightness reason. And, at least to judges, the values that figure in these reasons apparently qualify as intrinsic values, desirable for their own sake and not necessarily instrumental to the realization of other values allegedly "behind" them. Why then should these reasons not be considered autonomous?

Furthermore, judges commonly give rightness reasons as the primary grounds for their decisions. Often they do not even refer to goal reasons.[184] These judges apparently intend that their opinions be taken at face value, and they are usually so taken. In all such cases, the reductionist must argue that the rightness reason really derives its force from some implicit goal reason (available in the particular case, or generally). Yet even where a judge has found and explicitly referred to such an "underlying" goal reason,

[184] *See* illustrative cases cited in note 172 *supra*.

I know of no instance where he has acknowledged that it provides the sole support for the decision. Can we dismiss widespread and long-standing justificatory practices, common both inside and outside the law, as fragmentary and essentially unsophisticated? The reductionist seems to take this view.

C. *Differences Again*

The arguments I have considered here for the reducibility thesis are at best inconclusive. Whether rightness reasons are reducible to goal reasons is a complex question to which we do not have an answer. But it is undeniable that rightness reasons figure prominently in judicial justification and differ in substantial ways from goal reasons.

Nevertheless, even if the justificatory force of rightness reasons ultimately derives entirely from accompanying or implicit goal reasons, it still would not follow that judges could always dispense with constructing and evaluating any available rightness reasons, and concern themselves solely with goal reasons. For example, there might be a certain type of goal reason that only has justificatory force if it incorporates or is accompanied by a rightness reason. If so, the rightness reason would be an essential component or concomitant of the goal reason, and if any internal element of the rightness reason itself were absent or seriously deficient, the goal reason would accordingly lack force as well. Thus, if rightness reasons necessarily figure in at least some goal reasons, judges must understand the character of rightness reasons in order to construct and evaluate those goal reasons.

## VIII

## Significance of the Duality of Substantive Reasons

I have differentiated two basic types of substantive reasons and noted the possible importance of some specific differences between them. I now take up the general significance of this duality.

In the many cases that require resort to substantive reasons—*e.g.*, cases of first impression and cases that overrule precedent—judges must recognize and remain aware of this duality. The essential elements of good goal reasons and good rightness reasons are not identical. Moreover, the facts and decisional context of a case might generate one type of reason but not the other. The duality directs the attention of judges (and readers of opinions) to quite different facets of each case—those potentially relevant to the construction and evaluation of goal reasons (future-regarding aspects), and those potentially relevant to the construction and evaluation of rightness reasons (usually, past-regarding aspects). Judges who focus separately on these different justificatory source-beds are more likely to discover all available reasons, to incorporate all the necessary elements in their construction (while excluding all extraneous elements), and to evaluate correctly the strengths and weaknesses of each reason.

I have already noted that precedents are not self-defining and self-applying.[185] To apply a precedent rationally, judges must advert to the substantive reasons behind it. Sometimes the precedent fails to state these reasons, or fails to state them clearly. Or it might be possible to formulate new and better reasons for the precedent. If judges remain conscious of the duality of substantive reasons and choose the appropriate model, they are likely to be more faithful in reconstructing and interpreting reasons that are only implicit or poorly expressed. Similarly, they should do a better job of constructing reasons from scratch.

Furthermore, the rationales for following precedent are themselves susceptible to analysis in terms of rightness norms and goals.[186] The doctrine of stare decisis varies in force and effect depending on which type of rationale supports it most strongly in a given case.

Courts regularly reevaluate precedents in deciding whether to follow, modify, or overrule them. Yet courts cannot undertake this task without applying evaluative standards. These standards fall into two categories; precedents should be judged not only by relevant goal standards but by rightness standards as well. In addition, judges should recognize that time can take different tolls on the two types of reasons. The continued force of a good goal reason depends, for example, on the continued validity of particular hypotheses of social cause and effect—hypotheses that technological developments can undermine. The force of rightness reasons is also subject to decline. For example, growing sociomoral enlightenment may lead to the alteration or abandonment of the norm on which a rightness reason depends.

Good substantive reasons also have factual requirements that vary according to type. As a result, there may be areas of the law in which one type of reason should figure more prominently

---

[185] *See* Part III *supra*.

[186] I will consider this topic in forthcoming work.

than the other. For example, a "due care" rightness reason can support a course of decision only if certain "adjudicative" facts are regularly determinable. Yet many, perhaps most, high-speed accident cases suffer from a paucity of evidence relevant to the issue of due care, and consequently degenerate into "negligence lotteries."[187] This at least weakens the general case for resolving high-speed accident cases on due-care rightness grounds. Similarly, judges sometimes seek to base their decisions in water-law cases on goal reasons such as "development of regional productivity," yet frequently know too little about relevant causality to justify such reasoning.[188] Again, the introduction of sealed containers, preventing consumers from inspecting the contents, has largely undermined the factual basis for the familiar rightness principle of caveat emptor. Thus, a general failure to satisfy the factual requirements of a reason type argues against basing a course of decision on reasons of that type. Since judges in subsequent cases will be unable to determine reliably whether the resulting doctrine is applicable, the values to be served by that doctrine cannot be realized with regularity.

In deciding whether to alter the common law, judges sometimes find it relevant, in the name of uniformity, to consider trends across the country. The duality of substantive reasons provides a useful framework for identifying and interpreting trends. A judge might note that a particular rightness norm has gained or lost acceptance, or that courts have started to recognize and implement a particular goal, or that an increasing number of courts have concluded that a long-standing goal has been sufficiently realized.

The duality is also relevant when judges consider whether they should defer to the legislature.[189] For example, institutional reasons argue more strongly for deference to the legislature when a judge proposes to overrule a precedent for goal reasons alone. Rightness reasons, on the other hand, tend not to be politically controversial and so call less strongly for adoption solely by democratic bodies. In addition, rightness reasons rarely require factual inquiries beyond the fact-finding machinery of the courts. In most cases, courts also have sufficient powers to implement the values that typically figure in rightness reasons. Moreover, when judges

---

[187] *See generally* Franklin, *Replacing the Negligence Lottery: Compensation and Selective Reimbursement*, 53 Va. L. Rev. 774 (1967).

[188] *See, e.g.*, Irwin v. Phillips, 5 Cal. 140 (1855).

[189] I will deal in forthcoming work with this topic as well.

decide cases of first impression on the basis of genuine (as opposed to *merely* conventional) rightness reasons, litigants relying on old law can claim unfair surprise with far less credibility, at least when the rightness norms involved are widely shared in society.

The duality might even enhance the faith of some judges in the power of reason. Secure that they can resort to at least two legitimate wellsprings of reason, not just one, judges might refrain from watering down their opinions and generalizing their reasons simply to gain the votes of colleagues. Instead, more judges might write dissents or concurring opinions, which in the long run might well make for a better reasoned body of law.

Furthermore, a judge who recognizes the duality of substantive reasons will be a more effective advocate of his views. He will be better equipped not only to formulate reasons of his own, but also to predict what types of reasons his colleagues on the bench will marshall to support *their* positions in a case; for among the many judges who are willing to resort to substantive reasons, some may be primarily rightness-minded, some primarily goal-minded, and some a mixture of the two.[190] A judge who can anticipate the differing priorities and opposing arguments of his brethren stands in a better position to begin formulating counterarguments to win them over to his side. (This predictive capability, of course, will also aid trial and appellate advocates.)

Indeed, the duality provides a framework for analyzing the entire judicial philosophy of an individual judge. To develop this analysis we would ask not only whether the judge favored goal reasons, rightness reasons, or a combination of the two, but also: Which goals and rightness concepts figure in the judge's reasoning, which are most prominent, and how are they related?[191] (Judges

[190] For example, a preliminary analysis of the opinions written by Judge MacKinnon of the United States Court of Appeals for the District of Columbia Circuit suggests that he is predominantly a "rightness-minded" judge. *See, e.g,* Hooks v. Southeast Constr. Corp. , 538 F.2d 431 (D.C. Cir. 1976) (in determining scope of subcontractor's duty to insure and indemnify, emphasizes contract language and nature of parties' relationship, while ignoring possible goal question of appropriate allocation of risk); Berger v. Board of Psychologist Examiners, 521 F.2d 1056 (D.C. Cir. 1975) (focuses upon fairness in particular case; downplays social goals of reducing fraud and maintaining high professional standards); Kline v. 1500 Mass. Ave. Apt. Corp., 439 F.2d 477, 488 (D.C. Cir. 1970) (dissenting opinion) (attacks majority's risk-allocation goal reason by emphasizing rightness reason that decision imposes crushing economic burden on defendant).

[191] To complete the analysis, we would also have to study the judge's use of institutional reasons and the extent to which he relies on authority reasons. This would provide far more insight into a judge's attitude and philosophy than the mere application of such labels as "activist" or "passivist."

themselves might subject their opinions to this analysis to achieve a heightened self-awareness.) Having analyzed the philosophy of a particular judge, we might consider further whether this philosophy constitutes a recognizable type, and whether this type correlates with factors in the personal backgrounds of judges who espouse it. A great judge must be a giver of good reasons and a good critic of reasons. The duality helps to explain what these complex attributes entail.

Finally, the duality represents not just an accidental but, in my view, an essential feature of the ideal conception of common law. Thus, the theory of common-law justification I offer here serves not only as a descriptive account, but also as a justification of the common law itself. Both goal reasons and rightness reasons must thrive in a healthy and resourceful system of common law.

## Conclusion

I have set forth in this Article—tentatively and schematically—the core of a general theory of common-law justification. I have addressed myself to judges, and have focused on those reasons that have primacy in the common law—reasons of substance. But the potential ramifications of my theory extend beyond common-law justification, and, in some respects, beyond the law itself.[192] By way of conclusion, I will suggest some of the broader jurisprudential and theoretical implications.

(1) Judicial resort to substantive reasons may keep the common law more or less continuous with the morality of a society. Most substantive reasons have counterparts in daily life. That these show up in common-law justification should not be surprising. By attending to substantive reasons in the law one can discern specific and fundamental ways in which the law accommodates moral considerations (without necessarily becoming moralistic). One can thus avoid the temptation to *identify* law with morality in order to account for the bearing of morality on law.

(2) It is often said that the reasoning of judges and lawyers is esoteric or "artificial"—the province of an elite legal priesthood. But to the extent that substantive reasons spring from justificatory practices in daily life, they show themselves to be neither artificial nor the exclusive province of those trained in the law.

---

[192] The theory might even have certain educational implications. Why not require a fall-semester, first-year course entitled "Reasons"? (Holmes stressed that students should strive to "get to the bottom of their subject." What better way?)

(3) Most ideas of "justice" and "injustice" found in common-law cases appear in the work clothes of rightness reasons. By studying these reasons, we should achieve a fuller understanding of justice as a distinct standard for evaluating decisions. (Note, however, that not all rightness reasons embody concepts of justice or injustice.)

(4) Rightness reasons do not fit forward-looking instrumentalist theories of law, and thus do not sit well with most "social engineers." Such theories ignore the justificatory significance of the past, except insofar as it is relevant to shaping the future through goal subservience. A sufficiently detailed account of rightness reasons might therefore serve as a corrective to the myopias of crude utilitarianism as well. Bentham was wrong to think that "thank you" means "more, please."

(5) A faithful reconstruction of the justificatory practices of judges must, in large part, map the workings of the so-called "legal mind." How judges and lawyers think when they seek to justify common-law decisions is only one facet of the "legal mind," but it is an important one.

(6) By studying substantive reasons, and particularly goal reasons, we can see precisely where and how economics, sociology, and other "policy sciences" bear on the common law. Of course, contrary to what some practitioners of these sciences believe, not all reasons are "policy" reasons, and courts can make new law without "making public policy."

(7) If my theory of substantive reasons is basically right, the very integrity, tone, and spirit of a legal order intimately depend on the way in which judges view and use rightness reasons. A legal system without decisions based on rightness reasons is imaginable but, in my view, abhorrent.

(8) Although the law is only one field within which justificatory practices occur, it is a field of distinctive significance. Judges take pride in their ability to give good reasons and correctly view reason-giving as a basic judicial function. In addition, legal records and case reports provide unusually good sources for analyzing justificatory processes. Thus, students of justification will find substantive reasons articulated in common-law cases an extraordinarily rich quarry from which to extract materials for the construction of more general theories.

(9) Common-law reasons of substance should also interest value theorists, for, among other things, such reasons invoke a wide range of evaluative notions, including some that to date have

received only scant attention. Moreover, value theorists may well conclude from their study of substantive reasons that the categories of "justice" and "utility" are not really exhaustive or sufficiently refined.

(10) The theory should also cast light on our very concept of a "reason for deciding," as distinguished from a "reason for believing." Certainly we can no longer say that having a reason for deciding is merely a matter of knowing some facts, or of bringing values into play. Furthermore, there might be something distinctive about reasons for deciding as a separate subclass of reasons for acting.[193]

My ambitions, then, for the theory I offer are considerable. And the theory itself is ambitious. Bits and pieces of it may well fall at the hands of thoughtful scholars. Indeed, fundamentals of the theory might not survive.[194] But even so, the task will have been worthy of the effort. A general theory of common-law justification is long overdue. Any failure of mine can hardly signify that a theory of this nature lies beyond us.

---

[193] Note that a particular reason may have significance on three different levels, or from three separate points of view: (1) as a motive for an actor on the front line of human interaction; (2) as a reason for a judge's decision of a case; and (3) as a standard for evaluating the action taken in situations (1) and (2).

[194] Criticism of my theory of substantive reasons is, of course, invited. Such criticism might be addressed to at least the following issues:

(1) With respect to the two types of substantive reasons: (a) Does the theory account for and appropriately characterize each type's essential elements? (b) Are any of the listed elements unnecessary or readily collapsible into others? (c) Is the manner of their combination appropriately described? (d) How appropriate is it to conceptualize the evaluation of substantive reasons and their individual elements in terms of bi-polar continua? (e) Does the theory account for all the major forms of criticisms or weaknesses to which substantive reasons are subject?

(2) Are there major types of substantive reasons in the common law that the theory omits?

(3) Are institutional reasons appropriately accounted for?

(4) How genuine are the claimed differences between goal reasons and rightness reasons? Are there other differences?

(5) Are there major forms of the reducibility thesis other than the two considered here? Are there other responses to the thesis?

(6) Does the theory overstate the significance of the duality of substantive reasons? Does this duality have other forms of significance?

# [5]

# Good Faith in General Contract Law – A Philosophical Approach

*Men must be able to assume that those with whom they deal in the general intercourse of society will act in good faith.*[1]

## I. Introduction

THAT persons should behave in good faith is a minimal standard rather than a high ideal; yet, judging from the facts of litigated cases, contractual bad faith, in its many and varied forms, is a continuing problem. The law's solutions to the problem will be the concern of this Article. The topic is timely, for there is growing interest in devising legal standards of contractual morality—interest generated in part by enactment of the Uniform Commercial Code's express obligations of good faith.[2]

The doctrine of good faith purchase will not be considered;[3] rather,

---

*Associate Professor of Law, University of Oregon. B.S., 1955, University of Oregon; LL.B., 1959, Harvard University. The author wishes to record his substantial gratitude to Mr. Richard A. Carsel, third-year student at the University of Oregon School of Law, for research aid, and to Miss Kristen Nelson for secretarial assistance. The author also wishes to thank Professor Richard E. Speidel of the University of Virginia School of Law, who made helpful comments on an early version of this Article.

[1] R. Pound, An Introduction to the Philosophy of Law 188 (1922). Some judges have noted that businessmen generally do assume good faith. "Business men habitually . . . trust to luck or the good faith of the opposite party . . . ." Phoenix Ins. Co. v. DeMonchy, 141 L.T.R. (n.s.) 439, 445 (H.L. 1929) (Lord Atkin). It seems all the more probable that most nonbusinessmen similarly trust to luck or good faith.

[2] In particular, § 1-203, which provides: "Every contract or duty within this Act imposes a duty of good faith in its performance or enforcement." Uniform Commercial Code § 1-203 [hereinafter cited as UCC]. In addition, the Code utilizes good faith terminology in 60 of its 400 sections. Thirteen of these sections appear in article 2 on sales: §§ 2-305(2), 2-306(1), 2-311(1), 2-323(2)(b), 2-328(4), 2-402(2), 2-403(1), 2-506(2), 2-603(3), 2-615(a), 2-702(3), 2-706(1), (5), 2-712(1). The Code has now been enacted in all states but Louisiana.

[3] A classic study is Gilmore, *The Commercial Doctrine of Good Faith Purchase*,

this Article will deal with other requirements of good faith recognized in contract case law and in Code provisions on sales, a much neglected area of study.[4] The focus will be on three questions. First, what meaning have the courts and the Code draftsmen given to the phrase "good faith"? It will be argued that good faith, as used in the case law, is best understood as an "excluder" [5]—it is a phrase which has no general meaning or meanings of its own, but which serves to exclude many heterogeneous forms of bad faith. It will also be suggested that if the Code draftsmen had perceived this, they would not have given the term the general, invariant meaning: "honesty in fact in the conduct or transaction concerned." [6]

The second question is: In what circumstances do case law and the Code provisions on sales impose obligations of good faith? Although it has not been possible to do a comprehensive survey of the cases,[7] it

---

63 YALE L.J. 1057-1122 (1954). On good faith purchase of negotiable instruments under the Code, see Littlefield, *Good Faith Purchase of Consumer Paper: The Failure of the Subjective Test*, 39 SO. CALIF. L. REV. 48 (1966).

4 Only three general studies on these other requirements have been discovered. Farnsworth, *Good Faith Performance and Commercial Reasonableness Under the Uniform Commercial Code*, 30 U. CHI. L. REV. 666 (1963); Kessler & Fine, *Culpa in Contrahendo, Bargaining in Good Faith, and Freedom of Contract: A Comparative Study*, 77 HARV. L. REV. 401 (1964); Powell, *Good Faith in Contracts*, 9 CURRENT LEGAL PROBLEMS 16 (1956). As the latter two articles make clear, there are numerous studies of contractual good faith in other legal systems which have recognized legal obligations of contractual good faith more fully than Anglo-American legal systems have.

5 For a discussion of excluders generally, see Hall, *Excluders*, 20 ANALYSIS 1 (1959).

6 UCC § 1-201(19).

7 First of all, in the standard treatises and research tools, relevant good faith pigeonholes are sparse. It has, therefore, been necessary to resort to some hit-or-miss techniques. The cases expressly dealing with good faith which appear in three leading contracts casebooks were sorted out and shepardized. The most useful of these sources was JONES, FARNSWORTH & YOUNG, CASES AND MATERIALS ON CONTRACTS (1965). Another valuable source of cases was the late Professor Patterson's brief study in 1955 N.Y. LAW REVISION COMM'N REP. 310-315. Then there were articles and notes which dealt, in part, with good faith as it figured in the formulation of the particular legal doctrines under study. *E.g.*, Gellhorn, *Limitations on Contract Termination Rights—Franchise Cancellations*, 1967 DUKE L.J. 465, 495-505; Havighurst & Berman, *Requirement and Output Contracts*, 27 ILL. L. REV. 1 (1932).

Second, even if the usual research tools had been more helpful, it would not have been possible to do a comprehensive study without staying at the job for several years. For, as this Article shows, good faith is at least potentially relevant in a substantial percentage of the total accumulated contract cases to date. Though the study presented here is merely an Article, the following comment applies *mutatis mutandis:*

> The time has long since passed when it was possible for any treatise which deals with a broad field of law to pretend that it is exhaustive. A decorative

can be seen from the ones reviewed here that the duties judges have imposed in the name of contractual good faith are more varied and numerous than anyone has yet recognized in print. On the other hand, it will be seen that the Code's explicit requirements of good faith in sales transactions are less extensive than some scholars would have us believe.[8] It will also be suggested that extra-Code law on good faith—via section 1-103, which states that "general principles" are to supplement the Code's specific provisions[9]—will prove a more fertile source of Code requirements of good faith than will the Code sections which use these very words.[10]

The theories on which courts have afforded relief against contractual bad faith include contract, tort and quasi-contract. And the forms of such relief are highly varied, ranging from denial of any recovery to the award of punitive damages. Our final question is: What adjustments might be made in these theories and forms to provide more adequate relief? Several modest proposals will be set forth, not as final solutions, but as suggestions worthy of further consideration. Among other things, it will be argued that courts should resort to tort law more often than they have to combat bad faith.

Before taking up the first question, it is appropriate to explain in some detail why the imposition and refinement of legal standards of good faith are of potentially great significance in contractual contexts, commercial and noncommercial. First of all, in these contexts good faith has pervasive and distinctive relevance. It is natural for two

---

> feature of the treatises of a half century ago was the collections of cases from all the jurisdictions from Alabama to Wyoming. No such collections will be found here.

1 G. Gilmore, Security Interests in Personal Property (1965).

8 In particular, the requirements appear less extensive than indicated in Mentschikoff, *Highlights of the Uniform Commercial Code*, 27 Mod. L. Rev. 167, 168-70 (1964), and in Mooney, *Old Kontract Principles and Karl's New Kode: An Essay on the Jurisprudence of our New Commercial Law*, 11 Vill. L. Rev. 213, 247-53 (1966).

9 UCC § 1-103 provides:

> Unless displaced by the particular provisions of this Act, the principles of law and equity, including the law merchant and the law relative to capacity to contract, principal and agent, estoppel, fraud, misrepresentation, duress, coercion, mistake, bankruptcy, or other validating or invalidating cause shall supplement its provisions.

As the extra-Code case law on good faith grows, it can be fed into the Code via this section. What the section invites is not limited to law which exists as of the date of particular enactments of the Code.

10 For a perceptive account of the various ways in which "general principles" can be relevant under the Code, see Young, Book Review, 66 Colum. L. Rev. 1571 (1966).

parties to assume that each will act in good faith toward the other throughout the course of their contractual dealings.[11] Moreover, morals obligate them to act this way.[12] Yet, in one sense their interests will remain essentially antagonistic, for each will be expecting to get something from the other on advantageous terms. And, in a given case, misunderstandings may arise, unforeseen events occur, expected gains disappear or dislikes develop which may motivate one party to act in bad faith. If, however, such a party is legally as well as morally obligated to act in good faith, he will be significantly less likely to break faith.

Good faith is not only peculiarly and pervasively relevant in contractual matters, it is also part of a family of general legal doctrines, including implied promise, custom and usage, fraud, negligence and estoppel, which perform significant functions in this field.[13] These doctrines supplement, limit and qualify specific legal rules[14] and contract terms, and some of them also serve as substantive bases of liability independent of contract. The functions they perform further the most fundamental policy objectives of any legal system—justice, and justice according to law. By invoking good faith, implying a promise or working an estoppel it may be possible for a judge to do justice *and* do it according to law. Without legal resources of this general nature he might, in a particular case, be unable to do justice at all, or he might be able to do it only at the cost of fictionalizing existing legal concepts and rules, thereby snarling up the law for future cases. In begetting snarl, fiction may introduce inequity, unclarity or unpredictability.[15]

---

11 See note 1 *supra*. It is probable that this assumption is most often tacit rather than either implicit or explicit. On the role of tacit assumptions in contractual contexts, see L. Fuller & R. Braucher, Basic Contract Law 554-59 (1964).

12 At least, there is a general moral obligation not to act in bad faith toward those with whom one deals. This is not, of course, to say that moral good faith and legal good faith are identical. Moral good faith is, in one important respect, narrower. See pp. 204-06 *infra*.

13 *See generally* Kessler & Fine, *supra* note 4.

14 One important relationship of good faith to specific legal rules was aptly formulated as follows: "[Good faith is an] honest intention to abstain from taking any unconscientious advantage of another, even through the forms and technicalities of law . . . ." Warfield Natural Gas Co. v. Allen, 248 Ky. 646, 655, 59 S.W.2d 534, 538 (1933).

15 All of which led Bentham to vent his critical wrath in inimitable invective: "Fiction of use to justice? Exactly as swindling is to trade . . . . The most pertinacious and basest sort of lying . . . . It affords presumptive and conclusive evidence of moral turpitude . . . ." *Quoted in* L. Fuller, Legal Fictions 3 (1967).

In addition, fiction can divert analytical focus[16] or even cast aspersions on an innocent party.[17]

It should be emphasized that in the foregoing family of general doctrines, good faith has its own distinctive potential. For example, a judge may resort to it as an independent theory of liability for misconduct which is neither fraudulent nor negligent.[18] He may rely on it to enforce the unspecified "inner logic" of a deal when custom and usage are silent and when the true basis for implying a promise is that good faith requires as much.[19] He can also invoke it to help prevent the abuse of powers conferred by contract when the elements of estoppel are absent.[20] Thus good faith is both a pervasively relevant and an independently significant doctrine in the fields of contracts and sales.

## II. Nature of Acting in Good Faith

If the potential of the good faith requirement is to be realized in practice, judges and legislators must give meaning to the phrase and must impose specific duties of good faith. What good faith means in contract case law and in the Code provisions on sales will be considered in this section; when it is required, will be considered in the next.

### *A. Meaning of Good Faith in Contract Case Law*

What is the best way to determine a judge's meaning when he uses the phrase "good faith"? In the case law taken as a whole, does the term have a single general meaning of its own, or perhaps several such meanings?[21] (The answers to these questions are closely linked.) Sometimes what a judge means by good faith will be instantly obvious, but

16 See the discussion in Patterson, *An Apology for Consideration*, 58 Colum. L. Rev. 929, 936-38 (1958).

17 Anthony P. Miller, Inc. v. Wilmington Housing Authority, 179 F. Supp. 199, 204 (D. Del. 1959).

18 Hoffman v. Red Owl Stores, Inc., 26 Wis. 2d 683, 133 N.W.2d 267 (1965).

19 *E.g.*, Kirke La Shelle Co. v. Paul Armstrong Co., 263 N.Y. 79, 188 N.E. 163 (1933). It is not uncommonly recognized that good faith is often behind a finding of an implied promise. "[I]ts significance . . . [is] in implying terms in the agreement . . . ." Farnsworth, *supra* note 4, at 670.

20 *E.g.*, Chrysler Corp. v. Quimby, 51 Del. 264, 283-84, 144 A.2d 123, 134 (1958).

21 Apparently judges and others frequently assume that good faith has one general meaning of its own. *E.g.*, Peden Iron & Steel Co. v. Jenkins, 203 S.W. 180, 188 (Tex. Civ. App. 1918). When this does not turn out to be true it is natural to think that the phrase must, therefore, be an ambiguous one—one which has two or more general meanings of its own. *See* Farnsworth, *supra* note 4.

frequently it will not be. When not, it may be that he is using the phrase loosely. But even if he is using it with care, there may still be unclarity. He might indicate only that, in a given context, parties are to act in good faith[22] or that a party did or did not act in good faith,[23] without elaborating at all. Or he might elaborate without communicating in any specific way—for example, by laying down some very general definition of good faith, such as acting "honestly" [24] or "being faithful to one's duty or obligation." [25] The analyst of such an opinion is likely to inquire: What is the meaning of good faith itself? He seems to assume that the phrase has some general meaning or meanings, one of which the judge presumably intends.

One of the principal theses of this Article is that in cases of doubt, a lawyer will determine more accurately what the judge means by using the phrase "good faith" if he does not ask what good faith itself means,[26] but rather asks: What, in the actual or hypothetical situation, does the judge intend to rule out by his use of this phrase? Once the relevant form of bad faith is thus identified,[27] the lawyer can, if he wishes, assign a specific meaning to good faith by formulating an "opposite" [28] for the species of bad faith being ruled out.[29] For example, a judge may say: "A public authority must act in good faith in letting bids." And from the facts or the language of the opinion it may appear that the judge is, in effect, saying: "The defendant acted in bad faith because he let bids only as a pretense to conceal his purpose to award the contract to a favored bidder." It can then be said that "acting in good faith" here

---

22 *E.g.*, Frigaliment Importing Co. v. B.N.S. Int'l Sales Corp., 190 F. Supp. 116, 117 (S.D.N.Y. 1960).

23 *E.g.*, Dickey v. Philadelphia Minit-Man Corp., 377 Pa. 549, 556, 105 A.2d 580, 583 (1954).

24 Peden Iron & Steel Co. v. Jenkins, 203 S.W. 180, 188 (Tex. Civ. App. 1918).

25 Hilker v. Western Auto Ins. Co., 204 Wis. 1, 235 N.W. 413, 414 (1931).

26 This also is the approach of nearly all the commentators. *E.g.*, Farnsworth, *supra* note 4.

27 Throughout this Article the phrase "form of bad faith" is used. A more awkward substitute would be "form of breaking faith." For purposes of composition, the less awkward phrase inevitably wins out and is here used to cover many varieties of conduct, including some which do not involve bad motives. See 204-06 *infra*. It is recognized that some readers will resist this. For them, it would, therefore, be bettter to use the phrase "form of breaking faith," at least when referring to conduct which is not in good faith but which, nonetheless, does not involve a bad motive.

28 The word "opposite" is not being used here in any of the formal logician's technical senses of the word.

29 For purposes of communication, however, this additional step will seldom be necessary.

simply means: letting bids without a preconceived design to award the contract to a favored bidder.[30]

If good faith had a general meaning or meanings of its own—that is, if it were either univocal or ambiguous— there would seldom be occasion to derive a meaning for it from an opposite; its specific uses would almost always be readily and immediately understood. But good faith is not that kind of doctrine. In contract law, taken as a whole, good faith is an "excluder." [31] It is a phrase without general meaning (or meanings) of its own and serves to exclude a wide range of heterogeneous forms of bad faith.[32] In a particular context the phrase takes on specific meaning, but usually this is only by way of contrast with the specific form of bad faith actually or hypothetically ruled out. Aristotle was one of the first to recognize that the function of some words and phrases is not to convey general, "extractable" meanings of their own, but rather is to exclude one or more of a variety of things. He thought "voluntary" was such a word.[33] And the late Professor J. L. Austin

[30] This example is based on Heyer Prods. Co. v. United States, 140 F. Supp. 409 (Ct. Cl. 1956).

[31] In describing "excluders," Hall states: "Adjectives that have these features, i.e. (1) are attributive as opposed to predicative, (2) serve to rule out something without themselves adding anything, and (3) ambiguously rule out different things according to context, I call 'excluders.'" Hall, *Excluders*, 20 ANALYSIS 1 (1959). But it may be unwise to think of good faith as an adjective. It is true that within sentences good faith appears as if it were just another modifier like "ponderous" or "intentional," terms which themselves name, respectively, a positively definable property and a positively definable mental state. True, some have said that good faith in law is merely a state of mind. *E.g.*, Dallas Waste Mills v. Texas Cake & Linter Co., 204 S.W. 868, 869 (Tex. Civ. App. 1918). *Accord*, Honnold, *Buyer's Right of Rejection*, 97 U. PA. L. REV. 457, 475-76 (1949). *But see* Farnsworth, *supra* note 4, at 672. As this Article will show, good faith is not generally a phrase which names a particular property or state, as such. Rather, if it generally names anything, it names a whole dimension of appraisal. *Cf.* J. AUSTIN, PHILOSOPHICAL PAPERS 128 (1961). Lawyers too must fight against the bewitchment of their intelligence by means of language. That grammar and syntax can subtly mislead philosophers is well known. *See* L. WITTGENSTEIN, PHILOSOPHICAL INVESTIGATIONS 47e (1958); Ryle, *Systematically Misleading Expressions*, in LOGIC AND LANGUAGE 11 (1st ser., Flew ed. 1951).

[32] At least three different clues initially suggested the appropriateness of classifying good faith as an "excluder." (1) Judges sometimes write of lack of bad faith or absence of bad faith, as if it were the nonexistence of something else that constitutes good faith. (2) When a judge uses the phrase good faith, one is frequently unable to attach a definite meaning to it without knowing what, in context, the judge means to exclude and. (3) Even a cursory study of judicial usage reveals that the phrase is used to rule out a wide range of heterogeneous forms of conduct.

[33] 3 ARISTOTLE, NICOMACHEAN ETHICS (W. Ross transl. 1925). Hart also maintains that "the word 'voluntary' in fact serves to exclude a heterogeneous range of cases

of Oxford made much of "excluders." His discussion of the term "real" is instructive:

> That is, a definite sense attaches to the assertion that something is real, a real such-and-such, only in the light of a specific way in which it might be, or might have been, *not* real. "A real duck" differs from the simple "a duck" only in that it is used to exclude various ways of being not a real duck—but a dummy, a toy, a picture, a decoy, &c.; and moreover I don't know *just* how to take the assertion that it's a real duck unless I know *just* what, on that particular occasion, the speaker has it in mind to exclude. This, of course, is why the attempt to find a characteristic common to all things that are or could be called "real" is doomed to failure; the function of "real" is not to contribute positively to the characterization of anything, but to exclude possible ways of being *not* real—and these ways are both numerous for particular kinds of things, and liable to be quite different for things of different kinds. It is this identity of general function combined with immense diversity in specific applications which gives to the word "real" the, at first sight, baffling feature of having neither one single "meaning", nor yet ambiguity, a number of different meanings.[34]

But it is not only because good faith is an "excluder" that the case analyst will be wise to focus on what the phrase rules out, rather than on what it means. It is also because the typical judge who uses this phrase is primarily concerned with ruling out specific conduct, and only secondarily, or not at all, with formulating the positive content of a standard.

Good faith, then, takes on specific and variant meanings by way of contrast with the specific and variant forms of bad faith which judges decide to prohibit. From the cases it would be possible to compile a list of forms of bad faith, with an opposite for each listed as the corresponding specific meaning of good faith. The beginnings of such a list might look like this:

such as physical compulsion, coercion by threats, accidents, mistakes, etc., and not to designate a mental element or state . . . ." Hart, *The Ascription of Responsibility and Rights*, 49 Proceedings of the Aristotelian Soc'y 171, 180 (1949).

[34] J. Austin, Sense and Sensibilia 70-71 (Warnock ed. 1962). If good faith is an "excluder," the author of one recent study has done with the phrase just what Austin says is incorrect. Farnsworth says good faith is ambiguous and sets out to name two different general meanings: "good faith purchase" and "good faith performance." Farnsworth, *supra* note 4. His analysis prompts one to ask: What of "good faith interpretation"? "Settlement"? "Enforcement"? "Termination"? Are all of those separate meanings, too? Surely something has gone awry.

| *Form of Bad Faith Conduct* | *Meaning of Good Faith* |
|---|---|
| 1. seller concealing a defect in what he is selling[35] | fully disclosing material facts |
| 2. builder willfully failing to perform in full, though otherwise substantially performing[36] | substantially performing without knowingly deviating from specifications |
| 3. contractor openly abusing bargaining power to coerce an increase in the contract price[37] | refraining from abuse of bargaining power |
| 4. hiring a broker and then deliberately preventing him from consummating the deal[38] | acting cooperatively |
| 5. conscious lack of diligence in mitigating the other party's damages[39] | acting diligently |
| 6. arbitrarily and capriciously exercising a power to terminate a contract[40] | acting with some reason |
| 7. adopting an overreaching interpretation of contract language[41] | interpreting contract language fairly |
| 8. harassing the other party for repeated assurances of performance[42] | accepting adequate assurances |

This list could run on and on, but it is unnecessary to extend it for present purposes. As it stands, it shows how specific meanings for good

35 Stewart v. Wyoming Cattle Ranche Co., 128 U.S. 383, 388 (1888).

36 Dodge v. Kimball, 203 Mass. 364, 89 N.E. 542, 543 (1909).

37 Lingenfelder v. Wainwright Brewery Co., 103 Mo. 578, 595, 15 S.W. 844, 848 (1891) (only bad faith used).

38 Carns v. Bassick, 187 App. Div. 280, 284-85, 175 N.Y. Supp. 670, 673 (1st Dep't 1919).

39 Obrecht v. Crawford, 175 Md. 385, 395, 2 A.2d 1, 6 (1938).

40 J.R. Watkins Co. v. Rich, 254 Mich. 82, 85, 235 N.W. 845, 846 (1931).

41 Sylvan Crest Sand & Gravel Co. v. United States, 150 F.2d 642, 643-44 (1945).

42 James B. Berry's Sons v. Monark Gasoline & Oil Co., 32 F.2d 74 (1929). (Although the court does not talk of good or bad faith, see UCC § 2-609, Comment 4.)

faith can be derived and shows that this phrase rules out radically heterogeneous forms of bad faith.[43]

Given the specific meanings of good faith in the foregoing right-hand column, it may seem all the more natural to suppose, contrary to our "excluder" analysis, that there must be some single word or concise phrase which faithfully unifies all such specific meanings into one general meaning of the term.[44] What about "honesty"? Is not acting in good faith equivalent to acting honestly? Numerous judges appear to have thought so, but this is wrong unless, of course, the definition of honesty is stretched beyond recognition. Honesty only rules out dishonesty in its various forms.[45] But good faith, as used by many judges, excludes numerous forms of contractual bad faith besides dishonesty. For one thing, dishonesty is necessarily immoral, but in the eyes of many judges contractual bad faith is not necessarily immoral at all. A party may, for example, abuse his bargaining power, undercut the other party's efforts to perform, or act capriciously without having the "guilty mind" that would make his actions immoral–indeed, a party might even think this conduct is in the other party's own best interest. And despite this purity of mind, many judges could be counted on to say that such conduct conflicts with requirements of contractual good faith. As one judge stated, "Good faith in law . . . is not to be measured always by a man's own standard of right, but by that which it has adopted and prescribed as a standard for the observance of all men in their dealings with each other." [46]

[43] It should be noted that the distinction between "general positive meaning" and "excluder" is not the same as the distinction between affirmative and negative. Good faith may exclude not only affirmative action as such, it may also exclude refraining from affirmative action. That is, it may require affirmative action as well as forbearance. Duties of disclosure and of diligence are examples.

[44] Philosophers, legal and nonlegal, have not uncommonly erred in seeking such unity when it was not to be found. *See generally* Summers, *The New Analytical Jurists*, 41 N.Y.U.L. Rev. 861, 882-85 (1966). Judges seem to have fallen into the error of assuming that the instances to which the same term (*e.g.*, good faith) is applied must have some quality (*e.g.*, honesty) in common. Some judges have even spoken of good faith as a quality, as if it inhered in all conduct in good faith in the way that the quality of redness inheres in all things red (if it does). *See, e.g.*, Krone v. Snapout Forms Co., 360 Mo. 821, 827, 230 S.W.2d 865, 869 (1950).

[45] It might be argued that honesty not only rules out dishonesty, but also all that is not honest. But this is a mistake. Otherwise, honest and not honest must encompass everything. It would be very odd to say that a requirement of honesty rules out such conduct as abusing one's bargaining power. Rather, in such instances it is better to say that the issue of honesty versus dishonesty simply does not arise.

[46] First Nat. Bank v. F.C. Trebein Co., 59 Ohio St. 316, 324-25, 52 N.E. 834, 837

Even if it were conceded that conduct must be subjectively immoral before it can constitute bad faith, it still would not follow that dishonesty is the only form of contractual bad faith. Thus when a man openly and straightforwardly gives another a "raw deal," he does not necessarily act dishonestly. That is, he does not undertake to mislead or deceive.[47] Consider, for example, the conduct of a buyer who openly seizes upon trivial defects to justify his rejection of goods under a rule requiring perfect tender,[48] admitting all along that he is rejecting the

(1898). It must be conceded that some judges use the phrase good faith restrictively to rule out only immoral action. It seems that this usage comports with usage in moral discourse. But for the law's purposes it is often necessary, as many judges have done in the case of good faith, to depart from lay usage. The intentional torts are analogous. It will not do, for example, for a party to defend against a claim for damages for battery by saying that he meant no harm, and that he socked the plaintiff because he honestly believed this would, on balance, do the plaintiff more good than harm. Yet, in a sense, the defendant did not act immorally—at least he had no evil intent. As one commentator has put it, "It is now more or less generally recognized that the 'fault' upon which [tort] liability may rest is social fault, which may but does not necessarily coincide with personal immorality." W. PROSSER, TORTS 17 (3d ed. 1964). The strong tendency of some judges and lawyers to think of contractual bad faith as necessarily immoral is easy to explain: (1) this is its connotation in moral discourse, and the pull of ordinary language is always powerful, even in legal contexts, and (2) in the one legal context in which the phrase bad faith is used to the knowledge of almost all judges and lawyers, namely the purchase setting, it is commonly applied to a purchaser acquiring with actual notice of third party rights—a situation where the purchaser is trying to get away with something and thus is acting immorally.

47 It is not suggested that "undertaking to mislead or deceive" is a comprehensive explication of acting dishonestly. But this account does serve to differentiate acting dishonestly from many other forms of acting in bad faith, and, for present purposes, this is the only relevant realm of contrast. Nor is it suggested that everyone in fact uses "acting dishonestly" synonymously with "undertaking to mislead or deceive." But it is interesting to note that *Webster's Third New International Dictionary*, which in 1961 purported to be *au courant*, listed numerous other accounts of dishonest as obsolete, with "misleading, lying, cheating, untruthfulness, defrauding" then coming to the fore instead. By 1966, the *New Random House Dictionary of the English Langauge* did not even list other accounts of dishonest. Its story goes like this: "not honest; disposed to lie, cheat or steal; not worthy of trust or belief; a dishonest person . . . . proceeding from or exhibiting lack of honesty; fraudulent." It is not suggested that judges always look to lay usage to decide law cases. Often they do not and should not, even when there is a relevant lay use of the term or phrase. But often they do, too. And it is believed that with moral notions such as dishonesty, both the tendency to look to lay usage, and the pull of lay usage, are strong. One addendum: "Acting dishonestly" is not a "success" phrase. Thus, one can act dishonestly without succeeding at deceiving another. Hence the use of "undertaking" in the foregoing formulation. It is not suggested that this is exactly the right word, but it seems the best available.

48 Pre-Code law on the sale of goods generally required perfect tender. *See, e.g.*,

goods because the price has gone down and he wishes to buy more cheaply elsewhere. Such conduct is not dishonest. But it may well be thought immoral, and it is certainly commercial bad faith. In truth, good faith cannot be defined in terms of honesty. As numerous judges use the phrase, it excludes many forms of bad faith which a requirement of honesty alone does not.[49]

It is submitted that any but the most vacuous general definition of good faith will similarly fail to cover all the many and varied specific meanings that it is possible to assign to the phrase in light of the many and varied forms of bad faith recognized in the cases. Of course, a particular judge might declare that for him good faith does have a general, invariant meaning which he always intends when he uses the phrase. But if such a judge should have to pass on very many of the different forms of bad faith, it is most unlikely that he could stand by his definition for long.

To summarize, general definitions of good faith either spiral into the Charybdis of vacuous generality or collide with the Scylla of restrictive specificity. Moreover, the analyst who puts general definitions aside and tries to focus on the form of bad faith which a given judge intends to exclude by his use of the term is likely to get closer to that judge's meaning, for good faith functions as an "excluder," and judges are more interested in what they are proscribing than in characterizing what is generally allowed.

No effort has been made here to identify the criteria which judges ought to use in deciding whether particular conduct is in bad faith, although enough has been said to show that these criteria must vary from context to context. Nor has there been any attempt to catalog all the varieties of contractual bad faith, were this possible.[50] Instead, the aim has been to show that good faith is best conceptualized as an excluder, and that the lawyer should, therefore, focus on what judges rule out in using this phrase. What has been said may prove of value not just to lawyers, but to judges as well, and thus may also contribute to the accumulation of a viable body of case law on good faith. A judge who appreciates the implications of the excluder analysis should, in working with precedents, refuse to adopt restrictive definitions of good

Mitsubishi Goshi Kaisha v. J. Aron & Co., 16 F.2d 185, 186 (2d Cir. 1926) ("there is no room in commercial contracts for the doctrine of substantial performance").

49 Additional forms of bad faith which are not dishonest will be identified in Part III of this Article.

50 See note 7 *supra*.

faith; rather, he should focus on the forms of bad faith ruled out in previous opinions and work from these opinions either directly or by way of analogy. Likewise, the judge who sees that good faith functions as an excluder should not waste effort formulating his own reductionist definitions. Instead, he should characterize with care the particular forms of bad faith he chooses to rule out; bad faith rather than good wears the pants in this dichotomy.

### *B. Good Faith as Conceptualized in Uniform Commercial Code Provisions on Sales*

The Code imposes express obligations of good faith on parties to sales transactions via section 1-203, which provides that "[e]very contract or duty within this Act imposes an obligation of good faith in its performance or enforcement," and via thirteen sections in article 2, which expressly require good faith in sales transactions. Section 1-201 (19) defines good faith as used in all these sections to mean, at the least, "honesty in fact in the conduct or transaction concerned." How this narrow definition came to be adopted and the respects in which it is narrow will now be considered.

We may begin with the background of section 1-201 (19). Its predecessor in the 1949 draft of the Code read:

> unless otherwise agreed, in this Act: . . . 'Good faith' means honesty in fact in the conduct or transaction concerned. Good faith includes good faith toward all prior parties and observance by a person of the reasonable commercial standards of any business or trade in which he is engaged.[51]

It is evident that the Code draftsmen were not, in 1949, thinking of good faith as an "excluder." Rather, they viewed it as a positive concept, with a general, definable meaning of its own. However, in defining the term they did not substantially restrict it, at least as it applied to businessmen, for under the definition businessmen were required to observe their own "reasonable commercial standards," a seemingly far-reaching phrase. Almost any other synonym would have had a significant limiting effect, given the numerous and diverse forms of bad faith that a full-blown obligation of good faith can exclude.[52]

---

[51] UCC § 1-201(18) (May 1949 Draft).

[52] As it was, the 1949 definition did place some limits on the requirement. For example, its reasonableness test applied only to businessmen.

It is evident, too, that the foregoing definition of good faith must have been influenced by formulations of good faith in purchase contexts,[53] and especially in contexts involving the purchase of negotiable instruments. Every ex-law student knows that a person cannot be a holder in due course of a negotiable instrument if he does not purchase it in good faith.[54] But what must he prove to establish his good faith? For decades controversy has raged over whether (1) the purchaser needs only to show that, at the time of purchase, he was in fact ignorant of third party rights in or defenses to the instrument, or (2) he must show not only his ignorance, but also that he had no reason to know of any such rights or defenses. The first standard is frequently formulated in terms of "honesty in fact" and referred to as a subjective test of good faith. The second is often formulated in terms of "reasonableness" and referred to as an objective test.[55] Instead of choosing between these, as judges have commonly done in negotiable instruments cases, the Code draftsmen, in the 1949 draft of section 1-201(19), required at least "honesty in fact" and, of businessmen, compliance also with reasonable commercial standards of their businesses. Of course, the draftsmen doubtless recognized that this definition controlled the meaning of good faith not only in sections of article 3 on holders in due course,[56] but also in section 1-203, imposing a general Code obligation of good faith, and in other specific sections of article 2 using these words. But what will suffice in the purchase context should suffice in others as well. Good faith is good faith, or so the draftsmen seem to have thought.

In September 1950, the Committee on the Proposed Commercial Code

[53] In the early drafts, Karl N. Llewellyn, the chief draftsman of the Code, had the purchase context very much at the forefront of his mind in drafting good faith definitions. *See, e.g.*, UCC § 10, Comment (1948 Draft). No doubt many other scholars of commercial law were, at this time, thinking in the same vein. For example, one author stated: "In its customary setting in problems of *bona fide* purchase, a concept such as 'good faith' is necessary, and reasonably workable." Honnold, *Buyer's Right of Rejection*, 97 U. Pa. L. Rev. 457, 475 (1949).

[54] I fear that I speak only of every law student who graduated prior to the recent onset of the so-called elective curriculum. This development can only hasten the end of courses in bills and notes. One hesitates to imagine similarly catastrophic consequences of electivism.

[55] For discussion of the "objective-subjective" controversy, *see* W. Britton, Handbook on the Law of Bills and Notes 246 (2d ed. 1961); W. Hawkland, Cases and Materials on Commercial Paper and Bank Deposits and Collections 196-200 (1967); Rightmire, *The Doctrine of Bad Faith in the Law of Negotiable Instruments*, 18 Mich. L. Rev. 355 (1920).

[56] See, in particular, UCC § 3-302(1)(c).

of the Section on Corporation, Banking and Business Law of the American Bar Association recommended that the general Code definition of good faith be

> limited either to honesty in fact or at most this plus "commercial decency" or something akin to this concept. A possible definition would be:
>
> "(18) 'Good faith' means honesty in fact in the conduct or transaction concerned and the absence of trickery, deceit or improper purpose." [57]

The Committee gave three reasons for its recommendation:

> [(1)] Although we recognize that there are some court decisions that have added to "honesty in fact" in the meaning of "good faith" the requirement to observe some commercial standards of conduct, nevertheless we believe that to the average person and the average lawyer, "good faith" signifies primarily "honesty." [(2)] Assuming, however, that within the term there should be added to "honesty" some meaning of "commercial decency" the phrase "observance of reasonable commercial standards" carries with it the implication of usages, customs or practices. If this is true there immediately arises the very difficult problem of *what* usages, customs and practices are those intended to be included in the standard. Any lawyer who has ever attempted to prove what a usage or custom is will immediately recognize how litigious such a standard could grow to be. [(3)] More serious still is the possibility that "reasonable commercial standards" could mean usage, customs or practices existing at any particular time. This could have the very bad effect of freezing customs and practices into particular molds and thereby destroy the flexibility absolutely essential to the gradual evolution of commercial practices— a result which the Code draftsmen certainly would never desire.[58]

While the Code draftsmen did not adopt the ABA's recommended definition, they did delete all but the "honesty in fact" half of their 1949 definition of good faith,[59] so that in the 1952 final Official Draft section 1-201(19) read: " 'Good faith' means honesty in fact in the

[57] Malcolm, *The Proposed Commercial Code,* 6 BUS. LAW. 113, 128 (1951).

[58] *Id.*

[59] Braucher, *The Legislative History of the Uniform Commercial Code,* 58 COLUM. L. REV. 798, 812 (1958).

conduct or transaction concerned" [60]—today's definition. At the same time, the sponsors also inserted an objective test of good faith in several other provisions of the Code.[61]

With the objective half of the generally applicable section 1-201 definition of good faith lopped off, the remaining "honesty in fact" half took on more significance. In assessing the effect of the deletion, it is useful to distinguish the following classes of cases:

(1) cases in which a purchaser, payor or the like feigns ignorance of third party rights or defenses, pretends belief in their absence or willfully refrains from investigating;

(2) cases in which a purchaser, payor or the like negligently fails to ascertain the existence of third party rights or defenses;

(3) cases other than (1) in which a party feigns ignorance of or pretends belief in facts;

(4) other forms of dishonesty such as cheating, trickery, deviousness or the like, including fraud;

(5) cases other than (2) in which a party negligently fails to ascertain the existence of facts—for example, he negligently fails to discover a breach of warranty;

(6) other forms of negligent behavior unrelated to the ascertainment of facts at the moment of purchase—for example, the negligent failure to give timely notice;

(7) forms of bad faith that do not involve dishonesty, let alone negligence—for example, openly abusing the power to break off negotiations, openly taking unfair advantage of bargaining power, openly acting capriciously or openly undercutting another's performance.

Readers familiar with negotiable instruments law will immediately recognize cases in categories (1) and (2) as the ones which the subjective-objective controversy was largely all about. The subjective test of good faith only ruled out conduct that came within category (1),

60 UCC § 1-201(19) (1952 Draft with 1953 changes) [hereinafter cited as 1952 Draft].

61 UCC §§ 2-103(1)(b), 3-302(1)(b), 3-406, 3-419(3), 7-404, 7-501(4), 8-318. But there was precedent for defining "good faith" primarily in terms of honesty. Prior uniform acts had so defined it. *See, e.g.*, Uniform Sales Act § 76(2); Uniform Warehouse Receipts Act § 58(2); Uniform Bills of Lading Act § 53(2), all drafted by Professor Samuel Williston of the Harvard Law School. It is important to note that these prior uniform acts expected much less from definitions of good faith than the Code draftsmen. Hence, but little strain could have been thrown on them.

while the objective test ruled out conduct within both (1) and (2). It would have been natural for negotiable instruments-minded lawyers working on the Code in its early stages to think that the sole effect of the two-pronged definition of good faith in section 1-201(18) of the 1949 draft was merely to rule out cases in categories (1) and (2). A few of them may have perceived that the 1949 draft would also rule out cases in categories (3) and (5), and possibly those in (4) and (6). However, it seems likely that cases in category (7), forming, as we shall see, a large class, escaped the notice of nearly everyone. However, in ruling out unreasonableness, as well as dishonesty, the 1949 draft proscribed not only what negotiable instruments-minded men were aiming at—namely, cases in categories (1) and (2)—but also virtually all of the other remaining types of cases listed, including those in category (7).

But this blunderbuss effect was lost in 1952, when good faith was finally defined merely as "honesty in fact in the conduct or transaction concerned." Even then, negotiable instruments-minded lawyers could be expected to assume that the sole effect of lopping off the reasonableness half of the 1949 definition was merely to "make negligence irrelevant to good faith." Consider, for example, the following comment of Professor Braucher:

> Section 1-201(19) defines "good faith" as "honesty in fact," and thus follows a number of the uniform commercial acts in making negligence irrelevant to good faith. The adoption of this "subjective" test, sometimes known as the rule of "the pure heart and the empty head," dates back more than a hundred years in the law of negotiable instruments, to the abandonment of the "objective" standard announced in *Gill v. Cubitt.* In the Code the definition of "good faith" is also made applicable in the rather different context of section 1-203: "Every contract or duty within this Act imposes an obligation of good faith in its performance or enforcement."[62]

However, this deletion appears to have had a much more significant effect than merely that of "making negligence irrelevant to good faith." According to one observer, it left the Code's general obligation of good faith in section 1-203 "enfeebled";[63] good faith, as defined now in section 1-201(19), expressly rules out only cases in categories (1), (3) and (4).

62 Braucher, *supra* note 59, at 812.

63 Farnsworth, *Good Faith Performance and Commercial Reasonableness Under the Uniform Commercial Code*, 30 U. Chi. L. Rev. 666, 674 (1963).

What of cases in categories (2), (5), (6) and (7)? They appear to be left untouched by the express language of section 1-201(19). And since categories (2), (5) and (6) only include acts of negligence—conduct which is not, as such, a form of bad faith—they may be set to one side. This leaves the large class of cases which fall within category (7): forms of bad faith that do not, as such, involve dishonesty or negligence. Regardless of how bad such conduct may be, it is far from certain that judges will consider it dishonest and, therefore, in bad faith within the meaning of section 1-201(19).[64]

Should it be concluded, then, that the Code definitions of good faith, *in their entirety*, do not rule out conduct within category (7) when it occurs in sale-of-goods transactions? Not without two general qualifications.

First, there is a special definition of good faith applicable within article 2. Section 2-103(1)(b) provides:

> In this Article, unless the context otherwise requires . . . good faith in the case of a merchant means honesty in fact and the observance of reasonable commercial standards of fair dealing in the trade.

This definition obviously excludes far more than the section 1-201(19) "honesty" definition. But the Code seems to give this broader definition a rather limited scope. It appears to apply by its terms only when a specific provision in article 2 uses the phrase, "good faith." On this reading, its scope would be strikingly narrow since only thirteen of the 104 provisions of article 2 use these words. Code Comments[65] suggest, however, that this definition applies throughout the gamut of circumstances governed by article 2, as if it reached back into article 1 and defined good faith in section 1-203 for purposes of that section's general application to sales between merchants. But there is little justification in the text for this interpretation, and several of the relevant Comments

[64] Of course, judges could give the "honesty" definition a rubbery texture. But this, again, would be to indulge in fiction. See pp. 198-99 *supra*. Furthermore, this would be inconsistent with the legislative history of § 1-201(19), which is restrictive, not expansive. Indeed, the honesty definition of good faith, given its origins, could be read only to rule out very special forms of "undertaking to mislead or deceive," namely, "feigning ignorance of third party rights or defenses, or pretending belief in their absence." Of course, it is not suggested that the definition ought to be read this way. At least, it rules out all forms of undertaking to mislead or deceive. See the discussion in note 47 *supra*.

[65] UCC §§ 1-201(19), Comment 19; 1-203, Comment 1; 2-209, Comment 2; 2-609, Comment 6; 2-612, Comments 3, 7.

can be explained away as addressed to earlier versions of the Code in which good faith in section 1-201(19) was broadly defined both for purposes of section 1-203 and for specific provisions throughout the Code.[66] In the Code's evolution, Comments have not always kept pace with changes in the text.[67]

Another limiting feature of the special definition of good faith in article 2 is that it applies only "in the case of a merchant." Section 2-104(1) defines a merchant as

> a person who deals in goods of the kind or otherwise by his occupation holds himself out as having knowledge or skill peculiar to the practices or goods involved in the transaction or to whom such knowledge or skill may be attributed by his employment of an agent or broker or other intermediary who by his occupation holds himself out as having such knowledge or skill.

Furthermore, the article 2 definition of good faith presumably can operate only insofar as there are commercial standards of fair dealing in a given trade which are reasonable. It may be hard to determine what a trade is, and a given trade may not have any standards at all; it may be a jungle. In that event, the only forms of dealing ruled out under the article 2 definition would be those excluded by its "honesty" language—language which is already applicable to article 2 transactions via sections 1-203 and 1-201(19).

The second qualification—and the second avenue for retrieving ground lost because of the narrow definition in section 1-201(19)—involves use of the "unless the context otherwise requires" language prefacing this definition. This language allows a judge to apply section 1-203, the Code's general good faith provision, to rule out forms of contractual bad faith other than dishonesty. There is evidence that Karl Llewellyn, the Code's chief draftsman, was cognizant of forms of bad faith be-

---

[66] It must be admitted that UCC § 1-201(19), Comment 19 and the Comment to UCC § 1-203, cannot be explained away in this way. A quote from the Code's chief draftsman may be more appropriate here:

> I am ashamed of it in some ways; there are so many pieces that I could make a little better; there are so many beautiful ideas I tried to get in that would have been good for the law, but I was voted down. . . . When we weren't allowed to put in where we wanted to go . . . , we at least got the thing set up so that we are allowed to state in accompanying comments where the particular sections are trying to go.

Llewellyn, *Why a Commercial Code?*, 22 TENN. L. REV. 779, 784, 782 (1953).

[67] Skilton, *Some Comments on the Comments to the Uniform Commercial Code*, 1966 WIS. L. REV. 597.

sides dishonesty, and that he intended the Code's obligations of good faith to exclude conduct of this nature.[68] A judge bent on raising standards of contractual morality may implement Llewellyn's purpose via the "unless the context otherwise requires" language. But for good reasons other judges may refuse to take this route. The force of these reasons ought to lead the Code's Permanent Editorial Board to rework its treatment of good faith. First of all, a judge may think that the deletion of the reasonableness half of the 1949 definition, which left good faith defined solely in terms of honesty, manifested an intent to leave nondishonest bad faith untouched except insofar as other specific Code provisions deal with it.[69] Second, Professor Patterson plainly pointed out the narrowness of the honesty definition during the New York Law Revision Commission's review of the Code: "The purposes of Section 1-203 seem to go beyond the requirement of 'honesty in fact' . . . ." [70] Despite this, the Code sponsors did not revise the definition of good faith when they subsequently overhauled the Code in light of the Commission's work. This, a judge might conclude, shows that the Code sponsors have given up on more expansive doctrines of good faith. Third, under the foregoing approach, the instances in which it would be necessary to invoke the prefatory language of 1-201(19) might well outnumber the instances in which the honesty definition itself would be invoked, given the many and varied forms of nondishonest bad faith. Thus a judge tempted to adopt this approach might feel he would have to accept the paradoxical consequence that the "unless otherwise required" language of 1-201(19) is to do an even bigger job than the honesty definition itself. Understandably, he might not be willing to accept an interpretation which would have this effect. After all, such language is ordinarily inserted ahead of a definition only to

---

[68] See especially UCC § 10, Comment, and § 26 Comment (1948 Draft). In the 1962 Official Text, *see, e.g.*, the Comment to § 1-203; the Comment to § 2-209 on good faith in modifying a contract; Comment 4 to § 2-210 on good faith in exercising rights to specify requirements; Comment 3 to § 2-612 on good faith interpretation; Comment 5 to § 2-504 on good faith duties of co-operation; Comment 2 to § 2-601 on good faith in disposing of rejected goods; Comment 5 to § 2-607 on good faith duties to give notice of breach; Comment 7 to § 2-612 on negotiation in good faith; Comment 11 to § 2-615 on good faith in not discriminating between buyers.

[69] This intent is reinforced by the fact that the draftsmen have made an "objective" test applicable for some sections of the Code. See note 61 *supra*. When read along side such sections as 2-103(1)(b), there is at least a negative implication that § 1-201(19) deals only with dishonesty.

[70] 1955 N.Y. Law Revision Comm'n Rep. 310, 311.

deal with exceptional situations, and not to perform functions of the magnitude that the definition itself is to perform.

In sum, the Code's definitions restrictively distort the doctrine of good faith. A variety of factors account for this, including the draftsmen's failure to view good faith as an excluder, their urge to guide through definitions,[71] the influence of the subjective-objective controversy in the law of negotiable instruments, the precedent of prior uniform acts and an apparently compromising attitude toward an American Bar Association committee. The Code's Permanent Editorial Board should amend the Official Text to confine its definitions of good faith to purchase contexts alone,[72] leaving good faith otherwise wholly undefined, both for the purposes of the section 1-203 general requirement of good faith and for purposes of the various specific provisions which use these words in nonpurchase contexts. The Board should also amend section 1-203 to rule out all relevant forms of contractual bad faith, examples of which should be given.[73]

If an obligation of good faith is to do its job, it must be open-ended rather than sealed off in a definition. Courts should be left free, under the aegis of a statutory green light, to deal with any and all significant forms of contractual bad faith, familiar and unfamiliar. The legislature should grant only power; it should not try to guide through definitions —a fact Code draftsmen have recognized in other, analogous contexts.[74] Courts should determine the scope of the good faith requirement, partly because it is an unusually "circumstance-bound" doctrine and excludes highly varied forms of bad faith, many of which become identifiable only in the context of circumstantial detail of a kind that defies comprehensive statutory formulation. In addition, the requirement of good faith often functions as a kind of "safety valve" which may be turned to fill gaps and qualify or limit rights and duties arising under contracts

71 Definitions are frequently inspired by the desire to give specific guidance.

72 An argument can be made that the definitions are not even adequate in purchase contexts. But that controversy is beyond the scope of this study.

73 A possible substitute for § 1-203 might read:

> *Section 1-203. Obligation of Good Faith*
>
> (1) From the negotiation to discharge of contracts or duties this Act governs, parties shall act in good faith.
>
> (2) For purposes of subsection (1), "good faith" rules out all relevant breaches of faith, e.g., abusing the privilege to withdraw an offer, taking unfair advantage, evading the spirit of a contract, conjuring up a dispute to force a favorable modification, abusing a power to terminate a contractual relation.

74 In UCC § 2-302 the draftsmen did not undertake to define "unconscionability." Nor did they, in article 9, define "possession."

or rules of law. Judges, situated as they are in the midst of the relevant circumstantial detail, are in the best position to know when to turn this valve.

To treat the nature of good faith as conceptualized in the Code is inevitably to tell a significant part of the story of the scope of good faith obligations under article 2 of the Code. But there is still more to the story.

## III. Scope of Obligations to Act in Good Faith

Cases have been discovered which, if taken as a whole rather than by states, require good faith at every stage of the contractual process, from preliminary negotiation through performance to discharge, and in nearly all kinds of contracts. This is not to say that all cases agree as to when a duty of good faith should be imposed, for they do not. Nor, of course, is it to say that the jurisdictions are more or less uniform in the extent to which they require good faith. On some questions there is a fair sprinkling of decisions from different states, but on others—for example, whether contract negotiations must be conducted in good faith—case law is scant. Further research would probably turn up more cases, but it has not been possible to do a comprehensive survey of all the cases in which good faith could have figured.[75]

The cases discovered reveal that good faith is a highly versatile doctrine. Procedurally, it may figure in plaintiff's prima facie case for relief,[76] or it may be asserted as an affirmative defense.[77] Substantively, it may be invoked to rule out a wide variety of forms of bad faith, including negotiating without serious intent to contract, abusing the privilege to break off negotiations, entering a transaction without intending to perform or in reckless disregard of prospective inability to perform, nondisclosure of known defects in the subject of a sale, abusing superior bargaining power, evading the spirit of a transaction, lack of diligence, willfully rendering only substantial performance, and abusing the power to specify terms or to determine compliance. Other forms of

[75] See note 7 *supra*. It should be added that no effort has been made to collect statutes which require good faith. See, *e.g.*, Ga. Civ. Code, § 56-1206 (1960), allowing damages against an insurer for bad faith refusal to pay a loss; Cal. Civ. Code § 3306 (1954), allowing enhanced damages against a vendor of realty who refuses to convey in bad faith, and; the Automobile Dealers' Day in Court Act, under which a dealer may recover damages from a manufacturer who terminates a franchise not in good faith, § 2, 15 U.S.C. § 1222 (1964).

[76] *E.g.*, Ralston v. Mathew, 173 Kan. 550, 250 P.2d 841 (1952).

[77] *E.g.*, Doll v. Noble, 116 N.Y. 230, 22 N.E. 406 (1889).

bad faith which have been ruled out by the doctrine include interfering with or failing to cooperate in the other party's performance, pretending to dispute or arbitrarily disputing, adopting overreaching or "weaseling" interpretations or constructions of contract language, taking advantage of the other party's weaknesses to get a favorable readjustment or settlement of a dispute, abusing the right to adequate assurances of performance, refusing for ulterior reasons to accept the other party's slightly defective performance, willfully failing to mitigate the other party's damages, and abusing a privilege to terminate contractual relations.[78] Courts have not always ruled out the foregoing forms of bad faith solely in the name of good faith; some have been proscribed more commonly in the name of other doctrines—for example, deceit,[79] failure of constructive conditions of cooperation[80] and breach of implied promises.[81]

Code sources of specific duties of good faith are numerous and varied, although relevant Code case law to date is scant. First, the parties are free to include contract clauses requiring good faith.[82] Second, section 1-103 authorizes a judge to apply extra-Code case law on good faith if it rises to the status of a "supplemental general principle of law or equity." [83] What is such a principle? Must a jurisdiction's highest court state explicitly that good faith is generally required in matters contractual, or is it enough if that court recognizes explicitly several specific duties of good faith from which it could be generalized that good faith is a "general principle"? Only a few courts, notably those of New York[84] and California,[85] have said that good faith is generally required. It would seem that recognition of several specific duties is

78 Each of these forms of bad faith will be treated subsequently. In the course of this study, numerous other forms of contractual bad faith have been encountered. But for purposes of this Article, it is not necessary to discuss them.

79 For example, see the "false promise" cases at 227-28 *infra*.

80 See, *e.g.*, the "hindering of performance" cases at 241-42 *infra*.

81 See, *e.g.*, the "evasion of the spirit of the deal" cases at 234-35 *infra*, and the discussion of "implied promise" at 233 *infra*.

82 But the parties are not free to vary explicit Code duties of good faith. UCC § 1-102(3).

83 On the countervailing tendency in our law to view principles as less law than specific rules, see Dworkin, *The Case for Law—A Critique*, 1 VALPARAISO L. REV. 215-17 (1967). This factor presumably has impeded recognition of general obligations of good faith in our law.

84 Wigand v. Bachmann-Bechtel Brewing Co., 222 N.Y. 272, 277, 118 N.E. 618, 619 (1918).

85 Universal Sales Corp. v. California Press Mfg. Co., 20 Cal. 2d 751, 771, 128 P.2d 665, 677 (1942).

enough, but perhaps even this should not be necessary if the specific duty in question is one which several other states impose.

A third source is section 1-203, which provides: "Every contract or duty within this Act imposes an obligation of good faith in its performance or enforcement." Some writers would have us believe that this provision imposes a pervasive obligation of good faith in sales transactions.[86] Its reach is broad, but far from all-inclusive. As we have seen, the "honesty" definition of good faith appears to limit it significantly. And, by its terms, it does not rule out bad faith in the negotiation and formation of contracts, a fertile field for untoward conduct. The Code's Permanent Editorial Board should change this.[87]

A fourth source of duties of good faith under the Code is section 1-205(3), which provides:

> A course of dealing between parties and any usage of trade in the vocation or trade in which they are engaged or of which they are or should be aware give particular meaning to and supplement or qualify terms of an agreement.

This section will, in some cases, operate to require good faith, and one commentator has argued that it establishes a general duty of "commercial" good faith in sales transactions.[88] Yet when there is no prior course of dealing between the parties, an obligation of good faith cannot arise from this source. And when there is a prior course of dealing, it is far from clear that section 1-205 automatically holds the parties to a general obligation of good faith in their subsequent dealings. Subsection 1-205(1) says only that a course of dealing is

> a sequence of previous conduct between the parties to a particular transaction which is fairly to be regarded as establishing a common basis of understanding for interpreting their expressions and other conduct.

That parties have dealt with each other does not necessarily mean that they have "a common basis of understanding" to deal in good faith. Turning to "usage of trade" under subsection 1-205(2), in a particular

86 Mentschikoff, *Highlights of the Uniform Commercial Code*, 27 Mod. L. Rev. 167, 168-70 (1964).

87 See the proposed revision of § 1-203, note 73 *supra*.

88 Mooney, *Old Kontract Principles and Karl's New Kode: An Essay on the Jurisprudence of our New Commercial Law*, 11 Vill. L. Rev. 213, 247-53 (1966).

trade, dealing in good faith may have "such regularity of observance . . . as to justify an expectation that it will be observed with respect to the transaction in question." [89] But, even conceding as much, it does not follow that the Code thus imposes a general obligation of good faith in all trades.

A fifth source consists of specific provisions in article 2. Thirteen sections in the article expressly require good faith. Several more do not use these exact words, but clearly incorporate good faith requirements—for example, section 2-302 on unconscionability, section 2-206(1)(b) on the "unilateral contract trick," [90] section 2-311(3) on hindering the other party's performance and section 2-309 on abuse of termination powers.

A final source of Code obligations of good faith consists of the Official Comments for each section. The Comments are not law, but judges give them some weight. Numerous Comments in article 2 expressly require good faith,[91] include cross-references to section 1-203[92] or do both. Moreover, the lead Comment to section 1-102 expressly invites judges to apply Code sections by analogy when they are inapplicable by their terms.[93] Some judges will accept this invitation and will apply by analogy article 2 sections which explicitly or implicitly require good faith.

---

[89] UCC § 1-205(2).

[90] The unilateral contract trick has been described by Dean Hawkland:

> Suppose B offers to buy 100 units of x goods from S, and his offer clearly prescribes that the mode of acceptance is to be shipment of the goods. S, in response to the offer, ships to B 100 units of x goods. B discovers that the goods are defective and sues S for breach of the sales contract. S defends by asserting that no contract was ever consummated, because his non-conforming shipment did not give the offeror that for which he bargained, and, consequently, did not constitute an acceptance. A number of courts have been receptive to this defense. Subsection 2-206(1)(b) shatters the defense . . . .

W. Hawkland, Sales and Bulk Sales 6 (1958).

[91] Sections in article 2 which do not use the phrase good faith but whose Comments do are as follows: § 2-205, Comment 5; § 2-209, Comment 2; § 2-210, Comment 4; § 2-309, Comments 1, 3, 5, 8; § 2-312, Comments 1, 2, 3; § 2-313, Comments 4, 6; § 2-314, Comment 10; § 2-317, Comment 2; § 2-324, Comments 1, 4; § 2-326, Comment 2; § 2-327, Comment 4; § 2-504, Comments 2, 5; § 2-601, Comments 1, 2; § 2-604, Comment; § 2-607, Comments 4, 5; § 2-608, Comments 3, 5; § 2-609, Comments 2, 3, 4, 6; § 2-610, Comment 4; § 2-612, Comments 3, 5, 7; § 2-715, Comments 2, 3.

[92] The following sections in article 2 do not use the phrase good faith but have Comments which include a cross reference to § 1-203: §§ 2-209, 2-309, 2-312, 2-314, 2-324, 2-504, 2-609, 2-610, 2-612, 2-715.

[93] See Note, *The Uniform Commercial Code as a Premise for Judicial Reasoning*, 65 Colum. L. Rev. 880 (1965).

We may now profitably consider how particular forms of contractual bad faith have fared at the hands of courts, and how they would be likely to fare under relevant Code provisions. The main purposes of the extended, but far from exhaustive survey which follows are to show (1) that, contrary to the facile assumption that good faith is a nebulous doctrine, it is possible to pin down particular duties of good faith which rule out specific, concrete and characterizable forms of bad faith; (2) that these duties are more varied and numerous than has heretofore been recognized; (3) that a substantial body of case law exists on which courts may draw to recognize such duties in new contexts; (4) that section 1-103, which authorizes use of extra-Code law "supplementally," is likely to be the most fertile of the Code's sources of duties of good faith; (5) that the scope of section 1-203, expressly imposing a general Code obligation of good faith, apparently is limited significantly both by its own terms and by Code definitions of good faith; and (6) that other Code resources for combating bad faith can have an important bearing in particular contexts.[94]

### *A. Bad Faith in the Negotiation and Formation of Contracts*

Forms of bad faith at the negotiation and contract formation stage include negotiating without serious intent to contract, abusing the privilege to break off negotiations, entering into a contract without having the intent to perform, entering a deal recklessly disregarding prospective inability to perform, failing to disclose known defects in goods being sold, and taking undue advantage of superior bargaining power to strike an unconscionable bargain. The extent to which courts recognize such forms of bad faith for what they are, and act accordingly, varies widely. For example, except for cases ruling out a bad faith withdrawal of an offer, there is little case law on abuse in the negotiation process. On the other hand, there are many cases, in contract and in tort, on nondisclosure and misrepresentation.

Since section 1-203, which sets forth the general requirement of good faith, applies only to the "performance or enforcement" of a contract, it does not impose a duty of good faith in the negotiation and formation of sales contracts. Thus to the extent that the text of the Code rules out bad faith in the negotiation and formation stages it must be

[94] The potential bearing of custom and usage and of the "unless the context otherwise requires" language prefacing the honesty definition of good faith will be assumed but not discussed. On the latter, see 213-14 *supra*.

via section 1-103, on supplemental principles of law, or via specific sections in article 2. Like general contract case law, Code sections treat the foregoing forms of bad faith unevenly. For example, they neglect bad faith in the negotiation of sales contracts but invalidate unconscionable sales contracts or clauses.

*Negotiating Without Serious Intent to Contract*[95]

A party who negotiates without serious intent to contract might be trying to tie up the other party in order to stall for time or in order to keep him from competing in another venture or deal. He also might be going through the motions of negotiating merely to comply formally with some rule of law that requires him to shop around for the best deal.[96]

While the law requires parties to collective bargaining transactions to negotiate in good faith,[97] and while a few cases say that a party who has contracted to negotiate must do so in good faith,[98] only one case has been discovered in which a court has recognized, in the absence of a statutory or contractual duty to negotiate, that a cause of action exists against a party who negotiates without serious intent to contract. In *Heyer Products Co. v. United States*,[99] a 1956 decision, the Court of Claims held that a disappointed low bidder on a Government contract is entitled to recover the expenses he has incurred in preparing his bid whenever he can show that "bids were not invited in good faith, but as a pretense to conceal the purpose to let the contract to some favored bidder . . . ."[100] The potential implications of this case are far reaching. If bidders are protected in this way, then why not protect similarly any party who finds that he is the victim of another's ulterior negotiating purposes? A party to negotiations assumes the usual risk that business reasons may prevent consummation of a deal, but he does not assume

95 This category and the next (abusing the privilege to withdraw a proposal or an offer) are suggested in the admirable article by Kessler & Fine, *Culpa in Contrahendo, Bargaining in Good Faith, and Freedom of Contract: A Comparative Study*, 77 HARV. L. REV. 401, 419 (1964). The article deals with a wide variety of forms of bad faith in the negotiation and formation stage.

96 Obviously, there are still other possible reasons for such conduct.

97 Cox, *The Duty to Bargain in Good Faith*, 71 HARV. L. REV. 1401 (1958).

98 *E.g.*, Henry G. Meigs, Inc. v. Empire Petroleum Co., 171 F. Supp. 888, 892-93 (E.D. Wis. 1959), *aff'd*, 273 F.2d 424 (7th Cir. 1960).

99 140 F. Supp. 409 (Ct. Cl. 1956).

100 140 F. Supp. at 414.

the risk that the other party, having no serious intent to contract, will merely lead him on and then drop him.[101]

The *Heyer* decision does not seem to have had much influence in the ten years since it was handed down, or at least *Heyer*-type plaintiffs have not won any reported cases.[102] There are several possible explanations. No doubt a cause of action such as that in *Heyer* is hard to prove, and lawyers, thinking exclusively in terms of contract, may hastily dismiss the possibility of relief when the parties do not ultimately consummate a contract. Furthermore, courts may fear that by following *Heyer* they will deter parties from entering contract negotiations or will undesirably limit freedom to negotiate. Then, too, *Heyer* may seem easily distinguishable. Even those who would concede the soundness of the decision might try to distinguish it on any of the following grounds: (1) that, far from independently sanctioning a claim for damages flowing from a specific form of bad faith, the case turns on an interpretation of Section 3(b) of the Armed Services Procurement Act of 1947, which provides that unless the public interest requires the rejection of all bids, the one "most advantageous to the United States" shall be accepted;[103] (2) that bidders on Government contracts need special protections not afforded to other offerors "because of the large cost involved in preparing a bid";[104] or (3) that since federal regulations make Government contract bids irrevocable, considerations of "mutuality" justly "imply a correlative right in the bidder" to have the Government consider his bid in good faith.[105]

But none of these distinctions justifies limiting the *Heyer* doctrine. The first is not even a true distinction, for the case could not have turned on an interpretation of Section 3(b) of the Armed Services Procurement Act of 1947; the court recognized an independent cause of

101 The wrong here is aggravated, and becomes worthy of the legal system's concern, whenever a "negotiator" leads the negotiatee on and then refuses both to consummate and to compensate for the out-of-pocket expenses the negotiatee has been induced to incur. The negotiatee might incur even greater losses, as where he passes up other opportunities, reasonably assuming that the negotiations in progress with the negotiator will materialize.

102 See Robert F. Simmons & Associates v. United States, 360 F.2d 962 (Ct. Cl. 1966) and Edelman v. FHA, 251 F. Supp. 715 (E.D.N.Y. 1966) for the most recent cases of significance. Although plaintiffs have been unsuccessful in litigation, this does not mean that *Heyer* has had no impact upon the behavior of negotiating parties.

103 62 Stat. 22 (1948), *re-enacted*, 10 U.S.C. § 2305(c) (1964).

104 See Hawkland, *Contracts*, in 1957 ANN. SURV. AM. L. 267, 268 (Collings ed. 1958).

105 105 U. PA. L. REV. 756, 760 n.34 (1957).

action on an "implied contract." [106] Moreover, there is little force in the argument that bidders on Government contracts need protection not afforded other offerors; all offerors can, in particular cases, incur significant expenses in preparing proposals. Finally, in this age of asymmetry, considerations of "mutuality" can hardly serve to distinguish cases.

Because of its potential significance,[107] the *Heyer* case has been discussed at some length. How might a party who negotiates for a sales contract without serious intent fare under the Uniform Commercial Code? He could not be held liable under section 1-203, which imposes a general duty of good faith, for that provision does not cover the negotiation and formation of contracts. And article 2's specific provisions are silent on negotiating without serious intent. However, the Code does not preclude a tort recovery, based on general principles of deceit. Section 1-103 states that general principles of law and equity supplement the Code, including principles of "fraud" and "misrepresentation." [108] Moreover, section 2-721 specifically contemplates "remedies for fraud."

### *Abusing the Privilege to Withdraw a Proposal or an Offer*

Traditionally, a negotiating party who has made a proposal, but not an offer, has generally been allowed to break off negotiations with impunity, even when he has "agreed to agree" and has induced the other party to rely to his detriment.[109] But a recent case may foretell different law for the future and thus show the way to an important new legal duty of good faith in the conduct of contract negotiations. In *Hoffman v. Red Owl Stores, Inc.*[110] the Wisconsin Supreme Court allowed recovery against a party who walked away from contract negotiations after inducing the other party to rely on the prospect that a contract would materialize. Red Owl had represented to the plaintiff that it

---

106 140 F. Supp. 409, 413 (Ct. Cl. 1956).

107 "Negotiation" may be taking hold as a law school subject. *See, e.g.*, White, *The Lawyer as Negotiator: An Adventure in Understanding and Teaching the Art of Negotiation*, 19 J. LEG. ED. 337 (1967). If so, it is to be hoped that explicit attention will be given not only to the art of negotiating but also to the legal rights and wrongs of negotiating.

108 The dissenting judge in *Heyer* maintained that the Court of Claims lacked jurisdiction because the cause of action sounded in tort. 140 F. Supp. at 414. *See also* Edelman v. FHA, 251 F. Supp. 715, 719 n.7 (1966).

109 *See, e.g.*, Rosenfield v. United States Trust Co., 290 Mass. 210, 217, 195 N.E. 323, 326 (1935). *But see* Morris v. Ballard, 16 F.2d 175 (D.C. Cir. 1926).

110 26 Wis. 2d 683, 133 N.W. 2d 267 (1965).

would establish him as a franchise operator of a Red Owl grocery store if he would perform certain conditions and contribute 18,000 dollars. The plaintiff met all conditions—that is, he sold his bakery, bought and operated a small grocery store for a time to gain experience, secured an option to buy certain land for the proposed supermarket and rented a home close to the site. But Red Owl then insisted that he invest 34,000 dollars, instead of 18,000 dollars.[111] The plaintiff refused and brought an action to recover the damages he sustained in relying upon Red Owl's negotiating proposal.

The court granted relief on the theory of promissory estoppel, stating that to sustain this theory it is not necessary for a defendant's representations to

> embrace all essential details of a proposed transaction between promisor and promisee so as to be the equivalent of an offer that would result in a binding contract between the parties if the promisee were to accept the same.[112]

On the question of damages, the court remarked:

> Where damages are awarded in promissory estoppel instead of specifically enforcing the promisor's promise, they should be only such as in the opinion of the court are necessary to prevent injustice. Mechanical or rule of thumb approaches to the damage problem should be avoided.[113]

Concluding that recovery should not be allowed for lost profits, the court granted reimbursement only for the expenditures and losses the plaintiff incurred in preparing to take up the Red Owl franchise. This is a welcome departure from decisions which interpret Section 90 of the Restatement of Contracts inflexibly to require the award of full expectancy damages in all cases.[114] The potential significance of *Red Owl*

[111] It may be a common ploy for a party who wishes to break off to introduce a new and highly unreasonable condition into the negotiations, hoping thereby to induce the other to walk away.

[112] 26 Wis. 2d at 697, 133 N.W.2d at 274-75. Courts have usually viewed promissory estoppel as a substitute for consideration in cases in which the plaintiff has relied to his detriment on either a gratuitous promise or an offer.

[113] *Id.* at 701, 133 N.W.2d at 276.

[114] For cases and discussion, see Shattuck, *Gratuitous Promises—A New Writ?*, 35 Mich. L. Rev. 908 (1937).

is substantial.[115] If the decision is followed by other courts, it will no longer be possible for one party to scuttle contract negotiations with impunity when the other has been induced to rely to his detriment on the prospect that the negotiations will succeed.

What of the bad faith withdrawal of offers?[116] It is important to distinguish between the positions of unilateral and bilateral offerees. While it may once have been that a unilateral offeror could lawfully withdraw his offer at any time before the offeree fully completed the performance constituting his acceptance, this is no longer the general rule. Varying theories now deny the unilateral offeror the right to withdraw his offer after the offeree has begun performance.[117] Furthermore, the unilateral offeree who has merely prepared to perform may, according to some cases, recover any reasonably foreseeable expenses which he has incurred.[118]

When a bilateral offer is withdrawn after the offeree has relied on it to his detriment, without first accepting, the result should depend, in part, on the terms of the offer. Bilateral offers may be divided into three categories: (1) those which clearly call for a return promise from the offeree before reliance would be reasonable, (2) those which contemplate that the offeree will or may rely prior to making a return promise and (3) those which do not clearly specify any sequence of events. In cases of the first type, courts do not appear willing to protect the rely-

[115] As one observer put it, the case creates "a new right which looks very much like a cause of action for breach of an implied promise to negotiate in good faith." 51 CORNELL L.Q. 351, 355 (1966). The *Red Owl* court said Red Owl did not act in bad faith. 26 Wis. 2d at 695, 133 N.W.2d at 273. But from the context, it is clear that the court meant only that Red Owl had no fraudulent intent at the time of making its proposals. Under the circumstances of the cases it remains a violation of good faith for Red Owl to refuse both (a) to consummate the deal and (b) to compensate Hoffman for his losses.

[116] Some judges have, in so many words, invoked good faith to limit the power to revoke an offer. *E.g.*, Zwolanek v. Baker Mfg. Co., 150 Wis. 517, 525, 137 N.W. 769, 773 (1912). Corbin has objected to this conceptualization, stating: "In general, it is not thought to be bad faith to revoke any offer before it has been accepted, even though the purpose is to avoid contracting with the offeree . . . ." 1 A. CORBIN, CONTRACTS § 49, at 193 (1963). The author disagrees with Corbin's assertion, at least insofar as it applies to the withdrawal of an offer which reasonably and foreseeably induces detrimental reliance. An offeror who, without more, acts in this way breaks faith unless he agrees to compensate for such reliance.

[117] *See* Brackenbury v. Hodgkin, 116 Me. 399, 102 A. 106 (1917); Los Angeles Traction Co. v. Wilshire, 135 Cal. 654, 67 P. 1086 (1902); RESTATEMENT OF CONTRACTS § 45 (1932).

[118] 1 A. CORBIN, CONTRACTS § 51 (1963).

ing offeree.[119] This is sound, for the offeree who relies on such an offer without first closing the deal assumes the risk that the offeror will withdraw. In cases of the second kind, the doctrine of promissory estoppel is increasingly being invoked to protect the reasonably relying offeree against a withdrawal.[120] In cases of the third variety, the offeror's right to withdraw should be limited in a proper case.[121] At the least, out-of-pocket costs should be recoverable whenever the requirements of promissory estoppel are met.

Does the Code impose any duties not to abuse the privilege to withdraw? Section 1-203 is, as we have seen, silent with respect to the negotiation and formation stages. However, a court might use section 1-103, concerning supplemental principles of law, to bring any applicable extra-Code case law to bear. With two notable exceptions, specific provisions in article 2 do not require good faith negotiation. The first exception is section 2-205, which limits an offeror's power to withdraw a "firm" offer:

> An offer by a merchant to buy or sell goods in a signed writing which by its terms gives assurance that it will be held open is not revocable, for lack of consideration, during the time stated or if no time is stated for a reasonable time, but in no event may such period of irrevocability exceed three months; but any such term of assurance on a form supplied by the offeree must be separately signed by the offeror.

This section is narrow in scope and applies only if (1) there has actually been an offer (2) by a merchant (3) in a signed writing (4) which gives assurance that it will be held open and (5) which would, but for lack of consideration, otherwise be irrevocable. A meritorious plaintiff may well hang up on at least one of these requirements.[122]

[119] *E.g.*, White v. Corlies & Tift, 46 N.Y. 467 (1871).

[120] *See, e.g.*, Reynolds v. Texarkana Constr. Co., 237 Ark. 583, 374 S.W.2d 818 (1964); Drennan v. Star Paving Co., 51 Cal. 2d 409, 333 P.2d 757 (1958). The effect of invoking § 90 of the Restatement may be to compensate not merely loss of out-of-pocket expenses, but also, as in these very cases, loss of expected profits.

[121] No cases have been discovered which fit the "proper case" description. It should be noted that because the parties were not close enough together to justify awarding damages for loss of expectancy from the contemplated contract itself, it does not follow that no expectancy damages should ever be awarded in any such case. A meritorious plaintiff might have foregone other opportunities on the reasonable assumption that the deal at hand was "going through."

[122] There is little case law under this section to date. *See*, E.A. Coronis Associates v. M. Gordon Constr. Co., 90 N.J. Super. 69, 216 A.2d 246 (App. Div. 1966).

Section 2-207, the other notable exception, prohibits an offeror from abusing the privilege to break off by seizing upon an insignificant variance in a purported acceptance to establish that no contract was formed.[123] Thus under the Code contracts can be formed which, under general contract law, would fail because of conflict with the requirement that an acceptance match up perfectly[124] with an offer.[125]

*Entering A Deal Not Intending to Perform or Recklessly Disregarding Prospective Inability to Perform*

According to one authority, in the majority of states a party who promises without intending to perform will be liable in tort for deceit.[126] The purchase of goods without intent to pay is illustrative.[127] Let us suppose, though, that instead of making a false promise, the party makes a promise in reckless disregard of a substantial likelihood that he will be unable to perform when the time comes. Of course, if he ultimately fails to perform, he will usually be liable for breach of contract. But, for present purposes, the significant point is that the courts give special effect to the party's bad faith in recklessly disregarding substantial prospective inability to perform. For example, there is authority that a vendor of realty who ultimately is unable to convey good title must compensate the aggrieved party for the loss of his bargain if, when entering the contract, the vendor knew or had good reason to know of his substantial prospective inability to perform.[128] Otherwise, the

123 This section also purports to limit the power to withdraw in the face of a significant variance. *See* Roto-Lith, Ltd. v. F.P. Bartlett & Co., 297 F.2d 497 (1st Cir. 1962). *See also* UCC §§ 2-206(1)(a), (b), § 2-204(1), § 2-208, each of which can operate to prevent bad faith withdrawal.

124 Poel v. Brunswick-Balke-Collender Co., 216 N.Y. 310, 110 N.E. 619 (1915).

125 A form of bad faith cognate to those discussed in this section consists in backing out of a deal that is, in law, imperfectly formed. See the discussion at 259 *infra.* A deal may fail in law for a variety of reasons, including noncompliance with the statute of frauds or indefiniteness. Many courts refuse to require the party backing out to pay either expectancy damages or damages for detrimental reliance. However, quasi-contractual recovery has been allowed in some cases. Note, *Quasi Contractual Recovery for Part Performance of a Contract*, 44 HARV. L. REV. 623 (1931). Article 2 of the Code seeks to reduce the occasions on which this form of bad faith can occur in the first place. Its statute of frauds provisions are less stringent than earlier ones. UCC § 2-201. And it tolerates much indefiniteness in valid contracts of sale. See UCC § 2-204(3) and the numerous "gap filler" provisions in article 2.

126 W. PROSSER, SELECTED TOPICS ON THE LAW OF TORTS 380, 401 (1954).

127 *E.g.*, Donovan v. Clifford, 225 Mass. 435, 114 N.E. 681 (1917).

128 *See, e.g.*, Arentson v. Moreland, 122 Wis. 167, 99 N.W. 790 (1904).

vendor would be liable only for the amount necessary to restore the vendee to the status quo. To cite a second example, under pre-Code law a seller could, in some circumstances, reclaim goods sold on credit to an insolvent who bought without a reasonable expectation that he would be able to pay for them;[129] this relief was available in lieu of the usual remedy of money damages.

A party to a sales transaction under the Code who makes a false promise will be liable therefor in tort either independently or via section 1-103 on supplemental general principles. This same section might also be used to draw in extra-Code law giving special effect to the reckless disregard of prospective inability to perform. Among the specific sections of article 2 which may be relevant, section 2-702(2) should be singled out. It provides:

> Where the seller discovers that the buyer has received goods on credit while insolvent he may reclaim the goods upon demand made within ten days after the receipt, but if misrepresentation of solvency has been made to the particular seller in writing within three months before delivery the ten day limitation does not apply. Except as provided in this subsection the seller may not base a right to reclaim goods on the buyer's fraudulent or innocent misrepresentation of solvency or of intent to pay.

*Seller's Nondisclosure of Known Infirmities in Goods*

*Caveat emptor* was supposed to have been the prevailing rule at one time, notwithstanding that it can conflict with elementary requirements of good faith. But there is evidence that the courts are putting this doctrine to rest in some fields.[130] What of the sales field? Suppose a seller remains silent with respect to a known infirmity in his product under circumstances in which he knows his purchaser probably would not buy at all or would buy only at a lower price if he knew of the infirmity. Presumably, many would agree that the seller has acted in bad faith, but under the oft-stated general rule of pre-Code case law, he has incurred no liability in tort or in contract.[131] Of course, if the seller actively conceals the truth, he is liable in tort for the damage he

129 California Conserving Co. v. D'Avanzo, 62 F.2d 528 (2d Cir. 1933).

130 *See* Kessler & Fine, *Culpa in Contrahendo, Bargaining in Good Faith, and Freedom of Contract: A Comparative Study*, 77 Harv. L. Rev. 401, 441-44 (1964).

131 *See* W. Prosser, Torts 710-11 (1964).

causes,[132] but such is not the case when no more than passive nondisclosure is involved.

If the infirmity in question goes to title or to quality, the Code's warranty provisions may afford significant relief against a nondisclosing seller, especially when the buyer does not examine the goods before entering into the contract.[133] Of potentially greatest significance here is section 2-314, which defines the seller's obligation to sell "merchantable goods":

> (1) Unless excluded or modified (Section 2-316), a warranty that the goods shall be merchantable is implied in a contract for their sale if the seller is a merchant with respect to goods of that kind. Under this section the serving for value of food or drink to be consumed either on the premises or elsewhere is a sale.
>
> (2) Goods to be merchantable must be at least such as
>
> (a) pass without objection in the trade under the contract description; and
>
> (b) in the case of fungible goods, are of fair average quality within the description; and
>
> (c) are fit for the ordinary purposes for which such goods are used; and
>
> (d) run, within the variations permitted by the agreement, of even kind, quality and quantity within each unit and among all units involved; and
>
> (e) are adequately contained, packaged, and labeled as the agreement may require; and
>
> (f) conform to the promises or affirmations of fact made on the container or label if any.
>
> (3) Unless excluded or modified (Section 2-316) other implied warranties may arise from course of dealing or usage of trade.

Many cases of bad faith nondisclosure will generate valid claims for breach of the foregoing implied warranty of merchantability,[134] but

[132] *Id.* at 711.

[133] UCC § 2-316(3)(b) states:

> when the buyer before entering into the contract has examined the goods or the sample or model as fully as he desired or has refused to examine the goods there is no implied warranty with regard to defects which an examination ought in the circumstances to have revealed to him . . . .

[134] *See also* UCC § 2-315 on the related implied warranty of fitness.

this section will not afford relief for all meritorious claimants. Thus goods might be "merchantable" within the foregoing definition and yet have known infirmities which, if disclosed to the buyer, would at least have led him to insist on a lower price; section 2-314 does not necessarily afford relief under these circumstances. Furthermore, a seller has broad power under article 2 to disclaim warranties or to limit drastically remedies for their breach.[135] A nondisclosing seller who follows either or both of these tacks may leave the buyer without significant rights under the Code's warranty provisions.

Had the Code sponsors drafted section 1-203 to apply to the negotiation and formation of contracts, courts could have invoked it against the nondisclosing seller acting in bad faith.[136] But, as Professor Patterson pointed out to the Code draftsmen at the New York hearings in 1955:

> Good faith in the making of a commercial contract is not required by section 1-203 and . . . therefore . . . one party to such a contract is not required to disclose to the other a material fact relating to the prudence or value of the bargain, even though the one who knows this fact also is aware that the other party does not know it, and would not make the contract if he did.[137]

*Taking Advantage of Another in Driving a Bargain*

There are many ways, short of fraud, by which one party can take advantage of another in driving a bargain. For example, one may take advantage of another's lack of real alternatives,[138] his disinclination to read a printed form,[139] his inferior negotiating skill,[140] his lack of knowledge,[141] or his emotional state.[142] At the least, if a person con-

---

135 UCC §§ 2-316, 2-718, 2-719.

136 The section could have been invoked not only for undisclosed defects in quality but also, presumably, for failure to bring disclaimers and the like to the attention of the buyer. On what might be called a duty of good faith to disclose "defects in legal rights," see K. LLEWELLYN, THE COMMON LAW TRADITION: DECIDING APPEALS 370-71 (1960), and Kessler & Fine, *supra* note 128, at 442 n.173.

137 1955 N.Y. LAW REVISION COMM'N REP. 315.

138 *See, e.g.*, Henningson v. Bloomfield Motors, Inc., 32 N.J. 358, 161 A.2d 69 (1960).

139 *E.g.*, Klar v. H. & M. Parcel Room, Inc., 270 App. Div. 538, 61 N.Y.S.2d 285 (1st Dep't 1946), *aff'd*, 296 N.Y. 1044, 73 N.E.2d 912 (1947).

140 See cases cited and discussed in Collins, *Contracts*, in 1962 ANN. SURVEY OF AM L. 451, 459-62 (1963).

141 *E.g.*, Kellogg v. Iowa State Traveling Men's Ass'n, 239 Iowa 196, 211-12, 29 N.W.2d 559, 568 (1947).

142 *See, e.g.*, Newman & Snell's State Bank v. Hunter, 243 Mich. 331, 220 N.W. 665 (1928).

sciously takes advantage of such weaknesses, he acts in bad faith. When in this manner he not only strikes a bargain, but also strikes one that is unconscionable, his action becomes all the more the law's concern.

Some courts at times refuse to enforce some unconscionable contracts or contract clauses. But, except in a relatively few areas,[143] they seldom do this openly. Rather than invalidate openly in the name of public policy, fairness or good faith, they more often resort to back door techniques—for example, they base their decisions on contract interpretation or construction,[144] on specific rules of offer and acceptance,[145] on want of "mutuality,"[146] on lack of consideration,[147] or on mutual mistake.[148] This is all a notoriously open secret.[149] At the same time, it cannot be said that, in general, unconscionable contracts or contract clauses are, as such, invalid. The courts, as a whole, are not yet willing to go so far, and they certainly are not ready to go so far openly.

Under the Code relevant extra-Code law can be brought to bear via section 1-103 to afford relief to victims of unconscionable sales contracts. And section 1-203, though not applicable by its terms to the negotiation and formation of contracts, applies to prevent enforcement of unconscionable deals, at least when they are dishonest. Admittedly, this will be rare.[150] Some specific Code provisions may protect parties from binding themselves unwittingly to overreaching clauses.[151] More im-

143 Henningson v. Bloomfield Motors, Inc., 32 N.J. 358, 161 A.2d 69 (1960), is perhaps the most important recent example. In some fields, such as creditor-debtor relations, courts have long been willing openly to invalidate contract clauses. *See, e.g.*, Seasongood, *Drastic Pledge Agreements*, 29 HARV. L. REV. 277 (1916).

144 *See, e.g.*, Hardy v. General Motors Acceptance Corp., 38 Ga. App. 463, 144 S.E. 327 (1928).

145 *See, e.g.*, Cutler Corp. v. Latshaw, 374 Pa. 1, 97 A.2d 234 (1953).

146 *See, e.g.*, Weil v. Chicago Pneumatic Tool Co., 138 Ark. 534, 212 S.W. 313 (1919).

147 See cases cited and discussed in Note, *Species of Inadequacy of Consideration Which Have Induced Judicial Refusal to Attach Obligation to Promises*, 27 COLUM. L. REV. 178 (1927).

148 *See, e.g.*, Dansby v. Buck, 92 Ariz. 1, 373 P.2d 1 (1962).

149 See Siegelman v. Cunard White Star, Ltd., 221 F.2d 189, 206 (2d Cir. 1955); Llewellyn, Book Review, 52 HARV. L. REV. 700, 702 (1959).

150 While preparing this Article, the author spent a day at the University of Chicago School of Law perusing the Karl Llewellyn Papers. Among other things, he came across evidence that the Code's chief draftsman perceived the possible relevance of § 1-203 to problems of unconscionability. On what is presumably his copy of the 1949 Draft of the Code, the following question is hand-written opposite § 1-203: "Is an unfair bargain prohibited"? In the 1949 Draft the relevance of this section would have been even more obvious, for good faith was then defined to rule out much more than dishonesty. *See also* UCC § 1-205, Comment 6.

151 *See, e.g.*, UCC §§ 2-316(2), 2-209(2), 2-201(2).

portant are certain other provisions which parties cannot vary by agreement.[152] Most significant of all is section 2-302:[153]

> (1) If the court as a matter of law finds the contract or any clause of the contract to have been unconscionable at the time it was made the court may refuse to enforce the contract, or it may enforce the remainder of the contract without the unconscionable clause, or it may so limit the application of any unconscionable clause as to avoid any unconscionable result.
>
> (2) When it is claimed or appears to the court that the contract or any clause thereof may be unconscionable the parties shall be afforded a reasonable opportunity to present evidence as to its commercial setting, purpose and effect to aid the court in making the determination.

Case law under this section is scant. What little there is suggests that "unconscionable" at least means "excessively expensive,"[154] that an "add-on" clause in a secured consumer sale may be unconscionable,[155] that under some circumstances a franchise contract clause dispensing with advance notice of termination may be invalid,[156] and that a waiver-of-defense clause in a contract for the sale of consumer goods is, at least in some states, unenforceable.[157]

*B. Bad Faith in Performance*

Contract case law recognizes distinguishable types of bad faith in performance, including evasion of the spirit of the deal, lack of diligence

[152] One scholar has remarked that the "core task" of commercial law is "to determine the relatively few rules which are not subject to change by agreement, the rules which are designed to stake out the necessary minimum area of protection for parties whose bargaining power is inferior . . . ." Schlesinger, 1955 N.Y. Law Revision Comm'n Rep. 101. Among relevant Code provisions which cannot be varied by agreement are, "the obligations of good faith, diligence, reasonableness and care prescribed by this Act" (§ 1-102(3)), the provision which extends the seller's warranties to the buyer's family and guests (§ 2-318), and certain provisions of article 9 applicable to secured sales of goods (§ 9-501(3)).

[153] For an exhaustive study of this section, see Leff, *Unconscionability and the Code—The Emperor's New Clause*, 115 U. Pa. L. Rev. 485 (1967).

[154] American Home Improvement, Inc. v. MacIver, 105 N.H. 435, 201 A.2d 886 (1964); Frostifresh Corp. v. Reynoso, 3 UCC Calaghan Rep. 1058 (N.Y. Sup. Ct. 1966).

[155] Williams v. Walker-Thomas Furniture Co., 350 F.2d 445 (D.C. Cir. 1965).

[156] Sinkoff Beverage Co. v. J. Schlitz Brewing Co., 51 Misc. 2d 446, 273 N.Y.S.2d 364 (1966).

[157] Unico v. Owen, 50 N.J. 101, 232 A.2d 405 (1967).

and slacking off, willful rendering of only substantial performance, abuse of a power to specify terms, abuse of a power to determine compliance, and interference with or failure to cooperate in the other party's performance. Thus in addition to the more familiar sources of standards of performance—for example, the contract language itself, case law on how contract gaps are to be filled, and custom and usage—judges turn to specific concepts of good faith in deciding whether a party has or has not performed his agreement. Admittedly, judges frequently introduce these concepts as implied terms in contracts, and not as duties of good faith.[158] But it is almost always better to recognize something for what it is rather than to fictionalize it. And surely, how a doctrine is conceptualized can affect the outcome of cases. For example, it seems likely that a judge who thinks in terms of implied provisions will be less willing to enforce duties of good faith than the judge who thinks explicitly in terms of such duties; one who views himself as "implying terms" is more likely to think he is remaking a contract to some extent—something which judges are reluctant to do.[159] It seems, too, that a judge may be unduly hampered by the parol evidence rule if he considers himself to be implying terms instead of enforcing duties of good faith.[160]

Under the Code, performance of a sales agreement is similarly meas-

158 One writer has even suggested that the sole significance of good faith is "in implying terms in the agreement." Farnsworth, *Good Faith Performance and Commercial Reasonableness Under the Uniform Commercial Code*, 30 U. CHI. L. REV. 666, 670 (1963). It must be admitted that courts do not always mean the same thing when they speak of implying terms. No one has put this better than Glanville Williams:

> Judges are accustomed to read into documents and transactions many terms that are not logically implied in them. As an academic matter non-logical implication may be classified into three kinds: (i) of terms that the parties (the plural shall throughout include the singular) probably had in mind but did not trouble to express; (ii) of terms that the parties, whether or not they actually had them in mind, would probably have expressed if the question had been brought to their attention; and (iii) of terms that the parties, whether or not not they had them in mind or would have expressed them if they had foreseen the difficulty, are implied by the Court because of the Court's view of fairness or policy or in consequence of rules of law. Of these three kinds of non-logical implications (i) is an effort to arrive at actual intention; (ii) is an effort to arrive at hypothetical or conditional intention—the intention that the parties would have had if they had foreseen the difficulty; (iii) is not concerned with the intention of the parties except to the extent that the term implied by the Court may be excluded by an expression of positive intention to the contrary.

Williams, *Language and the Law—IV*, 61 L.Q. REV. 384, 401 (1945).

159 *See* Parev Prods. Co. v. I. Rokeach & Sons, 124 F.2d 147, 149 (2d Cir. 1941).

160 *See generally* Corbin, *The Interpretation of Words and the Parol Evidence Rule*, 50 CORNELL L.Q. 161 (1965).

ured against standards from varied sources. These sources include the language of the agreement itself, as well as specific Code provisions which may be used to fill gaps left by the contract language—for example, section 2-314, on warranties of merchantability; section 2-309, on "absence of specified time provisions"; section 1-103, on supplemental general principles, like the principle recognizing "constructive conditions of co-operation";[161] section 1-205, on course of dealing and usage of trade; section 2-208, on course of performance and practical construction; and section 1-203, imposing a general obligation of good faith in the performance of sales contracts. It will be recalled that section 1-201(19) defines good faith for the purposes of section 1-203 as "honesty in fact in the conduct or transaction concerned." Whether this definition "enfeebles" section 1-203[162] will largely depend on the willingness of courts to invoke the prefatory language of section 1-201(19): "unless the context otherwise requires." If courts are unwilling to invoke this language, Code requirements of good faith will be restricted significantly, for the more expansive special definition of good faith in article 2 apparently applies only to the thirteen sections of the article which use the phrase.[163]

*Evasion of the Spirit of the Deal*

Some judges recognize that to evade the spirit of a deal is to act in bad faith and thus is to commit a breach, even though the evasive conduct is within the letter of the agreement or the agreement is silent on the matter. Any form of bad faith may be contrary to the spirit of a transaction, but this section is addressed only to forms of bad faith that are also essentially evasive. A few illustrations will show what is meant. Courts will not permit a buyer under a requirements contract to "pretend not to have a requirement to avoid his obligation";[164] nor can he suddenly expand requirements to take advantage of the seller.[165] Evasive action of this nature conflicts with good faith. Further examples may

[161] Patterson, *Constructive Conditions in Contracts*, 42 Colum. L. Rev. 903 (1942).

[162] Farnsworth, *supra* note 158, at 674.

[163] See the discussion at 212-13 *supra*.

[164] Fort Wayne Corrugated Paper Co. v. Anchor Hocking Glass Corp., 130 F.2d 471, 473, (3d Cir. 1942); *see* Western Oil & Fuel Co. v. Kemp, 245 F.2d 633 (8th Cir. 1957).

[165] Cullinan v. Standard Light & Power Co., 65 S.W. 689, 690 (Tex. Civ. App. 1901). *See also* Loudenback Fertilizer Co. v. Tennessee Phosphate Co., 121 F. 298 (6th Cir. 1903).

be helpful. Suppose a seller develops and builds a market for product *X* and then sells his rights to manufacture and market it; the buyer of these rights is to pay royalties according to a rate based on the sales he makes. Later, the buyer develops product *Y*, which competes with *X*. Can the buyer keep *X* under his control until the market for *Y* has been built up and then safely forget *X*? The answer is "no," for the buyer would be evading the spirit of the deal and therefore would be acting in bad faith.[166] Or suppose a lessor rents premises to a lessee who agrees to pay a 2,000 dollar minimum rental plus a fixed percentage of receipts, in excess of this minimum, from sales and services "in the course of the aforesaid business on said premises." Subsequently, the lessee finds another location at a lower rental and moves enough of his business there to avoid payment of anything beyond the minimum rental. The lessee here may also be evading the spirit of the deal.[167]

Under the Uniform Commercial Code, some courts are likely to say there is a general principle of law that the spirit of a deal is, within limits, just as much a part of that deal as its letter and is always enforceable via section 1-103 on supplemental general principles. What is the likely bearing of section 1-203, the general good faith provision? Courts may try to use this provision despite the restrictive "honesty" definition of good faith, for evasion will often involve a state of mind sufficiently close to dishonesty to justify calling it that. Specific article 2 sections will also have bearing—for example, section 2-306, which imposes obligations of good faith on parties to requirements contracts. It will be recalled that whenever the words "good faith" appear in an article 2 section, they require, by virtue of section 2-103(1)(b), much more than honesty in fact.

### *Lack of Diligence and Slacking Off*

In a variety of contract cases courts have stated that good faith excludes lack of diligence and slacking off, even when that conduct does not violate the letter of the agreement. To cite an example of lack of diligence, a vendor who contracts to convey realty is guilty of bad

---

[166] This example is discussed in Parev Prods. Co. v. I. Rokeach & Sons, 124 F.2d 147, 150 (2d Cir. 1941); *accord*, Mechanical Ice Tray Corp. v. General Motors Corp., 144 F.2d 720 (2d Cir. 1944); cases cited in 3 A. Corbin, Contracts § 570, at 372 n.94 (1960).

[167] *Cf.* Food Fair Stores, Inc. v. Blumberg, 234 Md. 521, 534-35, 200 A.2d 166, 174 (1964); Dickey v. Philadelphia Minit-Man Corp., 377 Pa. 549, 105 A.2d 580 (1954).

faith if he acquiesces in a cloud on his title, such as a lien[168] or an adverse tenancy,[169] and does not strive to clear it so he can convey a good title. In some jurisdictions he also is subject to special damages. In one case an agreement between a power district and a contractor provided that the deal was not to become "effective" until the contractor had procured certain policies of insurance. After the contractor had failed not only to procure the insurance, but also to perform the agreement, the district sued the contractor's performance bond surety. Although the surety was successful in his defense that the contractor in good faith failed to get the insurance and thus was never obligated to perform the agreement, the court added that the contractor would have become obligated had he acted in bad faith by acquiescing in an obstacle within his power to remove.[170] In the course of contractual relations, occasions may arise when one party knows he should notify the other of some event that has occurred or of some intended action, even though the contract, by its terms, does not so require. A party who fails, for want of diligence, to give such notice or to give timely notice is guilty of bad faith and may be liable as for breach. For example, it has been held that good faith requires a party who intends to exercise a right to cancel to give reasonable notice of his intent.[171]

There are some "generalizable" insurance cases on slacking off in bad faith. In one case an insurer exercised a contract right to take over exclusive control of the defense of a claim against the insured. The contract did not explicitly require the insurer to appeal adverse judgments, and it refused to appeal an adverse judgment which went beyond the policy limits. The insured then prosecuted the appeal, obtained a reversal and successfully sued the insurer for the expenses of the appeal. The court stressed that

> there is a contractual obligation of universal force which underlies all written agreements. It is the obligation of good faith in carrying out what is written. The defendant's failure to observe this requirement of the contract in suit is the thing upon which its liability may safely

168 Kramer v. Mobley, 309 Ky. 143, 147, 216 S.W.2d 930, 934 (1949) (dictum).

169 *See* Sitlington v. Fulton, 281 F.2d 552 (10th Cir. 1960) (dictum).

170 Omaha Public Power Dist. v. Employers' Fire Ins. Co., 327 F.2d 912 (8th Cir. 1964).

171 Sylvan Crest Sand & Gravel Co. v. United States, 150 F.2d 642, 644 (2d Cir. 1945).

be predicated. Its failure to continue the defense of these cases was in effect a breach of its contract.[172]

Turning to the Uniform Commercial Code, some jurisdictions may have general principles which, via section 1-103, proscribe lack of diligence and slacking off in the performance of sales contracts. But it seems clear that the section 1-203 general requirement of good faith is not, given the "honesty" definition of the phrase, a useful weapon here. Unless it knowingly misleads, conduct of this kind is not dishonest, however bad it may otherwise be. Of course, whenever the words "good faith" expressly appear in an article 2 provision, they impose, in the case of a merchant, requirements of reasonableness.[173] Some of these provisions can operate to rule out lack of diligence or slacking off in a particular context. Section 2-306(2) on exclusive dealing contracts should be singled out, for it requires both buyer and seller not just to use ordinary efforts, but to use best efforts. Also, numerous provisions of article 2 expressly require one party to notify the other of certain facts or of certain intended acts.[174]

*Willfully Rendering Only "Substantial" Performance*

In some branches of contract law, a plaintiff who fails to perform in full is, nevertheless, entitled to recover on the contract if he has "substantially performed." [175] Recovery generally is for less than the full contract price since the plaintiff has not performed fully. This principle of "substantial performance" is most commonly applied in the field of construction contracts. Courts often say that for a contractor to qualify as one who has substantially performed, he must, among other things, establish that his noncompliance was not in bad faith. According to some cases, this means that he must show that his omissions or deviations were "the result of mistake or inadvertence, and were not intentional." [176] Otherwise, the contractor will be remitted to *quantum meruit* recovery—the reasonable value of the benefit he has conferred.

---

[172] Brassil v. Maryland Cas. Co., 210 N.Y. 235, 241, 104 N.E. 622, 624 (1914). An analogous form of slacking off occurs in the collective bargaining context when a union adopts a "slow down" or "work to rule" stance.

[173] UCC § 2-103(1)(b).

[174] UCC §§ 2-201(2), 2-206(2), 2-207(2)(c), 2-309(3), 2-311, 2-327, 2-503, 2-504, 2-508, 2-602, 2-607(3)(a), 2-615(c), 2-705(3)(a), 2-706(3), 2-717; *see* UCC § 1-205(6).

[175] A. Corbin, Contracts ch. 36 (1960).

[176] Odegaard v. Investors Oil, Inc., 118 N.W.2d 362, 375 (N.D. 1962).

For years the doctrine of substantial performance was not, at least in theory, recognized in the law of sales.[177] If the seller did not perform strictly, the buyer could reject the goods with impunity, even though the noncompliance was trivial.[178] The Uniform Commercial Code, however, allows the substantially performing seller to recover on the contract in some types of cases, despite his trivial breach. But in such cases "[t]he buyer on notifying the seller of his intention to do so may deduct all or any part of the damages resulting from any breach of the contract from any part of the price still due under the same contract." [179] An interesting question arises. Now that the Code recognizes the doctrine of substantial performance in some contexts, will judges draw on construction contract cases to impose, via section 1-103, a requirement that the otherwise substantially performing seller act in good faith? And if judges choose not to do this, will they invoke section 1-203, the general good faith provision? Willful breaches do go to state of mind and in some cases may be dishonest and, therefore, not in good faith. The effect of a finding of bad faith in this context would, if parallel to the usual result in general contract law, be to remit the seller to *quantum valebat* recovery—the reasonable value of the goods delivered.

But it is not clear that article 2 provisions leave any leeway for a good faith requirement. When the buyer accepts substantially conforming goods, he becomes liable "on the contract" under section 2-607, and the Code specifically contemplates that buyers may "accept" goods "in spite of their non-conformity." [180] This may indicate that *quantum valebat* is not to be the alternative in such cases even when the seller has acted in bad faith.[181] When a buyer rejects nonconforming goods wrongfully (because the Code tolerates the nonconformity), the Code's remedial scheme appears to allow the seller to recover "on the contract," whether or not his deviation was in bad faith. Still, since an essential function of the Code's general obligation of good faith is to modify rights and duties arising under a contract or under rules of law, a buyer may be able to convince a court that *quantum valebat* is the appropriate remedy for sellers who do not substantially perform in good faith.

177 48 COLUM. L. REV. 161 (1948).

178 *See generally* Honnold, *Buyer's Right of Rejection*, 97 U. PA. L. REV. 457 (1949).

179 UCC § 2-717.

180 UCC § 2-607(2).

181 *See* UCC § 2-703.

*Abuse of a Power to Specify Contract Terms*

A power to specify terms may be held jointly, as where parties to a contract agree to agree later on a given term, or severally, as where one party has the power to specify a term. Contract cases condemn the abuse of these powers as a form of bad faith in performance, even when the objectionable conduct is within the letter of the contract or when the contract says nothing at all about how the powers are to be exercised. For example, a farmer and a railroad agreed to agree at a later time on the location of a crossing that the railroad would maintain for the farmer. The parties failed to agree, and the farmer successfully sued the railroad for damages. On appeal, the court inquired into the good faith of the railroad and decided that its failure to agree "was not capricious or arbitrary." Presumably, however, the railroad would have been liable for damages if it had acted in bad faith.[182]

When only one party has the power to specify one or more terms of a deal, the opportunity—and the temptation—to take advantage of the other is likely to be greater. It should not be surprising, therefore, that courts require such a power to be exercised in good faith. Relevant cases deal with varied matters—for example, time of performance, price and quantity. In a New York case *A* offered to sell property and give *B* part of the proceeds if *B* would give *A* a release from any claims he might have against *A*. *B* agreed and gave *A* the release. Their contract did not specify when *A* should sell, and eight years went by without the sale of the property. The plaintiff, an assignee of *B*, sued *A*'s executors, who responded that the contract did not obligate *A* to sell before he "felt disposed to do so." The court disagreed:

> Every contract implies good faith and fair dealing between the parties to it . . . . When the contract between these parties is read in the light of this implication, it is obvious that the defendants assumed the obligation to sell within such reasonable time as the circumstances would permit.[183]

Similarly, good faith prohibits a party from setting unreasonably high (or low) prices under an "open price" provision,[184] and in a require-

[182] Chesapeake & O. Ry. v. Herringer, 158 Ky. 267, 164 S.W. 948 (1914).

[183] Simon v. Etgen, 213 N.Y. 589, 595, 107 N.E. 1066, 1067-68 (1915).

[184] Pillois v. Billingsley, 179 F.2d 205, 207 (2d Cir. 1950); California Lettuce Growers, Inc. v. Union Sugar Co., 45 Cal. 2d 474, 484, 289 P.2d 785, 791 (1955).

ments contract good faith requires the buyer not to demand unreasonable quantities.[185]

Under the Uniform Commercial Code, section 1-103 on supplemental general principles is available to remedy abuse of discretionary contract powers when warranted by extra-Code law. Section 1-203 is less likely to be useful, for however culpable an open abuse of discretionary power may be, many judges are not likely to think it dishonest. Article 2 contains relevant specific provisions, including sections 2-311(1), 2-305(2) and 2-306(1). The first of these is of prime significance:

> An agreement for sale which is otherwise sufficiently definite (subsection (3) of Section 2-204) to be a contract is not made invalid by the fact that it leaves particulars of performance to be specified by one of the parties. Any such specification must be made in good faith and within limits set by commercial reasonableness.

It will be recalled that when good faith is used expressly in an article 2 section, it means, in the case of a merchant, "honesty in fact and the observance of reasonable commercial standards of fair dealing in the trade." [186] Since the majority of contracts granting discretionary power to one party are between merchants, the foregoing requirement of good faith will find a wide scope for application here.

*Abuse of a Power to Determine Compliance*

Under the terms of a contract one party may, in effect, have power to determine whether the other party's performance complies. Thus a party may agree to perform not only in accordance with the contract plan, specification or description, but also to the "satisfaction" of the other party or a third party. Arrangements of this kind occur in a variety of contractual settings—for example, in contracts involving employment, lease, building, construction, land sale and sale of goods. Many courts say a party cannot arbitrarily and capriciously refuse to be satisfied, for this conflicts with good faith. Thus a buyer who declares that he is dissatisfied with a heating and hot water system, but is unable to say why, acts capriciously and in bad faith.[187] Similarly a

---

[185] See discussion and cases cited in Havighurst & Berman, *Requirement and Output Contracts*, 27 ILL. L. REV. 1, 13 (1932).

[186] UCC § 2-103(1)(b).

[187] O'Hare v. McGee, 116 Pa. Super. 318, 323, 176 A. 525, 526 (1935).

buyer of a piano acts in bad faith when his reasons for dissatisfaction have nothing to do with the piano.[188]

It should not be surprising that contract cases require a party to act in good faith in determining his own satisfaction, for a satisfaction clause, by its nature, affords him an unusual opportunity to take advantage of the other party.[189] The law under the Code will surely be the same. The wealth of pre-Code cases requiring good faith in satisfaction cases generally, and in sales of goods cases in particular,[190] can be introduced into the Code as a general principle of law via section 1-103. Moreover, section 1-203 will rule out all cases of feigned, and therefore dishonest, dissatisfaction.

*Interfering with or Failing to Cooperate in the Other Party's Performance*

It is one thing not to perform the consideration moving to the other party, and another to interfere with or fail to cooperate in his performance. Contract cases rule out the latter as well as the former, and often in the name of good faith. Indeed, deliberate interference with the other's performance is one of the most flagrant forms of bad faith. In one type of fact pattern, a seller of a product hires a broker to market it and, just as the broker is about to close the deal, steps in and closes it himself, thereby cutting out the broker. By the express language of the agreement the broker will have no rights if he has agreed that he is to receive a fee only for sales actually made. However, judges have held that a seller who intervenes in this way acts in bad faith and incurs liability for damages. Thus in a New York case the court stressed:

> The law reads good faith into every contract. Reasonableness is the rule for construing contracts and determining their implications. To hold that one may employ another at an agreed compensation to do a specific thing, and yet may with impunity deliberately prevent the other from doing that thing, is so plainly violative of good faith and reasonableness as to preclude extending the rule in ordinary brokerage cases to such a case as this.[191]

[188] Sears, Roebuck & Co. v. Kitchens, 31 Ga. App. 574, 121 S.E. 583 (1924).

[189] As with harems and eunuchs, where temptations are great, measures must correspond.

[190] Annot., 86 A.L.R.2d 200 (1962).

[191] Carns v. Bassick, 187 App. Div. 280, 284, 175 N.Y.S. 670, 673 (1st Dep't 1919).

In another New York case a vendor did not own land he contracted to convey, expecting to buy it at a foreclosure sale. The court refused to allow the buyer to get away with outbidding the seller at the foreclosure sale, stating that "[i]n the case of every contract there is an implied undertaking on the part of each party that he will not intentionally and purposely do anything to prevent the other party from carrying out the agreement on his part."[192]

Turning to cases which have required affirmative cooperation, the plaintiff in *Kehm Corp. v. United States*[193] agreed to manufacture practice bombs for the United States, which was to supply tail assemblies. The contract did not say when the assemblies were to be delivered. Unreasonable delays by the United States caused the plaintiff damages for which the court allowed recovery, holding that a party must "not only not hinder his promisor's performance, he must do whatever is necessary to enable him to perform."[194] Similarly, if an insured unsuccessfully attempts to comply with policy requirements as to notice and proof of loss, "[g]ood faith on the part of the insurer requires that it point out the details in which a notice or proof of loss is insufficient under the contract and give the insured an opportunity to correct these defects. Good faith does not permit an insurer to be silent and evasive under such circumstances."[195]

In contract law courts recognize a general principle of law imposing "constructive" terms of cooperation.[196] Judges, therefore, can invoke Code Section 1-103 to rule out the foregoing forms of bad faith. But the section 1-203 general requirement of good faith again seems of little utility, given its "honesty" definition; however blameworthy openly hindering or refusing to cooperate may be, it is not, as such, dishonest. On the other hand, when lack of cooperation is the issue, it is unlikely that a court will have to rely on either section 1-103 or 1-203 since section 2-311 provides that

> where one party's cooperation is necessary to the agreed performance of the other but is not seasonably forthcoming, the other party in addition to all other remedies

[192] Patterson v. Meyerhofer, 204 N.Y. 96, 100, 97 N.E. 472, 473 (1912).

[193] 93 F. Supp. 620 (Ct. Cl. 1950).

[194] *Id.* at 623.

[195] Johnson v. Scottish Union Ins. Co., 160 Tenn. 152, 156, 22 S.W.2d 362, 363 (1929). *Compare* UCC § 2-508.

[196] See Patterson, *supra* note 161.

(a) is excused for any resulting delay in his own performance; and

(b) may also either proceed to perform in any reasonable manner or after the time for a material part of his own performance treat the failure . . . to cooperate as a breach by failure to deliver or accept the goods.

### *C. Bad Faith In Raising and Resolving Contract Disputes*

Parties to a contract may engage in disputes over a variety of issues, including the meaning of contract language, compliance with applicable law and the existence of relevant facts. It may be a conservative guess that for each contract dispute resolved by an appellate court, a hundred others are settled before trial. Much can turn on a contract dispute, and thus a party may be tempted to act in bad faith, as by conjuring up a dispute, adopting an overreaching interpretation or taking advantage of the other party in order to get a favorable settlement. Case law rules out these and cognate forms of bad faith. Similarly, the Code includes provisions which can be brought to bear against such conduct.

#### *Conjuring up a Dispute*

A party acts in bad faith when, in an attempt to stall or bluff, he pretends to dispute, not really believing in his position. And a party who disputes capriciously is deemed to have acted in bad faith. A bad faith disputant may not even try to put up appearances—he may not try to base his position on anything. For example, in an early case a logger's employer refused to pay him wages plainly due then and there. The logger capitulated and agreed to take a lesser sum, the balance to be paid later. Shortly thereafter the logger sued for the balance, claiming that since there was no good faith dispute between the parties as to their rights, the employer gave no consideration for the agreement to delay payment. The court agreed, stating that the employer

> did not claim that the contract was different from what plaintiff asserted it to have been, or that by law the wages were not payable . . . . He simply asserted . . . that he would not pay all the money because it was not "the law of the company," or . . . because they "didn't settle that way," without giving any reason. A person cannot create a dispute sufficient as a consideration for a compromise by a mere refusal to pay an undisputed claim.[197]

[197] DeMars v. Musser-Sauntry Land, Logging & Mf'g Co., 37 Minn. 418, 419, 35 N.W. 1, 2 (1887); *accord*, Berger v. Lane, 190 Cal. 443, 450-51, 213 P. 45, 49 (1923).

More commonly, a party who conjures up a dispute tries to put up appearances—he tries to base his position on something. In some cases he will rely on contract language. But unless his position is "founded on some reasonably tenable or plausible ground," [198] any settlement he induces is not likely to stand up.

Many cases in which courts appear to require good faith in raising a dispute involve the validity of an accord and satisfaction. But this is not always the issue. For example, where an insurance company ceases disability payments, incorrectly claiming that the insured is no longer disabled, several courts have held the insurer liable only for the back payments and not for the value of all likely future payments as well.[199] A few courts have conditioned this limitation of liability on the good faith of the insurer in raising the dispute.[200] Presumably the insurer who disputes in bad faith is liable for something more—perhaps the whole value of the policy.

A party who conjures up a dispute will not fare well under the Code. Section 1-203 might even be invoked against him. For example, if he takes a position without really believing in it, but rather for some ulterior purpose, his action is deceptive, and therefore dishonest. There is one hitch in this. Section 1-203 applies only to bad faith in the performance or enforcement of contracts, and some judges may think that raising a dispute concerns neither performance nor enforcement. But, if he wishes, a judge can relate almost any dispute to performance or enforcement. No specific provisions of article 2 deal with the bad faith disputant, as such, but extra-Code law can be brought to bear via section 1-103.

*Adopting Overreaching or "Weaseling" Interpretations and Constructions of Contract Language*

Though not conjuring up a dispute, a party may take a position that is plainly a form of overreaching. In *Sylvan Crest Sand & Gravel Co. v. United States*[201] the United States adopted an overreaching construction of a contract which provided that the gravel company would

198 State v. Mass. Bonding & Ins. Co., 40 Del. 274, 9 A.2d 77 (1939); *accord*, Hogue v. National Automotive Parts Ass'n, 87 F. Supp. 816, 821 (E.D. Mich. 1949); Modern Dust Bag Co. v. Commercial Trust Co., 34 Del. Ch. 354, 104 A.2d 378 (1954); 6 A. Corbin, Contracts § 1287 (1962).

199 Annot., 99 A.L.R. 1171 (1935).

200 *See, e.g.*, New York Life Ins. Co. v. Viglas, 297 U.S. 672, 676 (1936).

201 150 F.2d 642 (2d Cir. 1945).

deliver rock to the United States and that "[c]ancellation by the Procurement Division may be effected at any time." The United States refused to request deliveries within a reasonable time and denied liability, citing this clause. Construing the agreement against the United States, the Second Circuit remarked:

> Surely . . . [the agreement] would not have been understood thus: "We accept your offer and bind you to your promise to deliver, but we do not promise either to take the rock or pay the price." The reservation of a power to effect cancellation at any time meant something different from this. We believe that the reasonable interpretation of the document is as follows: "We accept your offer to deliver within a reasonable time, and we promise to take the rock and pay the price unless we give you notice of cancellation within a reasonable time." Only on such an interpretation is the United States justified in expecting the plaintiff to prepare for performance and to remain ready and willing to deliver. Even so, the bidder is taking a great risk and the United States has an advantage. It is not "good faith" for the United States to insist upon more than this.[202]

Overreaching also takes the form of trying to do indirectly under a contract's language what obviously could not be done directly under it. For example, a contract which required Chrysler to give its dealer ninety days notice of franchise termination also provided: "All orders are subject to approval and acceptance by Chrysler at its principal place of business." Chrysler argued that this clause allowed it, in effect, to terminate the franchise without notice merely by not delivering cars. The court disagreed:

> To construe it as Chrysler now contends would result in making the agreement one terminable at will and thus rendering the 90-day termination clause meaningless. . . . [T]he right of termination must be exercised in good faith.[203]

"Weaseling out," another form of bad faith interpretation or construction, is commonly intertwined with the form of bad faith characterized earlier as "evasion of the spirit of the deal"—for example, pretending not to have a requirement, hoping thereby to evade one's true obliga-

[202] *Id.* at 644.

[203] Chrysler Corp. v. Quimby, 51 Del. 264, 284, 144 A.2d 123, 134 (1958).

tions under a requirements contract. As was seen, judges are not willing to allow such conduct.[204]

What, if anything, does the Code say about bad faith interpretation or construction? It is obvious from Code Comments that Llewellyn and company considered this species of bad faith a problem.[205] However, section 1-203 applies only to bad faith in performance or enforcement, and adopting overreaching or weaseling interpretations or constructions is not necessarily either. Whenever weaseling is accompanied by bad faith in performance, such as evading the spirit of the deal, it seems that section 1-203 could be invoked, for evasiveness is akin to dishonesty. But even if section 1-203 does not apply, it seems likely that courts will almost automatically turn to general principles of contract interpretation and construction—principles which already rule out these forms of bad faith. Few courts are likely even to cite section 1-103 on supplemental general principles as authority.

*Taking Advantage of Another to Get a Favorable Readjustment or Settlement of a Dispute*

Questionable techniques of negotiation, such as stalling or bluffing, have already been alluded to. In addition, some courts recognize a variety of "weaknesses" of which one party may not take advantage to procure a favorable settlement. It suffices to mention three such weaknesses. First, there are cases where one party has another "over a barrel," so to speak. For example, in *Lingenfelder v. Wainwright Brewing Co.*[206] plaintiff's testator was an architect who had drawn plans for and was supervising defendants' construction job. He walked off, thus threatening timely completion of the entire project, but later agreed to come back on condition that the defendants promise to pay him a bonus. The court refused to enforce this promise, for "[t]o permit plaintiff to recover under such circumstances, would be to offer a premium upon bad faith, and invite men to violate their most sacred contracts, that they may profit by their own wrong."[207]

In another category of cases courts have refused to permit one party to take advantage of the other's relative lack of knowledge of facts or law. For example, an insurer cannot hold an unknowing insured to a

---

[204] See p. 234 *supra*.

[205] *See, e.g.*, UCC § 2-313, Comment 4; § 2-314, Comment 4; § 2-504, Comment 2; § 2-612, Comment 3.

[206] 103 Mo. 578, 15 S.W. 844 (1891).

[207] *Id.* at 593, 15 S.W. at 848.

settlement procured by inducing him to accept and cash a check given "in full payment" when the insurer has failed to explain to the insured that the legal effect of cashing such a check is to give the insurer a valid defense to any subsequent claim by the insured for a larger sum.[208]

There also is authority for the proposition that a party cannot, in bad faith, take advantage of another's "necessitous circumstances." For example, one Headley sued one Hackley to recover full compensation for cutting, hauling and delivering a quantity of logs, after having earlier accepted a settlement for less. The flavor of the context should be appreciated:

> The amount [Headley] claimed was upwards of $6200, estimating the logs by the Scribner scale. He had an interview with Hackley in the morning, who insisted that the estimate should be according to the Doyle scale, and who also claimed that he had made payments to others amounting to some $1400 which Headley should allow. Headley did not admit these payments, and denied his liability for them if they had been made. . . . Hackley said to him: "My figures show there is 4260 and odd dollars in round numbers your due, and I will just give you $4000. I will give you our note for $4000." To this Headley replied: "I cannot take that; it is not right, and you know it. There is over $2000 besides that belongs to me, and you know it." Hackley replied: "That is the best I will do with you." Headley said: "I cannot take that, Mr. Hackley," and Hackley replied, "You do the next best thing you are a mind to. You can sue me if you please." Headley then said: "I cannot afford to sue you, because I have got to have the money, and I cannot wait for it. If I fail to get the money to-day, I shall probably be ruined financially, because I have made no other arrangement to get the money only on this particular matter." Finally he took the note and gave the receipt, because at the time he could do nothing better, and in the belief that he would be financially ruined unless he had immediately the money that was offered him, or paper by means of which the money might be obtained.
>
> If this statement is correct, the defendants not only took a most unjust advantage of Headley, but they obtained a receipt which, to the extent it assumed to discharge anything not honestly in dispute between the parties, and known by them to be owing to Headley beyond the sum received, was without consideration and ineffectual.[209]

[208] Kellogg v. Iowa State Traveling Men's Ass'n, 239 Iowa 196, 212-13, 29 N.W.2d 559, 568 (1947).

[209] Headley v. Hackley, 45 Mich. 569, 573-74, 8 N.W. 511, 512 (1881).

Ultimately, Headley recovered full compensation because Hackley had, in fact, not acted in good faith.[210]

We saw that in sales transactions one party may try to take advantage of another's weaknesses to strike a bargain, fair or unfair.[211] It is no different with modifications, readjustments, compromises or settlements under pre-existing contractual relations. The Code contains several relevant provisions. Section 2-209(1) provides that "[a]n agreement modifying a contract within this Article needs no consideration to be binding." The Comment states, however, that "modifications made thereunder must meet the test of good faith imposed by this Act."[212] Section 1-107 provides: "Any claim or right arising out of an alleged breach can be discharged in whole or in part without consideration by a written waiver or renunciation signed and delivered by the aggrieved party." The Comment to this section states that it "must be read in conjunction with the section imposing an obligation of good faith." These Code sections do not use the words "good faith." Accordingly, some courts are likely to conclude that the "honesty" definition of good faith applies, even in the case of merchants, and that the Code does not rule out forms of openly taking advantage in bad faith. One who openly takes advantage of someone he has over a barrel, someone less well informed or someone whose financial situation is "necessitous" certainly is a scoundrel, but this does not also make him dishonest. In such cases courts may have to fall back on section 1-103 and relevant extra-Code principles of law, or on section 2-302 on unconscionability, discussed earlier.[213]

### *D. Bad Faith in Taking Remedial Action*

Recognizing that a party may act in bad faith when seeking a remedy, courts specifically rule out various remedial actions, including abuse of the right to adequate assurances of performance, wrongful refusal to accept delivery, willful failure to mitigate damages and abuse of a power to terminate. The Code similarly imposes good faith limitations on remedial action.

#### *Abuse of Right to Adequate Assurances of Future Performance*

What can be done to protect a party faced with the prospect that

---

210 50 Mich. 43, 14 N.W. 693 (1883).

211 See pp. 230-32 *supra*.

212 UCC § 2-209, Comment 2.

213 See pp. 231-32 *supra*.

one with whom he has contracted may not be able to perform because of intervening circumstances? This problem can arise in almost any contractual context.[214] It should not be surprising, therefore, that legal techniques have been devised to deal with it. Section 2-609 of the Code gives the aggrieved party a right to demand and receive "adequate assurance of performance"; prior to the Code, lawyers wrote this same right into contracts. Any right of this kind may be abused. For example, a buyer who refuses to be satisfied with assurances given and unnecessarily harasses his seller for repeated assurances may really be trying to force an end to relations so that he can buy elsewhere on more favorable terms. Conduct of this kind plainly violates good faith, and cases hold that dissatisfaction with assurances given must be "actual, and based upon reason, and not arbitrary and capricious." [215]

Judges can apply such law under the Code via section 1-103. But section 1-203 is of little help since courts are not likely to say that open harassment is dishonest. However, if the party harassed can show that the harasser has an undisclosed ulterior motive, section 1-203 might apply.

*Wrongful Refusal to Accept the Other's Performance*

This, too, is a general problem,[216] for although not all types of wrongful refusals are in bad faith, some are. Suppose that a buyer has rejected goods ostensibly for minor nonconformities of tender or of quality, but in reality for another reason—for example, the price has fallen, and he wishes to buy elsewhere more cheaply. Under the letter of pre-Code law, which required perfect tender, the buyer would be free to do so. But in a few pre-Code cases judges appear to have denied him this right, partly on the ground that he was merely trying to get out of a deal because of a price break and was not motivated by the seller's slightly defective tender.[217]

Under Article 2 of the Code perfect tender is generally required,[218]

[214] *See generally* Wardrop, *Prospective Inability in the Law of Contracts*, 20 MINN. L. REV. 380 (1936).

[215] James B. Berry's Sons v. Monark Gasoline & Oil Co., 32 F.2d 74, 76 (8th Cir. 1929).

[216] See generally the cases discussed in Honnold, *Buyer's Right of Rejection*, 97 U. PA. L. REV. 457 (1949), and in Eno, *Price Movement and Unstated Objections to the Defective Performance of Sales Contracts*, 44 YALE L.J. 782 (1935).

[217] *See, e.g.*, Fielding v. Robertson, 141 Va. 123, 129, 126 S.E. 231, 233 (1925); Eno, *supra* note 215.

[218] UCC § 2-601.

though there are exceptions.[219] In cases not within these exceptions, how will bad faith rejections fare? A court might utilize section 1-103 to bring into play relevant extra-Code law. Beyond this, there is section 1-203, which should prove useful against buyers who pretend to be rejecting because of the admitted nonconformity. Against buyers who openly say they are rejecting because of the price break and cite the perfect tender rule as window dressing, the bearing of section 1-203 is less clear. Some judges may say that such conduct simply is not in bad faith, for it is not dishonest.

It seems paradoxical that section 2-601 on the buyer's right of rejection does not condition rejection on good faith, while section 2-603, imposing a duty on a merchant buyer to take over and care for or dispose of rejected goods under specified circumstances, does incorporate this language. Under the Code text, then, the merchant buyer is expressly held to a higher standard in handling rejected goods than he is in exercising the more fundamental right of rejecting them in the first place.

*Willful Failure to Mitigate Damages*

Contract law, in numerous contexts, denies a plaintiff recovery for damages attributable to his own failure to take reasonable steps to mitigate losses. In some sale-of-goods cases judges say the plaintiff must mitigate "in good faith." For example, in *Obrecht v. Crawford*[220] the court approved an instruction to the jury that plaintiff-seller could recover the difference between the price the buyer contracted to pay and the resale price to a third party, provided the resale was in good faith, which the court took to mean with "reasonable care, diligence and judgment." Obviously a plaintiff-seller ought not to be allowed to resell at a low price merely to increase damages recoverable from the buyer. This would be bad faith. But even without this motive, a resale would be in bad faith under the *Obrecht* instruction if it was unreasonable. The same kind of problem can arise when a buyer sues a seller for the difference between the price for which the defaulting seller agreed to deliver the goods and the price the buyer had to pay by going into the market and making a substitute purchase. To the extent that such "cover costs" were not incurred in good faith, they would not be recoverable.

[219] UCC §§ 2-504, 2-508, 2-612.
[220] 175 Md. 385, 394-96, 2 A.2d 1, 6-7 (1938).

The story is much the same under Article 2 of the Code, for specific provisions thereof expressly require good faith. Under section 2-706 an aggrieved seller may resell and charge the buyer at least the difference between the resale price and the contract price, provided the resale "is made in good faith and in a commercially reasonable manner." Likewise, an aggrieved buyer may go into the market and "cover," charging the seller at least the difference between the cost of cover and the contract price, provided the cover purchase is made "in good faith and without unreasonable delay" and is itself a "reasonable purchase."

*Abuse of a Power to Terminate*

Having begun this survey with bad faith in the initial stages of contracting, it is fitting to end with abuses of powers to terminate contract relations. In many different kinds of contracts, parties insert a clause giving one party an option to terminate, either "at will" or upon conditions. Most litigation appears to involve clauses of the first type. Not infrequently, courts assert that a party must act in good faith to terminate at will.[221] However, it must be admitted that the case law, taken as a whole, does not speak with one voice on good faith in the termination context, and some courts have even refused to adopt a good faith limitation.[222] In one context Congress has intervened and enacted a statute which provides that a dealer may recover damages for the failure of

[221] J.R. Watkins Co. v. Rich, 254 Mich. 82, 84-85, 235 N.W. 845, 846 (1931); *accord*, Busam Motor Sales v. Ford Motor Co., 203 F.2d 469, 472 (6th Cir. 1953).

[222] *See, e.g.*, Bushwick-Decatur Motors, Inc. v. Ford Motor Co., 116 F.2d 675 (2d Cir. 1940). *See generally* Gellhorn, *Limitations on Contract Termination Rights—Franchise Cancellations*, 1967 DUKE L.J. 465, 495-505. Gellhorn questions the "effectiveness of a good faith test" and whether "subjective terms should be imported into contracts. . . ." *Id.* at 505. He views good faith here as merely ruling out bad purposes and correctly notes that bad purpose and "harshness" of termination are not necessarily connected. *Id.* at 504. He also asserts that when a contract provides for termination "at will," so far as good faith is concerned, it can be so terminated, for "the parties can hardly be viewed as having intended to insert a good faith limitation." *Id.* at 502-03. Two comments are called for: first, Gellhorn assumes that good faith here is inevitably merely a matter of motives, which is false. Second, the usual explicit "at will" termination clause does not settle the issue. If anything, it gives rise to it. In agreeing to an "at will" termination power, a party presumably agrees merely to the grant of a power, and not also to the grant of a power to abuse that power. And if it should appear that he has been induced to agree to the latter, a case can be made that this should not be given effect. *Cf.* UCC §§ 1-102(3), 2-302.

an auto manufacturer "to act in good faith . . . in terminating, canceling or not renewing" a franchise.[223]

By invoking Code Section 1-103 courts can bring relevant extra-Code requirements of good faith to bear upon terminations of deals involving the sale of goods. Also, section 2-309(3) provides:

> Termination of a contract by one party except on the happening of an agreed event requires that reasonable notification be received by the other party and an agreement dispensing with notification is invalid if its operation would be unconscionable.

However, this provision only requires advance notice of termination; it does not protect against all forms of bad faith termination. What of section 1-203? That section may not apply at all, for to terminate obviously is neither to perform nor to enforce, and the section applies only to bad faith in the "performance or enforcement" of contracts. This aside, the section 1-201(19) "honesty" definition of good faith does not rule out arbitrary terminations, for however bad arbitrariness may be, it is hardly dishonest. This definition may proscribe terminations for bad motives, but these seem relatively uncommon.

## IV. Theories and Forms of Relief for Contractual Bad Faith—Some Modest Proposals

Case law and Code law, then, afford relief against many types of contractual bad faith. While tort theories play a part, especially with respect to fraud, and while quasi-contractual theory may be invoked if the defendant's bad faith enriches him at the plaintiff's expense, most relief against contractual bad faith is premised in contract, and it takes a variety of forms. For example, it is familiar that a defendant's bad faith can make him liable to pay damages, as for breach of an "implied term" in an enforceable contract.[224] Or he might be denied an affirmative defense, as where he conjures up a dispute merely to force an accord and satisfaction—a defense which is not available unless the accord is reached in settlement of a genuine dispute.[225] Or he might become subject to some form of specific relief. For example, goods which he

[223] The Automobile Dealer's Day in Court Act of 1956, 15 U.S.C. § 1222 (1964).

[224] His bad faith might even constitute an independent substantive basis on which he could be liable in damages, as where he abuses the privilege to break off negotiations. *See* Hoffman v. Red Owl Stores, Inc., 26 Wis. 2d 683, 133 N.W.2d 267 (1965). See also the discussion at 258 *infra*.

[225] 6 A. Corbin, Contracts § 1287 (1962).

bought on credit in reckless disregard of prospective inability to pay might be reclaimed.[226] Or bad faith might enhance a defendant's liability in damages, as where the court relaxes the plaintiff's duty to give proof of lost profits flowing from the defendant's willful breach.[227]

The significance of a finding that a plaintiff lacks good faith might be that he gets no remedy at all. A plaintiff who fails to show he was unaware of a mistake in an offer he "snapped up" would be a case in point.[228] Or the plaintiff's bad faith may arm the defendant with a valid affirmative defense, such as unconscionability.[229] The effect of his lack of good faith might be the denial of a particular substantive theory of contractual relief, as where a builder loses the right to sue for "substantial performance" and is remitted to *quantum meruit* because of his willful departure from contract specifications.[230] Or the effect of a plaintiff's bad faith might be the denial of a particular remedy. For example, the remedy of specific performance is not available to parties with "unclean hands." [231]

Contract theory, then, accords diverse significance to bad faith. But it does not adequately protect against all forms of contractual bad faith. Several proposals for reform will be offered here, not as final solutions, but as tentative suggestions worthy of further consideration. While these will be cast in the form of proposals for case law reform, they will not be without significance under the Code, especially in view of section 1-103 and several specific sections of relevance.

### A. Relief on Contractual Theory

A case can be made that we ought to enhance measures of recovery for some kinds of bad faith breach of contract. For example, there is no reason that recovery for consequential damages must always be limited to what the defendant had reason to foresee at the time of contracting.[232] Nor is it inevitable that punitive damages can never be awarded in contract.[233]

---

226 *E.g.*, California Conserving Co. v. D'Avanzo, 62 F.2d 528 (2d Cir. 1933).

227 5 A. Corbin, Contracts § 1020 (1964); Bauer, *The Degree of Moral Fault as Affecting Defendant's Liability*, 81 U. Pa. L. Rev. 586, 592 (1933).

228 *See, e.g.*, United States v. Jones, 176 F.2d 278, 287-88 (9th Cir. 1949).

229 *E.g.*, American Home Improvement, Inc. v. MacIver, 105 N.H. 435, 201 A.2d 886 (1964).

230 Odegaard v. Investors Oil Inc., 118 N.W.2d 362, 375 (N.D. 1962).

231 *See* Carmen v. Fox Film Corp., 269 F. 928 (2d Cir. 1920).

232 The rule is invariably so stated. 5 A. Corbin, Contracts § 1007 (1964).

233 But this is the general rule. *Id.* § 1077.

*Expanded Recovery for Consequential Damages*

In a proper case recovery should be allowed for consequential damages flowing from a defendant's bad faith breach even though, at the time of contracting, he had no reason to foresee such damages. The best possible case for this relief would be one in which the following factors are present: (1) the defendant's breach is malicious, (2) the damages ordinarily recoverable for such a breach are, under the circumstances, either not significant or highly difficult to prove, (3) the unforeseeable consequential loss to the plaintiff is significant so that if the ordinary measure of damages were applied, he would not be compensated for his true losses, (4) the award of greater damages is rationally limitable to something short of ruinous, runaway liability and (5) the loss is of such a nature that, had the parties thought of its possibility, they would not have agreed on a clause depriving the plaintiff of a right to recover therefor in the event of breach, and they would not have agreed on additional consideration for the defendant in return for his incurring greater potential liability. This last factor takes account of the rationale most commonly stated for the rule limiting contractual recovery for consequential losses to those which the parties had reason to foresee at the time of contracting—a party ought not to be liable for losses he had no opportunity to contract against.[234] This rationale loses its force in any case in which a party, given the opportunity, would very likely not have contracted against such losses.

Cases can be imagined which satisfy the foregoing criteria. One example will suffice, based as it is on the alleged facts of an actual case.[235] Suppose a free-lance author enters a contract whereby the publisher agrees to publish and promote the sale of a book which the author agrees to write; the publisher further agrees to pay royalties on copies sold. Prior to publication the publisher mails out advertisements announcing the book, but after copies of the book had been printed, the publisher refuses to publish because he has acquired a malicious and spiteful attitude toward the author. As a result, the author not only loses all royalties, whatever they might have been, but also suffers significant loss of reputation as an author—a loss not reasonably foreseeable at the time of contracting. This loss could manifest itself in various ways; for ex-

[234] Patterson v. Illinois Cent. Ry., 123 Ky. 783, 786, 97 S.W. 426, 427 (1906).

[235] Schisgall v. Fairchild Publications, Inc., 137 N.Y.S.2d 312 (Sup. Ct. 1955), 41 Cornell L.Q. 507 (1956).

ample, his sources of offers for placement of free-lance articles might dry up.

It is assumed that recovery in tort for defamation would not lie since no defamatory statement was made by the publisher.[236] But should not the author be entitled to recover in contract for his loss of reputation— a loss which flowed from the publisher's malicious breach of contract? While general damages in the form of lost royalties would be hard to prove,[237] the consequential loss of reputation is substantial and would be no more difficult of proof and valuation than is the case in many defamation actions in tort.[238] Furthermore, to require the publisher to compensate for this loss is not to impose ruinous, runaway liability for consequential losses either in this case or in similar cases. And it is most unlikely that the parties would have taken this kind of loss into account at the contracting stage, had the possibility occurred to them.

In sum, it is submitted that there are cases where recovery should be allowed in contract for losses flowing from bad faith breaches, even though the losses were not reasonably foreseeable at the time of contracting. There are analogous contractual contexts in which courts have, in effect, modified the measure of recovery, in part because of the bad faith of a party. In some jurisdictions a plaintiff-builder who willfully departs from specifications cannot recover in contract on the theory of substantial performance, but must sue in *quantum meruit*.[239] A party who contracts to sell realty and recklessly disregards his own prospective inability to convey good title is, upon breach, liable in some states for more than the ordinary defaulting vendor.[240] And some courts have relaxed the requirement of certainty of proof of lost profits when the defendant willfully breaks his contract.[241] Given the foregoing analogies, in a proper case it would not be a radical step for a court to grant recovery in contract for losses which flow from a bad faith breach, but which were not reasonably foreseeable at the time of contracting. Of course, a court could grant relief in tort where the applicable measure of recovery unquestionably includes such losses, but since they flow

236 W. PROSSER, TORTS 754 (3d ed. 1964).

237 And generally they must be proved with "reasonable certainty." 5 A. CORBIN, CONTRACTS § 1020 (1964).

238 Defamation cases which pose difficult problems of proof and valuation of damage are not uncommon. *E.g.*, Elms v. Crane, 118 Me. 261, 107 A. 852 (1919); Craney v. Donovan, 92 Conn. 236, 102 A. 640 (1917).

239 Annot., 6 A.L.R. 137 (1920).

240 *E.g.*, Arentsen v. Moreland, 122 Wis. 167, 99 N.W. 790 (1904).

241 See note 227 *supra*.

from what is plainly a breach of contract, it seems best to premise relief in contract.

*Punitive Damages*

The general rule is that punitive damages may not be awarded in contract.[242] But if the legal system is to allow punitive damages in civil actions at all, it is difficult to see why they should not be granted in contract actions. In tort law a proper case for punitive damages is generally said to be one in which

> the defendant's wrongdoing has been intentional and deliberate, and has the character of outrage . . . . such as spite or "malice," or a fraudulent or evil motive on the part of the defendant, or such a conscious and deliberate disregard of the interests of others that his conduct may be called wilful or wanton.[243]

There is no reason that such conduct cannot manifest itself in contract as well as in tort contexts, and it seems probable that a significant number of contract breaches actually fit the foregoing description. Allowing a punitive award in these cases would further the primary purposes of punitive damages, as stated in tort law—namely, to punish and to deter.[244] In fact, the calculating and malicious contract breaker is both more culpable and more deterrable than those tortfeasors who act impulsively or recklessly and end up having to pay punitive damages.[245] Furthermore, the institution of contract is no less important to society than many interests which tort law protects, partly via punitive damage awards. The thin end of the wedge may be in view already, for a growing minority of courts now grants punitive damages for some kinds of bad faith breaches.[246]

## B. *Noncontractual Theories of Relief*

Since contractual bad faith is contractual, it is tempting to assume that any relief therefor must be premised in contract. But the law seems never to have been that wrongs occurring in a contractual setting

242 5 A. Corbin, Contracts § 1077 (1964).

243 W. Prosser, Torts 9-10 (3d ed. 1964) (footnotes omitted).

244 *Id.* at 9.

245 *E.g.*, Booth v. Kirk, 381 S.W.2d 312 (Tenn. Ct. App. 1963).

246 Simpson, *Punitive Damages for Breach of Contract*, 20 Ohio St. L.J. 284 (1959); Note, *Exemplary Damages in the Law of Torts*, 70 Harv. L. Rev. 517, 531-33 (1957).

must be redressed, if at all, in contract. One who negligently performs a contract may incur liability in tort as well as in contract, and a party who, at the time of contracting, makes a promise without any intent to perform may become liable in tort for deceit.[247] A party also may commit the torts of fraudulent concealment and misrepresentation in contractual contexts. It should not, therefore, seem radical or iconoclastic to suggest that a noncontractual theory may be an appropriate basis for relief against some forms of contractual bad faith.[248] The contract-minded judge who accepts this suggestion might even be led to allow damages against a defendant whose bad faith does not take the form of breaking an enforceable contract. As the following examples will show, this is no mere academic matter.[249]

*Recovery for Bad Faith at the Negotiation Stage*

The victim of bad faith at the negotiation stage cannot recover in contract since a contract has never been formed. Recovery must be premised in tort, in quasi-contract or in some other theory. Two possible "negotiation" torts are negotiating without serious intent to contract and withdrawing a negotiating proposal after foreseeably inducing another to rely on it. As we have seen, authority that squarely recognizes these wrongs as actionable is scant. But it will be recalled that the Court of Claims in *Heyer Products Co. v. United States*[250] held that a disappointed low bidder may recover bid preparation expenses if he can show "that bids were not invited in good faith, but as a pretense to conceal the purpose to let the contract to some favored bidder . . . ."[251] The court, because it had no jurisdiction over tort claims, was forced

247 W. Prosser, *The Borderland of Tort and Contract*, in Selected Topics on the Law of Torts 380, 387-422 (1954).

248 It is not just that tort theory is already in use against contractual bad faith. The use of noncontractual theory in this way is even more widespread than the use of contractual theories. It has been said that the theory of unjust enrichment, in some of its applications, affords redress against losses flowing from contractual bad faith. R. Pound, Introduction to the Philosophy of Law 156, 188-89 (1922). As a possible example, see Matarese v. Moore-McCormack Lines, Inc., 158 F.2d 631 (2d Cir. 1946).

249 In what follows, distinctions between theories of liability will be taken more seriously than may seem becoming of a law teacher. My defense is that many lawyers and judges take these distinctions seriously. *Cf.* Shanker, *Strict Tort Theory of Products Liability and the Uniform Commercial Code: A Commentary on Jurisprudential Eclipses, Pigeonholes and Communication Barriers*, 17 W. Res. L. Rev. 5 (1965).

250 140 F. Supp. 409 (Ct. Cl. 1956).

251 *Id.* at 414.

to say that a cause of action for negotiating without serious intent sounds in contract rather than in tort, and in implied contract at that.[252] Yet the dissenting opinion,[253] and subsequent cases citing *Heyer*,[254] have pointed out that the appropriate theory is tort. Implied contract, as used here, is merely a fiction prompted by the jurisdictional peculiarities of the Court of Claims.

The Wisconsin Supreme Court in *Hoffman v. Red Owl Stores, Inc.*[255] required the defendant to compensate for losses the plaintiff reasonably incurred in reliance upon a negotiating proposal which the defendant subsequently withdrew. The court invoked promissory estoppel, but stated that "this is not a breach of contract action"[256] and that the withdrawn negotiating proposal did not constitute an offer to contract.[257] If a tort is defined as a civil wrong other than breach of contract, the Wisconsin Supreme Court plainly recognized a cause of action in tort, for the court did not invoke promissory estoppel as a "substitute for consideration in a binding contract." That inducing reliance and then walking away may be a tort is not a new idea.[258]

Some lawyers and judges have presumably failed to see that relief in tort might lie for bad faith in conducting contract negotiations—a factor that helps explain the dearth of case law.[259] Therefore, it is all the more important to recognize explicitly "negotiation wrongs" as tortious; otherwise, some victims will continue to bear losses unfairly for lack of contracts on which to base recovery. And these losses are not always confined to "out-of-pocket" expenses; loss of expectancy may occur, too, as where the defendant induces the plaintiff to pass up other lucrative opportunities in order to deal with him.

[252] *Id.* at 413.

[253] *Id.* at 414 (Laramore, J., dissenting).

[254] Edelman v. FHA, 251 F. Supp. 715, 719 n.7 (E.D.N.Y. 1966).

[255] 26 Wis. 2d 683, 133 N.W.2d 267 (1965).

[256] *Id.* at 701; 133 N.W.2d at 276.

[257] *Id.* at 697-98; 133 N.W.2d at 274-75.

[258] See Snyder, *Promissory Estoppel as Tort*, 35 Iowa L. Rev. 28 (1949). The precise characterization of the wrong as a tort or something else is not, of course, as important as the recognition that a breach of contract should not be necessary for relief.

[259] There are, of course, other factors. One, which goes to the assumed "nature" of contract, should be noted here. A judge who thinks of contract theory as the only possible basis for relief may, in some cases, be disinclined to grant recovery for the further reason that he thinks contract liability must inevitably be "all or nothing" in character—liability for full expectancy damages, or no liability at all. Such a judge will turn away a plaintiff seeking merely reliance damages if expectancy damages would not also be appropriate. This "all or nothing" approach is perceptively criticized in Fuller & Perdue, *The Reliance Interest in Contract Damages*, 46 Yale L.J. 373 (1937).

*Recovery Against a Party Who Backs Out of an Imperfectly Formed Deal*

The parties may enter a deal without realizing that it is legally unenforceable; for example, the agreement may be too indefinite, or it may not comply with the statute of frauds.[260] Later, when one party discovers he has an "out," he may take it, bad faith or no. At this stage it will not be uncommon that the aggrieved party will have partly performed or in some way relied to his detriment. He is allowed to recover in quasi-contract for the value of any unjust enrichment of the other party, but this measure is inadequate whenever his reliance expenditures and other reliance losses exceed the amount by which the defendant is enriched. It must be admitted that some courts have allowed plaintiffs to recover this excess, and in quasi-contract at that.[261] But this distorts theory.[262] In a proper case, recovery should be allowed in tort for that part of the loss which is not properly compensable in quasi-contract. This approach openly premises recovery on appropriate theory and makes it more likely that meritorious plaintiffs will prevail. However, it would be inconsistent with the rules denying enforceability to imperfectly formed deals if such a plaintiff were allowed to recover for loss of expected profits.[263] The losses appropriately compensable in tort would be only those measurable in terms of the "unjust impoorment" of the plaintiff at the defendant's instance.[264]

---

260 Of course, there are many other reasons why such a deal might turn out to be unenforceable.

261 See Note, *Quasi-Contractual Recovery for Part Performance of a Contract*, 44 HARV. L. REV. 623, 626 (1931).

262 The true concept underlying the decisions seems to be not one of restitution based on quasi-contractual principles, but rather one of indemnification sounding in tort: the plaintiff has made expenditures foreseen by the defendant, in reasonable reliance on the defendant's promise, which is unperformed because of the latter's fault; the plaintiff recovers such portion of that expenditure as is necessary to make him whole.

*Id.* at 627 (footnotes omitted).

263 Not that such consistency is all that important. Some of these rules may themselves be questionable in policy, such as the statute of frauds.

264 This is in contrast to unjust enrichment at the plaintiff's expense. The phrase "unjust impoorment" was suggested to me by my colleague, Professor Alfred P. Rubin, who, along with another colleague, Professor Herbert W. Titus, kindly commented on an earlier draft of this section of the Article. A noteworthy case openly and squarely granting relief for "unjust impoorment" as such, rather than via an extension of the unjust enrichment theory, is Kearns v. Andree, 107 Conn. 181, 139 A. 695 (1928).

*Affirmative Recovery Where Contract Theory Accords Only Defensive Significance to Bad Faith*

The only significance contract theory gives to some forms of bad faith is defensive in nature. For example, a party who in bad faith conjures up a dispute to induce an accord and satisfaction merely loses this defense upon being discovered; he does not become affirmatively liable in contract for any losses he causes.[265] Similarly, a party who overbears another and talks him into an unconscionable deal merely loses the right to enforce the agreement; he does not become affirmatively liable in contract for any losses he causes.[266] And yet it is clear that losses can occur which are traceable to such misconduct. A debtor who arbitrarily and capriciously refuses to pay a necessitous creditor in full, seeking thereby to induce him to settle for less, might cause the creditor financial ruin. As one creditor testified in an actual case: "If I fail to get the money to-day, I shall probably be ruined financially . . . ."[267] Similarly, a car dealer's repossession of a car, sold to a buyer pursuant to unconscionable price and credit terms which the buyer could not meet, might deprive the buyer of self-transportation and thereby cause him to lose his job. The relief afforded by contract theory in cases of the foregoing nature seems inadequate. In the first example the debtor is denied the defense of accord and satisfaction and remains liable merely for the amount of the debt plus interest; in the other the buyer acquires a defense of unconscionability which he may set up against the dealer should he try to recover any amount remaining unpaid on the price of the car. Contract theory might be modified to allow the creditor recovery for consequential losses specifically traceable to his debtor's bad faith since the debtor is in breach for failure to pay in the first place. But the debtor's bad faith consists of his capricious refusal to pay in order to force a favorable settlement. This misconduct, rather than mere nonpayment, constitutes the distinctive wrong. In the unconscionability case, contract theory cannot be modified to allow the buyer affirmative relief, for the seller is not in breach of his contract. Accordingly, the tort alternative offers itself as all the more worthy of consideration.[268]

265 No cases have been discovered in which the defendant has been held liable for such losses.

266 No cases have been discovered in which the defendant has been held liable for such losses. UCC § 2-302 specifies that an unconscionable contract is not enforceable. It neither grants nor denies other relief.

267 Hackley v. Headley, 45 Mich. 569, 574, 8 N.W. 511, 512 (1881).

268 Some judges may feel the need for a "doctrinal bridge" from unenforceability

*Some Objections*

Several proposals to expand relief for contractual bad faith have been outlined. It is appropriate to close this section by considering two general objections to such expansion. First, it might be said that the elements of "negotiation" torts, "backing out" torts, "unconscionability" torts and the like cannot be defined with sufficient precision.[269] But is this really true? The mental element in torts of this nature could, in each case, be defined in terms of an intent to do the acts constituting the wrong. If it is thought desirable to restrict liability during an initial period of experimentation, the mental element could be tightened up even further to require the intent not only to do the acts constituting the wrong, but also to do wrong as such—for example, the intent to string another along and drop him after inducing reliance, or the intent to impose a particular unconscionable bargain. Additional elements of these torts might consist of (1) doing the relevant acts, (2) causing damage thereby and (3) having no justification or excuse. Elements of this nature are no less definite than those analogous intentional wrongs which have long been actionable as torts. For example, the elements of the tort of "inducing breach of contract" consist of (1) intentionally (2) causing another (3) to break his contract (4) without justification or excuse.

A second general objection to more expansive liability for contractual bad faith is that there are counter-considerations which, it might be said, ought to carry the day. For example, it is arguable that the recog-

to affirmative recovery in damages: "Just as a whole field of law may be influenced by the accidental *presence* of a particular case at particular stage of its development, so a whole field of law may be influenced by the accidental *absence* of a decision which might serve as a sort of *doctrinal bridge* between existing rules and needed new law." Fuller, *American Legal Realism*, 82 U. PA. L. REV. 429, 441 (1934). The case of Williams v. Walker-Thomas Furniture Co., 350 F.2d 445 (D.C. Cir. 1965) can serve as a doctrinal bridge from recognition of unconscionability as a valid defense, to its use offensively to recover damages. In *Williams* the court decided that an "add-on" clause giving a seller a security interest not only in the goods then being sold on credit, but also in all goods previously sold to the buyer and for which he had not paid in full, could, in some circumstances, be unconscionable. When so, the seller could not then lawfully repossess the previously sold goods thus freed from the clause, and would be affirmatively liable in conversion to pay damages for thus seeking to enforce the unconscionable clause. In the *Williams* case, the buyer was resisting replevin, but she might just as well have been suing in conversion, had the facts been slightly different.

269 Another, more general, way to put this kind of objection is to say that since good faith is a phrase some judges use loosely and impressionistically, it should not figure significantly in our law.

nition of "negotiation" torts would conflict with the social policy favoring freedom to negotiate, and that some parties might decline to negotiate at all for fear that they would incur liability in tort. But while it is true that counter-considerations are at work, the crucial question is whether they outweigh the social interests to be protected—ensuring just compensation and maintaining appropriate standards of behavior in the contractual process. It is this kind of question which courts should face up to.[270]

## V. Conclusion

Q. You have used the phrase "good faith" throughout, but you still have not said what it means. What does it mean?

S. You and others persist in asking that question, which, as I have contended, misconceives good faith. Good faith, as judges generally use the term in matters contractual, is best understood as an "excluder"—a phrase with no general meaning or meanings of its own. Instead, it functions to rule out many different forms of bad faith. It is hard to get this point across to persons used to thinking that every word must have one or more general meanings of its own—must be either univocal or ambiguous.[271]

Q. You speak as if your conclusions were based on judges' uses of the phrase. Were the cases you cited all ones in which judges actually used these words?

S. No, but ninety per cent of them were.

Q. Is it your view that whether conduct is in bad faith must turn on something substantive rather than on what it is called?

S. Of course.[272]

---

[270] Certainly it should not be said, as it was in Bushwick-Decatur Motors, Inc. v. Ford Motor Co., 116 F.2d 675, 677 (2d Cir. 1940), that obligations of good faith are properly imposed only by legislators. For criticism of this view, see Gellhorn, *Limitations on Contract Termination Rights—Franchise Cancellations*, 1967 Duke L.J. 467, 503-04 (1967). *See generally* Peck, *The Role of the Courts and Legislatures in the Reform of Tort Law*, 48 Minn. L. Rev. 265 (1963).

[271] See pp. 199-209 *supra*. The excluder analysis is admittedly one developed by philosophers. But there is no a priori reason why it should not have application to problems of legal analysis.

[272] Cf. Kessler & Fine, *Culpa In Contrahendo, Bargaining in Good Faith, and Freedom of Contract: A Comparative Study*, 77 Harv. L. Rev. 401, 408 (1964) ("[t]he absence of good faith language is by no means conclusive") (nor is the *presence* of good faith language).

Q. Can you say what that is?

S. It is possible to say something general, but I doubt if it will satisfy you. In most cases the party acting in bad faith frustrates the justified expectations of another. As I have tried to show, the ways in which he may do this are numerous and radically diverse.[273] Moreover, whether an aggrieved party's expectations are justified must inevitably vary with attendant circumstances. For these reasons it is not fruitful to try to generalize further. It is easy enough to formulate examples of bad faith and work from them.[274] Besides, any general definition of good faith, if not vacuous, is sure to be unduly restrictive, especially if cast in statutory form.[275]

Q. I still can't pin you down. Aren't you, in Sartre-like fashion, really saying that good faith permeates all? At least, you put no limits on it. Doesn't this very promiscuity of good faith make it useless as a distinctive legal test?

S. I have not said good faith permeates all of contract law. Many rules of contract are not merely matters of good faith, and some have little, if anything, to do with good faith.[276] It is true that the general enforceability of promises, as such, can be derived from the basic principle that men should act in good faith towards others with whom they deal.[277] It is also true that good faith is pervasively relevant in contracting contexts, from the negotiation stage through to discharge.

Q. You welcome uncertainty in the law. Shouldn't the parties, especially in matters contractual, be able to tell where they stand? You won't let me have a definition of good faith, and you tell me good faith is "pervasively relevant." If courts adopt your theory, how am I supposed to be able to tell in advance when some judge will say I am acting in bad faith?

S. You say: "If courts adopt my theory." It is not my theory; it is a judicial and legislative theory. As for your certainty point, I think its

273 See Part III *supra*.

274 One of the important insights of Professor Fuller is that the bad can often be more usefully discussed than the good. Fuller, Book Review, 9 U. Chi. L. Rev. 759, 760 (1942).

275 See pp. 206-07 *supra*.

276 The examples range from relatively narrow rules, for example, "acceptance by post of an offer by post is effective on dispatch," to broad principles, for example, "the parties are generally free to make what contracts they wish."

277 *See* R. Pound, An Introduction to the Philosophy of Law 188 (1922).

merit meager. You seem to wish for more certainty than the nature of the case admits.[278] This apart, we already have, in regard to some problems, more uncertainty than I believe we would have if courts attacked such problems directly in terms of good faith rather than indirectly in terms of irrelevant contract rules. This seems true, for example, of the law on taking unfair advantage. Some courts have bent and twisted contract doctrines to reach just results;[279] other courts have refused to do this and have denied relief.[280] One can't be at all sure when to expect a court to take one line or the other.

Furthermore, once we accumulate a body of holdings on what forms of conduct are in bad faith, we should then have the certainty you want, at least as to those forms of conduct, shouldn't we?

Q. Yes, but even then the omnicompetent presence of good faith would always be with us for new situations. My friends teaching criminal law wouldn't stand for this sort of thing. They honor the maxim, *nulla poena sine lege*, and they insist on clarity and certainty in advance. To them, your doctrine would be "void for vagueness."

S. Good faith is not vague in its applications. Indeed, what good faith requires can only be defined usefully in the context of particulars. As I have tried to show, good faith takes on definite (and variant) meanings by way of contrast with definite (and variant) forms of bad faith.[281] Moreover, your criminal law anology is inapposite; the purposes and functions of criminal law and contract law are not the same.

Q. Maybe the criminal analogy isn't apt, but you still haven't convinced me that a requirement of good faith can really qualify as true law. It is far from a rule.

S. You reveal your prejudice in favor of rules: "If something can be formulated as a definite, detailed rule, then it can qualify as law, but if it is merely a general maxim, policy or principle, then it cannot qualify as law at all. Only rules can be laws." This is a common view.[282] But

---

278 Aristotle stressed that we should not seek more certainty than the subject matter allows—always sobering counsel. THE BASIC WORKS OF ARISTOTLE 936 (McKeon ed. 1941).

279 See, *e.g.*, pp. 257-58 *supra*.

280 *E.g.*, O'Callaghan v. Waller & Beckwith Realty Co., 15 Ill. 2d 436, 155 N.E.2d 545 (1958).

281 See pp. 202-04 *supra*.

282 For discussion of this view, see Dworkin, *The Case for Law—A Critique*, 1 VALPARAISO U. L. REV. 215, 216-17 (1967).

it is not in accord with relevant reality. In fact, a moment ago even you cited to me *nulla poena sine lege*, which surely is no more than a maxim. And what of our law of negligence? Aren't its formulations rather vague? And what of the principle of unjust enrichment? Of Section 90 of the Restatement? Of the "prima-facie tort" doctrine? Of the whole of equity, with its vague maxims, policies and principles? In point of fact, our law recognizes many kinds of non-rules as law.[283] Why not similarly recognize the principle requiring contractual good faith? Furthermore, if we are to have doctrines which, among other things, perform safety valve functions, then isn't it inevitable that they will take rather general form? Of course, in their specific applications they will generate rules.[284]

Q. You argue with conviction. Aren't you at bottom just a moralist trying to foist your ideas of good faith off on others?

S. So moralism concerns you, too. The ABA committee which induced the Code's sponsors to delete the expansive definition of good faith from Section 1-201(19) of the Code was plainly fearful of moralism.[285] Several comments must be made. First, I have tried to make it clear that legal good faith, in the case law, is not identical with moral good faith, though it must be admitted that the two overlap.[286] Second, insofar as legal good faith incorporates morals, which require a party to act in ways he ought to act anyway, I see nothing to object to. It may be true that many men, in their commercial dealings, do not think consciously in terms of right and wrong, but rather in terms of profit and loss and possibly of the standards of dealing that prevail in their businesses, however high or low. But to the extent this is so, it seems irrelevant. At the least, a judge should always be willing to intervene to enforce minimal standards of just dealing as well as the spirit of any consummated

[283] On maxims, policies and principles as law, see Dworkin, *Judicial Discretion*, 60 J. of Philosophy 624 (1963). See also the important recent study, P. Stein, Regulae Juris—From Juristic Rules to Legal Maxims (1966).

[284] "[T]he general requirement tends to be systematized into a series of rules." P. Devlin, The Enforcement of Morals 46 (1965).

[285] [I]t is of interest that this provision and certain others in the same vein have produced quite a violent reaction on the part of some businessmen and business lawyers. They say: "Why should the Code draftsmen tell us to be good? Businessmen, or at least most of them, carry on business ethically and did so long before the Code was ever conceived. The Code should not try to prescribe morals."

Malcolm, *The Proposed Commercial Code*, 6 Bus. Law. 113, 127 (1951).

[286] See pp. 204-06 *supra*.

deal. It is possible that a judge might, in the name of good faith, impose on a contracting party merely his own personal ideals of upright behavior. But this is a risk worth running. And it is not much of a risk, for good faith is more a minimal standard than a high ideal anyway.[287] Also, a party can appeal.

Q. If you are right in all this, then why haven't lawyers and judges made more of good faith than they have?

S. Any answer would, of course, have to be speculative. It should be noted first, though, that the influence of good faith is greater than your question implies. One reason people don't see its full reach is that it is sometimes clothed in other doctrinal garb. But to get on with my answer, no one has satisfactorily conceptualized good faith for the law's purpose. Flummoxed by the question, "What does good faith itself mean?" people may have decided that good faith is useless as a legal requirement. There has not been much study of cases to see how judges actually use the phrase. You have already mentioned other factors which presumably have impeded acceptance of good faith in our contract law—misplaced concern about uncertainty, prejudice favoring narrow, definite and detailed rules, and fear of judicial moralism. Anti-paternalism, the ideology of free contract, and regard for "arms-length" bargaining have no doubt played a part, too.[288] It has even been said that courts are not free to require good faith; only the legislature can.[289] Despite all this, we now have a considerable body of law. If all the cases cited here were on the books of a single state, that state would have a rather fully developed doctrine of good faith.[290] But it is true

[287] *Cf.* H. HART, THE CONCEPT OF LAW 176-80 (1961).

[288] If the Court were to interfere otherwise than as a referee to prevent fouls, or if it were to tender help to the party who appeared to be getting the worst of it, worse still if it engaged itself as an active promoter of fair dealing, sooner or later it would be telling both parties that it knew what was good for them better than they did themselves. That is an attitude that always has been and still is repugnant to lawyers . . . .

P. DEVLIN, THE ENFORCEMENT OF MORALS 47 (1965). "The traditional notion that parties when negotiating for a contract should look out for their own protection is still exercising a powerful pull . . . ." Kessler & Fine, *Culpa in Contrahendo, Bargaining in Good Faith, and Freedom of Contract: A Comparative Study*, 77 HARV. L. REV. 401, 419 (1964). "[M]andatory rules, not subject to agreement by the parties, are not ordinarily favored in our law . . . ." Farnsworth, *Good Faith Performance and Commercial Reasonableness Under the Uniform Commercial Code*, 30 U. CHI. L. REV. 666, 678 (1963).

[289] Bushwick-Decatur Motors, Inc. v. Ford Motor Co., 116 F.2d 675, 677 (2d Cir. 1940).

[290] New York appears to have the most fully developed doctrine of good faith.

that in most states the law of contractual good faith seems relatively undeveloped. Maybe the Code will serve as a stimulus, especially if it is amended as suggested.[291]

291 See note 73 *supra*.

# Supplemental Citations

Subsequent writings of the author on the themes of the 6 essays collected here.

**1. Methodological**

*Essays in Legal Philosophy*, Intro. (U. of Calif. Press and Blackwells), 1968.
*More Essays in Legal Philosophy*, Intro. (U. of Calif. Press and Blackwells), 1971.
'Professor H.L.A. Hart's Concept of Law', 1963 Duke L.J. (1963).
'H.L.A. Hart's The Concept of Law – Estimations, Reflections, and a Personal Memorial', 45 *J. Legal Ed.* 587, (1995).

**2. Form**

'The Practical and Theoretical Importance of the Formal Character of Law', forthcoming in *Rechtstheorie*.
'The Place of Form In the Fundamentals of Law', Stevens Lecture at the Cornell Law School, March 31, 1999, forthcominh in *Ratio Juris*.

**3. Substance, Content, etc.**

'Economists Reasons for Common Law Decisions – A Preliminary Inquiry', 1 *Oxford J. Legal Studies* 213 (1981).
'The General Duty of Good Faith – Its Recognition and Conceptualization in the New Restatement of Contracts', 67 *Cornell L. Rev.* 810 (1982).

# Name Index

For Product Safety Concerns and Information please contact our EU representative GPSR@taylorandfrancis.com Taylor & Francis Verlag GmbH, Kaufingerstraße 24, 80331 München, Germany

**Batch number: 10726013**

Printed by Printforce, the Netherlands